ALL AT SEA
Memories of a Coram Boy

Gordon Aspey

EMSEA PRESS

© 2010 Gordon Aspey
All At Sea ~ Memories of a Coram Boy

ISBN 978-0-9566424-0-0

Published by EMSEA PRESS
Motorcats Group
Unit 1a
Emsworth Yacht Harbour
Thorney Road
Emsworth
Hampshire PO10 8BP
email: emseapress@btinternet.com   www.all-at-sea.com

Book designed by Michael Walsh at
THE BETTER BOOK COMPANY
5 Lime Close Chichester PO19 6SW
www.thebetterbookcompany.com
and printed by
ASHFORD COLOUR PRESS
Unit 600 Fareham Reach Gosport Hants PO13 0FW

I have decided that *All At Sea*, a book that has taken me twenty years to write, should be my small tribute to this remarkable man.

Originally I started writing about my life in my own way to gratify my mother, who wanted to know all about me and what I had done in my life. We hadn't seen each other for over forty years and I hadn't known her at all until I was a teenager. Later, after discovering many documents, letters and photos that were held in the Foundling Hospital archives, I became more and more engrossed in writing my history. I discovered that writing about my past life gave me a much better understanding of the life I'd previously led and also helped to heal a lot of mental wounds that had been deeply buried. In addition I think that the story I have related tells a bit of social history that is worth knowing.

I, too, have developed a dogged belligerence and more than that in my life. I've rarely been in step with the establishment, there's no improvement there, I'm afraid. I tell my story as it came to me: unorthodox and earthy at times, but as honestly as I can remember. Occasionally the hurt of unhealed wounds shows through, but I hope the unjustified optimism that generally steered my thoughts and actions shines uppermost.

My father was born in 1865. It was the year LaMarcas Adna Thomson was busy inventing the fairground roller coaster ride, President Abraham Lincoln was busy getting assassinated and Sir Joseph Wilson Swan was busy sorting out the light bulb. By now you may well be thinking, *this bloke has to be older than Henry Allingham; that can't be right.* So I should explain that there was a fifty-two-year age gap between my under-age mother, who I think was either aged sixteen or seventeen and my father who was aged sixty-eight when I was conceived. These and other out of the ordinary facts would gradually be revealed to me over a long period of time.

* * *

My story starts with a boat delivery in the Atlantic. My eldest son, Victor, a yacht-master, had been commissioned to deliver a thirteen-metre catamaran from Southampton to Florida. He invited Robin (his younger brother), myself, and two others to help him on the first leg to the Canaries. We missed the 'English hurricane' in October 1987 by a whisker, but got hammered by a force ten storm off the North African coast soon afterwards. We were tested to the limits of our endurance. There were moments of mind-numbing panic when each second was a lifetime and our survival seemed to be in serious doubt. The experience had a profound effect on me, and I decided to break a promise I had made to myself over four decades earlier at the age of sixteen that I would never ever return home.

My children knew nothing of my secret past, so they were in for a few surprises. Even my wife would be astonished by some of the things that I later revealed and that are written about in this book.

I've changed some of the names and tweaked one or two of the situations described to avoid legal issues.

Gordon Aspey
May 2010

Captain Thomas Coram

Introduction

Captain Thomas Coram was an eighteenth-century seafaring philanthropist. He established the Foundling Hospital by Royal Charter in 1739, and I was one of the last children to benefit from the care and education that over 27,000 children received before the final closure of the foundling institution in 1953. I was number 24221 and still have the original identity disc that was placed around my neck when I was accepted into the institution's care in March 1934 at the age of three months.

Thomas Coram was by all accounts a belligerent and dogged character in early Georgian London. After his return to England from the Americas, where he had a shipbuilding business in Nova Scotia, he became shocked by the plight of London's children, having witnessed babies abandoned on manure heaps amongst dead animals. He decided to try to organise a foundling hospital, based on the system practised by the French, and spent seventeen years and much of his own money to achieve this objective. On 14 August 1739 George II signed a charter that established England's first charity for children. Coram targeted aristocratic ladies whom he hoped would sign his petition, probably thinking they would be more sympathetic to the plight of babies and children than their husbands. Eventually he garnered 1739 names for his Royal Charter including: 23 Dukes, 34 Earls, 7 Viscounts, 22 Lords, 45 Knights, 11, Doctors, the Archbishops of Canterbury and York, the Bishop of London and others.But he was not always well received. One Duchess was rumoured to have told him to sod off. He had a sharp temper and wasn't the easiest of men to get on with, but his persistence won him important friends such as George Frideric Handel, William Hogarth, Henry Fielding and the first Duke of Montagu, and their famous names still reverberate around the world in the twenty-first century.

ACKNOWLEDGEMENTS

The Foundling Museum staff

The Coram family

Old Coram Association and ex-foundlings for their support, with special mention for Tom Vale, Philip Taverner, Lilian Payne and Sam Mold

Ex RAF:

Graham H. Leavey (the bugler)

Mike O'Neill

Paul Bacon, his wife, and daughter Christine Durant

Ginger and Techie, who wish to remain anonymous

Pathicia Eve, Loulou Brown, Catherine Madina and Judith Worley for their tireless enthusiasm

Shipbourne villagers, with special thanks to Jenny Wakeman, Mrs Tapps' great grand-daughter

Jonathan Veale

To my wife and wonderful family.

1

I was married with three children, a nice house, living a comfortable, ordinary life. But things were about to change with a phone call from Victor, my eldest son.

'Dad,' he said, 'I have to deliver a catamaran to Florida. I'm collecting the owner and his family during Christmas week in the Canaries. I need crew for the first leg from Southampton. D'you fancy a bit of adventure? I could do with your experience.'

'When are you going?'

'End of August. The boatyard lads in Southampton are doing the finishing touches, and then we do a few trials to check her out.'

'Blimey! That's a bit late in the year, Victor. You don't want to be crossing the Bay of Biscay any later. Who else is going?'

'There's Hannah, my diving buddy, and Kevin, a navigation student. Oh, and Robin said he might come.'

'You're kidding! Your brother's never shown any enthusiasm for boating. Okay, I suppose I ought to keep an eye on the pair of you.'

'No, no, Dad. You're crew.'

'What? Me crewing for you? That's a bit of a turnaround!'

I was gingerly tiptoeing around the options for semi-retirement. I reckoned that the trip would give me the opportunity to further my strategy for a more leisurely lifestyle in the future. Also, the idea of crewing for my twenty-six-year-old son, in company with Robin his younger brother, appealed to me as a unique adventure.

* * *

The voyage from Southampton to the Canary Islands started full of excitement and somewhat apprehensive anticipation. To start with, the autumn of 1987 wasn't vintage in boating terms, with the continual march of Atlantic lows towards English shores bringing strong headwinds and big seas.

'I thought we'd take the classic route like the old three-masted schooners,' said Victor, studying the chart. '*Katehawk*' doesn't sail well to windward. I think we'll make for Kinsale in southern Ireland.'

The boatyard had delayed delivery of the boat by several weeks, supposedly on account of 'minor problems'. In fact, it had been delayed to display *Katehawk* at the Southampton Boat Show. Our departure date was now mid-September. This was not at all a good time to be crossing the Bay of Biscay.

'Have we got all the stores on board, Hannah?' I asked.

Vic's raven-haired girlfriend puffed out her cheeks in a mock grimace, wiping beads of perspiration from her forehead. 'Goodness knows where we're going to store everything,' she said, pointing to the mountain of boxes heaped in the cockpit. 'There's enough here to feed the proverbial army.'

'We'll soon get through it,' said Victor. 'You'll see.'

* * *

We were heading out of Southampton Water in thick fog towards the Needles Lighthouse when we heard an agitated voice on the radio: 'Coastguard? Coastguard! This is fishing boat *Dinkwell*. We've caught a mine in our nets – over.'

'Bloody hell! Well that's a good start,' said Kevin. Kevin was a brawny character who'd been invited along for his strength. He would have made a good extra in a pirate film. He would have had no need for make-up as he had a large gold earring and a close-shaven head, and came armed with jaw-dropping vocabulary.

'We'd better keep a lookout,' said Victor. 'According to my calculations he's only about eight hundred yards to the east. Do us a favour, Robin. Flick on the strobe light, second switch on the left, yeah? That's it; great. Let's hope they can see that.'

The conversation between coastguard and fishing boat had a mixture of panic-stricken dialogue and casual 'What's for breakfast?' type urgency. *Dinkwell* was finally assured by the coastguard that *HMS Warcry* was on its way to deal with the problem.

'I'll be glad when this fog clears,' muttered Kevin. 'This foghorn is doing my fucking head in.'

'Yeah, I can't see it's doing much good, Vic. Can you imagine the skipper of a big container ship a hundred feet up in the air being able to hear that? It'd sound more like a flea farting in a bowl of custard. It's a waste of time.'

'Well, we don't have radar, Dad, and we have to follow the rules of the road. The forecast was "fog banks in the Channel", but this seems to be nailed to our bleeding mast. I'll get an update from the coastguard.'

The VHF buzzed and crackled.

'*Katehawk*, this is Esso tanker *Falmouth*. I heard you calling for weather update – over.'

'Esso *Falmouth*, this is *Katehawk*. This fog bank seems to be widespread – over.'

'Yeah *Katehawk*, it's dense in the Channel. I think I may be astern of you. Can you confirm your position? I'm not getting a good target, if it's you on my radar – over ... Did you say 270 degrees – speed five knots? Please confirm *Katehawk* – over ... Thanks *Katehawk*. Gotcha! Yes, I'm half a mile astern of you, been following you for a while. Can you hold your course and I'll pass down your port side – over?'

We waited in silence, peering into the fog till we heard a muzzy fog signal.

'See, Vic,' I said, 'Collision regulations require every craft to give fog signals, the reality being, of course, that small foghorns are useless in the vicinity of large ships, which can't possibly hear them. If we were standing on his deck, it would bust your ear-drums.'

'That was on our starboard side,' said Robin.

Victor grinned. 'You can't always tell, Rob. Fog plays havoc with sound signals.'

'Put your nose over the port side, Robin; you can smell his diesel fumes coming on the breeze,' I said.

Victor switched off the engines as we strained our eyes and ears into the darkness.

'I can faintly hear his engines,' whispered Hannah. 'He's level with us.' We started to bounce up and down on her wash as she passed.

'That's dodgy if he couldn't pick us up on his radar. Are you sure the reflector is working, Vic?'

'I hope so. That tanker was getting a signal. The owner couldn't afford the extra cost of radar. Trouble is, Dad, you don't know if these reflectors work until something whacks you. They're only a bit of bent-up tin, you know.'

'Hmm, you're right there, Vic, and fibreglass doesn't make the best target in the world.'

The fog stayed with us all night and most of the following morning.

'That was some fog bank,' said Hannah. 'I hope we don't get too much of that in Biscay.'

She had hardly finished voicing her fears when there was an almighty bang that had us all scurrying on deck clutching our life jackets.

'Jesus!' yelled Kevin, his eyes wide with terror. 'What the hell was that?' We checked everything on board and scoured the horizon with the binoculars, but couldn't see any wreckage or anything untoward.

'I thought we'd hit that unexploded mine,' said Robin. 'Phew! I saw my whole life flashing by in Technicolor.

The mystery of the almighty bang was swept aside as the increasing wind strength gave us a few unpleasant hours of seasickness approaching the lighthouse at Crosshaven in the Republic of Ireland. Navigation had been reduced to Victor counting his fingers, trying to work out the speed required to cover the last eight miles to arrive at Kinsale by 0600.

The jolly bearded harbour master seemed puzzled when questioned about the loud bang. He suggested it might have been a military aircraft, or perhaps Concorde breaking the sound barrier. 'I've got some good news for you,' he boomed, tugging at his darkly whiskered face. 'We're doing a 20 per cent reduction on mooring charges this month.' He seemed disappointed by our lukewarm response to this outpouring of generosity, but the seasickness we'd suffered had nearly deprived us of the will to live. All we wanted to do was to abandon ship and bury ourselves in the stable countryside. The high cost of eating in the delightful local restaurants soon healed our seasickness, however. We bought a lot of Irish potatoes – and then scarpered.

During our first day after leaving Ireland to cross Biscay, Kevin made an important discovery. 'So where's the bread?' he demanded, banging cupboards open and shut. 'I can't find the bloody bread.'

Hannah had a passion for Italian food. Without so much as a 'What do you think, chaps?' she'd stuffed *Katehawk* to the gunwales with pasta and all things Italian. 'Don't worry, Kevin,' she assured him. 'I'm baking fresh bread every other day. We've plenty of Irish new potatoes ... and too much starch isn't good for you.'

Bad weather and ongoing seasickness soon scuppered this idea, though, and the galley began to look as though it was a redundant pottery, with assorted lumps of dough in varying stages of production scattered around the galley. Hannah's regular excursions with the clanging sick bucket became the signal for a no-bread day.

Kevin showed no sympathy for Hannah's suffering, saying, 'She's the ship's nurse. She should cure her bleeding sickness and get on with baking the bread.' In all his nineteen years he couldn't remember a single day without a pile of sarnies gracing the table at home. Now he was dying of malnutrition, clinging to life with a daily ration of fucking pasta shells. He said he felt as though he was crossing a gale-ridden Bay of Biscay in a bloody gondola.

I was already beginning to dislike Kevin.

* * *

Conditions proved to be a trial for the inexperienced crew, but *Katehawk* acquitted herself well, confirming her seaworthy qualities with only slight damage to a reefing support and the Navstar aerial. After brief stopovers at Lisbon and Vilamoura we continued down the Portuguese coast to Gibraltar.

We were fortunate to squeeze into the crowded Gibraltar outer harbour four hours before the 'English Hurricane' of 15–16 October struck. Even so, the edge of the weather system roughed up our anchorage during the early hours of the morning as the dinghy danced around, sawing through the ties of protective fenders. The skipper raised us crew from our warm bunks with an urgent call: 'Everyone on board! Hurry!'

In my haste to get on deck I forgot the practised method of getting out of my bunk and banged my head hard on a teak cross-member. Kevin thought it was extremely funny as I staggered into the cockpit holding my head and cursing.

'That's not funny, you ignoramus,' I growled.

'Oh I don't know; I could do with a laugh,' he chuckled.

With a sore head and a certain amount of resentment I helped to reset the anchor and keep a watchful eye on two schooners and several other large vessels in case their anchors dragged.

'You ought to get rid of that Kevin,' I muttered to Victor. 'He's really getting on my nerves.'

'I had noticed,' said Victor grinning broadly. 'But Dad, you too can be cantankerous at times.'

It was during a late breakfast that I lost my temper with Kevin. I was waiting for the toaster to finish toasting two slices of bread, which seemed to take forever. Then I noticed Kevin had cleared the table.

'Where's my boiled egg?' I demanded.

'Oh. I thought you'd finished,' he said. 'I chucked it overboard.'

'Maybe you've finished with these!' I said, grabbing his yellow wellies.

'Don't you dare, you prune-faced git, or I'll chuck you overboard!'

By the look on his face I felt sure he would do just that … and I didn't fancy a bath before breakfast. I grinned to myself, thinking about the unusual expression. I'd never heard it before, but realised it was a fair observation. I did look a bit like a corrugated lampshade. In fact, Kevin was not very different to me when I was his age: an unruly, self-opinionated, objectionable bigot.

The dinghy had to be repositioned several times to reduce the persistent lurching and banging against the hull. We should have brought the blasted thing on board and placed it into the davits, but instead Victor had to bale it out as it was waterlogged, and then row arduously across in it to the Spanish mainland to recover two of *Katehawk*'s expensive fenders. The continuous friction of the dinghy rubbing against the catamaran's hull had severed the ties and, with the help of the wind and the tide, they had floated off to the opposite shoreline.

'Have you heard the news?' he asked, breathing hard after his exertions. 'I've just spoken to Mum on the phone. They've had a hurricane in the UK; it's absolute mayhem. I'll tell you something else, too. If we'd delayed leaving Lisbon by another three or four hours we wouldn't be talking about it now.'

'Well it was grim here,' groaned Robin. 'I didn't sleep at all. I wondered what the hell was going on with all that banging and crashing around.'

'We were lucky, Robin. If we'd been out there, they'd be picking up our bodies on the beach, never mind the fenders.'

We later heard that the catamaran joining us for the Atlantic crossing had her hysterical crew taken off by lifeboat near Portland Bill.

'Christ, that's no place for a boat in a force four, never mind a bleeding hurricane.'

'You're right there, Dad,' said Victor. 'D'you know the skipper wouldn't get off? "This boat," he said, "is all I've got and I'm sticking with it. I didn't call out the lifeboat. It was one of my crew." The navy jettisoned a bit of oil on the water to smooth things down a bit and he sailed her into Weymouth harbour on his own. I bet he'll get another crew and turn up for the crossing. We'll see him in the Canaries, I'm sure. He's a real tough character.'

He did.

We were relaxing in one of the coffee shops, enjoying the early morning sun, when a familiar figure came darting along and paused for a short time at our table.

'Hi Gordon! What you doing here?' It was Charlie, an ex-bus driver from Greenwich, who'd been left a lot of money by his granny. I'd helped him in the previous December with a shakedown sail in his new yacht with Boris and Jasper, two mates from the yacht club. We had discovered he was a manic-depressive, and the experience had not been enjoyable. Yet now he looked bronzed and happy. Beside him stood a willowy, green-eyed blonde. 'This is Heidi, my new crew. She's a brilliant sailor, aren't you?' he said, gently squeezing her arm. 'She knows the whole thing A to Z. We're off to Gran Canaria once we've tanked up. We'll see you.'

Victor and Hannah had a couple of days off to improve their qualifications at the local diving establishment. I lazed in the open cockpit soaking up the sun, while Kevin and Robin investigated the shops. Victor had a long telephone discussion with the owner of the boat, who wanted it in the Canaries to enjoy a bit of sailing with his family before departing for Florida.

* * *

We left Gibraltar in a late afternoon and I bunked down in preparation for my first solitary watch. My dual watch with

Kevin had been abandoned after Victor had realised the friction between us was getting worse, and in any case the improved conditions didn't warrant two lookouts. When I stepped into the cockpit for my watch, the sea had settled and the night glowed with a North African candelabra sky. The gentle drum and burr of eager sail in warm, beamy winds promised a relaxing watch. Tightening the mainsheet, I watched a distant cruise liner, ablaze with light, gradually dip below the horizon, en route to warmer climes.

Jammy devils, I thought. *That's what I want: a few more degrees south.*

The boating grapevine had urged mariners to keep a good distance off the Moroccan coast because of reports of hostile activity. Yachts had reported gunshots being fired towards them from the shoreline. The droning voice at Lloyd's signal station at Europa Point that guarded the Gibraltar Straits was now out of range, which confirmed that we'd cleared twenty-five miles from the mainland. Apart from the strange Morse-code whistles of local fisherman, the VHF became silent except for the occasional crackle. Later we heard some discussion between two tugs that had been towing the ill-fated *Herald of Free Enterprise* on its journey to India. They had abandoned the tow on account of the extreme weather, and the urgency of their discussion seemed to focus on doubts as to her whereabouts.

Sucking on a toffee I waited for the moment when it would stick to my new half-denture. Normally a source of great irritation, this night I didn't care – I was happy. This despite the fact that somehow my half-denture had jumped upside down and bitten me in the tongue, drawing blood. I was pleased to be rid of Kevin and have the watch to myself.

Sipping a mug of peppermint cocoa, I settled comfortably at the helm and watched the moon appear above the horizon: scarlet-tinted orange, yellow to lemon, rising like a child's balloon gathered by the wind. *Katehawk* sailed majestically with noiseless grace, except for the assertive swish from twin hulls piercing the carpet of rippling silver. I was totally captivated by the magic.

This perfect night would later shine like a star in the ebb and flow of my memory.

I thought with amusement about my role reversal with Victor. I remembered the small, gurgling bundle on my lap aboard the *Corinthian* some twenty-five years previously, who was now a chunky, six-foot-three adult, and a qualified yachtmaster instructor with a university degree. Time had flown by so quickly. I hadn't settled well into the trappings of middle age, and suddenly I was nearing the fag end of my life.

According to the pilot books we could expect fair winds for the time of year in 30 degrees of latitude. Hannah in particular had good reason to hope for better conditions, having spent most of the Biscay crossing attached to the sick bucket.

'Don't worry,' said Victor. 'Forget about the Bay of Biscay. From now on, things can only get better. By the end of the week you'll be complaining about the sun.' To our collective dismay, however, by 1500 hours we were plunging into big seas against a steady 35 knots of wind. One of the stanchions compromised by earlier damage pulled clear of the deck, dislodging the Navstar aerial, although a temporary repair kept it in commission. The sick bucket continued with its irritating clanging with Hannah in regular tow. During the night we watched a distant electric storm that lit up the sky, and heard the rumbling of thunder which seemed to get nearer but never quite arrived.

By first light the wind had moderated and a warm, watery sun together with the smell of burnt toast greeted us. Kevin had purchased a personal supply of Liptons bread while we were in Gibraltar, and he wasted no time. With contented scrunching noises he downed one slice after another. For the first time he seemed a happy and completely different person. Encouraged by the better conditions, there was more light-hearted banter and we wondered how a shoal of squid had managed to leap over the seventeen-foot beam of the boat. Several didn't make it, but were enthusiastically helped back to the sea by Kevin, who dribbled them overboard with his yellow wellies. Occasionally small birds would land on the boat, and even bees and butterflies, often many miles from the nearest land. They would stay for a couple of hours, sometimes for a couple of days. The mystery as to where they came from and where they went remained – except for a chirpy robin that went nowhere, who took up residence above the chart table. Hannah thought he was highly intelligent because he kept focusing his bright, beady eyes on the chart as if studying our position. Victor, however, was less impressed, pointing at a limestone outcrop almost obliterating Madeira.

'Look at all that crap on my chart. Get him out of here.'

During the night the slumbering Kevin awoke with a loud shriek and discovered the robin nuzzling up to his left ear. He danced around shooing and shouting him out of his cabin. I discovered the robin in my shoe the following morning and presumed he'd died of fright. As the morning progressed we relaxed in earnest. Victor assaulted a gargantuan fruitcake, with mutterings of discontent from Kevin: 'Leave some bloody cake for us.'

Robin remained engrossed in a book about Watergate, with occasional gasps of 'Jesus! I don't believe it.'

Kevin read out passages from his book, a true-life tale of a shipwreck. He took particular delight in relating the scene where sharks were trying to nibble the buttocks of the unfortunate mariner through the dinghy's rubber floor.

Reclining in the cockpit, I considered my future. Perhaps it would be an 'icing on the cake' retirement: a nice house in the Solent with moorings at the end of the garden, and maybe a small flat in Spain to enjoy during the English winter months. My one and only insurance policy would soon mature. I was really looking forward to that, the culmination of a lifetime's savings that had nearly been cashed in so many times. I remembered the angry exchanges with the insurance company's agent when he told me the policy had expired because I'd failed to keep up the payments. The head office eventually agreed to credit me with all my payments, but insisted I took out a new policy extended by ten years. I wasn't happy, but didn't seem to have much choice. I smiled to myself as I recalled the wily insurance salesman from

Bridgwater whose main purpose in life was to sell me a policy all those years ago. It wouldn't buy a bigger boat, but I had earmarked it to cover a twelve-month sabbatical cruise through the French canals, and then winter in Spain: a long-held dream.

Hannah, ever helpful, had taken on the task of searching for my glasses. Her smiling, 'Here you are', however, was followed by a loud scream of terror as the glasses case clattered to the floor. She dashed out of the cockpit and hid in her cabin.

'What's all that about?' cried Victor, frantically brushing cake crumbs overboard. 'Hannah, what's the matter, for heaven's sake?'

'There's a horrible big spider in your dad's spectacle case.'

'A what?'

'This boat's turning into a bloody zoo,' said Kevin. 'Birds, bees, butterflies and now a monster spider.' He raised the lid to peer inside.

'Bugger me! How the hell did he get in there?' he gasped, snapping the lid shut. An uncomfortable silence followed as all eyes centred on the spectacle case.

'So how big is it?' queried Robin, nervously sliding the spectacle case away from himself across the cockpit floor.

'Well, it's the biggest spider I've ever seen,' said Kevin, spreading his palms like an optimistic fisherman.

'Get away,' said Robin, 'the case is only six inches long, for God's sake!'

'Yeah! But it's got a huge rucksack on its back.'

'Hmmm! Must be one of those plastic munching monsters, and he's scoffed Dad's glasses,' chuckled Robin.

'Throw it overboard,' said Victor.

'Hang on, Vic! What do you mean, "throw it overboard?"' I said. 'That's my glasses case, for Christ's sake. I need it. Surely it's possible to shake the thing into the drink?'

'I think we should adopt a more humane approach,' said Robin, rather enjoying the dilemma. 'We should set the spider adrift on a raft made up from the remaining pasta-shell packets.'

'That's a bloody brilliant idea,' said Kevin, showing a lot of enthusiasm for this solution.

'Yeah, and we can chuck in the dead bird to keep him company.'

The dead bird was neatly placed between two slices of burnt toast, held in place by elastic bands. The raft was ready to lower into the water, and Robin had even put together a few words to give the exercise a ceremonial flavour. The only problem would be to coax the occupant out of the spectacle case.

'Oh, for goodness sake!' said Victor, 'I'll toss a coin.' Further argument followed when Kevin won three calls on the trot and thought he was out of the reckoning. Victor, however, insisted he was the outright winner. 'Why do you think we invited you on this cruise if it wasn't an opportunity for you to display your courage and tenacity?'

Robin read out his departure note: 'Oh Lord, please accept this unfortunate pair into your kind and compassionate care and give them a really nice treat. Kit them out with fancy webbed feet. Amen.'

He gently lowered the raft into the water. 'NOW, KEVIN!' he shouted.

Kevin, startled by the unexpected volume of the command, fumbled with the case, then dropped it to the ground as the spider ran up his arm. With yells of terror he went into a rain dance as the spider crawled under his plum-coloured shirt.

'Ah, ah, eeeh; get it off!' he cried, twisting back and forth trying to locate its whereabouts, but the spider seemed to understand that the sea wasn't the place for him and scuttled up the backstay. The ungainly raft soon attracted a pair of seabirds.

'Tell you what, Kevin,' said Robin, 'the gulls are showing a lot of enthusiasm for your elasticised sarnie.'

'Yeah!' replied Kevin, white-faced and trying to compose himself. 'Look at all the good your bleeding prayers have done for your feathered friend.'

Victor called out to Hannah, 'It's all clear! The spider has gone for a swim.' He held his finger to his lips in a gesture to the crew to keep quiet on the subject.

Hannah, looking anxious, stepped into the cockpit. 'The barometer's falling!'

'What, again?' said Victor, surprised. 'It's been going up and down for the last hour. I'm not sure we can rely on it. I think it might be bust.' But all thoughts of a defective instrument were dismissed as Hannah, with a worried frown, pointed to a thick black line on the horizon; it looked as if a felt pen had drawn it. The mood of the crew changed instantly and the banter dissolved into an eerie silence.

Battening down had now become automatic, requiring little instruction, and we resigned ourselves with weary sullenness to the pain that lay ahead. Fear lurked in the shadows, an unobtrusive presence that tugged at our sleeves and sharpened the senses, helping to tighten the ship.

I volunteered to cook a meal; a later opportunity might not become available. I thought we needed something hot and satisfying, of blanket-clinging quality to adhere to plastic plates and inner stomach linings, that could be eaten with a spoon. Knives and forks are awkward in a pitching boat, and at 1600 hours conditions were becoming unbearable. I served up a shepherd's pie like an Indian scout playing shove-ha'penny, sliding plates and half-filled cups across the floor. The thud of solid water on the coach roof and decks, coupled with the unsteady wallowing in the steep troughs, told of worsening conditions outside. Day turned to night, as black as we had ever seen. The shepherd's pie clung to floor, ceiling, windows, winches and spectacles – everywhere except the stomach lining. Sleep became an almost impossible luxury.

When the autopilot gave up, we knew we had a long night ahead.

Victor thought it dangerous to continue battling into the huge seas; he was concerned the twin hulls might become overstressed and break in two. Our progress had dwindled to zero. We were bobbing up and down and going nowhere.

'I don't think we've any option but to run with the storm. What d'you think, Dad?'

'Steering downwind will be a bit hairy in these conditions. I think we should share the helming and hope things improve. Be careful turning her about, Victor. Wait for a decent gap. We don't want to shake hands with a big beamer.'

Although the motion became more tolerable running with the wind, our speed had accelerated, varying between four and six knots under bare poles, and *Katehawk* was flipping off the wave tops in scary fashion, threatening to pitch-pole into the troughs below. There was some discussion of using drogues to slow the boat speed, but the hull design made this awkward. Also the large dinghy strung across the stern created problems of access and visibility. We were now in a full-blown Atlantic storm, with gusts approaching forty-five knots. With no experience of such severe conditions the idea of ropes trailing astern had little appeal, and the fear of catching a rope round the propellers was something else we would have to worry about. There was some welcome relief when I managed to get the autopilot working again. The crew were showing signs of weariness from the constant battering and lack of sleep, coupled with seasickness. Speed became a constant worry, not only because of the danger of pitch-poling but also because of the dissipation of hard-won miles and the realisation that we would have insufficient fuel to get to Madeira.

A tap on the shoulder roused me from my warm bunk.

'It's your watch, Dad. It's really rough out there; don't forget to clip on.' Sleep had been shallow. I thought I'd only been in my bunk for ten minutes.

'Blimey! Already?' I had no enthusiasm for the three-hour dead man's watch that night. I wondered what on earth I was doing, crewing for my son on a boat in a howling Atlantic gale when I could have been snug at home in a comfortable bed.

I had little time or respect for some of the time-honoured traditions of the sea, regarding many as obsolete and egotistical nonsense. In the matter of watches, however, I had no quarrel. Watches had to be adhered to in a disciplined manner, and I took up my duty with yawning acceptance. Lying on the cockpit floor, I pulled a woolly hat over my ears and put on some warm gloves, a small investment in attire that had really proved its worth. Checking for the essential torch, I carefully came to my feet and lunged for the rope I had fastened across the canopy as a handhold. The small Yanmar diesels had proved most reliable and I almost enjoyed their music that mingled with the boat noises and storm. The noise created an unusual symphony, spoilt only by the strange noise at the stern of the boat, thought to be the hydraulic steering emulating the unnerving cry of a baby in distress.

I unwrapped another toffee and wished there'd been more chocolate peppermint drinks. The sachets had proved popular with all the crew, and were certainly one of Hannah's better decisions. But before I could raise the toffee to my mouth the stern lifted in the air, hovered unsteadily for a moment, then skittered down a wave that seemed to go on forever, followed by a bone-shaking judder as we slammed into the back of the previous wave. I was extremely alarmed as I realised we had almost pitch-poled. I studied the instruments and noted wind speed had increased to forty-six knots, gusting to fifty-two. Noise levels had increased, with the whine of singing steel in the rigging and humming halyards combining with stress noises I'd never heard before. The mast was flexing as if made of rubber and conditions were definitely getting worse. Once more the stern lifted, not so steeply, but I knew something had to be done – immediately. We were in grave danger unless we could reduce speed. Frantically I tried to figure the best course of action. I contemplated calling Victor from his bunk, but realised sleep was essential for him. I dithered about what to do next, and could feel I was starting to panic. I started to mutter to myself, 'Don't panic; don't panic'.

I suspected the wind was getting trapped in the large dinghy that was acting like a small spinnaker and causing the stern to lift at the top of a wave. It was no time to procrastinate – a pitch-pole seemed inevitable. I decided to alter course to bring the wind diagonally across the stern by about six degrees; anything more might bring us beam-on to the waves and into even more danger. If correct, my theory would let the wind spill more easily from the stern. Recalling the difficulties of getting the autopilot to accept any course earlier on did not make me feel very confident, yet it seemed to be managing so far. I realised that I couldn't hesitate any longer when once more the stern lifted alarmingly before a dizzy skittering dive down a wave. I made the decision to alter course with minor increments of one half-degree at a time. With trembling hands I applied the first half-degree. *Katehawk* faltered briefly, then steadied and held course. Then another and another till I had three whole degrees. The stern lifted again and she seemed to twist awkwardly, almost airborne, and then thudded into the trough below, banging my ribs against the console. Gut instinct told me to apply the other three degrees as quickly as possible. Holding my breath I added one whole degree, and stood ready to switch off the autopilot and take over the manual if she failed. I grew old watching her yaw back and forth threatening to slide into the boiling trough below, then she twitched her bow defiantly and straightened on to course. The motion improved almost instantly, as though a cushion had been strapped to the under hull. Even so there was still too much lift at the stern. In a brief moment I stopped concentrating on what I was doing and applied a full two more degrees all at once. *Katehawk* reared up and swung round like a bolting horse, threatening to flounder as she rejected the new course. I switched to manual and grabbed the wheel, fighting to get back on course, cursing my stupidity. With persistent tinkering she eventually settled down to the new course and I felt able to relax. I made a quick note of the course change in the log, knowing it was essential Vic should know what I'd done, and rewarded myself with a further two toffees, feeling the crew had much to thank me for.

There was still an hour of my watch to go; five minutes seemed like an hour. I became aware of drowsiness overtaking me as the pink glow of the compass started to dim to a tiny dot. I desperately wanted my warm bunk.

Twenty minutes passed on the ship's clock and *Katehawk* felt very much more comfortable on the new course. I gradually acclimatised to the noise and black fury of the sea, and defiantly started to hum Handel's Hallelujah Chorus. The humming exercise, which I found uplifting, had an unexpected soothing effect on my nerves. Then above the deafening noise there came an even louder roar, like a convoy of racing juggernauts, and a high-pitched whistle under the cockpit. There was a heavy, lurching thud and I was thrown across the floor. A solid wall of perceptibly green water burst through the canopy side screens rising up in front of me. I could only watch with terrified disbelief as the water swirled around me. It continued to pour in, quite calmly, as if with a perfect right to do so. Then it stopped, leaving a gaping black hole in the side of the canopy. There was a dull aching pain down my left thigh where I had been thrown against the port helm seat and two deep red tramlines under my fleshy forearm, almost piercing the skin, where I had wrapped it round the winch as the swirling water swept past me. In a daze I watched an apricot skin spiralling in the vortex of water swilling towards the large cockpit drain and wondered if the toffee wrapper would catch up with it. Knowing the importance of keeping the cockpit drains clear, yet unable to move, I glanced at the compass, thinking the auto-pilot had failed and that we had slid into a beam sea, but the lubber line seemed constant. Fear caught hold of both my mind and body and my thought processes became jumbled and incoherent. I disliked tinned apricots; so did Caroline, my daughter, and I wondered why. I wondered if the spider was still up the mast, and grinned at the thought of his discomfort; I wondered if he would survive and guessed we would never know. I remembered the police inspector's shock ultimatum: 'We don't want people like you settling on our patch! You've one week to get out of town.'

'Rat-a-tat-tat!' A noise like a machine gun brought me back to the present. I looked fearfully at the writhing black canopy. The wind was threatening to tear it off its supports. Another sickening thud – the bow rose into the air and a cloud of stinging spray burst into the cockpit. As a small boy at school I had constantly prayed to God: religion had been a seven-days-a-week preoccupation, but nothing in later life convinced me of its credibility. The gaping hole in the canopy meant we were in grave danger. The sea now had open access to flood and overwhelm the boat. The flimsy canvas may not have been a match for the odd freak wave, but at least it provided shelter and blotted out the black heaving terror from view. I knew we could not rely on prayer. The Almighty had turned on a wave machine and there seemed little likelihood of him switching it off any time soon. I had to try to sort out the problem myself – and quickly.

I felt anger welling up inside me as I wrestled with the canvas. The trimmer had made a solid job of the seams and the stitching had held together well, but two of the fasteners had been completely torn out. Fixing the canopy had always been a difficult task, even on a windless day, but now I had to release my lifeline, which was too short, and move outside. As a precautionary measure I tucked the bulky foghorn into my sailing jacket as a means of waking the crew if I went overboard. Realising its vulnerability to seawater, I covered it with a cellophane bag and tied it with a bungee strap, my thought being that I might just get two blasts out of it before the sea took over. I felt confident that even in these conditions the rest of the crew would hear it, although I had no illusions about my chances of survival. Even if they managed to scramble on deck in as little as two minutes, the boat would have travelled some two hundred and fifty yards from our present position. There would be little chance of recovery, but at least they would realise the boat was unmanned. The wind was so strong, like grappling arms trying to pull me into the raging sea. Clinging to the steel supports I felt them move ominously, and realised they couldn't possibly take my full weight of sixteen stone if I slipped. I stood deliberating about whether to climb back into the cockpit and tie a line around my waist and secure it to the base of the helm seat, and considered a short blast on the foghorn to make everyone else aware of my dangerous decision. Then I realised this action would require two hands. The anger welled up in me once more and I called myself a stupid idiot. I don't know how I managed to do this, but somehow I was able to tug the canvas towards me. Maybe I used the bungee strap that I had tied round the plastic bag holding the foghorn; in any event I was determined to reaffix what I could on to the fixing poppers. Having achieved a reasonable repair with some satisfaction, I carefully eased my way back into the cockpit. Then I became aware of something stopping my progress. The foghorn had become wedged between a deck stanchion and wire cable supports. I turned to free it, but it fell from my sailing jacket to the deck. Lurching downwards, I tried unsuccessfully to stop it falling into the sea, and almost fell overboard myself, but for fingertips still clutching the canvas. Finally I lay on the cockpit floor, my chest thumping like a bass drum, scared out of my wits at such a close call.

My growing list of mistakes was beginning to worry me. I had nearly thrown my life away for a few pounds of foghorn. I needed to focus and think clearly about making decisions. There was another rumbling roar, and I stared at the canopy. My tongue had stuck to the roof of my mouth, which was dry and swollen. Salt crystals were stinging my eyes and I thought of the young people in the cabins below: my two sons, Hannah and Kevin. I ached with fear for their safety.

I looked around the cockpit, trying to analyse the options. At the boatyard, great emphasis had been put on safety equipment; nothing had been left to chance. Yet I knew in the present conditions our best hope of seeing another dawn would rely more on good luck than anything else. A shuddering thud on the coach roof and *Katehawk* shook and trembled as a noise like a lorry dumping gravel startled me into action. Shining the torch into the lazarette, I focused on the heavy drum of coiled anchor rope, with some vague idea of tying the two hulls together fore and aft, the thought being that perhaps it would gain precious time if *Katehawk* broke in two. My greatest fear was that we might become separated. My hands shook violently in the torchlight as I went through the motions of trying to lift the drum, well knowing it was beyond me and would require two strong men to move it. Then I realised another dumb decision was forming in my head. To move out of the cockpit and on to the deck would be suicidal. The sensible solution was to stick with the boat, which was supposedly unsinkable. The breaking waves were like hammer blows on the shuddering hull as if to test its sea-worthiness, looking for a weakness. Panic and anger fused together as the full realisation of what could and might happen began to take a hold. I yearned for the supportive confident call of youth from the cabins below: 'Are you all right, Dad'?

But no voice came. I couldn't believe they could sleep in such pandemonium and guessed there would be white knuckles and fear below. I had always imagined myself as a strong, dependable person in a crisis, but now I felt helpless and terrified. Trying hard to fight the panic and muttering to myself, 'Keep calm', I seemed unable to react normally. It seemed as though the component parts of my body had become separated and were no longer attached to my brain.

Now a more formidable opponent confronted me. The ship's clock said there were another thirty minutes before my watch was finished. I stared intently at the hands, convinced it was slow or had stopped altogether. My legs started to buckle, my eyes kept closing and I experienced a previously unknown state of exhaustion. I tried to hold my eyelids open with my fingers, but merely filled my eyes with salt crystals. It was as though I had no further control over either brain or body. Stumbling below, scarcely able to stand, I knocked on Victor's cabin.

'Sorry, finished ... knackered ... danger to ship.'

I paused long enough to hear him answer, 'Okay, Dad.'

Despite the exhaustion, sleep didn't come easily. I heard voices during the night, a constant chattering, reminiscent of a school canteen, that went on and on. I tried to decipher the words without success. I had to be very careful getting into my bunk to avoid banging my head on the hardwood furniture. My head bounced around like a tennis ball, but I didn't feel any pain; even the bruising on my thigh had subsided. Then my mind started to fidget with a red-eyed, sobbing figure of forty-something years ago. This was very odd because until now I'd rarely thought of my mother. She belonged to the past, an unhappy period I'd long forgotten about. I'd shut her out of my life; my wife and children knew nothing about her. Now I couldn't get her out of my mind. I guiltily remembered the last time I saw her during the Christmas period of 1949. I'd thrown her Christmas presents – a white silk scarf and a pair of slippers – to the ground ... and swore I'd never return home.

All at once there was a crashing thud by my pillow and an angry, slithering noise like a growling serpent coming towards me. I jerked upright, thinking I was having a nightmare, and banged my head on the overhead beam, startled out of my semi-conscious state. Then the noise started to slide away from me as if it were disturbed by my presence and was trying to get away. My hands were shaking. What the hell was going on; was it a giant sea slug or something trying to get on board? I opened my mouth to shout, then heard another more familiar noise: the clink and clunk of metal. The anchor and its chain had shifted in the violent conditions. I buried my head in the pillow and once more groaned at my stupidity.

My thoughts kept returning to my mother; I couldn't get her out of my mind. Suddenly I desperately wanted to see her again, and hoped she was still alive. I swore that if we survived this storm I would find her. She would meet her grandchildren and their children. She would surely like that. I could then also truthfully answer the question Vic had asked me when he was a schoolboy: 'Dad, I've got to do a family tree for my homework. Can you help me?' His question had startled me and I had fobbed him off, saying I was too busy. He was upset and continued to ask questions about my family for several days.

I awoke from a shallow sleep. It was perhaps surprising that I'd slept at all, but exhaustion helped, and I found myself to be surprisingly refreshed considering the conditions. The sun was hot on my face and there were shouts from the cockpit.

'Jesus, look at that one!' It was Kevin's voice commenting on the size of the waves. Although the wind had slackened, the ship's motion had hardly improved. We were now back on a westerly course with well-reefed sails, reclaiming lost ground. I cupped my face to the perspex window and marvelled at nature's raw magnificence. I watched my tormentors of the night: huge, grey, tomb-like Niagaras cascading into pools of lobelia blue, ringed with frothy white alyssum. They were lacy-tailed predatory hounds with crusty manes, racing, chasing, coiling, curling, iridescent green; clouds of sparkling droplets, morphing into rainbow spray. It was a fascinating, fearsome panorama I felt privileged to witness, could never forget, or want to repeat.

Late in the afternoon Kevin yelled excitedly, 'Land ahead!' He pointed to a dull grey smudge on the horizon rising high into the sky.

'That's Porto Santo,' muttered Victor. He adjusted his binoculars, and sighed with relief. We rounded the headland into calmer waters, and while preparing to release the anchor into the bay we were surprised to see a marina.

'Are you sure this is Porto Santo, Vic?' asked Robin, scanning the chart.

'It's not on the chart, Robin, but I reckon this place has just been built. You can still see the cement lorries and stuff over there.'

I was overwhelmingly relieved as we moored up on the brand new pontoons. During the night I'd had my doubts that my feet would ever set on land again. The stark new concrete jetty caressed my feet like Kentish meadow grass; the snarling exhaust of a distant scooter sounded like Ravel's Bolero. Snow-white goats grazed on the emerald cliff-tops; red and pink geraniums grew wild by the roadside. There were no traffic wardens, yellow lines, or policemen. We needed to celebrate: to eat a four-course meal and get drunk.

The manager of the local restaurant, on overhearing we would have to go back to the boat to get more money, announced, 'It's no problem, my friends. You eat and drink now and be happy! Pay me tomorrow!'

Suddenly the world seemed a much better place.

2

We spent two days in Porto Santo recovering from the storm. During the first night I bought up the subject of the voices I'd heard during the storm. I couldn't believe that nobody else had heard them. Kevin, of course, made much of this. He whispered to Robin, 'So your Dad's hearing voices!' He used every opportunity he could to poke fun at me about this strange happening.

Several bedraggled mariners trickled into the harbour and recounted their hair-raising tales. A group of teenagers spilled out of a three-masted schooner. They looked drained and staggered along the jetty like zombies. The exhausted Norwegian skipper joined us for a drink.

He raised his glass. 'Salute! They are young offenders,' he confided. 'I try to teach them how to sail and become good citizens,' he added, scratching his stubbly chin and laughing, 'and how to be really sick. You know, they've hardly spoken a word for two days. I bought the boat from an Italian priest. He couldn't afford a thousand pounds a week for the moorings in Saint Tropez.'

'A thousand pounds!' gasped Victor. 'What's a priest doing with that sort of money and a boat like that?'

'Why not? The church has plenty of money.'

Another beautiful varnished ketch arrived, with a Scandinavian husband-and-wife crew. They tied up next to us and came aboard for a drink.

'The waves were so big!' she cried, drawing large, jagged hummocks in the sky. 'Yes, and the voices,' nodded her husband, clasping his hands to his ears, 'I kept hearing the voices.' I grasped his hand and replenished his glass. We became brothers, united in the proof of our own sanity.

Our next port, Funchal in Madeira, lay only twenty-five nautical miles south, but the journey seemed to go on forever.

Later we discovered that the bathing ladder hadn't been raised and that it was causing excessive drag. Kevin made the casual observation, 'We should've lowered the bathing ladder during the storm. It would've made a useful drogue.'

Seen from the sea at night, Madeira has a magical quality about it. It's a mountainous silhouette dotted with flickering lights; a delicate, dewy, sequinned spider's web, surrounded by clouds chasing the moon and stars. We anchored outside the harbour in the certain knowledge there'd be no room inside. With their broad girth, catamarans are not the most popular craft in crowded marinas. I relaxed in the aft cockpit, watching small fish dancing in a shaft of moonlight piercing a passing cloud.

'Come and look at these tiddlers,' I called out. 'They're dancing in unison in an aqua ballet. I reckon fish have more cultural instincts than we give them credit for.'

Kevin bent his chunky frame over the guard-rail, muttering, 'Nonsense, Gordon! You're talking bollocks. Fish are like some people I know, with a large space between the ears. They're not dancing; they're just trying to get out of the sewage.'

Most journeys in the dinghy were accompanied by rain. During my first dinghy trip in Madeira harbour, I experienced hailstones as big as conkers. Funchal is a popular stopover for the big cruise liners. *Canberra*, recently released from her duties in the 1982 British–Argentine war, looked resplendent after her decommissioning. Her paying passengers may have thought the sun had also gone for a refit, because we didn't see much of it during our stay, but they might have been a little excited when Eric Tabarly's forty-two-foot trimaran *Toria* was craned out just forward of *Canberra*'s bow sections. She had been towed into the harbour upside down by a fishing boat. The French crack yachtsman had won the Round Britain Race with her in 1966, had capsized in the same storm we'd been caught in, and had been rescued by the Portuguese navy. He said that the sea conditions were the worst he'd ever experienced.

* * *

Canberra in Madiera. Toria being craned out after the storm. Mark's catamaran at anchor.

One of the delights of cruising is the bonhomie and camaraderie. It's not uncommon to have visitors calling during the evening, and to hear the friendly 'Hello! Permission to come aboard?' Though caution is always advisable of course.

Mark and Juliet had a catamaran moored nearby, a workmanlike Wharram. 'We're on our way to Gambia,' said Mark with a casual grin. 'I have a signed letter from the president, granting me permission to charter the boat in the Gambia.'

'Not Pol Pot!' I gasped. 'He's murdered a quarter of a million people, for Christ's sake. That's a dangerous place.'

Juliet giggled aloud. 'Gordon! You're showing your ignorance. Gambia isn't Cambodia!'

27

'We're talking Africa,' laughed Mark. 'The Gambia River is a place of real opportunity. An up-and-coming tourist honey-pot.'

'Well, I don't know. The map of the world has changed so much since I left school.'

'We've had enough problems already,' said Juliet, a feisty, bubbly woman, with a great sense of humour. 'We've had a busted tiller, overheating, rigging problems, gales, and God knows what else. Luckily we've a couple of Israeli gorillas for crew. I don't know how we would have managed without them.'

'The anchor was the worst,' groaned Mark. It buried itself into an old rusting hulk on the seabed. We dived and dived, but couldn't release the blasted thing. It just wouldn't budge. We had to hire oxygen and cutting gear to release it.'

We sat in the aft cockpit exchanging yarns and sipping wine till late, watching the Wharram catamaran going up and down like a fairground switchback ride.

'Will you be all right with your dinghy?' asked the ever-caring Hannah, anxiously. 'It's so rough out there.'

'No problem,' said Mark, lowering himself over the side. 'We're well used to it. See you! Thanks for the drinks.'

A heavy swell and blustery conditions greeted us the following morning, making dinghy travel untenable. Victor decided to motor into the marina, knowing our appearance would cause some consternation. The yachts were rafted up to the harbour wall seven and eight deep, and audible groans were heard as we entered with our seventeen-foot beam. Victor called out, 'It's okay, we're not stopping. Just fuel and water.' Then a friendly voice called, 'Over here, Buddy. Throw us your line. Kinda rough out there, I bet.'

'You're not kidding,' said Kevin. 'Even the fucking seagulls are complaining.'

We spent a pleasant half-hour over a coffee with the American and his wife, while waiting for the fuel pontoon to open.

'The wife prefers this weather, don't you, dear?' He pointed to the large mushroom hat. 'Got a medical problem. Has to keep out of the sun, y'know.' She nodded, a snowy white face with a fine dusting of freckles.

'I like to feel the breeze on my face,' she said.

A buzz of excitement developed near the entrance to the harbour, followed by anxious voices building to a crescendo.

'Look out, look out!' A large French sailboat with a bowsprit like a redundant telephone pole was creaming down the main fairway. A dumpy, grey-haired woman with a look of sheer panic stood in the bow section with a long boat hook in one hand and a fender in the other, gesticulating to everyone to get out of the way. The American seemed to understand her agitated French.

'Busted gearbox. They can't stop, poor devils, they're in real trouble. Rather them than me. Hey! Jesus, what the heck are they doing now?' He rushed forward to get a better view of what was going on, then realised the telephone pole had angled in towards us. 'Oh shit!' Casting our lines aside, he shouted: 'Get outa here, that motherfucker's going to skewer us. Get your arse outa here,' he screamed at his deathly white wife, who was hesitating. 'C'mon, woman, let the frigging line go, will ya?'

We shunted *Katehawk* across to the other side of the fairway and wedged ourselves in amongst the fishing boats.

'What a to-do,' muttered Victor. 'We're well out of that.'

'This looks dodgy,' said Robin, pointing to a German catamaran slowly approaching the entrance, with a shapely blonde busily retrieving her smalls from the stanchion rails, oblivious to the trouble coming her way. A Swedish boat wanting to leave the harbour had let all the lines go of the boats rafted up to him. Soon the air became full of revving engines and loud swearing as boats zigzagged back and forth trying to keep out of harm's way. The loudest voice was the American, who stood in the bows of his boat with an armful of fenders, waving his boat hook and wanting to fuck everyone in the marina.

'Bugger off! You bunch of motherfuckers,' he screamed.

'It's like the Battle of Trafalgar,' laughed Robin.

Nevertheless, within half an hour complete serenity had

returned, without any apparent damage to anyone. The only voice was that of the softly spoken Frenchwoman, calling out to everyone who showed interest, 'So sorry, zer gearbox go puff puff.'

We tanked up with water and replenished our stores. As usual the diesel had its own set of problems; the fuel hose was too short, and we had the weary task of humping jerry cans across boat decks and other obstacles.

* * *

We left before daybreak the following morning for the Salvage Islands, an uninhabited volcanic archipelago a hundred and sixty-two nautical miles south of Madeira. We were told it was illegal to land without written permission from the Portuguese authorities. The chart confirmed it to be a rock-strewn area with a solitary white light at night. In true pioneering spirit, Victor decided to land at Selvagem Grande, just for the hell of it. At least the weather improved during the afternoon, so we splashed on the sun lotion and relaxed on a flat, oily sea. Two small birds joined us in the evening. One was a bright chirpy, yellow linnet-type bird that seemed unfazed by human contact and sat on Victor's shoulder, The other, with wagtail-like qualities, appeared more nervous and kept his distance, finally settling on a coil of rope for the night.

Robin decided to have a go at catching some fresh fish with a fancy lure. He had scarcely cast his line before his fishing rod was bent up like a U-bolt. There was a twang and the twenty-two-pound line snapped.

'Jesus!' cried Kevin. 'What the hell was that?'

Robin ruefully surveyed his line. 'I don't believe it!' he gasped. It's bitten right through the stainless-steel lure.'

'Come off it,' said Victor, 'that's impossible. I expect it was a conger eel. This is their type of habitat, although they haven't got titanium teeth as far as I know.'

'Well I'm glad I didn't catch him,' said Robin emphatically. 'I reckon he would have been really cross if we'd tried to eat him. I prefer tinned sardines. They're less confrontational.'

We motor-sailed all night with an irritating mainsail requiring constant attention in the fluky breeze. The hard lines of the islands appeared on our starboard side at daybreak, a dark, grey undulating hummock with streaks of white foam breaking on surrounding rocks. The wagtail fluttered out of the rope coil and settled on the stanchion rails, twitching his head and tail back and forth in exploratory fashion as if trying to establish his geographical position. Then he flew away. The yellow finch followed soon after. We then witnessed a most amazing sight. The sky filled with seabirds, thousands and thousands of them creating night out of daybreak. They didn't make a sound; it was a most eerie experience, like a curtain being drawn across the sky.

Victor scanned the surrounding area with binoculars for a suitable anchorage. 'We could try a landing over there,' he said, pointing to a small spot of sand and pebble on the rocky beach about the size of a dustbin lid. 'At least there's no surf breaking on it.'

'There's hardly room,' said Robin. 'Do you reckon it might be safer to go to Cambodia?'

'Landing there will be hazardous. You're taking unnecessary risks,' I said. Despite all my parental protestations, within half an hour I was the only member of the crew left on board. They sat awkwardly huddled together on the small patch of sand and shingle, twiddling their thumbs and with the occasional self-conscious wave in my direction. I settled down with a cup of tea. Half dozing, twenty minutes passed, and then I became aware of a change in wind direction. Peering through the binoculars at the wave pattern, I noticed the breakers were gradually moving along the island in a more southerly direction. I sounded the horn and pointed to the breaking surf moving towards them.

Victor realised the danger immediately and ushered Hannah into the dinghy. By the time he returned to collect Robin the breakers were already looking ominous, and he still had to go back for Kevin. The three of us watched anxiously as he weaved through the huge waves. Then Kevin cupped his hands together and yelled out his idea of the best approach.

'I'll hold the bow of the dinghy when you come in with the surf, then push you out as the next wave comes in, and then I'll climb on board. Okay?'

Kevin waded into the breaking surf like Colossus with outstretched arms ready to impose his superiority over the sea. He lunged at the pitching dinghy and disappeared in the bubbling surf.

'Oh no!' gasped Hannah.

Moments later the two of them were on the beach spitting out sand and pebbles with the dinghy on top of them.

'Now we've got a real problem,' I muttered. 'I think we might have to raise the anchor and try to get in closer. Perhaps if we tie the mooring lines together with a fender tied to one end to keep it afloat, they can secure it to the dinghy and we can winch them back.'

'Hang on, Dad. There are a couple of blokes coming down the cliff towards them. They're probably wardens or something. They seem to be giving instructions of some sort. They're going to have another go... ooh... er... Jesus, just look at those breakers. Where are they coming from? They're past the first one,' said Robin. 'If they can get through this next one they might be all right.'

'Here it comes ... Wowee!' yelled Hannah. 'Look at that. That was a real biggy.' Kevin looked humbled as he collapsed into the cockpit with fear still flickering in his eyes.

'Talk about dicing with death,' mumbled Kevin. 'That was bloody dangerous. I'm covered in bruises.'

'Okay, Dad,' panted Victor, wringing out his sodden shirt. 'I hear you loud and clear. We were lucky to get away with that.'

We were now heading for Las Palmas in the Canaries, the largest of the seven islands. Its commercial harbour had the dubious reputation of being one of the most oil-polluted in the world. Despite the floating boom separating the yacht marina from the commercial harbour, yachts and dinghies were seldom free from the oily sludge.

Even with the benefits of the so-called Portuguese current, worth about one-and-a- half knots, and extensive use of our cruising chute, the eighty-something miles seemed inordinately long.

'I think we've collected a bit of growth on our bottom,' said Victor. 'They'll have a scrubbing berth in the marina. We can sort it out there.'

As we arrived in the hours of darkness, we saw the tragic *Herald of Free Enterprise* berthed along the harbour wall. A car and passenger ferry, she had sunk in Zeebrugge on 6 March 1987 when her bow doors were accidentally left open. It was sobering to think of the near two hundred souls trapped and drowned in the cabins. I shuddered at the thought of their agony. Our storm would have been like a paddle in a municipal swimming pool compared to their suffering. After refloating in April 1987 she was renamed *Flushing Range*. We were told she was on her way to Alang in India.

* * *

'What about inviting Mum out here for a few days, Vic, while the sun is still shining?' I ventured.

'She doesn't like sailing, Dad.'

'Well, you didn't help – taking her out in the English Channel in a force eight, for Christ's sake. Out here it's different. She'd like the stability of a catamaran, I'm sure. Anyway, just ask her.'

Almost every other day we would meet interesting people with fascinating tales of extended voyages and reasons for taking them. One couple, Tom and Anita, had flown from America to buy a used Prout catamaran in Southampton. They were in the process of sailing it back to the States. They were disenchanted with the rat race.

'So what sort of work d'you do in the States?' enquired Kevin.

Without flinching, Tom answered, 'I'm a lawyer.' A suitable silence followed.

'So how's the trip been?' asked Victor. 'Many gales?'

'It's been rough most of the way. The wife's been on a diet of toasted popcorn and aspirin in equal measure since leaving the States. Although you cut out the popcorn in Biscay, huh?'

Anita nodded with a grimace. 'Yeah! The only thing I'm really missing is the unbearable misery and stress we enjoyed so much at home, before starting out on this crazy venture.'

Tom laughed. 'Me too. We had intended to sail around the UK a bit before coming out here, but we're new to this game and you Brits – well, your boating is kinda strange. I just don't understand how you can be sailing in twenty metres of water one minute, and then find yourself stranded in a sandcastle competition an hour later. It's crazy. We Yanks would dredge and concrete the whole damn English Channel, and neutralise this tidal nonsense. My only real regret is that I can't remember the animal who gave me this rotten idea in the first place. I feel I should be suing somebody.'

'Apart from that?' quipped Robin.

'Wouldn't change a thing,' said Anita. 'Now, can I offer you folks some toasted popcorn? We're a bit overstocked.'

* * *

The rest of the crew had gone into town as I sat dozing in the cockpit.

'Hello Gord! You got here, then? When did you arrive? Come and have a coffee, Mate.' Charlie looked like a tramp in scruffy jeans and T-shirt, with an enviable suntan. Loading four brown sugars into his cup, he stirred vigorously as he unravelled his painful chain of events. 'You met Heidi, didn't you?'

'Briefly, in Gibraltar,'

'She was great, Gordon. Bloody good sailor, too. I returned to the boat with the shopping and she'd gone. Not a note or anything. Just packed her bags and left. I don't understand it.'

'Come on, Charlie. She must have had a reason.' I resisted the temptation to mention his depression. 'You weren't getting frisky with her?'

'No Gord! It wasn't like that, though the chance would've been nice. She probably found herself a bloke, or another boat, or something. Then I had a couple of blokes who crewed for me to Madeira. A right lazy useless pair they were, just looking for a good time at my expense. Things got quite nasty with them. They cut my mooring lines during the night, caused me a whole lot of aggro, that did. I decided to sail solo down here.'

'That must have been a bit hairy, doing it solo. How did you get a kip?'

He shuddered. 'I wouldn't do it again. Too much of a worry. There's a lot of traffic round these parts, and the fishing boats are a real pain; you don't know whether they're coming or going. I'm not sure they do, either. Then the Salvage Islands. Jesus! You need to be wide-awake round there. I arrived at night in a hard blow. I was absolutely knackered. I wet myself. So how long you staying ? Are you doing the Arc crossing.

'No, I'm just waiting for Babs my wife to join us for a few days sailing, then I'll be returning to the UK.'

Victor got permission from the owner for her to join us for a quick sail round the islands. Fortunately the sun was in a good mood, and Babs enjoyed a few days of truly agreeable sailing. Our first stop was Santa Cruz in La Palma or the Green Island. There were limited moorings within the harbour but we were able to raft up to a German charter boat. The Germans were well represented in the Canaries, having bought large chunks of land (to the annoyance of many locals), and were building holiday villas en masse. La Palma had a good reputation for fresh fruit and vegetables, which we were keen to exploit, and also a rather smart township of well-stocked shops, bars and restaurants. Babs was particularly impressed with one large store that was on a par with Harrods. Our purchases were packed in gift-box fashion with ribbons and delivered to our boat. The island also boasted one of the largest volcanic craters in the world. We hired a car to explore. A tunnel had been cut out of the volcanic rock with a narrow, winding road climbing to the volcano's rim. We travelled across banana plantations, orange groves and small shantytowns, and passed through another tunnel thick with mountain mist where the temperature dropped rapidly. Then we rose above the clouds and were bathed in sunshine. We parked the car on the outer rim of the crater and admired the magnificence of the volcano. The air seemed so still, clean and fresh, and there was complete silence all around. Coniferous trees had sunk their shallow roots into the volcanic soil, creating a vast emerald carpet.

Hannah spoke my thoughts: 'I could pull up a deck-chair and just sit here all day.'

Trouble returned as we drove to the other side of the Island. Victor groaned, 'What do we do now?' A landslide of volcanic rock had collapsed on to the road, blocking our path. Workmen were hurriedly trying to clear the debris while an old man observed us from above. The front door of his home had fallen away and the foundations of his house were crumbling. Our problem seemed minuscule by comparison.

We liked Palma and would have stayed longer, but our schedule was tight. Our final call was to the island of Gomera. The pilot book warned against entering the harbour at night – which seemed a good reason for trying – but we became worried when we heard the yacht *Stilchea* put out a distress call over the VHF on our approach to the harbour.

The Danish crew were mightily relieved when we appeared on the scene and towed them into the harbour; they had struck a rock and buckled their shaft and propeller. 'You must come aboard and we will enjoy a nice bottle of brandy,' said the skipper. Having spent the better part of six months on a stable catamaran platform, we found it extremely uncomfortable in a monohull. There was only a slight swell running but we were being tossed all over the place and had to get off quickly and abandon the brandy.

* * *

Babs found it very difficult to get on and off the landing stage at the end of the jetty; there is a knack in skipping across a small armada of moving rubber dinghies without falling over. She insisted I should help her, and we looked an ungainly pair of clowns clinging to each other. The natural law of boating will ensure a large crowd will gather to be amused without paying an entrance fee, and so it was. The dinghy moorings became a constant source of comedy for local fishermen and those with time on their hands.

The catamaran owner and family decided they didn't want to join the boat to sail to America, and Victor had to get two more crew as apart from my not being available he'd also asked Kevin to leave.

Kevin joined a large French catamaran, saying untruthfully that he was a fully qualified navigator. They landed on the wrong island.

Charlie, the manic depressive, took on two Canadians for the crossing and won first prize for being the most unpopular skipper. He accepted it.

I stood on the quay in Gran Canaria watching the crews preparing for the annual Arc race across the Atlantic. There was excitement in the air, with horns blaring and shouts of encouragement as they set off. I felt very emotional as I said goodbye to my two sons. I felt I should be going with them for such a wonderful adventure, but I'd been away from home for nearly six months and Babs didn't want to spend Christmas on her own. For a while I was stuck in Gran Canaria without a bean. That meant I had to visit the British Embassy – who were much more helpful once they'd seen my bank statement. (In those days, getting your money out of the UK when abroad was very difficult and time-consuming.)

* * *

We were able to telephone a special number supplied by the race authorities who told us about Victor's progress. He took thirty days to cross the Atlantic and had his twenty-seventh birthday on 13 December halfway across.

3

I returned home to the UK in December 1987 just before Christmas. My first task was to find my mother and introduce her to the grandchildren she had never seen.

My initial, feeble attempts to find her were unsuccessful, though I had more luck in finding the Foundling Hospital offices. They were still at Brunswick Square in London, where I had been baptised in the courtroom. Even more surprisingly, they had an enthusiastic (albeit diminishing) membership of old boys and girls. They even held an annual school reunion. I discovered that the secretary lived a short distance from my front door, and she came to see me. I continued with my enquiries at the Foundling Hospital offices and uncovered a complete history of my past. Every letter my mother had ever written, including birthday cards and other documents, had been filed.

* * *

It was in February 1990, nearly two-and-a-half years after the bad storm, that I got into contact with my mother. I was dozing in an easy chair, when Babs called out, 'Phone!'

'Oh… Who is it?' I said, with mild irritation.

'Your mother.'

'My what? Are you sure?'

'Hello…'

'Is that you, Son? How are you?'

'Um… all right. And you?'

'Look, Son, I can't stop. I'm in a bit of a hurry. I'm off to a tea party and I don't want to be late. Give me a call tomorrow, all right?'

'Okay, er, Mum. Bye.' Then to Babs, 'Where the hell did she come from?'

Babs cupped her hand to her face and smiled apologetically. 'I've been doing a bit of detective work and I found her telephone number in the library. I knew you wanted to speak with her. I hope you don't mind.'

'N... no... no, that's fine. D'you know what she said? "I'm in a hurry, Son. I'm going to a tea party and I don't want to be late. Ring me tomorrow." What sort of a mother is that? I haven't seen her since I was sixteen years old. That's forty-odd years ago, and she's more interested in a tea party, for Christ's sake.'

**

There were extreme weather warnings telling people not to travel unless their journeys were absolutely necessary. I've always resented authoritarian instructions about the risks I should take in my life. I had to see my mother before she became distracted by another tea party. The snowploughs had been busy during the night, leaving high banks of brown, slushy snow by the roadside. As I sped down the motorway I wondered what she would look like. I guessed she would be nearly eighty years old, thin, grey hair, frail, with thick-lensed glasses.

I thought about what to call her. How could I call her Mum or Mother? She'd handed me over when I was three months old. Apart from a twelve-month stay with her after leaving school, I scarcely knew the woman. We had blood ties, yes, but Mother? I felt uncomfortable. I practised saying 'Mum' and 'Mother' to myself.

'Hello Mum, hello Mother, hi Mum...' It was incongruous and sounded ridiculous. I would soon be entering bus-pass territory. After wrestling with the problem for a while and nearly missing my turn-off, I decided I would give her the Mr Tapp treatment. He was my foster dad, but I never called him Dad. He became a person without a title.

Branching off the motorway, I followed the coastal road towards Dover. With all the roadworks temporarily abandoned, I became confused and almost missed another turn off to Sheerness. I remembered the landscape as flat, marshy and low-lying. Despite the heavy snowfall I could clearly see the Kingsferry Bridge with its four high concrete columns.

The old bridge had been replaced with a more modern structure. I remembered the old, clanking arrangement as it slowly opened to let through large ships and cargo vessels bound for the paper mills and the River Swale. I recalled the sooty smell of the steam trains and the clatter of wheels on steel tracks as they chuffed towards Sittingbourne and then on to London. I was surprised to see the remnants of a swan's nest that still survived near the entrance to the bridge, almost hidden by the snow. I remembered pausing on my bike as a boy, watching the cygnets majestically following their mother around and Uncle Dick calling out, 'Come on Gordon, we'll never get to Faversham at this rate.' Uncle Dick would be long dead, like most of the family.

Then I saw a warning sign in the middle of the bridge: 'Danger – road closed – snow drifts.' I considered turning back. I was having second thoughts and wondering whether it was such a good idea to be stirring up the past. It seemed a legitimate excuse to turn round with the bridge closed. Besides, my mother hadn't seemed overwhelmed at the sound of my voice. Going to a tea party, indeed!

I wandered along the bridge on foot, couldn't see anything too forbidding, and wondered why a few snowflakes justified the bridge being closed and all the subsequent inconvenience to the public. I started to make a three-point turn to abandon the journey, but there seemed to be a magnetic pull drawing me across the bridge and I changed my mind.

Despite the heavy snowfall I was proud that I'd been able to pinpoint my position after so many years. Though it was nearly nine o'clock there was hardly anyone about. Pausing at the traffic lights, I watched a muffled figure with vaporising breath grating his steel shovel across the concrete path clearing the snow. He waved to me in a friendly fashion as though we were the only inhabitants left on the island.

'Morning. Looks pretty, don't it?'

I waved back, nodding with a smile. The old house and sign studio with its black timber cladding had been demolished, as had much of the old high street. I briefly wondered about my nine o'clock goddess. I had admired her each morning as she'd passed the workshop window. She was gorgeous, with her neat, figure-hugging costume of burgundy with white angora jumper, Betty Grable legs and black high heels. One day she'd surprised me, turning quickly with a wave of the hand and the most wonderful smile.

Progressing down the high street I came to the clock tower, an elegant picture postcard in winter dress. Easing carefully past the piled-up snow, I could just make out the name: Hope Street, a turning to the left. It was a road with so many memories. Now it was an integral part of Tesco's supermarket and its car park.

Ahead I could see a large conglomerate of drab council flats. Climbing four flights of concrete steps I arrived at number 13, which had a wonderful view of Sheerness Harbour. As I pressed the bell I saw a shadowy figure with bowed shoulders moving on the other side of the glass-panelled door. I felt both excited and wary, wondering if I was doing the right thing. The door opened and my mother stood looking at me for a moment. Her eyes grew misty with tears and she raised her arms towards me. 'It's been such a long time,' she whispered.

'Hey, steady on,' I laughed. 'You're cutting off my air supply. Are you going to invite me in or what? It's freezing out here.'

'Come in, come in, Son,' she sobbed, dabbing at her face with a handkerchief. She straightened her shoulders and looked at me more intently. 'Good God, you ain't changed a bit, 'ave yer? I'd never've recognised yer!'

Contrary to my expectations, her hair still remained a fine gingery gold and she didn't wear spectacles. Neither was she thin or frail. She just looked like anybody's grandmother. I settled into the rust-coloured settee that had a slightly familiar look. The contents had a 1950s feel, with the telltale signs of an old person: a woollen cosy over the teapot, neatly folded plastic bags, and newspapers stacked in the corner.

'You just make yourself nice and comfy,' she said. 'I'll make us a cup of tea and then I'll cook you a nice dinner.'

'Okay Mum.' God, that sounded ridiculous.

Forty-two years had not improved her cooking. Three pork sausages, three rashers of bacon, macerated egg and a heap of greasy chips: a cholesterol nightmare.

'Jesus! I can't possibly eat all that lot.'

'Get it down yer, Son. You're a growing lad; it'll keep the chill out.'

'For Christ's sake! I'm practically an OAP.'

'You're not!' she said, showing genuine amazement. 'Well I never. I can't believe it! Why did you leave home like you did, Son? I was devastated. Mum told me not to worry, saying you'd be back tomorrow. "He knows what side his bread is buttered on," she kept saying. "He'll be back soon enough." But you never came back. I'd spent fourteen years trying to get you back home after they first took you away as a baby, but I had no say in anything, being under age.'

'Hey, c'mon Flossy. I don't want to churn all this stuff up. You weren't a happy family. As I recall, it was all rows and arguments, day after day. I wasn't used to it.'

'No it wasn't. Mum gave you that new bicycle and you had everything you wanted. You were given nothing but love and affection. That was so cruel, leaving me like you did. You're not going to leave all that food after all the trouble I went to cooking it, are you?'

'You're arguing already! I'm not very hungry. I was sixteen years old, remember? You do all sorts of daft things at that age. I'm not a baby any more. Man has landed on the moon. I've got three grown-up children. I have dentures, glasses, and according to the charts I'm clinically obese.'

'What's that? You're in the political police?'

'Eh? N... n... no. I'm a bit overweight – what's that whistling noise?'

'It's this hearing aid thing. It's useless. You should do more exercise.' Then she spotted a ship coming into the harbour. 'Just look at her, Gordon. Isn't she beautiful? I always like watching her coming and going, especially at night when she's all lit up. I sailed on her once to visit Bernard, your half-brother, and his German wife in Hamburg. It's a huge boat. They've got everything on board. Bernard lives in Dortmund now, you know. I don't see him any more. I wish things had been different, but there we are. I've only been with two men in my whole life. They both made me pregnant and I've shed enough tears to float the *Titanic*. I've had a bloody miserable life. I even went up to the offices in London with Pop and begged them to let you come home. They were a load of whisker-faced old fogeys sitting round a great long table in an enormous room. They called it the courtroom; anyways, they wouldn't let you back. Pop threatened to take legal action, and then the war started.'

'Yeah! There's a lot of history in that courtroom. If you'd delayed my birth by another thirty years you'd have had a nice council house, a barrow-load of benefits and I could have had a university education. But cheer up, Flossy, for Christ's sake. You're making me depressed. I'm happy; I'm pleased with my life; and I've no complaints.'

'Well, you put a smile on things, Gordon, but I'm sure you had a hard time at that boarding school. That Mrs Tapp, your foster mother, said you did. We had a right bust-up. We thought you'd gone to live with her. I was sure she was hiding you. She said she did everything she could to make you come home. But we didn't believe her.'

'That's true enough; she kept telling me my home was now in Sheerness. She even told me not to visit her any more.'

'She *didn't*! Did you see her again?'

'Just the once, eleven years later.'

I'd had enough of the way the conversation was going. I wanted to talk about other things. 'For heaven's sake, leave it, Flossy,' I begged. 'You don't owe me anything. You were a victim of the times. Do you mind if I call you Flossy?'

'Whatever you're comfortable with. I've hardly earned the title of Mum, have I? I'm just so happy to see you again.'

'What happened to Pop? He's not still around, is he?'

'Lord no, he passed away when he was well into his eighties. He often talked about you and said you'd do well in life. He gave me a shock, he did. I went round to his bedsitter on the seafront one morning to cook his breakfast herrings; he liked his herrings. He was dozing in his armchair as usual, or so I thought. "Come on, Pop," I said. "Wakey! Wakey!" He looked so peaceful. I took his hand. It was like marble, and icy cold. It didn't half give me a shock. I panicked and rushed out to the hotel a couple of doors away. I even left the herrings frying in the pan.'

'What about Gran?' I said.

'Oh she died soon after you left, when we had the big floods. I still miss her. She was a much better mum than I've been to you. The sea was up to the front door you know. That's when I moved into this new flat. She never knew; she died of pneumonia. What did you do when you left Sheerness, Son?'

'It's a long, long story, Flossy, and I'm not sure you'd like to know.'

'That's nonsense, Son. I've got plenty of time on my hands and I'm a good listener. I want to know everything. I want to share a little bit of your life with the time I have left, and meet your children. I know Mum didn't like me talking about the past, that school and your Mrs Tapp, but you never told me anything.'

'Hang on, Flossy, I was only three months old when I went to Mrs Tapp. I stayed there until I was aged five. The governors gave me a new name: Edwin Uphill – what foresight, eh? Mrs Tapp was getting on even then. She had a load of kids of her own. They're now married, with children of their own. We lived in a large cottage in Shipbourne that belonged to a Mr Cazalet. I really enjoyed my time in Kent as a kid.'

Flossy sat listening intently as I continued to relay my earliest memories. 'Mrs Tapp had very blue eyes and long, silver hair which hung down to her waist when she combed it. Then she would twirl it round into a sort of double bun that made her look six inches taller. She was bandy-legged through carrying heavy weights when she was a child – or so she said. Mr Tapp was an agricultural worker. Like everyone else in the village he worked for Mr Cazalet. I can still see him now, with his sweat-stained hat, bushy moustache and watery eyes, puffing on his short, stubby pipe. The village is now part of a large conservation area, you know.'

'Yes, I went to see your Mrs Tapp several times. That was when they said I could have you back, just before you left school. She was far too old to be a foster mother. She could hardly stand up straight with her rheumatic legs. Her old man was no better. They were a right crotchety pair. I could have looked after you much better than they did. I sent them money in a registered envelope to give to you when you left home, but it came back "return to sender".'

'Mrs Tapp never mentioned that to me, Flossy. I could have done with a few quid.'

I told Flossy all that I could remember about my childhood spent at the white cottage called 'The Brookers'. 'Mrs Tapp had a preference for the nickname "Smiler". According to her I was always smiling, even when I was miserable. My facial muscles became fixed when I fell from the upstairs bedroom window on to my head.'

'You fell out of the window?'

'Yeah! I carry lots of scars. I seemed to have been accident prone as a kid. I had quite a few before my fifth birthday. Apart from falling on my head, I collided with Mrs Tapp and a saucepan of boiling water, which left scars around my neck, chest and shoulders. I can remember lying in bed with a pleasant sensation of floating on puffy white clouds, going round and round. I expect it was morphine or some other painkiller. Oh, no. C'mon Flossy, you're getting all upset.'

'No... no, it's all right Gordon. It's just when I think of all the years that have passed by and how I missed all your growing up and the pleasure I could have had looking after you and your children. You should've been a big part of my life. You're my son, but I know nothing about you. It makes me feel so bloody miserable; you never told me nothing the short time you was home. We never had time to talk, with me still working at the dockyard.'

'It's all history, Flossy; it's gone and past and there's nothing we can do about it, so let's forget it and move on, for Christ's sake.'

'That's what Mum used to say to me. Stop it, Flossy, for heaven's sake. It's all in the past.'

'I'll tell you what I'll do, Flossy; I'll try and write it down from beginning to end, and you can read it in your own time. You can think of it as a journey back in time and you're with me all the way. How about that? It'll fill in the blank years, and you won't have missed anything.'

Her eyes lit up and she started to smile. 'Could you really do that? Write a book?'

'Yeah! Why not? They say everyone's got a book in them.'

'How long will it take you, Son?'

'Blimey, give us a chance... I don't know; I'll do it in instalments. I'll write it as I remember the story. It'll be our personal history, just you and me. Some things'll upset you, make you sad, even angry; I'm no angel – d'you know what I'm saying?'

'Angels don't live down here, Gordon. You do this writing thing. Promise?'

'I promise. Well, I must be going; I've a business to run and I have to earn a crust. One other thing, Flossy: I'd rather Babs and the kids didn't know about my father and the more sordid details.'

'I understand, Son. Don't worry.'

'I'm away on boat trips quite a bit, but I'll come and see you as often as I can. Keep smiling. Bye.

* * *

Over the following years, Flossy met her grandchildren and came to stay with us on many occasions. Often at weekends we would take her to Minster cliffs and have dinner in the Whitehouse, a restaurant overlooking the Thames estuary.

She told me of the horrible shock when she found herself in the workhouse and didn't know what was happening. 'I begged and begged Mum to get me out,' she groaned. 'It was terrible. The place was full of mad people. One of the nuns gave me a right ticking off for giving a biscuit to an old woman. She said it was bad for her.'

We'd walk along Sheerness promenade and she'd tell stories of her past and how difficult life had been, how often there was no food in the house, and how her mum had no money. Her stories didn't always match up with the documentation I collected from the school authorities, however.

'See that pub down there?' she said. 'As a girl, I remember having a delicious meat pie and half a glass of Guinness in there. It was wonderful.'

I found it incredible that a meat pie and a Guinness could remain so firmly fixed in her memory for sixty-five years. Surely there must be something more earth-shattering for her to remember? If there was I never discovered it.

Flossy was an unhappy soul. She disliked men, had little sense of humour, and regarded the world generally as a God-awful place. She was, however, genuinely delighted with the first few pages of our book. 'It's hard work reading your writing, Gordon. It's really interesting, but do you have to scribble it on the back of old invoice pads?'

'You mean you want it typed?'

'Well, yes. I'd like to read it like a proper written book, but hurry up. I don't want to kick the bucket before you've finished. And have you been doing more exercise lately?'

'Oh for Christ's sake!'

Flossy died in 2003

* * *

4

There were several families in Shipbourne, East Kent who fostered for the Foundling Hospital, mainly for the extra income. They looked after us kids as if we were their own. The governors took care to ensure nothing should complicate, or interfere with, the foster mother's task. Gifts and birthday cards from the birth mother were regarded as unacceptable and were withheld, though some presents might be delivered as if they were gifts from the foster mother. Every effort was made to hide the true identity of us kids from our birth mothers, even to the extent of us being supplied with different names and birth certificates. We had no idea of who had really given birth to us. An effort was made by the authorities to reduce the stigma of those born in the workhouse by substituting place of birth as 'Cliff House', as in my case. The birth mother could reclaim her child, but only at the discretion of the governors. She had to prove beyond any doubt that the child would benefit by being reclaimed. Such action was rare, and there was ample evidence that it was not encouraged. Flossy, my sparky mother, was a rare exception. Although I'm certain she couldn't have done anything without Pop and Gran's support, I'm also certain she wanted me back home. There were many letters, and although she didn't write them – she was nearly illiterate – the words used and the way they were expressed were hers. She displayed a gritty determination over a fourteen-year period in her attempts to reclaim me. A small parchment document was given to her with precise instructions on how to make her enquiry, quoting a particular letter of the alphabet followed by the year of baptism (usually within three months of birth). She knew me as P34.

My early years with Mrs Tapp, my foster mother, comprised a period of great happiness and contentment. Her grown-up children became my aunts and uncles. Uncle Jim was my favourite and a regular visitor. He was always laughing, often giving me a

above: 'Fairlawne', Shipbourne's manor house
Below: the shop, pub and church

49

HOSPITAL *for the Maintenance and Education of Exposed and Deserted Young Children.*

The *Eighth*   Day of *March 1934.*

RECEIVED a *male*   Child **P.34**

Reginald H. Nichols

Secretary.

This must be produced whenever a personal enquiry is made after the Health of the Child (which may be done on Mondays, between the Hours of Ten and Four), and also in case the Child should be claimed: if enquiry is made by letter, the full date of admission, the sex of the Child, and the letter of the Alphabet must be stated, but this parchment must not be sent.

The Foundling Hospital receipt for receiving a child into their care penny to buy a bag of sweets at the village shop. He spent hours tinkering with his motorbike, which seemed to be in bits most of the time. It used to make a lot of noise when it was going, roaring back and forth down Back Lane leaving behind clouds of black smoke. 'There he goes again,' Mrs Tapp would sigh. 'Never buy a motorbike, Smiler; they're nothing but trouble.'

My greatest pleasure was the freedom to roam where I wanted, across fields, in woods, up to the village green, chasing pheasants and rabbits, peering into birds' nests, picking primroses, bluebells and blackberries. All around me seemed to be sunshine and smiling faces. Mrs Tapp stood at the centre of my happiness, a frail, silver-haired figure, with cornflower-blue eyes and a wonderful soft, singing voice. She taught me about the countryside: the names of flowers, different birds, the hunting men on horses with red jackets and dogs with waggy tails, and how to pump the fresh spring water from the creaking old iron pump. I helped her on washing day, learning to light the fire under the copper with faggots of wood, feeding the clothes through the mangle. There was always plenty to do.

There was the tall man with a brown coat, brown hat, brown boots and big brown shiny van, full of pots and pans and all sorts of other things. 'Now! What have we here, Smiler? What about some chocolate flakes, or sherbet; maybe some biscuits – these are nice.' I looked forward to his visits.

I don't recall Mr Tapp being a dad. An occasional smile and friendly pat on the head – 'How are you, Smiler?' – seemed to be the only contact.

Then everything changed. Mrs Tapp made me look extra smart, and I sensed there was something wrong. She kept saying, 'You be brave, Smiler, you be brave, now.' She had an unusual sadness about her. We walked down to Puttenden Corner. It was a well-known meeting place for hop-pickers, and the meeting place for the foster mothers when collecting or returning their charges. She always pushed a pram to help support her rheumatic legs. She made a lot of fuss and kept kissing me. She was crying. I'd never seen her do that before.

I subsequently discovered that Mrs Tapp had no say in how her foster children were to be brought up. She followed the well-established convention of sending Coram foundlings to boarding school at the age of five.

I vaguely recall stepping into a green bus with other children. Every time we came to a bridge the driver would call out 'Ready, boys and girls?' and then he would shout out excitedly, 'Wheeee!' and we would all join in as the bus came down on the other side of the road.

I didn't see Mrs Tapp again for seven years.

* * *

Left: photo of me at 5 just before going to school standing at front gate of Brookers.

Above: Me sitting on the grass in front of the white fence recovering from my fall from the bedroom window.

A Coram boy and girl

The Foundling Hospital School, Berkhampsted   53

I was five years old in the spring of 1939 when I arrived at the Foundling Hospital School, (latercalled the Thomas Coram School) in Berkhamsted, Hertfordshire. It was a huge, newly built boarding school, a very posh place, described by *Picture Post* as 'the working man's Eton', and it became my home for the next ten years up to the age of fifteen. It was self-sufficient, with a swimming pool, church, infirmary, gymnasium, concert hall, orchard, vegetable gardens, sport's field and tennis courts. The entire area of two hundred acres was fenced around with iron railings, completely insulating us kids from the outside world.

Many outsiders thought we were the offspring of film stars and important people, but, as I later discovered, in fact we were 'foundlings', that is, abandoned bastards. Since its inception in 1739, the Foundling Hospital had cared for twenty-seven thousand bastards. According to Captain Thomas Coram, the philanthropist founder, he had seen foundlings dumped on manure heaps. It seems foundlings were thought to be the lowest form of human existence. Slaves, regarded as a mere commodity, were at least worth a bit of money and deserved to be cosseted to retain their value. But the foundling was regarded as a financial encumbrance, a drain on parish resources, and something to be quickly disposed of.

As babies, we had numbered discs tied around our necks. I was number 24221. After baptism, a member of the Foundling governor's staff gave us new names. The earliest foundlings were named after the famous, righteous and good: Shakespeare, Chaucer, Handel, Coram and many other 'worthies', perhaps a compensation for being of low birth. This practice, however, was later abandoned after a few problems with contested wills. A law introduced certain prohibitions: foundlings were not permitted to own land or to become policemen or freemasons.

To his credit, in later years the namesmith also avoided common-as-muck names such as Brown, Davis, Smith and Jones. Some evidence of his outside interests can be gleaned from a scattering of names such as Taverna, Alesmore and Hopgood. One boy had the misfortune to be saddled with the name Nut,

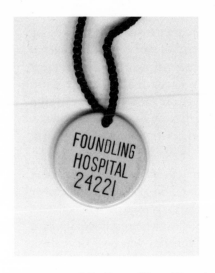

My Foundling Hospital name tag no 24221

the added misfortune being further compounded by marrying a woman named Hazel. Foster mothers and, for some, wet nurses looked after us until we became full-time boarders at the age of five. This was the accepted convention for all the foundlings. The facilities were of an exceptionally high standard, but the education proved to be a long way below Etonian standards.

The school ceased to operate in 1953.

* * *

My earliest memory of the place was of sitting on freshly mown grass, hearing the blackbirds singing, and staring at a bunch of daffodils. The first few days left me totally bewildered and utterly miserable. The daffodils were the only tangible way I could connect to Mrs Tapp and her neatly kept garden, often full of flowers. A softly spoken lady kept asking me to join the others in the group, but I kept returning to sit and stare at the daffodils, expecting Mrs Tapp to reappear at any moment.

We were all bathed on the day of our arrival like lambs being herded through a sheep dip. The smell of carbolic soap lingered for days and seemed to permeate everything. I can remember the crinkly black hair and puffy white face of a nurse with dark, irritable eyes who shoved my head under the bath water to stop me crying. Then I can recall a kinder young Norwegian primary-school teacher with brown eyes and a soft voice, trying to coax us out of our ongoing misery.

'I want you all to listen to me carefully and I am going to tell you the date of your birthday and you must remember it, otherwise you won't get a birthday present.' When it was somebody's birthday she would put a piece of chocolate or a sweet in their desk. She told me my birthday was on 3 December. (Ten years later I discovered that this was incorrect; my birthday was actually on 23 December.) Such treatment by the Norwegian teacher made life more bearable.

To start with we were housed on the girls' side of the school, but after a short period of assimilation we were transferred to the boys' side as juniors, and became subject to the bullying of monitors. Fear of the monitors became the predominant feature of my early schooldays. I remember a song about a hermit that we juniors had to memorise and sing from start to finish. I can still remember it:

Once in a blithe green wood
lived a hermit wise and good
whom the folks from far and near
for his counsel sought, knowing well that what he taught.
The dreariest of hearts would cheer
though his hair was white
his eyes were clear and bright...

There was one monitor who would apply a cricket stump to our bare-soled feet to speed up the process of recital. Other monitors gave us electric shocks, with out fingers being forced into light switches with the covers off. I have no idea why we had to learn this song, and I can't remember ever having to sing it again, but the power of pain is well proven. I remember learning the catechism in religious instruction without a cricket stump. The learning took much longer, and I can't remember a single syllable.

The first seven years at the school were grim and I couldn't wait for the day I would be able to leave. We had religious instruction seven days a week, and I hated that, too. Over time I gradually acclimatised to the harsh discipline of the regime. There wasn't anything we could do. Nevertheless, despite the negative features of my schooling I think we were most fortunate. Mercifully we were not subjected to the sexual abuse experienced in many boarding schools of the time that were reported much later in the press. If they had been able to curb the bullying, I think that today's youth who are brought up in council care might have found it a more acceptable alternative to the poor quality of today's schools.

The school catered for approximately 500 pupils, roughly divided into a near equal number of boys and girls. The school building had been designed to allow complete segregation of the sexes. This even extended to the dining room, where frosted glass doors slid on runners down through the centre, effectively dividing the area into two. Girls were shadowy figures, gliding around in the distance. We boys would grab any opportunity to peer at the girls through the gaps in the sliding doors. During meal times a master would walk up and down the tables. 'No talking' was an ongoing command, along with 'I want to see every plate clean'. This proved less of a problem than the opportunist with nimble fingers who could swiftly clean up the plate of the unwary. I hated fat, and despite the master's insistence, 'Eat it, Uphill!' I would spit it into my handkerchief when he wasn't looking. I would then throw it into the back garden of one of the teacher's houses at the side of the sports field.

The cane was a regular feature for any really bad behaviour, while lesser wrongdoing was punished by the miscreant being humiliated. This entailed standing on a chair or bench for the whole of a mealtime period. Strangely, perhaps, I feared being humiliated more than the cane, and I experienced both.

The school diet was well balanced and healthy by today's standards. Obesity was unknown. Hunger seemed to be a constant companion because food rationing had a huge impact. The emphasis on sports and exercise meant we were burning up far more calories than most kids of that time were. Extra calories came with eating small green leaves (vinegar leaves), blackberries, sloes, crab apples and quinces from around the extensive grounds, and raw vegetables were pinched from the school kitchen and vegetable store, together with green almonds without the bitter kernel. The green almonds had a soft outer shell when immature that offered extra calories, although they turned the tongue a violent green colour – underpants as well if you ate too many. The monitors augmented their calories by telling us juniors to 'dob up', slang for handing over. You didn't argue.

There were special days for a very few, when foster mothers could visit the school and give presents and food parcels, but Mrs Tapp never came on visiting day because the journey was too far. Occasionally she would write a letter, although she had taken on three more foundlings that kept her busy.

The most exciting time was Christmas. There would be no lessons over the holiday period; many of the staff would spend Christmas with their own families in the staff houses nearby. Prior to Christmas Day we spent a lot of time making decorations with strips of coloured paper that would be hung in chains around the classroom. There would be carol singing in the church, and on rare occasions the public would be invited to raise funds for buying Christmas presents. My earliest recollection of Christmas Day was a pillowcase at the end of each bed containing one apple, one orange, one pomegranate and a packet of Lexicon cards. I think everybody had the same. The pomegranates produced a few strange looks, and nobody, including the monitors, knew quite what to do with them. In later years I remember a large Christmas tree would be erected in the concert hall together with coloured lights and decorations, with Christmas presents all around the base. We would be marched into the concert hall and wait for our names to be called, then hurry towards the tree to collect our presents. But having recently spoken to a couple of boys I hadn't seen for over fifty years, their memories of Christmas presents were quite different from mine. Tom Vale, who was several years older than me, recalls a basket at the bottom of each bed. The early risers would quickly do a survey of the contents of each basket and switch their own presents for those that were more desirable. The last to wake up would finish with the worst presents.

Philip Taverner, in the same group as me, remembers receiving a bright red fire engine. 'Lucky you!' I said. 'I don't remember that; I reckon it was wishful thinking.'

The dining hall was decorated with the most beautiful Chinese lanterns. The first year I spent Christmas at the school I was totally mesmerised, and spent much of the mealtime just gazing at them. They seemed to project a sense of hope, for something better just around the corner. During Christmas meals the sliding doors between the boys' and girls' dining rooms would move back, revealing staring faces as we gazed at each other wistfully. There were no crackers, turkey or Christmas pudding, but there were Charlie Chaplin and Will Hay films in the concert hall, which had me in fits of laughter for days afterwards. On a more serious note, there was the annual film about Handel writing the *Messiah*. He did a lot for the foundling school with charity recitals to raise money, and also gave his organ and a fair copy of the Messiah to the school.

I spent seven Christmases at the school. Thereafter Christmas holidays were spent at home with my foster parents.

The standard of education was basic, served with an abundance of religious instruction and sport. I languished in the mediocre lane of intellectual achievement, much preferring the ad hoc offerings of Mr Bavister. I'm not sure what his speciality subject was, since he had a habit of wandering into various subjects before the end of his lessons. For example, one day after handing out geography books, he said, holding up a large glass jar, 'Right, boys, who can tell me what's in here? Any ideas?' He then walked quickly up and down the columns of desks displaying the jar.

Several boys replied: 'A bit of a tree; a twig; some green leaves...'

He took off the lid and prodded the object inside ... that moved.

'It's a stick insect,' he replied, re-fixing the lid. In that lesson I learnt a great deal about stick insects that I found really interesting, and still do to this day. Much of his teaching remains firmly nailed to the mast of my brain. None more so than his insistence that all teaching, including his own, should be questioned and scrutinised, and that we should apply logic and common sense in our arguments, and train our minds by constant questioning. I remember one lesson about the law of gravity that required several experiments. One of them involved swinging a bucket of water around his head without spilling a drop of water. We were all very impressed, eagerly waiting for the water to spill all over him, but it didn't.

It must have been in the early 1940s when he made a masterful attempt to explain Nurse May's outrageous suggestion that a new wireless had been invented where you could see people walking around inside. I wasn't entirely convinced. Beware of pills, he said. They are made from chemicals; they may lower the discomfort and pain but they don't cure the condition. I thought Mr Bavister was a great teacher who knew how to fire up the enthusiasm of us pupils, although we weren't smart enough to take as much notice as we should have done. He was many years ahead of his time.

There were no grades or certificates, but illiteracy was rare. In contrast to much of Mr Bavister's teaching, emphasis was placed on obedience aimed to encourage us to contemplate future military service to serve King and Country. First names were never used. Tears were frowned upon; if someone wept he would be called 'blubbing' and would incur disdainful names such as 'sissy'. The projected role model required a straight back, chin in, chest out and no whinging – you just had to get on with it.

Learning to swim was a fearsome experience; we were taught by a no-nonsense man, later sacked for his brutality. Tuition was swift, and effective. Mr Gordon would push the learners to the deep end of the pool with a large broom. Then he would shout, 'Let go of the broom and swim!'

Usually he had to repeat this command several times. If the boys still didn't let go of the broom, as was invariably the case, he would get angry.

'This is your last chance. If you don't let go of the broom, I will.' The surface of the water would boil with panic-stricken learners desperately lunging towards the sides of the pool and safety. They would then be rewarded with him saying, 'There you are! Now you can swim.' Sometimes the swimmer was too terrified to do anything and gradually sank. One of the stronger swimmers would be ordered into the pool to bring him out, and Mr Gordon would then comfort the half-drowned boy with the words, 'You will learn to swim even if we both drown in the process.'

As time passed the monitors would leave the school and go off to fight for King and Country. We juniors did not wish them well.

The teachers kept us up to date with the war and its progress. One day we became much more involved with the outside world when we discovered the playground was full of soldiers and motorbikes. The soldiers seemed to be learning to ride the motorbikes, and one of them fell off. We thought he had just broken his arm, but one of the teachers said he subsequently died in hospital. Then there were air raids and noisy sirens, which meant that we had to hurry to the shelters that were based under the main school building, a large cellar-like area. The shelter also doubled as the area where Mr Hickman taught carpentry. A section had been set up where palliasses, pillows and blankets were stored. Often there would be an unpleasant smell of boiled glue crystals and methylated spirits, used for sticking and polishing. Sometimes the all-clear siren would go early and we would be sent back to the dormitory, only to return later half-asleep, bumping and banging into things. Undisturbed sleep became hard to come by.

The soldiers left the playground, but the American Air force moved into Bovingdon Airfield a short distance away. They were very kind and generous to the foundlings, giving us presents and providing the odd tea party. We thought they were very brave with their Flying Fortresses and tried to count them as they set off, peering out of the window as they left with a droning roar to bomb Germany. Then we would count them again as they returned in the early morning, often with heavy losses. When in the shelter I would frequently sneak outside and watch the search-lights criss-crossing in the sky, marvelling at the powerful beams of light and listening to the loud bangs of distant guns shooting at the enemy. Miss Fuller, who said she was a friend of George Bernard Shaw, looked very glum. She told us the war wasn't going very well; we were taking heavy casualties and the shipping convoys were being sunk in large numbers. In direct contrast another teacher showed us on a map how powerful Britain was, and all the countries we dominated. He assured us we couldn't possibly lose the war and that there was no need to worry. Miss Fuller, however, managed to sow a few seeds of doubt about this.

The enthusiasm for counting money almost eliminated the need for Mr Wall's painful raps on the knuckles. I ran a brewery in the school dormitory at the age of fourteen; I sold Andrews Liver Salts and lemonade for a penny ha'penny a glass. I sold marbles, picture cards ... anything to make a profit. Even though there was still food rationing and I always felt hungry, I could never eat baked beans, tapioca or tinned apricots. I sold them all to the highest bidder. I was like a primitive forerunner of eBay without the mouse.

Every member of the school would receive a sum of pocket money related to how long he or she had been there. I eventually received two shillings and sixpence a month. There was also the proviso that any boy or girl causing any damage would automatically lose all his or her pocket money.

A new headmaster arrived in 1945, shortly after the end of the war, and made sweeping changes to the school environment. We were now free to walk into the town at weekends unaccompanied and bullying was forbidden, with the added assurance that cruel monitors would be severely dealt with. New lessons such as gardening, science and French were introduced, together with properly trained young teachers, although the French teacher, a most attractive lady, didn't stay long. (She was rumoured to have been the victim of unwanted advances from one of the male teachers.)

The change – almost overnight – was dramatic, and school life suddenly became not only bearable but also enjoyable. The sheer excitement of going to Chesham Common without master or monitor, with just a mate or on your own, was wonderful. Picking wild strawberries, blackberries, sloes and crab apples or whatever was in season, the smell of the bracken and colourful foxgloves and sticky buds as we called them that stuck to shirts, trousers, jackets and shoes; all this was a great joy.

A military man came to the school to warn us about special bombs the Germans had dropped over Chesham Common. He called them butterfly bombs with silver paper wings. We were told not to touch them but to report any sightings immediately.

Then came the most exciting change of all. For the first time since I'd arrived at the school I spent the summer holiday with Mrs Tapp in 1946. I was twelve years old. Previous holidays had been spent at the school playing cricket and football or rounders. Every day had seemed to be the same. I can recall lying on the grass hour after hour when it was warm and sunny, just staring up at the blue sky. I would project my gaze higher and higher as if on a long journey without end, wondering if my eyes would suddenly alight on some object that had never been seen before.

Another significant change had been the decision gradually to mingle the boys and girls together in the lower classes and dining room. Sex had never figured in the curriculum before, but suddenly this taboo subject fell to Mr McClellan, who seemed to be the general dogsbody in teaching terms. He was a dedicated teacher and put a lot of effort into his teaching, despite the often bored reception he received from his pupils. He taught history, geography, music appreciation, even how to ride and maintain a bicycle ... and sex.

He told us that when we got married and if we intended to have children, we had to make sure we married ladies with fulsome hips.

5

The excitement was intense as the bright green Maidstone and District line coaches rumbled into the school grounds to take us foundlings home to our foster mothers.

The foster mothers for the Shipbourne and Hadlow district had gathered at Puttenden Corner. I soon recognised the frail, bent figure pushing an empty pram to carry the cases, the smiling cornflower-blue eyes, the silver hair heaped into a double bun, glinting in the sunshine. She closed her arms around me, kissing me on the cheek. 'Goodness! Just look at you!' in her wonderful lanolin voice. 'You're so tall.' But I couldn't answer. I had a lump in my throat the size of a golf ball and was terrified I might start to cry.

As we turned off towards Back Lane, the main highway that passed our front door, memories of my early childhood came flooding back. The Brookers, a grey-slated, white-painted cottage I once thought of as home, came into view. A blackbird skipped along the white-slatted fence, pausing to sing a tune. 'Well look at 'im,' smiled Mrs Tapp. 'That's a nice welcome.'

The wooden stile immediately opposite the front door had been renewed, and looked very much smaller than I remembered, as did almost everything else. When I was small, the stile had been my gateway to the world. I paused to look over the field; it looked no bigger than the school playground, although I'd remembered it as a vast plain. I had an almost irresistible urge to leap over the stile, race up to the village shop and buy a bag of bull's-eye mints. Mr Tapp was leaning on his garden fork by the pond as we approached. He nodded a smiling welcome and raised his arm in a hesitant, awkward wave. The runner beans were full of flower and almost as tall as he was when he straightened his back. They were the source of much pride for him, and were always the best in the village. He was a kind, unobtrusive man, and looked exactly as I remembered him from seven years previously, with brown trilby hat, heavy grey moustache, brown corduroy trousers, watery grey eyes, and with a pipe permanently gripped between his teeth. He suffered from rheumatism and walked with a bowed back, often clutching his left knee in an awkward, shuffling walk, but never complained. He never raised his voice or chastised anyone, and seemed to carry an air of contentment with the suggestion of a smile permanently etched on his parchment face.

I plucked up the courage to show him Mr Bavister's gravity trick with a bucket of water. He seemed genuinely astonished and called out: 'Nomi! Come and see Smiler do this trick.' He used to call her 'Mother', and I couldn't remember him calling her Nomi before. Mrs Tapp proved to be equally impressed, and I decided to show off my dexterity by alternating the bucket from my left hand to my right.

'Well I never! ... Bless my soul, aren't you a clever one?' she laughed.

As is the way with young people, when on a winning streak there was a need to go just a little bit further than one should. I did the same exercise with two buckets. They collided at their highest point with a clanging crash and I fell in a crumpled heap, soaked to the skin. The noise of the runaway buckets bouncing along the cobblestone path was as nothing compared to the Tapps' uncontrollable laughter. Mr Tapp never quite seemed the same afterwards, and for much of the rest of the holiday his mild smile developed into a permanent fixed grin that would often explode into convulsions of laughter.

I had discovered the benefits of pocket money, and it became vital for me to get as much as I could. To this end I was recommended to approach the near neighbours. They were two farmers with the name of Jenner, Jim and his brother, Fred. I vaguely remembered both, and they seemed a likely duo in front of which I could rattle my moneybox. Jim was a tall, thin man, bald-headed with no teeth, but a ready smile for all the local children. His farm was a bit of a mess because he lived on his own and spent most of his time trying to catch his two horses, which showed no willingness to help him. Sometimes he would ask Mr Tapp to help and I would join in. The horses spent most of their time grazing in the field at the back of the Tapps' cottage, part of which also served as the burial ground for waste from the outside privy. The horses seemed to have a sixth sense and know this to be a good haven to head for when their master tried to harness them up for work. There was a large black dog called Nigger who always greeted me with a wild, wagging tail, and there was also a glass of fresh milk still warm from the cow as a treat. Jim had a passion for the plump, rosy-cheeked lady in the post office, and I collected a few pennies from him for ferrying sealed messages between them when I got his cigarettes.

Fred, a short, tidily dressed man with a severe expression, lived at the other end of Back Lane, and his farm was always spotless. Entering his yard I was immediately aware of a clean, orderly environment. The large stones bordering the immaculate flowerbeds were whitewashed, the windows were always sparkling clean, and everything looked freshly painted. Even the chickens had a hoity-toity manner and appeared to march in pairs.

One day Fred stretched out his arm towards a field covered with yellow weed-like flowers. He said, 'Get rid of that lot, lad, and I'll give you three half-crowns.'

Though impressed with the equivalent of three months' pocket money, I felt overwhelmed by the size of the field, which appeared to stretch as far as the eye could see. After two days of arduous back-aching work I became convinced there were more yellow flowers than when I started.

Mr Tapp displayed a look of disbelief on hearing about the contract, and for once abandoned his fixed grin. Then he engaged in one of his rare conversations.

'There's no end to that job, Smiler, not if you worked through your entire holiday till Christmas. They're like chalk and cheese, those Jenner brothers, and Fred is real sharp. You tell him to keep his half-crowns.'

Unable to accept the pain of working for nothing, I settled on a plan to try and cut my losses. I told Fred I had weeded most of the field, that what he could now see were another lot that hadn't been there before, and that therefore could he give me five shillings for the work I'd already done.

'That's not what we agreed, young man; I can't see any progress.' But after a lengthy lecture on the meaning of contracts, honest labour and other stuff, he gave me half-a-crown.

My greatest pleasure, apart from an exciting ride on Uncle Jim's new Thunderbird motorbike that I'd missed so much since going to school, was the freedom to roam where I wanted through woods and meadows. At school we had to march everywhere, or walk in long crocodiles. Now I had the freedom to clamber over the stile, then run up to the village green and thence to the solitary village shop, next to the only pub, and buy a bag of sweets. I loved to hear the church bells on a Sunday and the birds singing, as well as the gurgling noise of running water from a nearby stream. The sights and sounds of the country had been ingrained in me from a very young age. I saw a stoat flee gracefully from a spot close by the Tapps' house, and discovered a large rabbit still warm with a perforation in its neck where the stoat had killed it. Mrs Tapp was delighted.

'He'll make a nice pie. Goodness, just look at the meat on 'im!'

The Tapps had their own fruit trees, an extensive vegetable plot that sustained them throughout the year, and a large walk-in pantry bulging with home-made jams, cakes, cheese, with scarcely a tin in sight. I helped with picking the plums and damsons, feeding the chickens, collecting the eggs, the shopping and the washing, lighting the copper, chopping wood, and collecting the infamous buckets to replenish the water supply from the creaking pump; there was always plenty to do. The only task I didn't like was making butter. I hated that. It was a very tiring job, requiring a large glass container full of cream that had to be whisked by a turning handle fixed to the lid that seemed to go on forever. Sometimes I would stop for a rest, but Mrs Tapp would say, 'Keep going, or you'll spoil the butter.'

The harvesting brought much fun and excitement. The whole village seemed to be involved, because there was always an urgent need to ensure the crop wasn't spoilt by the weather. The combine harvester would go round the field in ever-diminishing circles, until only a small circle of wheat remained standing. In the centre there were always lots of rabbits, and the locals would be at the ready with their dogs for the free meat. Together with the village children, I helped load the hay on to the carts, and sat with them on the top of the hay cart as it bounced along unsteadily towards its destination, pulled by a large snorting horse.

Mr and Mrs Tapp always went to bed immediately after the nine o'clock news. I was pleased to be allowed to stay up with them, although my newly acquainted younger foster brothers, Cleaver, Muir and Griffin, also foundlings, went to bed much earlier. (I cannot remember their first names, as these were never used at school.) During the evening after the dishes and chores had been done there would be little conversation, just the droning voices on the radio and the odd comedy. Mr Tapp would sit in his personal chair and spread out his smoking apparatus, consisting of a cigarette-rolling machine, several pipes, packets of tobacco and an empty tin. His first task would be to swallow two small, white circular pills (Carter's 'Little Liver Pills'), and then start rolling the cigarettes for the next day. At the end of the nine o'clock news the national anthem would be played, and we would all stand solemnly to attention till it was finished. Removing his well-worn, sweat-stained hat, Mr Tapp would turn dutifully towards King George V1's portrait on the kitchen mantelpiece that mingled with a collection of coronation mugs and other royal paraphernalia. He would noisily clear his throat, grunt and grimace, holding his rheumatic knee. Then he and Mrs Tapp would begin their creaking ascent of the narrow, winding stairs to their bedroom, with a flickering candle stub stuck to a saucer because there was only one electric light bulb in the house.

One evening he leant towards me, gently rubbing his grey moustache, saying, 'S'pose you'll be fishing at the lakes tomorrow, Lad? I've got to give Jim a hand saddling Mabel.'

I hesitated and looked towards Mrs Tapp.

'He'll give you a hand, won't you, Smiler?' she said. 'You've got the whole holiday to go fishing.'

Mr Tapp nodded gratefully. 'Mabel's getting on in years, but she's still too darned lively for me these days.' He started to feed one of the small papers into the tobacco machine, then looked up and grinned. 'There'll be two shillings for your trouble.' I nodded my thanks eagerly and watched fascinated as he continued to roll the cigarettes with his little machine. He would examine each cigarette, and if it matched up to his requirements he would lick the rolled paper at its edges and seal it, tapping both ends on the table. Afterwards he would count the cigarettes he'd made several times before loading them into his special tin.

The old grandfather clock must have been one of the noisiest timepieces ever made, and despite its comfortable familiarity it would make me jump when it chimed. When Mr Tapp rewound it I was sure its works would burst out of its inside, since every turn of the key sounded as though the clock was being stretched to its limit. There was now a new addition to the living area: a heavy-looking gun suspended from the ceiling by two hooks that hung uncomfortably over the dining table, reputedly from the 1948 Israel-Palestine war in which Uncle Dave had been a participant.

'Did Uncle Dave kill anyone with that gun?' I asked. Mrs Tapp looked startled and glanced up at the ceiling.

'Well now, that's a strange question, Smiler. He's never said, as far as I know.'

Mr Tapp cleared his throat and fidgeted on his chair. 'Guns are for killing, Smiler. Don't you fill your head with such things.'

More familiar were the stag's antlers, perched above the reception room door that led into a room smelling of polish and scented with herbs that was reserved for Christmas or special guest occasions. On the mantelpiece stood two stuffed birds enclosed in domed glass cases, and on the wall opposite was a picture showing a Scotsman in kilt surrounded by dead and dying soldiers holding a flag high above his head with the title

'No Surrender'. In the centre of the room there was a highly polished circular mahogany table and six ornate polished chairs that were rarely ever sat upon.

My first summer holiday spent with the Tapps was a real joy, and I can remember it to this day, even though it was interrupted halfway through.

* * *

Shipbourne hadn't entirely escaped the war. Mrs Tapp often talked about the occasion when a six-inch canon shell rammed through the slate roof and buried itself in her pillow only moments before she was about to go to bed. She'd hurried down to Jim Jenner's farm, clutching the live shell to her bosom. Jim screamed at her to put it in the barn and run.

Mrs Tapp might well have had palpitations if she'd found out that my foster brothers and I had been roaming around the empty wood house overlooking Back Lane. During the war Americans had used the premises, and we'd discovered two live bullets. We spent a morning trying to fire them off without success by banging them with a hammer.

The stables at Fairlawn had suffered extensive bomb damage, and one of the Tapps' sons had been badly injured by a flying bomb that had landed on a building he'd been working on. His wounds eventually became gangrenous, and he died at The Brookers when I was there. I remember his strange behaviour the day before he died. He was waving a large Union Jack out of the window and singing the national anthem ... very badly. Mrs Tapp then sent Cleaver, Griffin, Muir and me to Auntie Helen's house in Hildenborough for the rest of the holiday.

* * *

I regarded the return to school with some trepidation. My worries were largely groundless, but even so, fear of the older boys was always present. I was worried about the monitors; there were still one or two who had the capacity to make my life miserable.

The school governors sent me to another foster home in Chertsey for the Christmas of 1946 because Mrs Tapp was still grieving for her son. I spent one Christmas with the Tapps in 1947. It was most exciting, with silver threepenny bits buried in the Christmas pudding. The front room was opened up, with decorations everywhere. The local tradespeople would pop in and have a glass of sherry and wish everyone a Happy New Year. We had a constant stream of visitors, and people seemed so friendly.

* * *

The following year I was allowed to take one of the school's pet rabbits with me to the Tapps for the Easter holiday. It was the first time Mr Tapp was angry with me. The rabbit, a Belgian Hare, got out of his cage and gobbled up two rows of lettuces. He said, 'If I catch that dratted rabbit in the garden again, Smiler, I'll put him in a pot for the dinner table.'

* * *

It was in the early summer of 1948 that I was summoned to the headmaster's study. He had a big surprise for me.

6

It was 1948 and I was fourteen years old.

I have always had an illogical deference for people with long, double-barrelled names. The possible need for a second breath to complete their name creates mingled feelings of inferiority and subservience in me. What do you have to do to get a hyphen jammed in the middle of your name – or, worse still, two hyphens, like my headmaster, Mr Blankerton-White-Widdenshaw? The teaching staff chickened out of anything other than calling him 'Headmaster' – all, that is, except the geography teacher, who called him 'Mr White'. We pupils were saved from the gasping experience because of the time-honoured requirement to call him 'Sir'.

I was summoned to 'Sir's' study. I fearfully knocked on the door, trying to work out what I'd done wrong.

'Ah yes, Uphill. Sit down. I have some good news for you. Your real mother wants to claim you.' He studied my reaction with disdain, as if to marvel that any woman could be daft enough to admit to giving birth to me. Three weeks previously he had promoted me to prefect. A week later he had caned me in front of the whole school for playing hide and seek in the church. He called it 'God's sanctuary'. The ignominy had been unbearable.

'Well?' he said, squinting over his spectacles at my open-mouthed amazement. 'So, would you like to meet your real mother?'

'Er… I think so. Yes, Sir.'

'Well, give it some thought, Uphill. The decision is yours; maybe the governors will let you join her for the summer holiday. You'll need to sign some forms, a legal requirement. Report back here tomorrow afternoon at three o'clock and we can proceed further with the matter.'

'Thank you, Sir.'

So who's this other mother, I thought. Where the heck did she spring from?

I now had two surnames, Uphill and Aspey. The latter was my birth mother's surname.

Crikey! I thought. *That's better than the double-barrel thing.*

My schoolmates only knew me as Uphill. Being too chummy wasn't encouraged. We were replacement fighting fodder, moving along the conveyor belt in preparation to fight for King and Country. (It was customary for the boys to become army apprentices until they were old enough for compulsory conscription.) The options when leaving were limited to joining the army or Wallingford Farm, an agricultural establishment.

The girls had only one option: domestic service.

I felt extremely lucky in the timing of events – and not only in the timing. I found I had two mothers, two birth certificates and two names (the latter subsequently proved to be very useful), with the possibility of a double-barrelled version. I had dodged the toe-to-toe confrontation with the Bosch, farming and the army. Almost overnight I felt as though I'd been elevated from a charity brat to a person of substance. My future was looking good. And there were more goodies to come: parcels and money. The visit to the headmaster's study had been a real surprise. What was in it for me? Did my real mother have money?

Even so, my feelings for Mrs Tapp were genuine; I truly felt for her as a son feels for a mother, and I didn't want to lose her. I did wish that Mr Tapp had been more like a real dad. He'd remained very detached from me, although he'd sometimes be pleased with some small task I'd done, and would ruffle my hair and smile at me with his watery eyes, saying, 'Well done, Smiler!' I liked that.

* * *

A letter from my mother told me when she would be arriving at the school and said she would take me to the theatre to see the

The Thomas Coram School
Berkhamsted
Herts

Dear Mum,

I hope you are well, and got back safely on Sunday as I did, I am hoping that you will come up on Saturdays instead of Sunday because I nearly always miss the cricket matches on Sundays that includes House Matches. I have got an airplane model as well as a master to help me, considering I could not make head nor tail of it, but I hope to have it flying in about a weeks time. My garden is getting along alright even though it is thick with overgrown weeds, I have got some pretty good flowers coming up to such as Sweet Williams Chrysantheums Single wallflower mixed wallflowers and a couple of red dahlias as well as a flower that resembles a cup and saucer, I forget the name of it now but that does not matter as long as they come up. I am looking forward to the Summer Holidays when I go fishing cycling and have a good old go at the amusements. By the way tell Margaret I will have to tell her of if she doesn't come next time.

I am looking forward to your next coming Parcels Letters welcome

From Your Ever Loving Son Edwin give my love to all xxxxxxxxxxxx

75

June 13
1948

My Dear Flo
Just a line hoping you are all
well as I am quite well, now
my Dear I have been looking for a
letter from you I hope you got back
quite safe, now my Dear I must
till you I had a letter from
Edwin and your photos they are good
aint they I was very pleased to hear
from him I am sending him some
plants for his garden at the
School but I am very pleased he
wont have much longer there
bless him, now my Dear I must
thank you very much for those little
overalls, O I wished I had put Keith
on a pair while you was here he
does look a nib in them and he
plead with them he went home them
all all day, and he sits in his car
and goes to and through the

76

matinee performance of *The Pirates of Penzance*. Afterwards she would take me to the Windmill tea rooms for a cream bun tea. I could barely contain my excitement when a note was handed to Mr Bavister during a geography lesson. 'Uphill, you have visitors', he said. 'Report to the headmaster's study.' At the end of a long corridor I saw three figures talking to the headmaster outside his study. The man was tall with a trilby hat and a long black overcoat. The woman seemed very young and was wearing a yellow flowered frock. She appeared to be hardly old enough to be anybody's mother. There was also a tall, very pretty, raven-haired girl named Margaret, though everybody called her Chick. Although she was only a few months older than I was, she was in fact my Auntie.

They waved goodbye to the headmaster and hurried towards me. My mother had golden, gingery hair with brown eyes. She made a right fuss, flinging her arms around me, kissing and cuddling; her breath smelt unpleasant. I felt embarrassed.

She and Chick called the tall man with a trilby 'Pop'.

I asked him, 'Are you my father?'

For a moment he looked uncomfortable, and then he pulled out a one-pound note, pushing it into my jacket pocket. 'Never you mind about that, lad; all in good time.'

The largest amount of money I'd ever owned was half-a-crown. Several boys stood at the edge of the playground watching me enviously. I pulled the pound note out of my pocket, feeling the crisp paper between my fingers, and fluttered it towards them, grinning with triumph.

Pop and Chick called my mother Flossy. I showed them around the school and my garden plot with vegetables and flowers.

We never got around to seeing *The Pirates of Penzance*, and we never had the cream bun tea. I would soon discover that promises rarely came to fruition in this new family.

* * *

The school governors decreed that my last summer holiday should be arranged so that I spent half the time with each mother, but Mrs Tapp insisted I should spend the whole holiday with Flossy and only return to her the day before going back to school.

The house in Sheerness seemed very small compared to my foster mother's cottage in Shipbourne. Pop used the house as part of his business. He made a lot of signs for the war department in the local army barracks, and there was a regular demand for his skills in the funfair. He had an agreement with the local cinema to advertise their programmes on the front of the house in exchange for a bundle of complimentary tickets. The front of the house was therefore used as a billboard, advertising his sign and poster business and displaying what films were on at the cinema. He used the complimentary tickets as prizes in the weekly tombola at the British Legion. He was the MC and often manipulated the prizes. He would swap the first prize, 'a large plump chicken', for a smaller one. We would have the large one for our Sunday lunch.

There was a small garden at the rear of the house, overgrown with weeds apart from a solitary, pink lily-like flower that had established its tenuous existence alongside the crumbling brick wall. I dug up the garden and planted some vegetables, but the family didn't show much interest in my endeavours.

Pop's house, studio and workshop

78

'It's not worth mucking about with,' said Pop. 'We've got a good greengrocer down the road.'

At the extreme end of the garden lay a half-domed mound of earth offering a fair degree of camouflage to the disused Anderson bomb shelter, which by all accounts had seen busy times. I soon discovered my new family was not very good at mending things. I also detected an awkwardness about some of the questions I asked, especially about my father, though I didn't attach any significance to this at the time. I was on holiday and wanted to enjoy myself.

Gran had given me a brand-new bicycle and I couldn't wait to go riding around on it.

'This is really your Christmas present,' she said. 'But you might as well have it now for your holiday, but don't expect Father Christmas to come round twice.' This was said with her eyebrows arched.

The first day of the summer holidays was warm and sunny. I awoke to the distant rattle of milk bottles. My room had recently been decorated with light-blue wallpaper covered with dark blue leaves and multi-coloured flowers. On the narrow mantelpiece stood a dented alarm clock with hands that no longer told the time. I carefully took the clock apart with my penknife, and then fiddled about with it before putting it back together. To my surprise it worked and went 'tick-tock-tick-tock'. But my surprise was nothing compared to other members of the family who thought they had a mechanical genius on their hands.

'Do you know them hands haven't moved for five years or more?' said Gran. The clock was then placed on the mantelpiece in the front room. Anyone unfortunate enough to find him or herself in the front room would be subjected to a tick-tocking exaggeration of my abilities as a clock mender.

At that time Sheerness was a seaside town buzzing with holidaymakers, mainly from South London. Pop had agreed with the school governors that I could bring my mate Endsleigh with me for the holiday. It was a bit awkward because Endsleigh didn't have a bike, so we had to walk to the amusement arcade. We revelled in the holiday atmosphere, with the loud music, jingling coin machines and brightly painted bumper cars. We spent most of the holiday on the beach, swimming and sunbathing and watching the dolphins two hundred yards offshore leaping out of the water We also enjoyed watching the paddle steamers, decked out with coloured lights, that blasted out loud music on their way to Southend from Queenborough Pier. I was always first out of bed in the morning and would rush off to the Co-op fishmongers on my bike to get Pop's breakfast herrings. Pop always had herrings for breakfast, attributing his thick black hair to his herring diet.

''Ain't got anything to do with herrings,' Gran insisted. 'It's all that bloody ale you drink.'

Flossy still worked in the dockyard where she had worked during the war with Uncle Dick, the charge hand and her boss. I was later shocked to discover that not only was he married with two daughters but that he was also Bernard's father. Bernard was about four years old at that time and he called Flossy 'Mum'. He lived in the house with Pop, Gran, Flossy, Chick and myself.

One of the most exciting things we did during the holiday was to take a trip to the Kursel fun fair in Southend. We crossed the Thames Estuary in one of the paddle steamers I had seen earlier. On arrival we went into a small café and had bangers and mash with peas, although Pop had jellied eels, a real favourite with him, before going on the machines and rides.

There were also other aunties and uncles in the family. One of them lived in Queenborough opposite the glue works; she invited just me over for Sunday tea. It was a small terrace house and the unpleasant stink from the glue works mingled with fish and seaweed throughout the house. On the dining room table stood a bowl of winkles, crusty bread, butter and jam and a large brown steaming teapot. The food on the table had attracted a lot of buzzing flies whose interest seemed equally divided between the winkles and jam. I took the opportunity to set about the flies with the occasional wild swipe.

80

'Don't you worry about them, ducky! I get them all in the end.' She pointed to several strips of sticky brown paper hanging from the ceiling covered with dead and dying flies. 'I cremate them in the fire.' I wasn't too keen on eating winkles, a new experience for me. The idea of sticking a pin in the backside of the occupant and dragging it out to be devoured in a short, munching swallow seemed a bit barbaric. And the persistent flies did nothing to boost my waning appetite.

The holiday came to an end. I had returned to Mrs Tapp and caught the coach for my last term at school. My excitement became intense as I ticked the days off to my final day and departure. But I was soon to discover that the world of work was not so jolly as I'd anticipated; there were many problems that I had to deal with.

7

It was December 1948 and I was fifteen years old. I didn't have a clue about what an apprentice sign-writer had to do. The world of work involved a lot of learning. Within a few weeks I wasn't sure it was a job I wanted to do. Pop, my boss, spent most of his time in the Bricklayer's Arms, and was anxious I should master the craft quickly so he could devote more time to the pub.

'Come on, Gordon, you can do it. Practise! Practise! Practise!'

He cajoled me, day after day, to do better and better. I spent hours and hours with pencil and paper, sketching alphabets, cleaning palettes and gallipots, learning to use a mahl stick, chalk lines, sable writers, mixing and matching paints. Twice a week I had to go to night school to learn allied subjects such as lining, glass gilding, French polishing, paint and its manufacture.

One morning I told him, 'I've had enough! I can't do it, I'm not artistic enough; it's too difficult.'

'Don't be so stupid, lad. You don't know how lucky you are. I've had parents offering to pay me hundreds of pounds to teach their sons this craft. You're doing very well – you've come on in leaps and bounds; you just need to stick at it. Master this craft and you'll never go hungry.'

I soon established who held high office in this new family of mine. I was very disappointed that I had to give over my wages of one pound a week to Gran to pay for my keep. She gave me one shilling pocket money. My mother also handed over her unopened wage packets to Gran, as did Chick, and they also received pocket money. Gran had a pet saying, 'We ain't rich and we ain't poor – but we're all right.'

This statement didn't seem to ring true.

She sent me to the Co-op fishmonger to get some mackerel for tea, but the shop was on the point of closing and the man said, 'Sorry, Son, we haven't any fish left; we've sold out. How about some crab? That'll make a tasty tea.'

'Okay,' I said, counting out the exact money, which included a few coppers of my own.

Gran was livid.

'This isn't the Savoy Hotel! You go straight back there and get my money back.'

I refused to go back and argued that the shop would anyway be shut.

'Right!' yelled Gran. 'You selfish little bugger; you can sit there and eat the lot yourself.'

The rest of the family sat round the tea table eating bread and jam while watching me trying to eat two crabs. Flossy told me to crack open the claws and not to eat a particular part of the crab because it would make me ill. At that point I lost my appetite and rushed out of the kitchen, slamming the door behind me, and went for a ride on my bicycle.

All the rows that went on revolved around money, and they became ever more frequent and increased in intensity. On one occasion while I was eating my dinner Pop and Gran were hurling lumps of coal at each other across the dining-room table. I was getting so fed up I mischievously said to Gran, 'I've still got my shilling from last week; you can have it, if that's any help. I can't think of anything to spend it on.'

Gran focused a most withering grey-eyed look on me, saying, 'You are an ungrateful, selfish, lazy little bugger.'

Pop also put in his two-penneth: 'You have a poor attitude; you're too argumentative; and you're grossly overpaid. You should be paying me!'

* * *

I decided to try and get back to my foster mother. I couldn't recall any arguments in her house; the atmosphere had always been happy there. I went to see her and was very shocked and upset when I kissed her goodbye. Her words cut into me as she whispered, 'Smiler, you mustn't come here any more; you must go back home.' Her cornflower eyes had turned to a rainy grey and were swimming with tears. Her heavily lined face was etched with pain, and she suddenly looked very old. I couldn't speak or understand what she was saying. I walked down to the bus stop in a daze, thinking perhaps that I'd misunderstood what she'd said. She'd often told me I was broad-shouldered and strong, and I certainly didn't think there was much that could make me cry. Now the tears were streaming down my face and I felt so wretched, worthless, and so isolated. The words 'love' and 'affection' didn't exactly pirouette on my tongue, but I'd held the deepest feelings for Mrs Tapp that I had ever held for another human being. Now she'd rejected me, and it was hard to understand why.

It was eleven years before I would see her again, for the last time, with my wife and infant son.

I stood leaning against the request bus stop, my misery mingling with rising anger at the abruptness of my dismissal. The silence was broken by the drone of the bus in the distance turning left at the village green. From the opposite direction I could hear whistling. I knew the tune well. A slightly built, uniformed figure came swaggering towards me. Through my tears I noticed brass buttons glinting in the sunshine and a kit bag on his shoulder. I hurriedly wiped my face with my jacket sleeve and looked the other way.

'Strewth... Uphill, isn't it? You've shot up since I left school. What's up with you, mate?'

I knew the voice and face well enough, even with the added thin, black moustache. It was a face that belonged to my days at junior school. The man offered his hand in a gesture of friendship. I glared at him as the memories came flooding back, feeling an almost uncontrollable urge to punch him in the face.

'I'm Steve Ember...'

'I know who you are,' I yelled. 'I remember the electric shocks, the coconut shies, the cricket stump and the beatings, you bastard.' I moved towards him with clenched fist and he stepped back, his eyes widening and voice wavering.

'St-St-Steady on Uphill, we all had the same grief. That's how things w...'

The green double-decker bus rumbled into view and screeched to a halt. The conductor looked quizzically at us as we stood like contenders in a pistols-at-dawn drama.

'You coming or not?' said the conductor, hand poised on the bell button.

The former monitor swung his kit bag on to his shoulder and hurried upstairs to the upper deck with a wary backward glance. I watched him ascending, hardly able to believe I could have been so frightened of him at school. He looked so ordinary; a pathetic little rat. The conductor hovered beside me with his ticket machine as I fumbled for the fare. The machine whirred and he gave me my ticket. He smiled.

'You made it just in time, lad,' he said, pointing to the heavy droplets of rain beating on the window.

The bus nearly emptied at Gravesend. I heard the clatter of heavy boots on tarmac as Ember hurried past the window, his kit bag hiding his face. It had stopped raining and the sun shone warmly through the window. I started to hum the tune he had been whistling earlier.

Once in a blithe green wood
lived a hermit wise and good
whom the folks from far and near
for his counsel sought ...

I think it was on that day, the most miserable day of my life, I realised that my future, however it turned out, would depend mainly on me. There seemed to be no option but to try and stick it out in Sheerness. I tried to keep out of the house as much as possible. If the sea was rough I would cycle up to Minster and watch the large breakers with their roar and power bursting over the rocks below.

Flossy tried to keep me out of the family turmoil, but she didn't seem to have much influence over anything. Uncle Dick was a regular visitor to the house, but I wasn't sure where he fitted into the scheme of things. My mother would get him to take me cycling to Faversham or Sittingbourne to get me out of the house. He was a quiet, easy-going man, but I felt nervous when I was with him; there was something that didn't seem right about him. He was my mother's boss and a lot older than her, but they seemed closer than I really liked. He had a technique of avoiding my questions with a tut-tutting smile and a shrugging of his shoulders.

There was one question I repeated time and time again, but no one seemed to want to talk about it, or whatever answer was given was fudged: 'So who's my father, and where is he?'

Then a photograph appeared on the mantelpiece. It was a faded sepia print of a soldier. Gran turned her head towards the photograph and sighed. 'He was your father. He was killed during the war. We all miss him.' The sepia photograph looked old, though the picture showed a young man in his mid-twenties. The face looked serious and the eyes stared out with laser-like quality and appeared to follow me around the room. Often when I was in the house on my own I would gaze into the picture and try to imagine what he was like, how his voice would have sounded and how he would look when laughing. I imagined him playing cricket and football with me and mending punctures.

* * *

Some of Pop's customers were very interesting. Mr Clay, a well-respected and relatively rich man, had his own fleet of lorries, all elaborately sign-written in gold leaf with outline and shadow. He told me how poor they had been as children and how they had often gone hungry with no food in the house. His mother had worked her socks off taking in laundry, and his father used to walk for miles every day delivering coal in a wheelbarrow.

'My biggest regret,' he said, 'was that my parents didn't live long enough to enjoy the benefit of all their hard work.'

Pop did a lot of signs for the war department. He liked that work, because it was lucrative. Payment was based on the height of the lettering – at tuppence an inch. This encouraged him to paint bigger letters than were really necessary. One day a man in authority enquired why the lettering on the fire hydrant signs in the army barracks seemed so large. Pop said, 'It's important that fire service personnel can see these points as a matter of urgency.'

'Is that so?' said the other man. 'Well, all the firemen I know have wonderful vision. What's more, according to the specification in my office, the permitted size of lettering on fire hydrants is strictly three inches. Please make your adjustments accordingly.'

I once found myself repainting signs in situ at the top of Minster cliffs – the wording read 'DANGER, unexploded mines, keep out!' It occurred to me that perhaps there might be an element of danger involved that Pop didn't know about. 'Is there any risk involved with me doing this work?' I asked.

'There is risk in every business, Gordon. It's something we have to live with. If a mine exploded, I wouldn't get paid for the sign and I'd have to get another apprentice.'

I was telling my woes to Mr Drawl, one of Pop's customers who had a small upholstery business; he'd always seemed friendly and helpful. But he threw his hammer across the bench and shouted, 'Stop feeling so bloody sorry for yourself! The world's not interested in your problems, and neither am I. I've got enough of my own. For God's sake, you're a young man. It's your life. Get on with it!'

I was badly shaken by his outburst, and slunk out of his workshop like a scalded cat, yet his piercing blue eyes shone out of his wrinkled, mahogany face with a fiery energy that I couldn't forget. His image and words still remain with me to this day. They seem to surface automatically in moments of despair and weakness. They would burst into my consciousness like bubbles rising in a fizzy glass of lemonade, chivvying me to get on with it.

Soon after the outburst Mr Drawl died from cancer.

My most difficult job was at the Fountain Hotel in Bluetown, where Lord Nelson and Lady Hamilton were alleged to have spent many nights together. The builders had erected scaffolding and ladders to get to the roof. The name had to be painted across the building at the very top. I had never felt so afraid in my life. Pop told me to relax – he would mark it out, and all I had to do was fill in the letters. He then left me to it, saying, 'You be careful now! And for God's sake don't step back to admire your work.'

It was then that I discovered my fear of heights. I was too scared to climb down for dinner. Although I finished the task, every brush stroke was hell.

The site manager called me over and pointed skywards. 'Look, lad, those two 'O's look like a couple of deflated tyres. Get back up there with a bicycle pump and sort it.'

Sometimes Pop would send me off to collect debts, and I soon discovered the hostility that may exist between creditor and debtor. I also discovered that an apprentice trying to throw his weight around might collect a few bruises.

'If you haven't got the money, you shouldn't have ordered the work in the first place,' I said.

Two men manhandled me out of the office and threw me on to the pavement, threatening me with something extremely unpleasant if I showed my face again.

Nursing my bruises and my indignation, I told Pop about my treatment, expecting the men to be arrested, but all he said was: 'I'm sorry about that, Gordon; these things happen in business. Don't tell Gran, for heaven's sake. Anyway, you're not hurt. Here's an extra half-crown; you've made good progress lately. You did an excellent job with that glass gilding at Burtons; the manager is delighted. That work's not easy; I struggle with it myself. Keep it up and well done.'

Pop rarely paid me compliments, so I felt six foot tall, and the extra money had me whistling all day.

If something was broken in the house, it remained broken. The toilet cistern had been defective for a long time, but nobody complained or did anything about it. Sometimes it would make a noise like a sick goat, dribbling all over the place; sometimes the rusty chain would break free and clatter to the ground. On a bad day if the chain were pulled it would move the cistern lid and shower water everywhere.

Flossy proved herself to be very impractical, with a succession of minor mishaps. She put an extra pair of creases down the side of my best trousers, which made me look like a matelot, the result being that I couldn't go to the Saturday night dance. Then she asked me to light the gas copper, but she'd forgotten to turn off the gas tap. I lost my eyebrows and most of my hair, thus missing further Saturday night dances.

At this time there were lots of private thoughts scurrying around my brain. I had a crush on many women – who remained completely unaware of this – such as the two assistants who worked in Featherstone's Decorating Supplies, as well as the woman in the greengrocer's shop who contrived to change her appearance on a daily basis. She changed so frequently I often didn't recognise her. Then there were the delightful twin sisters in St George's Avenue. The brightest star of them all, amongst a growing bevy of misty nymphs, was my nine o'clock goddess, a blue-eyed, blonde angel who roamed around my head like Veronica Lake hitchhiking from heaven. Each morning I eagerly waited for her to pass by the workshop window, wondering whether she would be wearing her pale blue-flowered frock or one of her close-fitting costumes. My favourite was the burgundy outfit with the white angora sweater. She was a real class act, with sensuous, swaying hips, gently bouncing breasts, elegant clicking high-heeled shoes supporting her Betty Grable legs – oooh!

One day Gran had some exciting news: we were moving to a brand new council house in Thames Street. Flossy and Gran were busy putting up new curtains and adjusting the furniture. The bad-tempered arguments became less and the household seemed to be going through a more settled period. Uncle Dick helped me dig up the new large garden, and designed a flowerbed that sloped down from the front room windowsill almost to the pavement. The neighbours thought it booked like a burial site and called the flower bed 'The 'Orses Coffin', while the local dog population regarded it as an all-purpose meeting place: somewhere to do their business, spray a bit of scent around, fight, and bark their heads off all day long.

I felt pleased in knowing my work had improved to a standard that needed very little adjustment. Then Pop in a menacing way asked me to spell the word 'dinners'.

'What's the matter with you, Gordon? How can you mess up like that? Three 'en's in dinners, for God's sake? What were you thinking of? You take one step forward and two backwards. You get down to Len's café and sort it out – now!'

The problem escalated out of all proportion, however, when the owner refused to let me correct what I'd done. He maintained the error had proved good for business. People kept coming into the café to tell him about the mistake, and he would feign mock astonishment – and then sell them a cup of tea and a sandwich, sometimes a full dinner. Pop, however, was adamant he wanted the error put right. He was pleased his client's business had taken an upward turn, but thought it unreasonable that his reputation should accelerate in the opposite direction because of three 'en's and a naff apprentice. The scowling owner was equally adamant. 'I've paid for the work, I'm well satisfied with it, and I don't want no bugger 'hinterfering with my 'hens.' Pop chewed angrily on his manikin cigar and asked if he could get his naff apprentice to put three bleedin' 'e's in 'teas' as well.

Pop let me continue to garden at the old house where I had sown a variety of vegetables. I think he owned it. (Later he rented it out to a woman friend.) One afternoon while doing some weeding I became aware of Mrs Lowe, the old lady from next door, staring over the fence at me:

'You're Flossy's other boy, ain't yer?'

I nodded.

'Well I'm blessed! I'll say this – you're a real smart-looking young fella. You ain't a bit like your father. God, he was an ugly bugger!'

'You knew my father?' I said, feeling a mixture of disquiet and excitement.

'I certainly did. He had a small shop down Hope Street, used to sell broken biscuits and stuff, mostly pinched out of the dockyard. He was a mean, dirty old bleeder. He only had one friend, a bloke who was one of the chief witnesses in the Nuremberg Trials. I can't remember his name. 'Course, that was after the war, long after your dad hung his-self in the shed.'

I stared open mouthed at the old lady. She wore a grubby pinafore about her skinny frame, with stockings loosely rolled at the ankles in an untidy collar. A freshly lit cigarette bobbled awkwardly on her lower lip as she spoke, half turning her wrinkled face away from the smoke drifting across her eyes.

'What d'you mean, "hung himself"?'

'Well, he would've gone to prison, wouldn't he?' she said. 'Flossy, your mum, was under age when he raped her, the dirty old bugger. He was sixty-eight years old.'

'You're wrong,' I shouted. 'He died in the war. He was in the Army.'

'No, he didn't. That's the truth I'm tellin' you; didn't they tell you nothing about it?' Then, in a more subdued tone, sensing the impact of her words, she said, 'I'm not making it up, Lad, you'll see.' Rubbing her hands on a grubby pinafore she slouched away muttering, 'It were all in the papers anyway.'

Anger welled up inside me, mingled with dejection and despair. I went into the old house and looked at the mantelpiece where the photo used to be, before the move to Thames Street. I wondered if perhaps Mrs Lowe had got him mixed up with somebody else, but deep down I knew her story was true. I remembered the awkwardness when I'd asked Gran about my father. I felt such an idiot, and there and then made up my mind to leave the family as soon as I could and get away from Sheerness forever.

Later at teatime I called Gran a liar.

'Don't you speak to me like that!' she shouted, rising up from the table and boxing me around the ears.

The heavy rings on her fingers cut into my forehead, and I jumped up angrily shouting 'liar, liar!' I shoved her roughly against the wall. Pop, Chick and my mother pushed me out of the way. I ran upstairs to pack my belongings. I told Flossy I'd be leaving in the morning and that I wouldn't ever come back.

Gran shouted up the stairs, 'Don't think you're taking the bike with you, you ungrateful bastard.' This was a severe blow; I'd intended to sell the bike to help me get to London.

You can shove the bike up your arse, you lying old cow.

8

Pop seemed strangely supportive of me, and only mildly rebuked me for my behaviour. I had a suspicion that he was enjoying all the aggravation and was using me to hit back at Gran.

'So, what are you going to do now?' he said. 'It's going to be very awkward. I suggest you take the day off and have a good think about it.'

I found lodgings in a smart-looking guesthouse with a fearsome landlady, Mrs Trip. After a thorough interrogation about my circumstances, she agreed I could stay for one pound a week, which was a 60 per cent reduction off the normal tariff. In return, I would be expected to help her: prepare meals, dust, clean, and other odd jobs. And in busy times I would have to give up my room and sleep in the shed, although she said she thought that that would be a fairly rare event. Then she said, 'I think you need to ask your employer to raise your wages by five shillings a week, otherwise you'll have no spending money.'

Pop puffed hard on his manikin cigar. 'So you're definitely leaving then?'

'Yes, and I'm not coming back.'

'Five shillings is a lot of money; I'm not sure I can afford to pay you that much. Hmm... you'll need to put a lot more effort into your work to justify that sort of increase. We'll see how we get on.'

He also agreed not to tell the family where I was staying.

Mrs Trip proved to be a demanding landlady, determined to make up for the 60 per cent shortfall. Sleeping in the shed in fact turned out to be a permanent feature, and the extra chores lasted well into the evening. Even so, the relief from all the family rows and squabbling made it almost enjoyable.

One day there was a knock on the door; it was the tallyman demanding two shillings and sixpence – one month's arrears for a pair of trousers I'd bought using up all my clothing coupons (at this time rationing was still in existence). Mrs Trip didn't like him calling and told him so in her outspoken way: 'You sod off and find somewhere more suitable to carry out your business. Don't come knocking on my bloody door.'

The tallyman retaliated angrily: 'Don't you tell me what to do, you stuck up fat cow; this is my job: knocking on fucking doors.'

Anxious to remain where I was, I gave him half-a-crown and asked him to call at Pop's workshop in future. Entering the payment in his ledger, he assured me he would call at the high street, but that if there was any difficulty he might be forced to return to this pretentious palace.

Pop seemed amazed I had no intention of returning home, but then confessed he had wanted to make the same decision himself, many years earlier. 'It takes a lot of guts to do what you've done, Gordon. I'm not saying it's the right thing, but I take my hat off to you. The rest of the family are expecting you to come back. Gran said you would be back soon enough when you realised on what side your bread was buttered.'

Mrs Trip's guests were a mixed bunch: commercial travellers, naval officers, policemen, businessmen and a variety of holidaymakers. Often they would talk to me, and they seemed curious about my relationship with Mrs Trip.

'Are you a relative or do you work for her?' they would ask. They noticed how I ate my meals in the kitchen and how she did everything she could to stop me talking to them.

Although I wasn't bothered by her efforts to isolate me from the guests, there was one thing that did emerge from my limited contact with them. They all seemed shocked at the treatment I received from my landlady, and the amount of work I was doing. One day a policeman came round and asked me lots of questions, and then spoke to Mrs Trip for quite a long time. After he'd finished talking to her, she had a very red face and looked angry.

'Nosy blighter,' she muttered. 'It's none of his bloody business.'

The policeman, Inspector Kieran, said to me, 'You shouldn't be working like this. That woman is taking advantage of your circumstances. If I were you, young man, I would go back to your parents. You shouldn't be living in a shed.'

Mrs Trip gave me my room back, on a temporary basis as she put it, while a builder extended the shed. The builder's merchant dumped half a yard of sand outside on the pavement. Mrs Trip wanted me to move the sand, but didn't like the idea of me trudging through the house with buckets of it messing up her carpet. She thought a better solution would be for me to take the two-hundred-yard trudge round by the back alley and the rear entrance. After eight trips I felt exhausted, and I was upset to find that the pile of sand looked just as big as when I had started the job. Mrs Trip, realising it would soon be dark, tried to hustle me along. 'Come on, get a move on, for heaven's sake.'

'I'm going as fast as I can,' I argued. 'There's a lot of sand here.' I was becoming increasingly irritated by her persistent nagging and was almost at the point of telling her to do it herself. Returning for another refill, I spied the tallyman striding purposefully towards the front gate.

Oh no, I thought. *Now there's going to be real trouble.*

The tallyman deliberately waded through the sandcastle, depositing the residue aggressively on the porch mat whilst rattling the front door knocker. The strong language brought the neighbours into the street. In a desperate effort to remove him from the scene, I emptied my pockets into his outstretched hand. Mrs Trip leaned out of the upstairs window, stuttering with rage: 'Never mind paying him, get on with shifting the sand!'

'Don't put up with that fat cow,' shouted the tally man. 'Let her get off her fat arse and shift her own bloody sand. She's treating you like a bit of shit, kid.'

I placed the buckets in the front garden and walked towards the porch entrance, 'Just a minute!' she shouted. 'Where do you think you're going? That sand has got to be shifted tonight.'

I shrugged my shoulders. 'I'm tired. I'm going to bed.'

'No you're not!' and she started to throw my belongings into the front garden.

The woman next door, who had spoken to me over the fence on several occasions, called out to me, 'You can come in here, young man. She's a wicked cow! You shouldn't be living under those conditions.'

The following day Pop agreed I could stay temporarily at the old house. My bedroom had been turned into a paint store, the windowpanes had been broken, and it looked very dilapidated. Uncle Dick came round, advising me to go home, saying my mother was most upset and that Gran had forgiven me. I refused, having vowed I would never return. The next day Uncle Dick returned with a broken camp bed that he thought might be useful and told me that the family knew where I'd been all the time. The middle strut was missing but I put my suitcase under it, which gave it adequate support. I used an old shirt stuffed with rags and newspapers for a pillow. The conditions were not as comfortable as they'd been at Mrs Trip's, and the mosquitoes were almost unbearable, but on the plus side I had twenty-five shillings spending money, a gas ring, and the basic requirements to feed myself. Earlier labours in the garden also provided some vegetables, although garden pests had already eaten their share.

Mrs Lowe apologised to me for all the upset she had caused, telling me that Gran had been round and given her a right earful. But she added that what she'd said about my father was the truth; it was all in the newspapers and I would anyway have found out sooner or later. Finally she said that I really ought to go back to my mum.

I had another shock when Uncle Dick said he had something to tell me.

'I'm Bernard's father.'

Again I felt angry, although I wasn't sure why. I had seen Uncle Dick once in the garden with his hand up my mother's skirt. I didn't like seeing this because he seemed so much older than she did, but then I felt totally confused about the whole family.

Mrs Lowe often chatted to me as I worked in the garden and would give me leftovers of food. She gave the impression of feeling really sorry for me, and even washed some of my clothes. I picked up bits of gossip about Gran during the war having a secret lover when Pop was a special constable on night duty.

'He was a tall bloke in the marines. God, he was a good-looking fella. He used to run like the clappers down the garden and over the back gate in one giant leap when Pop came home. For God's sake don't tell your Gran I told you this. I don't want another earful from her.'

The family was a real mystery to me. I could barely work out who was who. Gran had originally been Pop's housekeeper, but later became his common-law wife. Chick was Pop and Gran's daughter. Flossy was Gran's daughter by another man who left home and never returned. Bernard was Flossy's illegitimate son with Uncle Dick as his father.

I enjoyed my independence, going to the butcher for a pound of sausages, cooking bacon and eggs, and using my own vegetables. Sometimes Pop would complain about the cooking smells in his workshop, but admitted to admiring my spirit and often gave me advice on how to cook things. As the weeks went by, however, the novelty began to wear off and my appearance started to deteriorate. I hadn't much in the way of clothes and they seemed to wear out very quickly. The tallyman tried to sell me another pair of trousers, saying that I didn't need to worry about the clothing coupons; he could fiddle those. I reminded him that he had got me kicked out of my digs in the middle of the night and that he'd previously chased me all over the place.

'I done you a big favour, you silly bugger! You'd still be shelling peas in a pinafore for that miserable cow if it weren't for me.'

But although tempted, I didn't want the hassle.

***

I started to feel sorry for myself. I realised I didn't know anyone in the town, and I was becoming depressed. There were days when the only person I spoke to was Mrs Lowe next door. Then she told me something that really upset me and made me even more determined not to return home. She said that Gran had claimed me from the school in order to jump the queue for a council house: without me, they wouldn't have been eligible.

I made friends with a young bloke from the Salvation Army who invited me to play table tennis in the local youth club. A man from the Salvation Army had come into the shop wanting some posters. Pop usually made posters for them on a charitable basis, but always had a good moan afterwards: 'How am I supposed to make a living and pay the bills if I spend half of my time doing charitable work?' This time turning to me, he said, 'I reckon you're up to standard – you can do them, and justify that huge rise!'

The Salvation Army man seemed pleased with the posters and started asking all sorts of personal questions, including about where I lived. I ignored most of them with a shrug of the shoulders, saying that I wasn't interested in religion and stuff.

'That doesn't matter! You're good at table tennis – I've watched you play. I'd like to help you, if you'll let me.' He wrote a name and address down on a piece of paper. 'Please, go and see this lady, and say Ray Allen sent you. There are no strings attached; we just want to help.' Although I didn't want to get involved with Bible punchers, I was getting really fed up with the mosquitoes. It was as though they regarded me as some sort of food hamper, just waiting to be devoured. Every morning I would wake up covered in bites.

I had good reason to be grateful to the Salvation Army. They were most supportive during a difficult period. Mrs Thorne was a devout member. She was a quietly spoken, grey-haired woman, and she let me come and live with her in her small terraced cottage. There was a hairy cat of dog-like proportions that she doted on. I took an immediate dislike to the beast; it was an over-fed, ill-tempered feline with a tendency to use its claws when moved out of a comfortable chair. It also had the ability to growl like a dog, and bit me on the hand when I shoved it off my bed. Mrs Thorne made no attempt to influence my thinking in any way regarding religion or anything else, but gave me space to work out my own problems. Regarding lodgings, she said I could pay whatever I could reasonably afford. She even gave me clothes belonging to her youngest son. 'He won't miss them,' she said smiling. 'They'll be out of fashion by the time he comes home. Anyway, he's plenty of clothes.'

On one occasion she let me paint a large sign in the scullery, which must have caused her much inconvenience, but she never complained. I was concerned about the sign since I was doing it privately for a customer only two doors away from Pop's workshop. The customer said he would give me eight pounds ten shillings if I did a really good job, which seemed a phenomenal sum of money. I felt guilty about doing the job behind Pop's back, but the customer said Pop was far too expensive. When it was finished, Mrs Thorne said, 'That's a real work of art; you must sign it with your name.' Then, realising the problem with Pop, she said, 'You can use a nom-de-plume.' After much thought I decided to sign it as 'Nodrog', my Christian name in reverse. The customer was delighted with the sign, but soon afterwards Pop came into the workshop looking really angry.

'Somebody else has started up a sign business,' he fumed. 'There's not enough work for us, never mind bleeding outsiders. Nodrog Signs, they call themselves. What sort of a bloody name is that? Have you ever heard of them?' he asked.

'Well, yes,' I lied, 'a bloke at night school from Eastchurch had a weird name a bit like that.'

'Well, tell him to sod off,' said Pop, clearly upset at the prospect of competition.

I collected the money for the sign work and, feeling rich, I gave an extra three pounds to Mrs Thorne and treated myself to a large bunch of bananas. On returning from the high street I came upon Ray Allen from the Salvation Army smiling broadly.

'Goodness me. What have we here? How are you getting on?' He gently removed the fruit from my grasp. 'The old folk will certainly enjoy these.'

'What do you mean, the old folk? They're mine!'

'Oh no!' he smiled, 'it's self-denial week.'

I soon got over the banana loss, especially when my nine o'clock goddess turned and waved to me as she passed the workshop. I dared to hope that some day soon we might exchange pleasantries.

Pop entered the workshop unnoticed whilst I was ascending the higher octaves of Mario Lanza's latest hit record. My arms were spread above as though acknowledging the acclaim of an ecstatic audience. Pop did not look pleased.

'Good morning, 'Nodrog'. You're fired, GET OUT NOW!'

That was a hard knock; I wondered who'd told him.

* * *

Not wanting to go on the dole, I had no option but to trudge around on foot and try to get some work. My perseverance paid off with my first job for Schillings, a German ice-cream company. This was to paint, sign-write and service six 'stop me and buy one' tricycles, for the princely sum of three pounds ten shillings each.

Two weeks later, Pop called at my lodgings and told me he was very impressed with the way I was standing on my own feet. He was also impressed with my ability to get work and the improving standard of my workmanship. He offered me my job back, saying he had been wrong to sack me and that he would give me a 50 per cent increase in wages. Also that I needed to understand that the business would be mine when he retired, so I shouldn't be working against him. I told him I needed time to think about what he'd said, as I wasn't sure I wanted to stay in Sheerness. In fact I'd already decided to go to London when I had a bit more money.

Mrs Thorne announced that both her sons would be coming home for Christmas. The elder one was in the merchant navy; he had a good sense of humour and a fond attachment for the Bricklayer's Arms. He made me most welcome. But the younger one, a cadet in the Fleet Air Arm, twelve months older than me and his mother's favourite, was a real problem. He told me to replace the orange I'd taken from the fruit bowl. 'You are the lodger; you ask permission if you want an orange.'

'Fair enough. May I please have an orange?'

He seemed surprised at my easy acceptance of his rules.

'Er... all right.'

'Thanks.'

He reminded me of a monitor at school and I just knew we were going to have a punch-up, but realising my limited options for finding somewhere else to live with Christmas being so near, I decided to put up with his nonsense. I most definitely did not want to go home for Christmas. My mother came to see me and begged me to go back. She tried to give me presents – a pair of slippers and a white silk scarf – but I threw them on the floor without speaking. The tears were streaming down her face and I felt sad for her, but I knew I would never go back.

The landlady's younger son became more and more objectionable. The situation was brought more quickly to a head than I had anticipated. I still had to work to get enough money to support myself for a minimum of two weeks in London while looking for work. On returning from the pictures one night, I discovered my belongings had been scattered all over the floor of my bedroom. I rushed into his room, just in time to see him rising from his bed as if expecting trouble. I kept hitting him without stopping; he had no chance to retaliate. Mrs Thorne and her elder son dragged me away, pinning my hands behind my back and demanding to know what was going on.

'Have a look at what he's done in my room. He's chucked all my stuff on the floor. He's a stupid lunatic.'

Mrs Thorne shouted at me angrily. 'Gordon, I'm sorry you can't get on with Brian, but he's family; he's my son. You'll have to leave after Christmas.'

9

Ihad celebrated my sixteenth birthday with a punch up with Brian, and I would never see most of my family ever again.

I spent my last day in Kent in the Isle of Sheppey in a small guesthouse overlooking the Thames Estuary. I had hoped to be better funded for my journey to London, but my departure had been brought forward on account of my fight with Brian. A northerly wind rattled the sash windows as I emptied a jug of cold water into the wash basin. Shuddering as the icy cold swept the sleep from my eyes, I dabbed my face with a towel as I stared into the mirror and thought about my future.

'There you are, young man,' said the landlady. 'A nice hot breakfast to set you on your way.' I warmed to her smile, which reminded me of my foster mother, and nodded my appreciation. 'London is a big place; you'll need to be careful there,' she warned.

I filled my mouth with toast to avoid answering any further questions. I was worried that she was going to ask me about my family, which was the last thing I wanted to talk about. I didn't want anything more to do with them.

Though excited at the prospect of starting a new life in London, I had no illusions about the difficulties that might lie ahead. I would need to get work and accommodation very quickly. The train rattled across the Kings Ferry Bridge, past oystercatchers pecking voraciously on the muddy banks of the River Medway. Christmas decorations and tinsel-decked trees, the remnants of a most miserable Christmas, became blurred as the puffing engine gained speed.

Over forty years would pass before I came this way again.

There were two women sharing my carriage, and they gave me a good looking-over as though questioning my right to travel independently. The younger of the two, in her thirties, looked as though she might have some connection with the theatre. Her face was heavily made up with mascara and bright red lipstick. She had painted nails and long eyelashes. The other woman huddled in a corner seat opposite with her head buried in a book. I settled down to the chuffing and hissing of the train, taking in the passing panorama of back gardens and countryside. Speeding along on a train was a new experience for me. Apart from the occasional plume of sooty smoke entering through the open window, I found it quite exciting.

* * *

London proved a revelation after my closeted upbringing at the Foundling Hospital School. I marvelled at all the hustle and bustle, the big red buses, the taxis hooting and rushing around. There were all sorts of different-looking people. I stared at a small group of men with shiny, black faces, draped in creamy-looking nightgowns, with round hats draped with dancing tassels. I had never seen black people before except in geography books at school. Everybody seemed in such a hurry, which made me realise that I needed to get a move on and sort out my problems.

The Labour Exchange was my first taste of bureaucracy. I wasn't impressed. The dark-haired lady I spoke to became impatient with my inability to answer her questions. She didn't seem to understand that it was all a new experience for me and that I didn't know anything about the procedure. I couldn't disguise my frustration, and raised my voice. She shrugged her shoulders and with an irritable sigh turned away from me.

Despite the cold winter chill, I could feel the perspiration running down my face as I tramped around with my heavy suitcase. The same question kept being repeated: 'Have you got a union card?'

'No'

'Sorry, you must have a union card.'

What was a union card, and why did I need one? Resting my aching feet, I tried to work out my next move. I clearly didn't have enough money to stay in London – even for one night – and the possibility of getting a job quickly seemed unlikely.

I'd been determined to avoid Mr Kirk, the Foundling Welfare Officer, who worked at the foundling offices at Brunswick Square. I'd been told he had a reputation for treating us boys as though we came from reformatory school. He was the last-ditch call, but that's where I ended up. He asked me numerous questions and then gave me a good ticking off.

'You should've telephoned the office earlier; it's going to be difficult sorting everything out this late in the day. Have you got enough money for the fare to Reigate? You have? Well, wait for me there.'

After a short car journey from Reigate railway station we arrived at St Joseph's, a large, rambling house with a thatched roof in a tiny hamlet in Surrey called Duxhurst. It had previously been owned by an American temperance society during the prohibition era in the 1920s and early 1930s, and had later been used as a rehabilitation centre for 'fallen' women. The Foundling School had some connection with the property, and was currently using it for awkward cases like me. There were five other inmates I remembered from school; two were slightly backward. Despite feeling disappointed and defeated after my brief London adventure, I was nevertheless pleased to be among familiar faces, with food in my belly, and a roof over my head. In fact Mr Kirk proved to be more helpful than I'd expected.

Once more I was under the protective arm of the Foundling Hospital.

Each morning, the blousy landlady, Mrs Chesswell, gave us four marmalade sandwiches for lunch that had to last all day. Hunger became a problem well before lunchtime. I asked one of the other boys about trying to get more food, but he thought we would all finish up in a tangled heap in the thatched roof if we complained and preferred to go hungry. One evening I plucked up the courage to ask Mr Chesswell, who gave the impression of being a fair-minded. I casually enquired in a throwaway manner, 'I don't suppose you get any bits and pieces or leftovers in the kitchen, that you could, er... just, er... shove in my lunchbox?'

He looked at me open-mouthed with indignation, saying, 'Nobody else is complaining.'

'Oh Christ, no... no. I'm not complaining; I'm just saying that if there are any leftovers, sort of thing.'

He started to speak, and then stopped, removing his glasses and polishing the lenses furiously. 'I will have a word,' he said, and hurried away.

Mr Kirk fixed me up with a job at a coach works in Redhill. The shop steward came to see me on my second day at work, asking for my union dues. I told him I couldn't afford it. He was very annoyed with me.

'Can't afford it? What d'you mean, can't afford it? Everybody joins the union. It's only a tanner a week, for God's sake. I'll come and collect it on Friday.'

The older workers often brought their breakfast to work half an hour early, for fear of being late and getting the sack. I decided I had to get a bicycle because the buses were too unreliable – and I, too, didn't want to get the sack. Fortunately the plumbing system in the cottage doubled as an efficient alarm clock. Every morning, when Mrs Chesswell filled the giant kettle with water, the pipes would go into a rattling musical routine that made sure that even the most determined effort to linger a little longer in bed was thwarted.

Two of the other boys supplemented their wages by working at Miss Tithers' Dairy in their spare time. They helped on the milk round, stacking crates, cleaning and bottle-washing.

'Why don't you go up to her house and ask her for a part-time job?' said Sheldrake. I remembered him as one of my accomplices in a shameful sweet-pinching incident while at school before sweets came off ration, after the new headmaster had come to the school and had given us a lot more freedom to roam around outside. He had squealed like a stuck pig when he was caned. He was a lively, dark-haired character with thick-lensed glasses and serious acne. He had skipped the army option when leaving school and worked at British Monotype.

Miss Tithers seemed strange, like a middle-aged man with a slight moustache. She had a short haircut with a central parting and drove her car like Stirling Moss. Her father was rumoured to own most of the cinemas in Wales. She spoke with a deep masculine voice ... except when she spoke to her father on the phone. Her voice would then escalate several octaves and bubble with excitement. I didn't care; I needed the work.

Mr Chesswell must have had words with his wife because I discovered a piece of meat pie wedged between the sandwiches. The oozing gravy didn't improve the flavour of the marmalade, but the extra calories were welcome. There soon followed more extras: broken biscuits, the odd apple, or a piece of bread pudding that was almost inedible. The bread pudding became a regular feature with the other boys too, who were curious about what made it so heavy.

A lot of what I did at the coach works Tate and Marriott involved unbolting large lorry wheels with a spider wrench, then painting them with special black spirit paint with a horrible smell that lingered for days. The coarse sandpaper used in the preparation work made my fingers bleed as it rubbed away the skin on my fingertips. The spray shop attracted a large following of wasps and I hated them. I took every opportunity to spray them with whatever colour was in the spray gun. One day the manager caught me spraying a wasp a bright poppy red.

'Report to my office,' he said.

I thought, *Uh uh, here we go; I'm going to get the sack.*

'I've had a chat with the foreman,' said the manager. 'He tells me you are making good progress and are hard working. How would you like to sign up for an apprenticeship with us?'

An apprenticeship? I thought. *Why would I want an apprenticeship? They'll be dragging me off to the army soon; what's the point?*

'Can I think about it, Sir?'

'Of course! But you'll have to join the union; that's obligatory. By the way, Gordon, I don't like wasps either, but let's leave that to pest control, okay?'

One morning, before I set off for work, the landlady called me into the kitchen to have a little chat. She assured me there would be other little treats in my sandwich box, but that it was imperative to keep my mouth shut and not to tell the other boys.

'They're like a bunch of gannets – they'd eat the lino off the floor, given the chance.' Then she lowered her voice to a whisper. 'I've something to tell you in confidence. Mr Kirk the Welfare Officer and I, we're going into business, to start a pig-breeding farm. So you understand, Gordon, there's a need for profit. But I'll give you a few extras in your lunchbox when I can.'

During the week I worked at the dairy mainly in the evenings, bottle washing and preparing the vans for the deliveries the following day. At the weekend I usually helped with the early morning deliveries. The bottle-washing operation took a bit of getting used to. It consisted of two spinning brushes fixed to a wall. The bottles were submerged in a sink of very hot water with added soda, and then pushed over the whirring brushes fixed above the sink to cleanse their insides before they were plunged into another sink of icy cold water. Then they were stacked in crates. At first it was difficult to get both bottles on the brushes simultaneously. Invariably I would get one bottle on one brush, but the other bottle would get pushed out of the way by the spinning brush, making me become unbalanced, and I would be awkwardly bumbling around, waving a spare milk bottle above my head. With practice, however, I was soon able to push two milk bottles on to the brushes at the same time before plunging them into the hot water sink, followed by a rinse in the cold sink. The bottles would then be clattered into the crates ready for filling and delivery the following day. The extra money that came from working in the dairy encouraged me to look for a bicycle, which became essential for getting me to my main job on time as the buses were often on strike. Mr Chesswell recommended I try the bicycle shop in Horley.

'He's in an invalid chair, but I think he's fair-minded.'

The shopkeeper's lack of mobility didn't stop him from driving a hard bargain, however. He charged me well over the top for a second-hand bike. The only consolation was that he was prepared to accept instalments. He warned me that any failure to keep up the payments would result in immediate repossession.

The bicycle proved to be a real asset and considerably improved my lifestyle. There was now no need to rush off to work and hang around waiting for buses. The extra fifteen minutes each morning yielded a bigger breakfast clearing the leftovers, and an extra mug of tea. A friendly chat with the landlady sometimes produced an extra piece of cake or a couple of biscuits, with the finger-wagging warning, 'Don't you tell them others, mind.'

There was a girl I passed every day on her bicycle. She had shoulder-length black hair and a blue flowered dress that billowed around her thighs as she struggled with her free hand to stop it rising in the wind. Her bicycle looked expensive and virtually new. One morning I took a crafty peek over my shoulder as we passed, and she did the same. Our eyes met and we exchanged a shy smile. The next day she tinkled her bicycle bell and waved to me. I was very excited and decided, if I could pluck up courage, to ask her to come to the pictures with me. Despite my precarious finances, I bought a new sports jacket on instalments to impress her. This purchase, however, impacted badly on the bicycle repayments and I became entrenched at the wrong end of a Mr Micawber-style dilemma. I kept receiving demand letters and threats from the invalid bicycle man. Mr Chesswell criticised me for buying the jacket.

'You make it bad for us,' he complained. You should've finished paying for the bicycle before buying that jacket and getting into further debt.'

'I'll pay the arrears by the end of the month,' I assured him.

When asked if I would like to earn extra money by working more hours at the dairy, I quickly seized the opportunity, but the continual twirling brushes, combined with plunging bottles into hot caustic water, then icy cold water, started to take their toll. My fingers began to look like sticks of crabmeat, and the caustic soda stung my fingertips painfully.

I looked forward to seeing the dark-haired girl with the flashy bicycle every morning, and she seemed pleased to see me too. We would ring our bells and wave at one another. Then one morning she slowed and stopped, calling out to me, but an overtaking lorry got in the way and I couldn't hear what she was saying. When the lorry had passed she had gone. I felt so disappointed and cursed myself.

The shop steward continued to press me to join the union, insisting I was the only worker in the firm who wasn't a member and that it was an unacceptable situation. I persisted with my argument that I couldn't afford it. I claimed that every penny I earned went on food, but that if I was given a rise I might join the union. In fact, I'd made up my mind not to join; I resented the threatening tactics, and had also decided against an apprenticeship.

I came to hear of a local boy who'd received his call-up papers for national service who had a motorbike for sale.

'I won't take less than £20,' he said. 'I'd rather burn it than sell it for less.'

The dairy manager thought it was a real bargain. I went to see it, with some vague notion that the money would drop out of the sky and I might be able to buy it. Although too young to ride on the public highway, I could at least ride it around the dairy. The girl with the chromium bicycle would really be impressed with my having a motorbike.

The bike was displayed in the owner's family's front room, with a cat's milk saucer used to catch the minor oil drip from the gearbox. The boy's mother had been furious that he'd bought it, and was determined to get it out of the house before he went into the army.

I stood admiring the heavy chunk of shiny black machinery

with elegant gold lines and sparkling chrome. It was a 1936 BSA 350 with the gear changes on the fuel tank. I thought of Uncle Jim and remembered the exciting ride on his new Triumph Thunderbird during the school holidays. He had one of the first models off the production line, with innovative independent suspension, or something or other. I remembered the throaty roar of the exhaust, the wind rushing through my hair, the yellow blur of Jenner's buttercup meadow. There was the exhilaration and excitement as we roared down Back Lane and up the hill to the village green and back.

'Well, do you want it or not?' said the mother, showing some impatience at my daydreaming. 'I want it out of my living room; it's got to go. You can have it for a tenner.'

'Ten pounds?' I gasped. 'I'll need a few days to draw out my savings, but I'll certainly buy it.'

'Where the hell are you going to get ten quid from?' asked Sheldrake. 'You owe money all over the place.'

'I don't know. But that motorbike has got my name on it, and somehow I'm going to buy it.'

One of the men in the dairy told me of a local woman who wanted her front room painted. 'You might earn enough there to help buy the motorbike if you could get the job. They call her Mrs F. It isn't her real name, but you won't want to know what it is – it's Polish and longer than Epsom High Street.'

I was suspicious about all the laughing, and why one of the dairy drivers thought it was worth ten pounds just to press her front door bell. I felt nervous about getting the job because I knew nothing about decorating.

'What do you mean you don't know anything about decorating?' said the dairy manager. 'You don't have to be a Rembrandt! If you can piddle, you can paint. For heaven's sake don't tell her you know nothing about painting, or you won't get the job. If you want that motorbike, you'll have to pull out all the stops! I reckon that at ten pounds it's a give-away. If you're not careful, I'll go and buy it myself.'

The house was a converted stable that once belonged to Arthur Rank, the film producer. Mrs F certainly gave me the tremors, and I quickly understood the quip about ten pounds just to press the doorbell. She was unusually tall for a woman and her height was further emphasised by a double bun of steel-grey hair shrouding her hawkish, bespectacled face. Her voice was high-pitched and threatening, reminding me of the air-raid sirens used during the war. 'It must be blush cream,' she shrilled.

Mr F was quite the opposite of his wife. He was an easy-going man, short-legged, round-shouldered, with a shiny bald head, and reputed to be a sub-editor for some national newspaper. I told them I had done quite a bit of house painting and that I would ensure the blush cream exactly matched the curtains. My confidence grew in the certain knowledge that Mr and Mrs F knew even less about painting than I did.

Mr F showed much interest in my proposed purchase of the motorbike. 'I had a motorbike when I was your age. Ruddy awful thing; the damned leather belt used to come off every time I climbed a hill; utterly unreliable as I recall. I imagine things must have improved since those early days. Tell you what, young man. Make a good paint job of our front room and I'll give you the tenner for the bike. Is that all right, dear?'

'It must be blush cream,' Mrs F shrilled again.

The man in the decorator's shop explained they didn't sell blush cream. 'No, you have to mix it yourself, Mate. You need umber, yellow ochre, red vermilion and white distemper. It'll be hit and miss at first. Probably best to mix a bit at a time till you get the right shade. By the way, be careful with the vermilion; that's real powerful stuff. Keep stirring when you're using it – don't let it settle, for God's sake!'

Mrs F's voice hit the ceiling after the first coat had been applied. Her husband told me all was not well with my painting. 'The requirement is for a blush cream, not an Indian sunset. There's far too much red and it looks an awful mess. You'd better sort it out. We'll not pay you until it's done properly.' Then she became more hostile. Not content with removing the tea and biscuits and the small, everyday courtesies such as discussing the weather, she aired her annoyance by slamming doors and windows and beating the doormat till the dust rose above the chimneystack. Realising my dream of buying the motorbike was beginning to fade, I slapped on coat after coat in a desperate attempt to retrieve the situation.

My mixing had improved to some degree, and there was ample evidence of blush cream. But the overall effect had an awkward look about it. I tried shutting one eye and squinting at it from different angles but I couldn't improve the paint's appearance. The vermilion red from the first coat just kept grinning through each successive coat. In one last desperate effort to salvage something, I told Mr F the walls needed to dry out. Once that had occurred, a final coat should be applied, and, once settled, it would all tone down to a nice blush cream. Whereupon Mr F, who had earlier been in a heated discussion with his wife, took an untidy gulp of whisky, pulled out his wallet and gave me ten pounds. In a voice trembling with anger, he said, 'Don't be under any illusion as to what the ten pounds is for. You've worked hard, I'll grant you that. But you haven't the slightest idea of what you're doing. I also take exception to your bullshit about the paint settling down to a nice blush cream.'

'Well, it's no good blaming me; it's the blooming rotten paint. It doesn't mix properly,' I argued.

Mr F took another long gulp of whisky. 'Get out! Go on, get out! You've ruined our front room. We should've got a proper decorator at the outset. I've paid you ten pounds to get your arse out of my house. I'm not a malicious man, but I hope you fall off your blasted motorbike on a regular basis. I hope you get no better reliability or pleasure from it than I did with mine.'

But I was delirious with excitement at my new purchase, even with the tongue-lashing I'd received and mild shame on account of wrecking the couple's front room.

Sheldrake was beside himself with envy. 'I'm buggered if I know how you got away with it. You're up to your elbows in debt; you wreck the man's house; and poor old Kevin was forced by his mum to accept ten measly quid. Kevin is really, really upset. Ten quid! I can't believe it.'

The other boys took it in turns to sit on the motorbike and have their photos taken. The motorbike could only be used around the dairy estate because I had no licence and couldn't afford all the other expenses required such as insurance and road tax. I also found it difficult to manage as it defied even the most determined attempts to get it going. But eventually, with the help of one of the dairy drivers who had his own motor bike, it started with a roar and clouds of choking smoke. My momentary excitement turned to pain as I applied the brake; seconds later I was on the ground with the exhaust pipe burning my arm.

'Those brake pads are knackered,' puffed the dairy driver. 'You want to get them fixed or you'll finish up in a hospital bed.'

Miss Tithers temporarily let me leave the motorbike in the dairy garage, which enabled me to practise riding it around the estate. Then one evening I lost control on a bend and found myself in Earlsfield Hospital. One of the van drivers had witnessed the accident and had taken me to the hospital in a milk float; I couldn't remember anything.

I first realised that something was wrong when I woke up to see a nurse standing beside the bed, hands on hips with a bemused expression on her face. 'So we're awake, are we?'

My head felt heavy as I raised my hand to discover it was almost mummified with bandages.

'Are you in any pain?'

'No. What's happened?'

'Just relax; you fell off your motorbike, you're okay.'

A matron-like figure came towards me. 'Well, young man, you need to be more careful. How did you get that scar on your head?'

'I fell out of the bedroom window when I was a kid.'

'Hmm... You've taken a nasty knock and we're going to keep you in for a couple of days. What're all those other scars around your neck and shoulders? Were you in a fire?'

'That was years ago, I collided with a saucepan of boiling water.'

'You really are accident-prone. Anyway, you've been very fortunate. Your sports jacket got wrapped round your head somehow, and saved you from a worse injury, judging by the state of it, although the gravel did manage to take a lump out of your cheek. It's not serious, but you'll have another scar to add to your collection.'

'Oh no! For Christ's sake!' I groaned. 'I've only worn that jacket twice; I'll be paying for that for another year.'

My despair was diverted as I squinted through my bandages. I jerked upright, pointing at the wall opposite with disbelief. 'For fuck's sake!' I cried.

'What did you say?' snapped the matron.

'Th... th... that wall. There's acres of it. It's all bleeding blush cream!'

Mrs Chesswell practically doubled my food intake. For the next two weeks I discovered a bandaged head has many pluses. People take notice of you, feel sorry for you, and even joke with you. 'Did you have a go at Turpin?' they would ask. (Randolph Turpin had just won the world title from Joe Louis.)

The young girl from the posh house across the road started to take notice of me. The bandages hid the worrying increase of spots on my face and gave me extra courage to chat to her. Although she was nearly three years younger than I was, I noticed her well-proportioned figure with great satisfaction. Her voice was confident and mature for her age, and I liked the way her face puckered with concern as I exaggerated the details of my accident. Soon afterwards she invited me into her house and introduced me to her parents. I often played table tennis with her and her dad; he was pretty good. They had a large garden at the rear of the house full of fruit trees, and they grew most of their own produce. They also kept a large pig that terrified her mother, whose task was to feed the animal when her husband was at work, but often the pig would burst out of its pen and chase her all over the orchard. Her husband thought this was funny and told her not to worry about being chased as the pig would soon be turned into bacon rashers and they would then receive a nice fat cheque from the Ministry.

There were also lots of bantams running freely around the orchard that always seemed to be fighting. I made an utter fool of myself by trying to separate a bantam cock and hen that I thought were fighting. The Wayne family were doubled up with laughter, and Moira couldn't stop giggling as she explained that the bantams were doing the mummy and daddy thing. I felt such a prat.

I spent much of my time with Moira – I only made one feeble pass that was instantly rebuffed – and her parents started to treat me like one of the family. I promised to respray the family car for them if they borrowed a portable compressor and cleared some space in the garage. I also made myself generally helpful any way I could.

The Chesswells disapproved of my continual presence in the Wayne's house as they thought this was sponging. Mrs Chesswell had also discovered the books I had bought from a bookshop in Reigate a few weeks earlier. I had been impressed with the gilt lettering on the cover and reckoned the four of them were a real bargain for ten shillings. I jokingly called them my ten-bob library. In retrospect they proved to be one of my better purchases.

I tried to read secretly, knowing the other lodgers would ridicule me, but Mrs Chesswell caught me reading in bed one evening. 'University reading course, what nonsense!' she sneered. 'You're getting ideas above your station ... those books are a waste of money.'

'It's not nonsense. There's nothing wrong with trying to improve myself.' I omitted to mention my difficulty in understanding much of their content.

'You should pay for that bike,' said Mrs Chesswell. 'Now that would be a big improvement. The man is extremely angry with you. You've the cheek to go out and buy a motorbike. And don't think you are going to leave that mangled mess in our garage.'

Mr Chesswell stepped in with his two-penneth. 'Another thing you need to be extremely careful about is that girl over the road. She's under age. There'll be serious repercussions if you're not careful.'

'What d'you mean?'

'Well, you be careful; that's all.'

The men at work seemed pleased to see me again, joking about the large plaster under my left eye. They never lost an opportunity to gain amusement at the expense of the young apprentices, but nevertheless seemed to treat me differently. The hospital had removed the bandages .The foreman said there was a debt collector looking for me, something to do with money for a bicycle. That cheered me up no end.

I kept a lookout for the girl on the chrome bicycle, but never saw her again.

Mr Wayne had a visit from a Ministry man about his pig. 'We require much leaner pigs,' he said. 'Your pig is the largest and most violent I've ever come across. I'll have to reduce the offer price accordingly.' Mrs Wayne was furious when she recalled the worry and turmoil trying to feed the beast, and insisted they would never take on another pig under any circumstances.

Mr Wayne wasn't happy in his work. For many years his boss had been an old workmate. After the war he'd offered him the chance to join him in a business venture, but Mr Wayne had declined, saying it was too risky and he anyway didn't think it was a viable proposition. His friend went ahead with the project and soon developed a substantial and profitable electrical business. Some years later they had met and his friend had offered him the job as his works manager. Mr Wayne took up the offer like a shot because he didn't like his existing job, but soon afterwards became disgruntled and found himself, as he put it, 'working his nuts off to make the boss even richer'. Mr

Wayne's main aim in life was to win the football pools and buy the largest and most luxurious American Packard ever built. He would then park his car next to his boss's smaller Packard and tell him to get knotted. Mrs Wayne observed that the workplace wasn't terribly busy and the boss might tell him to move on – which she thought would be the more likely outcome.

Mr Chesswell kept nagging me. 'You must pay the man for the bicycle, even if you no longer want it. Twice we've had the debt collector knocking on our door; it's not good enough.'

'Okay, okay! I'll send him some money next week, but I still think he overcharged me.'

'He's determined to take you to court if you don't pay.'

Mrs Chesswell had reverted to the four-marmalade-sandwich routine, without any perks. I realised this was her way of telling me that I was no longer the favoured lodger. I showed my sandwiches to the foreman and asked him if he could do a hard day's work on such a diet, and that I really needed a rise to help sustain body and soul. Unbeknown to me the manager wrote to the foundling offices and told them I was starving. They sent Mr Kirk to investigate the four marmalade sandwiches claim.

Mr Chesswell had previously said I could borrow his 410 shotgun to get a brace of rabbits if I liked. Knowing my popularity was in decline, I decided to grab the opportunity before he withdrew the offer. I decided the most productive area would be the private game reserve down the road.

Sam lived in London; he was one of my school friends and had written to say he would be in Reigate the following weekend and why didn't we meet up. He jumped at the opportunity to do a bit of poaching.

'We'll have to be very quiet, Sam,' I whispered, when we were on the game reserve. 'The gamekeeper's a pretty sharp individual with a keen ear.'

'Stop worrying, Gordon, for heaven's sake; it's not like you.'

Sam was an awkward character with a permanent toothy grin. He had an exuberant voice, and laughter came to him uncontrolled, loud and long. Usually he was great fun to be with.

Neither of us had any experience of shooting, but we were both convinced there was nothing to it. Sam sounded like an approaching tank, crashing through the undergrowth. 'Sh! Sam, for Christ's sake, keep quiet.'

All God's creatures seemed to be aware of our presence and scampered for cover. Then I spied a woodpigeon settling on to its nest, ten feet up in a tree.

'Let me have first pot!' Sam cried, grabbing the gun from my grasp. He fired two cartridges in quick succession. The pigeon never moved, but just sat blinking at us. I looked at Sam in amazement.

'For Christ's sake, Sam, how can you miss from ten feet?'

He reloaded and fired off two more cartridges. The pigeon continued to sit staring at us. 'I don't believe it,' cried Sam. 'What's it made of? Concrete?' The pigeon stood up and swooped towards the ground, curving away to our right, then climbed sharply and settled on branches higher up the tree.

'Come on, Sam, let's go. The gamekeeper'll be on to us any moment. Come on, let's go now.'

'Just one more go, Gordon, I'll get him this time,' he yelled, loading one cartridge after another into the gun and ignoring my pleas.

'Gotcha!' The gamekeeper jumped out from behind a tree. 'I'll take that,' he said, snatching the gun out of Sam's hand. 'I want all your cartridges, and you'll be prosecuted for poaching. As you know, this is a private game reserve.' He took out a pen and notebook and wrote down our names and addresses. 'What've you shot? I know you've fired eight cartridges.'

'It was me!' said Sam with his toothy grin. 'I got a bit excited, but we ain't killed anything.' He pointed up the tree. 'There's the bastard I've been shooting at – he must be armour-plated.'

'We don't know anything about shooting; it's our first time,' I said.

119

The gamekeeper grinned. 'Well, you sure chose a hard task. Their breast feathers are like a bulletproof jacket.' He squinted down the barrel of the 410 and gasped. 'This is a death trap. Jesus, just look at the kink in the barrel. I'm amazed you didn't blow your head off.'

'Can I have the gun back, please? It belongs to my landlord and I'm already in the doghouse.'

'Okay, but I'm confiscating the cartridges. My governor will be writing to him, and probably the local police as well, about the condition of the gun.'

* * *

On returning from work one evening I was shocked to find Mr Kirk, the school welfare officer, in the house and all the other boys lined up in the kitchen with solemn faces. Mrs Chesswell ran into the kitchen screaming, 'You ungrateful bastard! After all I've done for you. Get out of my house ... Now!'

'Blimey! What's going on?'

The welfare officer read out the letter he had received from the manager at Tate and Marriott. 'This letter says you are suffering from an advanced state of malnutrition and are too weak to work, but you look extremely well-nourished from where I'm standing.'

I began to worry I would not be in the line-up for dinner that evening. My thoughts could scarcely carry any further. I was starving!

'What about you other boys?' enquired Mr Kirk. 'Has anybody else got any complaints?' There was an uncomfortable, shuffling silence. 'Well, Uphill, you appear to be the only one with a grievance.'

'I want him out of my house NOW!' screamed Mrs Chesswell.

Then she hurried into the kitchen, returning with a large joint of meat.

'Look at that!' she shouted triumphantly, shoving it under my nose. 'Does that look like starvation rations? He also had extra sandwiches, biscuits and fruit that the others didn't have. I gave him special treatment and that's how he repays me, the ungrateful sod.'

Accusing faces turned towards me, and I knew my popularity was at an all-time low.

'So what do you have to say for yourself?' demanded Mr Kirk, pointing to the large joint.

I realised my departure was imminent. I argued defiantly.

'That joint will last for a whole week. After the Sunday roast we'll have stewed bones. The others're just as hungry as me, but they haven't the guts to say so.'

'Get him out now!' fumed Mrs Chesswell, raising her arm as if to strike. Mr Kirk quickly stepped in. With persistent cajoling she agreed to let me stay for one more week while I looked for somewhere else to live. 'Providing he keeps out of my way and keeps his mouth shut.'

Mr Kirk turned towards Mrs Chesswell and assured her he'd tell the school authorities that I was a persistent troublemaker. He was satisfied that all the boys were well fed and in excellent health. He'd also write to Tate and Marriott and inform them that he'd thoroughly investigated the complaints and found them to be unfounded.

'You're not interested in the truth,' I snapped. 'You're only interested in running this pig farm. The two of you are in cahoots.'

'That's enough, Lad. You're not helping your cause. Your mouth is going to get you into serious trouble.'

The other inmates of the Chesswell household, already aggrieved at knowing about my extra rations, were nervous about being seen talking to me. Noise levels at meal times became comparable to that in the local library, although there was a welcome increase in dinner portions.

The Wayne family were astonished that I was being thrown out of the lodgings, and without hesitation offered me accommodation in their house. Mrs Chesswell's grim-faced satisfaction turned to disbelief as I staggered with my belongings across the road and into the sanctuary of the posh house opposite.

The volume of work at Tate and Marriott had started to slow down and all overtime was stopped. The overtime rates had been the cause of much anger among the younger workers; there was scarcely any improvement to the pay packet after tax had been deducted. Some of the older workers expressed their fears about getting the sack as rumours filtered down the pipeline that the workforce would be cut owing to an ongoing lack of fresh orders. One of the directors decided to take advantage of the lull and had a custom sports saloon built on a Lagonda chassis. The design emulated the Jaguar of the period: a sleek, racy-looking machine. The workers in the body shop were very amused when it was realised that no allowance had been made in the elegant design for changing the wheels in the event of a puncture.

I had no illusions about my chances of survival. The principle of last in first out was the accepted practice. There was also an earlier incident which was not going to help matters: the works manager had witnessed me taking aim with a piece of bread pudding, and had watched its delivery as it smacked on to the back of another boy's head.

'Your days of working in this firm are numbered,' he'd said.

As I'd expected, he called me into his office and explained that things were not going very well for the firm. The management had decided to reduce the wage bill and make other difficult cost reductions. After a prolonged and encouraging résumé of my general progress, punctuated with long silences as he stared out of the window, he finally gave me a week's notice, although he wanted me to understand that my dismissal had nothing to do with bread pudding. The lack of work was the only reason. If conditions improved he would be pleased to re-employ me...

'Although you must join the union.'

Then, smiling pleasantly, he shook me by the hand and said he sincerely hoped I was getting enough to eat.

Being unemployed created the ideal opportunity to respray

Mr Wayne's old Morris Ten car. I was determined to make a really good professional job of it; I didn't want a repeat of the blush-cream debacle. I assured Mr Wayne that by the time I was finished their 1935 Morris would look as good as new. I followed all the procedures exactly as I had followed them at Tate and Marriott, but the results were most disappointing. I seemed unable to replicate the lustrous high-gloss finish I'd achieved at Tate and Marriott. Mr Wayne ruefully accepted his disappointment in good-humoured vein, and confirmed with a grimace that he had at least received excellent value for money. Not only had I re-sprayed the car, but I'd also sprayed the garage and most of its contents, as well as half the orchard and two bantam cocks.

Mrs Wayne's concern was more for my appearance. 'Just look at the poor boy. All that horrible black stuff in his eyes, ears and lungs,' she cried.

Mrs Chesswell could hardly avoid seeing me as I was unemployed and living immediately opposite. Her glaring looks confirmed she wasn't too happy about the arrangement. Instructions were given to the other boys that they were not to talk to me.

I met up with Sheldrake on several occasions and enjoyed comparing our food intake. He groaned at my superior menus, but said there had been an improvement since my departure. Marmite and meat paste had been added to the marmalade menu. He also bought my mangled motorbike for five pounds, which didn't endear him to Mrs Chesswell.

I wasn't too surprised to find Mr Kirk, the welfare officer, knocking on the Wayne's front door. He had an unusually aggressive manner about him and demanded to know what I was doing, where I was working, had I been stamping my National Insurance card, and so on.

I told him it was none of his business. I was eighteen years old and could look after myself. I hoped his farm worked out all right and also hoped the old cow didn't overfeed the pigs. He left in a foul temper, assuring me he would be back soon.

10

I was most grateful to the Wayne family for taking me in; I no longer had to put up with marmalade sandwiches every day.

'I think you ought to get another job, or sign on and bring in a bit of dole money to help with your keep,' said Mr Wayne.

'He could decorate the kitchen in our bungalow while it's still empty,' volunteered Mrs Wayne. 'It really needs doing; it's in very poor condition.'

I didn't want to scrounge, but neither did I want to sign on at the Labour Exchange. I was still smarting from the frustration of my London experience, even though this was now two years previously. I hoped to God that it wasn't blush cream they wanted in the kitchen.

'Hmm, I suppose you're right,' muttered Mr Wayne.

Once more I took up the brush, determined to do a good job. It proved to be quite straightforward and the Waynes were very pleased with the outcome, showing that I had made amends for the disappointment with the car.

Soon afterwards papers arrived for me to report to the Labour Exchange for National Service. I kept putting this off and started to get warning notices.

'You're going to get into serious trouble if you keep ignoring the warnings,' said Mr Wayne.

'The war's over,' I argued. 'What's the point?' Then a postcard arrived, saying I would be put under arrest.

The man at the Labour Exchange gave me a right rollicking. 'You're nearly three months overdue. Your conscription starts at the age of eighteen. If you'd left it any longer you'd've been sent to prison.' There were forms to fill in and various other assessments. I was then told that my preference to join the RAF had been accepted, subject to a medical.

There were eight of us, shuffling uncomfortably in an empty office near the labour exchange. A bossy-looking man pushed some documents into my hand. 'You're to deliver these documents to the administration at Cardington, near Luton in Bedfordshire. It's your responsibility to make sure these men arrive on schedule and don't get lost. Is that within your capabilities? I was the oldest because of my delayed conscription, but not the most vociferous. That title belonged to a cheeky, bespectacled short arse, who demanded to know why I had been put in charge.

The short arse soon started to argue with me about what train we should catch on the underground to tie up with the train to Luton. 'There's a much quicker route,' he argued.

'I'm in charge,' I said. 'If you think you know better, you can bugger off and go your own way.' To my astonishment he went, and two of the others joined him. 'Well, they're in for a shock,' I laughed, 'they'll have to buy their own train tickets.'

The Administration Sergeant at Cardington was not impressed with my explanation four hours later of why I was delivering only five of my group of eight recruits.

'It's nothing to laugh about, you idiot. You've lost half a regiment already, and you're not even signed up. Go and find them. God help us!' he cried. I never found the missing conscripts; I can only presume they were dealt with in a different administration office.

We joined another large group of recruits, and a flight sergeant addressed us. He went through the procedures for taking the oath of allegiance. On completion, his tone of voice changed to a more disdainful note, with a few more decibels thrown in. He told us, 'You are now employed by His Majesty the King, twenty-four hours a day, seven days a week. Your whole existence is devoted to the service of His Majesty. You are not permitted to pull your pudding either, as you won't have time.'

He noted the puzzled looks, including my own, and enlightened us. Tea and coffee would be suitably spiked with bromide to discourage any handling of the flesh. I worried about this. I was a prolific tea drinker, so reasoned I would be more affected than most. Shortly afterwards we were herded on to trains bound for West Kirby training camp near Liverpool for the obligatory eight-week instruction course.

The instructor for my billet was a venomous little man, ably supported by an equally obnoxious sergeant. As we stood by our bunks listening to a tirade of abuse, I thought he'd turned his attention towards me.

'You with the tache, come here!'

I stepped forward smartly, as did the recruit standing next to me. The instructor glared at me and demanded to know where my tache was. I pointed to my attaché case and realised, too late, that he was referring to the bushy growth on my neighbour's lip.

'So you want to take the mick, do you?' he boomed. 'Well, we have eight weeks to sort you out.'

My popularity with the drill instructor took another dive when filling in the next-of-kin form, which I had some real difficulty with. I left the question blank, hoping it might be passed over. I felt acutely embarrassed as the corporal in loudhailer fashion started to air my personal records in front of the whole billet.

'I will ask you once more and then I am going to get really angry. Who is your next of kin?'

'I'm not really sure,' I said with reddening face.

There was a howl of laughter from the other inmates.

'What d'you mean, you're not sure? You must have some bloody idea,' he growled, with hovering pen at the ready.

'I don't know,' I said, injecting a note of angry defiance. A few giggles went up from the other recruits, and the corporal, sensing for the first time he was on awkward ground, announced, 'We'll be sorting this out later.' He never did.

At least the drill instruction was familiar territory. My schooling had been based on military service, with great emphasis on discipline and self-reliance. But having benefited from three years of relative freedom since my school days, I didn't realise how difficult it would be to step back into that environment. For me, the drill instructors had now become the much-hated monitors, and my resentment started to build. Orders were issued in high-pitched shouts and everything had to be done at the double. The object was to put the fear of God into everyone. A measure of their success was the unexpected interest shown by many in one of the recruits who turned out to be a religious missionary. He was able to conduct lengthy discussions with a bunch of cynical squaddies whose only experience of the church was passing en route to the local pub. Yet he held their interest and pushed the other topic of conversation, sex, into second place, possibly helped by the bromide. His religion didn't help when it came to marching, however, as he was the leading member of a small band who couldn't co-ordinate the proper sequence between arm and leg movements. The drill instructor, who seemed to be a lot nearer to God than the missionary, showed little reverence for the devout Christian. He gave him a really hard time. The Christian later collapsed on the assault course, had a nervous breakdown, and was discharged on medical grounds.

The weather proved more of a hardship than the training, with hail, snow, ice and biting cold winds to contend with. We progressed from marching to rifle drill to bayonet practice, and then had sessions with live ammunition that didn't do my eardrums any good. One airman was a worry to all of us, including the instructor. He would take up the correct position on the ground, but at the critical moment when squeezing the trigger he would lose control and end up firing bullets all over the place. It was rumoured he had been responsible for shooting a cow in a nearby field.

The only relief from marching up and down and exercising in freezing conditions came with the coffee breaks and meal times. The squaddie looking after the coffee trolley had a worrying task. On the order from the drill instructor, 'Dis ...miss', he'd see an army of bodies hurtling towards him at great speed, whose sole purpose was to be first in line. All the common niceties of human behaviour were abandoned. Sometimes the trolley man would leave his post and seek shelter in some discreet doorway rather than risk being trampled on.

One of the better-known pieces of advice generally accepted in all three services was never to volunteer for anything. I was quite upset with my neighbour with the hairy lip when the corporal entered the billet. 'Anyone here play the piano?' Hairy-Lip focused his gaze on me. I knew absolutely nothing about pianos, but his gaze was so intense that the corporal took it to be a yes.

'Right, Aspey, you can put in some piano practice by painting these fifty bayonet scabbards. They must be dry by Sunday morning so you'll do them on Saturday.'

I scowled at Hairy-Lip. 'Thanks very much. Why were you staring at me? I can't play the piano, for Christ's sake.'

'Well how was I to know?' he said, grinning from ear to ear.

Some time later the glossy black scabbards were neatly hung to dry on a line I had fixed across the room and tied to the window catch. I was still feeling the resentment of spending Saturday afternoon painting when a loud voice boomed out: 'Hey yooo, square head!'

A ginger-headed face appeared at the window. I recognised him as one of the other drill instructors, a nasty little Scotsman. He had some clothes folded over his arm ready to hang out to dry.

'Open the window,' he commanded.

'I've got these bay...'

'Open the bloody window,' he yelled. I didn't want to upset him so I opened the window. I was prepared to sacrifice my labours to the better good. The shiny black bayonet scabbards clattered to the floor. I stood to attention as he vented his spleen.

The hassle with the scabbards was nothing compared to the nightmare with the bayonet. I seemed to have the only 303 rifle in His Majesty's Service that wouldn't lock properly on to the bayonet. Drill instruction with fixed bayonet required maximum concentration, trying to blend swift and positive movements without the wobbling bayonet dislodging itself from the rifle. This problem would give me a nightmare at the passing out parade.

As we approached the last two weeks of our training, some of the restrictions were lifted and passes were granted to go into town with a time curfew. The most popular venue proved to be the local dance hall, and there was great excitement at the thought of meeting the local girls.

I normally didn't drink or smoke, but I needed two or three rum and Cokes and a good choke on a fag to pluck up the courage to get on to the dance floor. I was still a virgin, painfully shy and unworldly with girls. Bolstered by the alcohol I selected a girl who looked no less shy and awkward. I bought her a drink after a brief and ungainly shuffle. She then sat on my lap, since there was a lack of chairs. Her scent reminded me of the art teacher at school who had made such an impression on me with my one and only dance lesson. Shortly before I left school, somebody decided that us older boys should be introduced to dancing the waltz and foxtrot. I had one dance with the girls' art teacher. It was a memorable experience that unzipped a case of erotic fantasy. Her body language and her smile left me feeling that paradise was around the corner. I left school wishing there had been more lessons, but that had been the only one. I remembered her warmth pressing against me and how randy I'd felt, and the erotic dreams that had followed. Now the same urgent feelings came to the fore.

The girl showed her innocence when she asked, 'What've you got in your pocket?'

I wriggled uncomfortably and looked at the ceiling. 'Shall we go outside and get a bit of fresh air? The smoke is making my eyes water.'

'It's starting to pong too,' she said, pinching her nose.

I nervously raised my hand to her breast, expecting her

to object. But she made a hesitant sighing noise and pressed more firmly into me. Her breasts were small, soft and warm and her nipples were long and firm. I felt she was enjoying my exploration as much as I was. I became more daring and caressed her thighs, pressing my palms into her dampness as she moaned with pleasure. I guessed it was her first time too.

Then she sighed, saying, 'I really must go; I mustn't miss the last bus.'

'Just a bit longer,' I said, fumbling with the buttons on my greatcoat.

'No... no, no, I must go now or I'll get into trouble with my parents.'

I felt irritable and frustrated, but I didn't want to upset her. 'Okay... what about next Saturday? Can I see you here at the dance again? Or perhaps we can go to the pictures?'

She quickly kissed me on the cheek. 'I'll be here, don't worry.'

'You promise?'

'I promise,' she said, hurrying away.

I was frustrated to have got so far without getting my oats. The tone of her voice seemed full of promise. I felt sure my virginity would take a tumble next Saturday and so would hers; I couldn't wait.

I was late getting back to camp – and horrified to have my pass confiscated. Christ ... what was I going to do? I couldn't miss such an important date. This was the most important day in my life. Marching back and forth on the parade ground was becoming really boring, and the cold wind didn't help. I felt depressed and lethargic. Surely there had to be a solution to the problem?

There was a moment in the middle of the week that gave me immense pleasure. The commanding officer had ordered an inspection, wanting to see the progress of the new squaddies as we approached the end of our eight-week training period. The ginger-headed drill instructor who'd asked me to open the window in order to dry his clothes had been designated to instruct the whole group and put us through our paces. He took up his position next to the commander immediately opposite me, and I noticed the snotty-nosed git had a very square head. His voice echoed around the parade ground.

'Left, right, left, right, slope arms,' then, pausing briefly, 'Present ar-r-r-rms!' As he did so, with great gusto the rifle flew out of his hands and crashed to the ground. His face turned deep crimson as he sheepishly retrieved his rifle, with the ranks giggling with delight.

The commanding officer gave him a long, meaningful look, and then leant towards him, saying, 'You stupid pillock!'

So the day finished on a high note, and the billet filled with howling laughter at the instructor's ear-bashing.

'What's up with you, mate?' asked Hairy-Lip. 'You look as though you've lost a fiver and found a tanner.'

'It's a long story,' I said, and then told him about my terrible problem.

'Tell you what,' he said with a big grin on his face. 'As a special favour to you, mate, I'm willing to look after her for you.' Annoyingly, he announced my problem to the whole billet to hoots of laughter.

'Anyone got any ideas how Gordon can get to the dance and have his way with a local girl on Saturday? Although hang on, I think I know the best way out of this little problem,' said Lippy. 'Go to the sergeant's office, and just say "Please, Sergeant, can I have my pass back?" It's so simple. Tell him it's a matter of urgency, that you have some business with a bit of local crumpet.' There was a brief silence, followed by uncontrolled laughter.

It might be worth a try, I thought. After all, he couldn't kill me – well, not officially anyway. I remembered the advice of Mr Bavister, my geography teacher: 'Learn to solve your own problems in life. You don't have to adopt the sheep mentality. Exercise your brain, think horizontal.' *Sod it*, I thought, *I'll do it*.

The sergeant had an awesome reputation and a voice like an erupting volcano. I was getting into unknown territory and

I wasn't looking forward to the challenge. He sat in his chair with his mouth gaping open in disbelief. He slid his cap to the back of his head and called in the corporal.

'Give this airman a pencil and a piece of paper, Corporal. I want him to write down his "extra special request". I think he's got some sort of speech impediment.'

The corporal peered over my shoulder as I wrote the words, CAN I HAVE MY PASS BACK? I heard a sharp intake of breath.

'Can you read it out gently, Corporal. Read it twice, just to confirm I'm not having a horrible nightmare.' The corporal read out what I'd written slowly and deliberately, then leant across the desk and whispered, 'Sergeant, it doesn't even say "please".'

'No? Really Corporal!' His eyes filled with horror, then he opened the top drawer of his desk and scrutinised the pass.

'You see – what's your name?'

'Aspey, Sergeant.'

'Well, Aspey, I have a little problem here. I took your pass away because you broke the rules. The idea being it's a punishment, a tradition if you like. You don't seem to reckon with this idea, do you? In the old days we had whips, firing squads, hangings and other more interesting stuff. Yeah! Things have really gone downhill in recent years. I've got a dilemma, here. Tell me, Aspey; is there any particular reason for wanting your pass for this weekend?'

'Well, I... I've always, er, been sort of interested in historical buildings, Sergeant, and there are a lot in Liverpool.'

'Any particular building spring to mind, Aspey?'

'Not really, sergeant, it's just the whole place is steeped...'

'So you think these historical buildings are going to do a runner after this weekend?'

'No, Sergeant, but there's a lot of them and I haven't much time.'

'Have any of these historical buildings got big tits, Aspey?'

'Huh? I don't know what you mean, Sergeant.'

'Pick up your pass, Aspey. I don't want to hear any more of this bollocks.' He placed his mouth close to my ear and screamed, 'If you ever enter my office again I will bury you in bloody history. NOW GET OUT – AT THE DOUBLE – LEFT-RIGHT-LEFT...'

The inmates fell silent as I entered the billet. 'Blimey,' said Hairy-Lip, 'you've really upset our sergeant.'(His office was at the end of billet, and everyone had overheard what had been said.)

'Well, I took your advice, Mate,' I said, pulling out my pass and doing a Highland fling while waving it triumphantly in the air. 'Da-de-da-de-da.'

* * *

The corporal warned us of a special changeover parade that meant we had to be at our best, since it would be attended by the big cheese. He wanted everybody to look extra smart and focused his gaze on me. 'I don't want any cock-ups or I'll get really cross. Is that understood?'

'Yes, Corporal.'

I only had one thing on my mind: the shy-faced, delicious, delightful Jean, with her soft brown eyes and curly dark hair. Sex on Saturday pervaded and extinguished every other thought in my head. Saturday could not come soon enough.

I was surprised by the attitude of some of the inmates in my billet. They started to *like* the venomous little drill instructor. The general consensus seemed to be that he was only doing his job and that he'd made our group the smartest on the camp. They even made a collection for the little shit.

The changeover parade proved to be a bit more sophisticated than I had allowed for, involving dress rehearsals with full dress uniform, blancoed webbing and fixed bayonet. On the big day I found myself in the front line almost opposite the main guardroom, eyeball to eyeball with the camp commander. My wobbly bayonet played on my mind as I desperately tried to carry out the rifle drill in quick positive sequence without the bayonet clattering to the ground. Everything went reasonably well, and I was just beginning to think that I'd cracked it when the sergeant gave the final order, 'Present arms!'

This entailed thrusting the rifle away from the chest in an upward motion, but my bayonet somehow became wedged into my webbing strap, and, despite frenzied efforts to disentangle it, it was stuck. While all the other rifles pointed skywards in perfect unison, mine was lying diagonally across my chest as if it was having a siesta. The redcaps at the guardroom window looked at each other in amazement. The commander groaned aloud and shut his eyes.

'Dismiss these men, Sergeant,' he shouted, and scurried away muttering to himself.

'That was a bloody shambles,' shouted the sergeant. 'Aspey ... you're on a charge. Report to the guardroom.'

I started towards the guardroom, cursing my rotten luck and accepting that my date with Jean had failed at the last fence. Then a moment of madness came over me and I turned off towards the billets, running as fast as I could. A voice shouted, 'Oy, come back here,' but I ran even faster, clutching the dodgy bayonet in my hand. I hid in the washroom, determined to make the Saturday night dance at any cost. I thought that perhaps the NCOs might be too busy looking after the new arrivals to waste time on me. Then Hairy-Lip told me the depressing news: 'The corporal's going ballistic; he's going to have your guts for garters; he's looking all over the place for you.' I mingled with the large crowd passing the guardroom, hoping I wouldn't be spotted. I was jubilant. I'd made it to the dance.

Jean looked even more attractive than I remembered. With a lingering kiss on my cheek she admitted getting into a lot of bother at home after our last meeting. 'I missed the last bus and had to get a taxi. I didn't even have enough money to pay the driver. My parents were furious. I must be home by ten-thirty at the latest tonight.' I wrapped my arms about her, inhaling her heady perfume as I kissed her on both cheeks.

'I'm really sorry about that; it was my fault. I got into a spot of bother myself.' We shuffled on to the floor and embraced passionately in the dimmed lighting. I could hardly contain my excitement. 'We don't have to hang around here,' I said. Shall we go for a walk?' I hoped I wasn't rushing things.

The lights came on and an older girl grabbed my arm roughly. 'You can't dance with her; she's under age; she's my sister. But you can dance with me if you want.'

'No thanks. What d'you mean, under age?'

'Well my brother has told me to tell you that if you ever stick your grubby hand up her skirt again, he'll come and smash your fucking head in.'

I lost interest in dancing and left the sisters shouting abuse at one another. I then spent most of the time at the bar where I downed more rum and Coke than I either liked or could afford.

'Hello Mate! How the hell did you get past the guardroom? The corporal's gone mad looking for you. He was sharpening his bayonet last time I saw him.'

'Oh dear! Have I upset the little shit? Blimey, Lippy, what have you done? You've shaved your tache off! You don't half look different.'

'Well some birds just don't like the moustache, so I thought as it's my last night up this way, I'll give it a whirl ... So where's this crumpet you risked your neck for, Gordon?'

'There she is, Mate, smooching with that corporal. Just look at her. You'd think they were on honeymoon.'

'And after all that trouble getting your pass. I'd hate to be in your shoes tomorrow. The corporal is going to give you the full works.' That's what I expected, but it didn't happen. I can only conclude that they had a new intake of recruits and they wanted to be shot of me.

Before the end of the evening I latched on to a girl for the last waltz. 'You've had too much to drink, and you're standing on my toes. Just sway with the music and behave yourself.' Renee was a smashing girl. We arranged to meet under the clock tower at Preston station the following week on Saturday.

The corporal came into the billet on the final day of training and thanked us for all our hard work. He announced that, 'Despite the stupidity of one particular individual, this billet has gained top marks with a commendation from the group commander.'

There was a brief bit of hand clapping, and one of the inmates ventured to say, 'Three cheers for the Corporal, hip, hip, hooray,' and proffered the cardboard box with the coin collection.

'It's against the rules,' said the corporal. 'I'm not allowed to take either gifts or money' and threw the contents all over the floor. He came towards me, prodding his finger into my chest. With clenched teeth, he said, 'If I had my way, you'd be spending the next two weeks in the cells. This time you've got away with it, but I guarantee you'll spend time in the cells before you finish your service. Ah yes, and something else: I phoned the guardroom at St Athan and gave them your name. I asked them to be especially nice to you when you arrive.'

'Thanks, Corporal, that was good of you. By the way, I didn't put any money in your moneybox.'

The train to Preston was an hour late. I was gutted. It was common practice for girls not to turn up on dates. Some would turn up, get their entrance to the cinema for free, and then vanish once they were inside. Many other tricks were used to cover their spending on a night out, well aired by the more knowledgeable recruits in the dating game.

'Blimey!' I said when I saw her. 'I didn't expect to find you still waiting. Sorry about the del....'

'Don't worry, I know all about trains,' she said as she smiled, tapping me on the nose with her finger. 'My dad works on the railways. I knew you'd turn up.'

We spent our first date in Blackpool and went dancing in the Tower Ballroom. I discovered Renee was a fanatical, and very accomplished, dancer. Her swirling satin burgundy frock fascinated me, swishing around her white thighs. She had sparkling grey eyes couched in a mane of flowing black hair that whisked back and forth to the rhythm of the music.

Renee became my regular girl.

* * *

After the drill instruction I was sent to St Athan, in South Wales, where I underwent an extensive training programme in the assembly and repair of fabric-covered aircraft such as Tiger Moths, Oxfords and Ansons. I also became the camp sign-writer. I was given further educational instruction and assorted lectures on atomic warfare and mustard gas. I was promoted from Aircraftman (AC) to Leading Aircraftman (LAC). I was what was known as a Painter and Doper. With the introduction of jet aircraft like the Meteor and Vampires, my job description was changed to that of Aircraft Finisher.

One of the perks for the new trainees was the opportunity to join clubs and other activities. Encouraged by Renee, I even learned to dance – or at least I went to dancing lessons in Cardiff. My training then became much more intensive and I had to learn about parachutes, and high-speed finishes for non-fabric aircraft such as Vampires and Meteors. We also had education in the three Rs; our training was of a good standard and served me well in later years. In spite of the best efforts of the square-bashing corporal, I survived my posting to St Athan without spending too much time locked in the cells.

One of the female education officers was most impressed with my ten-bob library. 'If you only read half of those volumes Aspey, you will have gained an excellent education. You only need a good dictionary to improve your spelling and you'll be set up for life. How much did you pay for them?'

'Ten bob from a bookstall in Reigate.'

'Well done! You won't regret it.'

Despite being surrounded with my fellow RAF recruits, I felt a nagging isolation and loneliness. I became very conscious that most of them seemed to get letters by the handful and was envious of this. I realised that outside the camp I had nowhere to go: no family, no relations, no nothing. Renee's letters were a real joy. They were full of warmth and feeling, very caring and compassionate. I read them over and over again, and started to feel a genuine and deep liking for her.

I managed to get on some flying trips in a twin engine Oxford and an Anson. There wasn't much room for proper seating in the Oxford and I found myself sitting on a laundry basket, but my main interest centred on the fuel cap that seemed to be spurting out fuel. I thought I ought to tell the pilot immediately.

'There's fuel coming out of the filler cap and it's running down the wing,' I said.

'Thanks, Lad. Return to your perch and hold on tight; we're entering a wind pocket. Continue with your observations, and if the wing falls off, pop back and tell me, okay?'

The trainees were getting excited as Christmas approached. There were no Christmas cards for me, but I was used to this particular deprivation.

Spending Christmas alone was a different matter all together, however and I really worried about the prospect. The sergeant assured me the station didn't close down for Christmas; there would be a skeleton staff; and that the food was excellent. There was also another bonus: it was the tradition for officers to wait upon non-commissioned personnel. Even so, I wasn't too excited at the prospect. Belatedly, I wrote to Renee asking her to share Christmas with me, and to my delight and amazement she agreed. With her parents approval we arranged to meet at the Railway Hotel in Chester. The bar was crowded with eager, smiling faces, the noise of tinkling glasses, mingled with the background chatter and punctuated by occasional, raucous laughter. Colourful festive lights and decorations camouflaged the nicotine-stained ceiling. The smell of cigars and tobacco smoke hung heavy in the air, swirling around as the heavy mahogany doors creaked back and forth, letting in the cold night air.

Almost nine months had passed since my last meeting with

Renee. I sipped a glass of port and thought about what might happen. The previous day had been my nineteenth birthday and I was still short of sexual manhood; she had always been a touch on the prim and proper side – and there hadn't been anyone else. I was concerned about the way my plan would work. Surely by agreeing to spend time with me in a hotel she would expect to make some larger concessions? There were times when I thought I was the only bloke in the billet without The Knowledge.

'Penny for your thoughts,' said Renee smiling, tapping me on the nose with her finger. Her question took me by surprise and I could feel the colour rising in my cheeks.

'You're always tapping me on the nose like that; I'm not a bloody piano.'

'Oh dear, what's the matter with you? ... Have you gone all moody?'

'No... no, I'm only kidding. I wonder if they'll give us crackers with our dinner, with some nice little things inside? By the way, what was your parents' reaction when you mentioned spending Christmas with me? I bet they were surprised!'

'Mum wasn't overjoyed; she felt Christmas should be spent at home, but Dad said, "Why not? There won't be too much excitement going on here."'

My courage was beginning to ebb; I needed a couple more ports to put my plan into operation. I excused myself on the pretext of going to the washroom and headed towards reception. My hand shook as I signed the register 'Mr and Mrs Uphill' and booked a double room. This was daring stuff in the 1950s.

The grey-haired receptionist enquired in a matter-of-fact voice, 'Will you be having breakfast, Sir?'

I mumbled, 'Er... yes, we might do.'

Then, sensing my discomfort, with a worldly look on her face, she said, 'Follow me, sir.'

I stood in the doorway my heart thumping and clutching the room keys in my sweaty hands, when Renee appeared.

'Where's my room?' she demanded with uncharacteristic firmness. The receptionist hesitated with an 'Uh-oh!' expression on her face, and hurried quickly down the stairs.

The room had a large double bed, wardrobe, chest-of-drawers with mirror, and a small single bed. 'That's your bed,' I said, pointing to the double bed. 'And that's mine. It's a question of money; it's much cheaper with a single room.'

I'd never seen Renee look so angry. 'What do you think you're doing? You go downstairs NOW and book another room, and I'll pay for it.'

'Renee, hang on a minute. There's no need to make such a bleeding fuss; it's purely a question of money. Okay I should've asked, but I promise I'll not try anything. I really promise. Look, it's Christmas, for Christ sake. Let's relax and enjoy ourselves.'

Gradually she simmered down and agreed to leave things as they were.

After two more ports I felt disappointed about the clarity of her speech and her surefootedness as we walked along the canal towpath prior to retiring to bed. I felt quite dizzy as the fresh night air hit me, and I was conscious of slurring my speech. She seemed to be able to cope with alcohol much better than I could, and I realised that getting into her bed was going to be a monolithic task. Also she had threatened to scream her head off if I came anywhere near it. Christmas was already developing a lack-lustre look, and I was beginning to think that officers serving up dinner at the barracks might have been a more attractive alternative.

Renee's prissy attitude continued as we entered our room. 'You go to the bathroom while I get into bed,' she said in a bossy voice.

I sat on the toilet fully clothed and tried to imagine her undressing, easing her lemon angora jumper over her head, unzipping her brown velvet skirt, lowering her bra and her everything bobbling all over the place, God, I felt so horny. My penis twitched like a conductor's baton; Jesus, I couldn't wait.

At the same time I became aware of feeling very drowsy; the alcohol was really beginning to get to me.

I called out, 'Ok now?' and went into the bedroom without waiting for a reply. Renee was sitting up in bed with her shoulder-length black hair in contrast with the lemon jumper that she was still wearing. Unable to contain my disappointment, I shouted at her angrily, 'What are you? A bloody nun or something?'

Stripping down to my pants, I switched off the lights and jumped into my single bed. I lay wondering how I was going to get into Renee's bed without causing pandemonium. I listened intently for sounds of her undressing, then pretended to be asleep by breathing heavily. I started to feel myself going off to sleep and panic started to well up in me as I realised that if I did so this would deprive me of any opportunity of getting into bed with her.

'Is it all right if I come over and kiss you goodnight?' I whispered, slipping out of bed towards her. She gathered the bedclothes tightly about her while cautiously turning her cheek towards me.

'Just a little cuddle,' I pleaded, but she didn't answer.

'Oh bugger you then!' I said and returned to my bed. I struggled to remain awake. I imagined all the blokes in the billet gathered around my bed laughing their socks off:

'How's it going, Gord? They've got some nice historical buildings up here!'

This was crazy; I couldn't bear it any longer. I removed my pants and slid into her bed.

'What are you do... Get out!'

'It's all right... it's all right, I'm not going to do anything; I just want a little cuddle.'

'You promised... you promised!'

'I know, but come on, Renee; we're grown ups, for Christ's sake. All I'm asking is for a little cuddle like we've done in the past; a little Christmas cuddle.'

Eventually, with a long drawn out sigh, she accepted me in

bed with her.

I made a lot of drowsy promises and agreed to confine my activities to her upper regions. I pleasured myself with her breasts, hungrily mouthing the soft mounds of flesh in turn. My hand cautiously caressed her stomach, and I felt her body stiffen as my fingers clipped the outer periphery of her silky pubic hair. I set up a pattern of stroking her, sometimes missing her pubic hair, and at other times glancing at it as if by accident, and I could feel her melting beside me and her breathing become more intense. I felt her body stiffen, and she dug her nails into my back as I slid on top of her, kissing her full on the lips. I felt the moistness of her passion as I squeezed my knee into her groin. Gasping with pleasure as the warmth of our bodies met, her erratic breathing turned to a low hissing moan as I spilled over her. We lay silent and exhausted as sleep overcame us.

On waking up in the morning I was disappointed to discover her sitting on the edge of the bed, fully dressed.

'I've got a good mind to go home, after all your promises.'

'I'm sorry, but look, why all the fuss? Nothing much happened. I had too much to drink and I couldn't stop myself. All we did was have a necking session. Anyway, I was knackered. Look, Renee, I'm just a bloke; what am I supposed to do? Play bloody snakes and ladders? I consider you to be my woman.'

'I'll see you at breakfast,' she snapped, slamming the door behind her.

At the breakfast table she hardly said a word, and I was beginning to wonder what I could do to retrieve the situation.

'You've dropped some egg on your jumper,' I said casually.

'Where?' she leapt to her feet, frantically scanning her jumper.

'It's very small,' I said. 'You can hardly see it. Just there,' and I prodded her left breast. 'Only joking!'

'You devil!' she laughed, threatening to punch me on the nose.

After breakfast, in an arm-in-arm walk by the canal, we

made up with a kiss and a cuddle.

Renee made major concessions in the bedroom for our last night, on the understanding that she might be old-fashioned but that she had principles. If I slept in her bed, it would be a firm commitment to an official engagement. I must not attempt to go beyond caressing in the lower regions. Any attempt to have full intercourse and she would create mayhem.

On the return train journey to St Athan I thought about the Christmas holiday, which although it had been enjoyable was nevertheless disappointing. I was distraught to think how it could be possible to spend two nights in a double bed with a naked girl and remain a virgin. I realised that my knowledge about sex was severely lacking – then remembered the incident with Mrs Wayne's daughter and the bonking bantams that had embarrassed me so much. There were many gaps in my knowledge, and the answers were not to be found in my ten-bob library. Anyway the bottom line was that I was still a virgin – officially engaged to marry, according to Renee.

My disenchantment with the RAF started when I returned from leave on a forty-eight-hour pass. The train had broken down, which meant that I was an hour late. I was put on a charge, and the sergeant in the guardroom assured me he would do everything possible to ensure I enjoyed the experience. The smart-arsed officer gave me five days' jankers, a traditional punishment of polishing brassware in the guardroom and other unpopular duties. His cryptic and grinning advice was: 'Perhaps next time you'll catch the earlier train!' From that moment onwards, my dislike of authority developed into a major problem. I decided to take the first available posting abroad. I packed in the lessons in Cardiff; I couldn't get the hang of the fancy dancing. There were also far too many blokes in the billet with the potential to go professional. The dance teacher in Cardiff told everyone in her class that they had outstanding potential.

The NCOs were looking for more people to join the St Athan's boxing team, because there was a lack of volunteers. I insisted I wasn't any good at that sort of thing, and didn't approve of hitting people. It wasn't nice.

'You'll love it, Aspey!' said the corporal, 'and now it's compulsory. The sergeant in the guardhouse at West Kirby tells me you're really keen on boxing and need a lot of practice.'

'Yeah! I bet he did, the bastard.'

I hid behind a pillar during the boxing sessions, and groaned when the instructor winkled me out for a three-rounder.

'Now look, Aspey,' he said, as he laced up my boxing gloves. 'When you get in the ring I want to see fireworks. I want you to get stuck in straight away and put on a good show. I don't want any pussyfooting around like that last pair of muffins. Is that understood?'

'Okay,' I sighed.

My opponent was a short, stocky bloke with a face like a mangled swede. He was hopping up and down, making blowing noises as though he were inflating a box of balloons. He stopped and glared at me as though I'd escaped off the bottom of his shoe. I decided to get it over and done with as quickly as possible. I walked over to him, nodding in friendly fashion, then wacked him on the nose. The audience of recruits hooted with laughter. My opponent howled with anger and came at me with raised fist. The corporal intervened, wedging his body between us.

'You stupid idiot,' he yelled. 'That's not funny. You pay attention and wait till I ring the bell.'

'But Corp, you told me to get stuck in strai...'

From that point onwards I hardly knew what was happening. My opponent danced around the ring like a fairy, sticking his fist in my face time and time again. He was treating me like a punch bag. Every time I tried to hit him, he'd gone. By the end of the second round I'd scarcely landed a punch. My gloves felt like sacks of potatoes; my legs were like jelly; and my face was puffy and sore. Early in the third and final round I lost my temper. I'd had enough. I rushed at my opponent and wedged him into the corner of the ring. I then rained blows on top of his head as hard as I could, rat-a-tat-a-tat, as though I was knocking in a fencing post and followed up with a couple of rabbit punches. He looked bewildered and turned towards the corporal as if to query my unusual approach. I took the opportunity to smack him in the mouth. To my amazement, the corporal ignored his protest and gave me every encouragement.

'Well done, Aspey! Now you're thinking.' This seemed to slow my opponent down a bit, as he kept looking up at the ceiling. I was on the point of developing another innovative approach by kicking him in the bollocks, because by now I was really angry. Fortunately the final bell went and the corporal raised my opponent's hand as the winner.

'You know, Aspey,' said the corporal, oozing sarcasm as he removed my boxing gloves, 'you ought to take up fencing; you've real potential.'

I later learnt that the fleet-footed face-pummeller was a leading light in the St Athan's boxing team.

Passing the Administration Office one morning, I noticed some postings available on the notice board, my eye having settled on what I thought was West of Zoyland. I snapped it up. I'd had a previous conversation on a train with a bronzed flight sergeant, who'd told me what a magnificent country Kenya was.

'If you ever get the opportunity to go to Africa, Mate, take it. You'll never regret it. It's as near to paradise as you'll ever get on this godforsaken planet.'

With great enthusiasm I announced my imminent departure to my mates in the billet. 'Yoo-hoo! Listen here, folks. I'll soon be departing from this cloudy, rain- sodden hell island. In a couple of weeks I'll be thousands of miles away, sitting on my bum soaking up the sun.'

'So where're you going?' said Chalky.

'Africa,' I said.

'Africa?' said several voices at once, showing surprise that there were postings available in that part of the world.

'Whereabouts in Africa?' said Chalky with rising interest.

'Somewhere called West of zoyland,' I announced triumphantly.

'Then you'd better take an umbrella, Mate,' chuckled Chalky. 'You sure won't be getting sunburnt, 'cos I were born there. You mean Westonzoyland. It be near Bridgwater in Somerset; it's not much more than shouting distance from here.'

11

I was posted to the jet training flying school in Westonzoyland. I think my job was to administer the high-speed specification called DT772. The high-speed finish was important on the leading edges of the wings and tailplane, reputedly increasing the speed by as much as ten knots. I looked after about fourteen Meteors housed in the main hangar. The work was always urgent, to ensure the aircraft were not grounded and that maximum flying hours were maintained. I was promoted to senior aircraftman (SAC) and provided with a helper, Taffy, an air compressor and the keys to the paint and petrol store. I also painted those nice red, white and blue roundels on the wings and fuselage, and other warning signs on the aircraft. Later I was demoted back to LAC as a punishment, together with seven days in the cells and the loss of a week's pay.

Westonzoyland was a small station where everybody seemed to ride around on bicycles. The distance between the workshops and living area made this almost mandatory, and a bike was also useful for visiting Bridgwater, the nearest town. Soon after my arrival at the camp I discovered a gap in the hedge at the end of the runway. This useful facility gave me the freedom to come and go by bike as I pleased without being observed by the keen-eyed inmates at the guardroom.

But I wanted a car. I'd seen a 1934 Morris 10 saloon for sale in a garage near the cinema in Bridgewater. I was determined to raise the thirty pounds required to buy it. With tongue in cheek I wrote to the Foundling Hospital offices in January 1953, asking for a loan. I offered to pay the going rate of interest, but wasn't surprised when they didn't reply. I was, however, prepared to explore every avenue. I decided to try and pass my driving test quickly and then run a taxi service during the evenings and weekends on the camp to boost my income.

4093644 ASPEY (LAC)
SPRAY SHOP
AIR WING
32 M.U.
St. ATHAN
BARRY
GLAM.

Dear Mr. Nichols,

The request I have to make may read a little unusual and perhaps a trifle unreasonable. That I do not deny but would add it is for a purpose. My request is for the loan of the sum of £80, eighty pounds. For security all I have to offer is my word of honour to repay at the rate of £4 four pounds per month by registered post. In the event of consideration there will, no doubt be a little matter of interest, that I leave to you. This is no emergency and I am in no trouble, but am merely attempting to procure a bargain which will eventually prove its worth by my financial betterment.

I Remain Yours Truly
Gordon Aspey.

Letter to Foundling Offices asking for a loan to buy a car.

I was on my way back to the camp after a lazy day in town, waiting at the bus stop and daydreaming about the car. An airman slowed down on his bike, pointing behind him.

'There's a smashing bit of crumpet coming this way. She's an absolute cracker. Low-cut dress, nice boobs, the lot.'

'Yeah!' I said, with a mock yawn, 'You just can't get away from them, can you?'

'No, for real. You wait and see. She's a real corker and she's coming this way.'

The sun was warm. I felt fresh and relaxed after my dip in the municipal swimming pool. Birds were singing; insects buzzing in the hedgerows: summer was on its way. In the distance I could hear the chimes of an ice-cream van. I looked with mounting interest as the van turned the corner. It briefly obscured a female figure as it passed. *Christ*! I thought. *She looks gorgeous*! The airman hadn't been kidding.

A pale cream frock patterned with tiny poppy-like flowers swayed and swirled in the summer breeze. Blonde curls bobbled on her shoulders, synchronising with fulsome breasts. I was reminded of an early war film, a girl with windswept blonde hair and billowing cotton frock hurrying towards her hero. He is hobbling along on crutches with eager face raised towards her, returning from the war. I wanted to be him, her hero, but without the crutches. As she came closer I studied every ripple of her sensuous figure. Blue-green eyes shone out from her lightly tanned, pink-lipped face. The airman's description had done her an injustice: she was stunning, even more luscious than the nine o'clock goddess I had worshipped behind the window of the Sheerness workshop. I worked out a way to engage her in a conversation. Stopping the ice-cream driver, I bought two cones.

'Two?' he said, raising his eyes with surprise. Then he looked over his shoulder to see the woman coming towards us. 'Ahah!' he said with a smile, 'your friend?'

Her eyes fixed upon me, a questioning, unswerving look that demanded an explanation for my existence. I nervously licked my the ice cream and wondered what on earth to say. Her footsteps quickened and grew louder as she drew level. Fearing she would quickly disappear, the words tumbled out of me.

'I've... um... bought you an ice cream.'

'Pardon?' She looked both startled and amused.

'I've bought you an ice cream.'

'No thanks,' she laughed.

Disappointed by her rejection yet encouraged by her cheerful manner, I followed behind with an outstretched ice cream. 'I can't eat them both; it would be a shame to waste it.'

She paused with one hand on her hip. 'Then why buy two in the first place?'

'Well, a bloke's got to have a chat-up line.'

'You're funny,' she chuckled, sweeping her long, pink tongue around the melting ice cream.

Conversation came easily and I relaxed; it was as though we had known each other for years.

'Isn't this your bus?' she asked anxiously.

'I'm in no hurry. So what's a lovely lady like you doing, wandering around in the middle of nowhere?'

She paused, clearly uncomfortable with the question.

'Is this a bit more of your chat-up repertoire?'

'No, no; I'm just being nosy.'

'Well, it's a long story. What's your name?'

'Gordon.'

'My name's Sarah, and I'm married. I've got problems, but I don't want to talk about them right now.'

Oh sod it! I thought. *How could I have imagined a ravishing girl like her would be wandering around in the middle of nowhere dying to fulfil my sexual urges? Of course she was married.*

'Isn't a problem shared a problem halved?' I ventured, trying to expand my input into the problem.

'So they say,' Sarah sighed, flicking her hair over her shoulder. 'My husband is having an affair. I caught them in the front room. I'd gone to see my Mum, but returned home because I'd left her birthday card behind. I couldn't believe it. I was so angry I chucked all his belongings into the street.'

'Blimey! That must have been a shock for you.'

'Yes. I'd seen her many times delivering letters. She often stopped to chat with me, but I never suspected anything was going on. I think she must have packed in her job with the post office; I haven't seen her for weeks.'

I wondered about the sanity of a man who was frigging about with some girl in the post office while he had such a sparkling jewel.

'I've a little boy at home; the babysitter will be waiting. I'd invite you in for a cup of tea, but they're such gossips around here. Thanks for the ice cream and keeping me company; perhaps we'll meet again some time. Must go now. Bye.'

I couldn't hide my disappointment.

'I'm sorry,' she smiled, pausing to scrutinise my face. 'You'd better get your bus; they don't run that often.'

Sarah stepped off the pavement and hurried towards a row of terraced cottages. I watched her intently, admiring her shapely form moving sensuously with every step. I felt an overwhelming despair that our meeting had come to nothing. Every time she'd laughed and turned her face towards me I'd experienced a tingling excitement. Now she was gone, and probably I would never see her again. In the fading light I watched her cross the road, but suddenly she stopped, turned, and waved in my direction. I waved back, and then realised she was beckoning me. I hurried towards her with almost delirious excitement.

'Gordon... Give me half an hour to sort things out with the babysitter and make sure Michael is settled. If I come to the window and pull the curtains, you can let yourself in. If I don't draw the curtains, that means Michael is not yet settled and I can't let you in, and the bolt'll be on the door. But *please* Gordon, don't make a noise or any fuss if I can't let you in.'

'I won't; I promise, Sarah.'

The street was narrow and poorly lit, and there were shadows everywhere. It seemed strangely quiet for a summer's evening. I started to worry that I might be looking at the wrong house, because they all looked the same and I hadn't made a note of the door number. Half an hour passed. I started to think Sarah was playing games and had no intention of seeing me. Then I noticed a movement immediately opposite. Her face appeared and the curtains swung across. I looked up and down. The street was deserted. I wondered about the babysitter because I hadn't seen anyone leave. Crossing the road, I noticed an alleyway at the side. I carefully turned the brass knob and eased myself through the door. My hands were hot and sweaty and my excitement mingled with fear as I remembered that Sarah had a husband. I thought that perhaps she intended to give me a cup of tea as remuneration for the ice cream. I'd also sensed that she liked me; perhaps something exciting might happen.

'Just a minute,' she whispered, striking a match. The gas filament spluttered and hissed, then gradually filled the room with light. Her front room was small, with the remnants of a coal fire reflected in a large circular mirror on the wall. She pointed to a solitary seat, a shabby, black leather settee. There was a smell of laundry and behind the door I could see an assortment of coloured bricks and toys.

'Would you like a sandwich or some biscuits?' she said, handing me a mug of tea.

'A sandwich would be great.'

'Corned beef?'

'Whatever's going? Corned beef would be nice. Please.'

I munched through the thick sandwich and watched her out of the corner of my eye. Corned beef had never figured prominently in my diet; it was take it or leave it. But that evening corned beef was elevated to the top of what I wanted to eat. Thereafter, the very mention of corn beef would cause a stirring in my groin for a long time afterwards.

Sarah busied herself tidying up bricks and other toys, then suddenly raised her head and caught me looking at her. Her smile was uncertain, as if questioning her own judgement in letting this complete stranger into her house. She was now hesitant and had lost her confident poise. I desperately wanted her, but didn't want to make her fearful or anxious.

I handed her my mug and plate, 'Thanks; you make a nice sandwich.'

I stood up and looked at the photographs on the mantelpiece, pointing to the little boy.

'That's Michael,' she said.

'He looks just a weenie bit like you,' I laughed, trying to avoid the awkwardness hanging in the air. I sensed her nervousness and my courage started to fail. I was almost on the point of leaving, but then took a deep breath and moved towards the gas mantle and with trembling hands pulled the chain downwards until the gaslight was almost extinguished. I pulled Sarah towards me, kissing her cheeks and burying my face on her neck and bare shoulders. I luxuriated in the faint perfume that mingled with her fresh, soapy softness.

'Gordon, I do like you, but it would be nice to know you better first,' she whispered, pressing her hands against my chest.

'I feel I've known you all my life; why should we wait?' I said. I held her firmly, pressing into her softness and warmth. 'Sarah!' I whispered. 'I want you. Now.'

She didn't answer, but her arms gradually slipped round my neck as I unclipped her bra. I sucked hard on one of her nipples as her frock fell to the floor. Her mild resistance evaporated as I caressed and kissed her all over. We lay on the settee and I experienced the most luxurious warmth, an ongoing floating sensation of pure pleasure. The lust oozed out of me as I kept pushing into her, burying past disappointment and frustration. She moaned in a dreamy, distant way.

'You are one randy monster,' she said slowly, stroking my back and licking the beads of perspiration off my forehead with her tongue. Our bodies stuck to the leather settee, causing a ripping noise like tearing surgical plaster whenever we moved.

'Let's get more comfortable,' she beckoned. The image of her climbing the stairs was the most erotic and beautiful picture I'd ever seen in my life.

I remembered hearing a doctor talking on the radio: 'Only very strong men such as professional boxers and athletes can make love more than twice in one night.' I wondered how such people obtained this knowledge. Surely they didn't sit around with biros and clipboards counting on their fingers? Or was it mere establishment propaganda and guesswork? And where did I fit into scheme of things? Perhaps I was sexually unique.

That night I really became a man.

* * *

Three weeks later I bought the car with the proceeds of some private work. I'd resprayed a couple of the officers' cars and had also borrowed money from Ginger, who charged extortionate interest.

My work on the camp went to pot after my first rapturous night. I didn't know whether I was working on aeroplanes, cars, or garden gnomes. There were noises, voices and people all around me, but my mind and body were totally entwined with Sarah, plunging up and down between white sheets in Market Street. Taffy, who helped me in the preparation of the aircraft before I sprayed on the finish, kept asking, 'Are you all right, Gordon? You don't look well.' The bed in the billet wasn't slept in. I had to fill in a form for permission to live outside the camp, which had been granted grudgingly after I'd hastily concocted details about an imminent marriage. Even so, it was a mad dash to get back to camp. There were parades and occasional kit inspections that I had to attend, especially when the Mighty Mouse, our squadron leader, arrived on the scene. I was hollow-eyed and haggard, and questions and comments were ongoing. 'On the tiles again? You don't 'arf look rough. Who is she?'

I kept silent about Sarah. I took a dim view of some of my colleagues, who willy nilly bandied names around of local women they had supposedly scored with. I thought it unfair to defame a woman's reputation purely on account of fictional stories and wishful thinking.

12

An auntie had told me many years previously that my father had sold broken biscuits as a speciality from his tumbledown shop. Flossy, my mother, worked for him as a domestic servant. One of her jobs was to make paper cornets from old newspapers and fill them with broken biscuits to sell to the local children. He scolded her on many occasions for being too generous.

'Two inches below the rim, girl; I'm not running a bloody charity!'

I must have inherited his business acumen. I was a primitive forerunner of eBay without the mouse. This entrepreneurial streak accompanied me during my national service. I stood in the cinema car park with my best mate Ginger. We had met on the train when I was posted from St Athan. Our attention was focused on a mobile tea trolley with a 'For Sale' notice in its window. It looked like a converted caravan with a large serving hatch down one side, with all the internal fittings to run a teashop. It seemed a bit tatty, but I could soon fix that.

'Well? Are you going to buy it?' Ginger asked.

'I already have. That is, I've not actually paid for it, but I've given the owner the nod. Anyway, Ginger, I need a favour. I want to run it round to Starman's candle factory tonight. I've rented a space in the yard so I can spruce it up and get it operational as quickly as possible.'

'Gordon, you're a nutter. You want to run a taxi service, and you haven't even passed your driving test. Now you want to run a tea-trolley business. Where're you going to put it?'

'In the London Inn car park, right beside the camp. I reckon that's a good spot.' (It belonged to Mr Uphill, my nom de plume.)

'Hang on! You haven't paid for it; you can't just take it away like that. You're not allowed to run a business in the Service – its illegal. And another thing: you should be displaying L-plates as a learner driver.'

'Never mind bloody L-plates, Ginger! Show a bit of enthusiasm! The owner'll find me soon enough – when he wants his money. Are you going to give me a hand? Can you... er... drive? You've more experience than me; I'm a bit nervous.'

'Okay. Who's going to run it?'

'That's all sorted. Just give us a hand to hitch this up.' My car wasn't well suited to towing tea trolleys, and the tea trolley was a real pig to tow; it swayed all over the place and Ginger was most relieved when we arrived at our destination.

Mr Starman was a distinguished-looking toff from another era. He had all the mannerisms of somebody accustomed to the better things in life, but outwardly he looked short of a bob or two. In the course of haggling over the rental money, which he insisted had to be paid immediately, he grumbled about the introduction of electricity. He thought Mr Faraday had been born prematurely by a hundred years, thus depriving him of the comfortable living promised by his father.

'There's no demand for candles any more,' he moaned. 'This business has become a liability. I'll never sell it. I'll finish up living like a pauper. I have to rely on renting out the yard.'

He pointed to a pair of scruffy-looking ice-cream vans. 'There's no demand for ice cream, either. Ralph struggles to pay me his rent. I don't know where it's all going to end.'

The other tenant in Starman's yard was a travelling showman, complete with merry-go-round, all beautifully painted and gilded with the help of his two sisters who lived with him in the caravan. They worked on the dismantled merry-go-round during the winter months and toured during the summer. They were highly skilled in their craft, handed down from numerous generations of show people, but admitted they were the last in a long line and would soon be retiring.

They were impressed with my sign-writing skills, and watched me intently as I painted the name 'Sarah's Snack Bar' in a flowing script with blended grey shadow. The showman nodded approvingly. 'You be well taught, young man, that's nicely done.'

Ginger's negative attitude continued. 'You'll have to sell a lot of cups of tea to make a fiver. Apart from that, I can't see the brewers being too excited at you selling tea and sticky buns from their pub car park.'

'Try and give us a bit of encouragement, Mate – this could be my future we're discussing. This is a starting point. If it takes off, I'll buy a second tea trolley, and a third, and so on. Who knows?'

'Highly unlikely, Gord.'

'Haven't you heard of acorns and oak trees? Joe Lyons' teashops had to start somewhere, you know. I've got everything organised; I've written to the brewers; I've done a feasibility study. Sarah's going to run it for me, and I reckon I can get a nice little earner going by the time I get demobbed.'

'Who's going to run it?' asked Ginger, his eyes widening with disbelief. 'Sarah? Jesus, not that married girl you've moved in with? You're really sticking your neck out. Her husband will go berserk when he finds out.

* * *

The publican, Mr Blenham, seemed surprised when I towed the trolley into the London Inn car park.

'So the brewers be given yer permission already?'

'Yep,' I lied, trying to look as blasé as I could. 'They'll be confirming it in the post in a few days. Oh, and this is Sarah – she'll be running it for me.'

'Hmm… Well, ain't you one smart young lady,' he said, shaking her hand. His face brightened as he looked her up and down. 'If you's wants anything, anything at all, mind, you just come a-knocking on my door.'

'I don't trust that lecherous old bleeder,' I said. 'He must be nearly fifty years old. Did you see the way he was looking at you? The dirty old beggar; he was salivating.'

Sarah flipped her long blonde curls over her shoulder. 'I thought he was nice,' she said. 'Older men know how to treat a lady.'

Sarah and I got on very well together, and her young son accepted me. When I knocked on the door Michael would giggle with delight and demand to be lifted up and given a big hug. We looked like an ideal family in all but name. Although I was concerned about Sarah's husband she never mentioned him, and soon I forgot all about him.

The news of a gorgeous blonde bird with a tea trolley rapidly spread through the camp. I felt a mixture of satisfaction and anger at my early success. I didn't like to hear the inmates talking about Sarah in such a lecherous and crude manner. Ginger had agreed to keep my involvement a secret, knowing the camp inmates wouldn't like the idea of my lining my pockets. The manageress of the NAAFI couldn't understand why sales had plummeted, and she gave Sarah a bit of a grilling about who owned the tea trolley. She'd been told in the village that an airman in the camp owned it. Sarah assured her that this wasn't the case and that it belonged to a Mr Uphill.

Petrol rationing caused me a lot of problems. It messed up my plans for running a taxi service. I could only use the car for emergencies, collecting supplies and ferrying Sarah back and forth to the tea trolley. I eased the fuel problem by pinching a few gallons of aircraft high octane and mixing it with petrol. The fuel bowsers often had fuel remaining in the filler hose clipped alongside the tank, which I drained into cans late at night, and a small bucket tied to the rear of the fuel bowser, used for catching spills and cleaning, produced a few more useful pints. My car's performance went down a notch or two, and it produced clouds of choking black smoke. Techie, another mate in the engineering section, was an expert in all things mechanical and he said knowingly, 'You'll have to de-coke the engine every week and replace your exhaust valves.' He showed real concern for my illegal activities. 'Gordon, you're a real chancer. One of these days you're going to finish up in a cell; you'll get caught for sure.'

'As far as I am concerned, Techie, these little extras are merely payment for services rendered. The establishment deprives me of my liberty, has me marching up and down like a prat, polishing buttons, blancoing paving stones, sticks bromide in my tea, exposes me to gas without a mask, and expects me to fight to the death for king and country for thirty bob a week. Sod that. My life belongs to me. You tell me, Techie, did God decree that these morons should push us around like this? How did we get into this crazy situation?'

'We have to have laws, Gordon. If everyone thought like you, the world would be in a dreadful state.'

'Techie, the world *is* in a dreadful state. Marching around covered in blanco and saluting bastards with scrambled egg on their headgear isn't going to change anything.'

'Blimey, what's brought all this anger on? Has the Mighty Mouse put you on another charge, Gordon?'

In order to eke out the fuel situation I was forced to use a RAF bicycle more often than I liked. The daily cycle ride, coupled with all my other exertions, left me knackered at the end of the day. During a six-month period I lost nine pounds in weight.

* * *

The man who had sold me the tea trolley puzzled me. Not that I was anxious to pay him, but his brand new replacement tea trolley had been closed for nearly two months and I wondered if perhaps he was ill. He had offered to give me tuition on how to run the snack bar and advice on pricing and other tips. I had declined the offer owing to service commitments, but then he'd vanished. This, however, was a minor problem compared to the letter I received from the brewers, Starkey, Knight and Ford. It was an aggressive missive of unfettered indignation, refusing me permission to site the tea trolley at the London Inn.

Mr Blenham, unaware of the brewers' refusal, had an issue with the local council about the drainage from the trolley. He told Sarah, 'Don't you worry, my dear, I gave the man a right flea in the ear. I told him to sort out the annual flooding problem in the area and not to complain about a few tealeaves.'

'Blimey! That's bad news,' said Ginger when he heard about the brewer's refusal. 'What are you going to do? Still, it hasn't cost you anything; you can always return the trolley.'

'No .... Sod it, I'm going up to their head office in Bridgwater and try to get them to change their mind.'

'No chance, Mate!'

'Ginger, I need some encouragement!'

I had my first bust-up with Sarah. 'Look,' I argued, 'that red Oxo tin and the takings are my department. I need that money to buy stock and keep the business going. I can't afford it if you buy shoes and perfume. I already pay you housekeeping. It's not a lot, I know, but give us a chance to get things going.'

'Well, I think it's poor reward for serving those over-sexed, lecherous airmen. Most of them have only one thing on their mind. One officer bloke even tried to get into the trolley, for heaven's sake.'

'What d'you mean, 'officer bloke'? What was he like?'

'Well, he had a lot of gold on his hat.'

'Gold on his hat?' I yelped.

'Yes. He drank about ten cups of tea and invited me to his flat in Bridgwater. He said no expense would be spared and that he would give me a really good time. If you're going to be so mean, I'll be tempted to take him up on his offer.'

'All I'm saying, Sarah, is let's get the thing going first, and then we can talk about money later. That's fair, isn't it? ... What was he like, this bloke?'

'About six foot, slim, grey hair and blueish-grey eyes. Oh yes, and he had three gold rings on his jacket sleeves.'

'Three gold rings? ... I don't believe it! Did he have a wart on his nose?'

'Yes, that's him. He had a big wart on the right side of his nose.'

'The bastard. That's my wing commander. I'll bash his head in.'

I was still smarting from an interview in his office when I'd tried to buy myself out of the RAF.

'So why do you want to buy yourself out? You've only ten months service left to do.'

'Well, Sir, I think I'm wasting my time here. I'm not much good at playing soldiers, the war's over, and I don't reckon on all the marching, polishing, saluting stuff, Sir.'

I knew he would be annoyed, but I didn't expect such a violent reaction. He called me a shitty, whining wimp, and told me to bugger off and stop wasting his time. He practically chased me out of his office.

Mr Blenham was quite pleased about the tea trolley as he'd seen a noticeable improvement in the bar takings. He thought it would be a good idea if we sold cigarettes as he thought it'd shorten the queue at the bar. He didn't want people hanging around for ten Woodbines holding up more profitable customers. He said that he'd supply the cigarettes and that we'd split the profit down the middle.

'If that'd be all right with you,' he said, patting Sarah on the backside.

'Why don't you tell that randy old sod to leave your bum alone; he's always doing that. It really annoys me.'

'He's harmless. It don't mean nothing.'

'Harmless? You should see the look on his face! He looks like a mongrel that's stumbled into a poodle parlour.'

'What's the matter? You're getting very edgy these days. You're jealous,' she teased, pinching my nose.

I called at the offices of Starkey, Knight and Ford to try and get them to change their mind and give me permission to keep the tea trolley at the London Inn. I waited for ages in reception and was feeling really fed up, when a benign old gentleman came to the front office, shook hands and apologised for the long delay.

'So... you're the young man who wants to put a tea trolley on our premises?'

'That's me!' I said, bubbling with enthusiasm. 'The idea is that on market days the farmers can spend more time in the pub, while the wives can have a cup of tea and a natter. And there are cream buns and biscuits to please the kids.'

'Now look, young man, I has no personal objections to the idea, in fact, I reckon you should be given every encouragement in these difficult times. But in all honesty, I can't let my company become involved with selling tea and biscuits. It's totally contrary to our prime object, which is selling beer. That's what we do and will continue to do. Can you understand what I'm saying, young man?'

I argued fervently. 'Mr Blenham will be most disappointed. He has asked his customers, and they are very excited about the idea. Everybody is most enthusiastic. We wouldn't affect the workings of the pub as we'd be in the car park. In the short time we've been operating, Mr Blenham has already noticed an increase in beer sales.'

'Y... y... you mean the tea trolley is already trading?' he exclaimed with increasing irritation.

'Well, yes. I didn't think there could possibly be any objection, so I took a chance. But of course if you object I have no option but to remove it, and I think that would be a shame.'

'You shouldn't have done that, Lad! That's not right. You ca... can't go round shoving tea trolleys in public house car parks without getting permission. It's ju... just not done,' he stuttered. 'Hmm... hmm... you say he is selling more beer?'

'Loads more.'

'Hmm... well, I suppose that's what we're in business for, but you're a cheeky blighter and you tell a fine tale. You'd better carry on, then, and we'll be looking at the publican's figures in due course.'

'Can you give me permission in writing, please? So I can show it to Mr Blenham? He says I must have written permission.'

'No... no. I won't do that. As far as I'm co... co... concerned, I've never set eyes on you. I don't know anything about tea trolleys and st... sticky buns. I am, as they say, turning a blind eye.'

Ginger was gob-smacked. 'You got permission from the brewers? Well, I'll say this, Gord, that's bloody amazing. I'd written you off on that. I just couldn't imagine the brewers agreeing to have a teashop on pub premises. I reckon that director must have been asleep or half-pissed. I'm amazed.'

* * *

Things seemed to be going along quite nicely. I'd repaid Ginger's loan and had abandoned my intention to annihilate the Mighty Mouse by blowing his fucking brains out. I'd decided to let him live, albeit in a restricted form.

But then thieves broke into the tea trolley, stealing all the cigarettes, soft drinks, tea and confectionery. They stripped it clean, and the next few weeks became very complicated indeed.

I was summoned to the guardroom as the civil police wanted to take my fingerprints for elimination purposes, because Sarah had told them I'd done some jobs on the trailer for Mr Uphill who was the owner. While they were dabbing black stuff all over my hands the military police started firing questions at me.

'So who's this Uphill bloke and where is he? D'you have an interest in this tea trolley?'

'Who, me? No way!'

'Well how come Mr Blenham the publican says you own it?'

'Oh no. It belongs to Mr Uphill, but I said I might buy it from him when I am demobbed.'

A plainclothes man arrived in the guardroom and wanted to speak to Mr Uphill.

'Where's this man Uphill? We need to speak to him urgently. We have reason to believe the tea trolley was stolen from a cinema car park several weeks ago. The owner is serving a prison sentence and he can't identify the property at the present time.'

Rumour spread fast that the tea trolley belonged to an airman, and custom plummeted. There was an ongoing search for Mr Uphill, who was thought to be involved in the criminal underworld. Sarah got fed up with all the interrogations and decided to quit running the outfit. I was determined to keep the venture going for as long as possible, so I went to the employment exchange to get a replacement for Sarah, leaving a postcard with my requirements and Sarah's address for any replies.

Ginger had some news for me. With a huge grin on his face he asked whether I had read the local paper. He was busting his sides with laughter.

'Come on, Ginger. Don't keep me in suspense. What's so funny?'

'Well! You know the tea trolley bloke who never collected his money?'

'Yeah, I know. He's in prison.'

'Ah. So you do know. He got three years for buggery with a sixteen-year-old boy, teaching him the intricacies of running a tea trolley.'

'What? You're kidding!'

'No, straight up!'

'Well bugger me, no… no… Jesus, forget I said that… Phew! That's not funny, Ginger. There's something you don't know. The owner reported the tea trolley stolen, and I have a few problems to sort out there. The police are looking for a Mr Uphill. In fact everybody's looking for Mr Bleeding Uphill.'

'Blimey. How are you going to wriggle out of that?'

'I don't know, Mate, but I haven't been sleeping well lately. And the thought of the tea trolley man will not improve my sheep-counting remedy.'

Sarah had found a possible replacement to run things at the snack bar, sent along by the employment exchange. Her main interest centred on the often-repeated question, 'So 'ow much be payin' then?'

'Well, that depends,' I said.

'On what?'

'Well, I need to establish that you're a suitable person for the job. I mean, how much experience have you had in the catering trade?' I was thinking I had to get rid of this applicant pronto. I was annoyed with Sarah. My advertisement had said: 'Wanted urgently. An attractive, energetic young lady with lots of initiative to run a small snack bar. Initially two days a week. Remuneration according to experience.' This particular applicant, a short, dumpy granny with an unsightly crop of warts on her chin, didn't remotely fill the bill.

'Look, Sonny,' she said. 'I've had six kids, three husbands, and nine grandchildren. I knows all about caterin'. There 'ain't much else to learn, I can tell yer. 'Ow much be payin', anyway?'

Realising she was the only applicant, I seemed to have no option but to take a chance. To my delight she turned out to be a bit of a wizard with the sandwiches and tea. In contrast to Sarah's often stewed tea and navvy sandwiches, she offered variety, and the farmers' wives enjoyed chatting and seeking her advice on all manner of things – from cooking and home-made wine to growing rhubarb and washing nappies. Trade from the camp had dwindled but Granny kept things going with the farming community and managed a regular small profit.

Mr Blenham was disappointed by Sarah's leaving – and didn't show any inclination to go into bum-patting mode with her replacement. 'I 'ain't happy with you selling soft drinks,' he said, waggling a finger of disapproval at me. 'That's contrary to the agreement. Another thing: who's this Uphill bloke? Does he own this trolley or you?'

'Well it's mine sort of; it's a bit complicated. I think we ought to give the police a chance to find the thieves, and then maybe we'll get the cigarettes back.'

'Look 'ere, young man, when things go missing in these parts, they don't come back, so you be thinking about giving me my money back real soon for them fags and bringing your arrears of rent up to date.' Shortly afterwards things started to unravel. Sarah had another visit from the police – who now suspected Uphill and Aspey were one and the same person. Their questions became more complicated.

'So what happened to the day's takings? Who paid your wages?'

'I don't know all the ins and outs of what he does and doesn't do. He's his own man. Go and ask him. I don't work there no more.'

The civil police then notified the military police of their findings. I was marched up to the wing commander's office, who was the same bastard who'd tried to get his leg over Sarah. He was at his desk twiddling a pencil and scowling at me.

'Do you own this mobile snack bar at the London Inn?'

'No Sir.'

'The publican says you do.'

'He's mistaken, Sir. I think it belongs to Mr Uphill.'

'This Mr Uphill – you seem to be the only person that has ever set eyes on him, Aspey. Perhaps you can describe him to me. Is he tall, short, fat, thin, a liar, an idiot, or what?'

'He's just an ordinary sort of man, Sir. He's about my height, with fair hair. Oh yes, and he's got a large wart on his chin, Sir.'

The wing commander banged his fist down on the desk and yelled, 'Don't you try and get clever with me. Your fingerprints have been found all over that snack bar. I will ask you again. Who owns the snack bar?'

'According to the local paper, Sir, the owner is in prison. I've agreed to buy it when I'm demobbed.'

'So who is Mr Uphill? The local police say you are Mr Uphill. I think you are Mr Uphill. It was you who wrote to the brewers, asking for permission to site it at the London Inn. They didn't give you permission to put it there and you have ignored them.'

I now realised that no amount of wriggling would resolve this issue.

'I will ask you once more. For the last time, Aspey, who is Mr Uphill?'

'Me!' I snapped, injecting a note of defiance.

'So you are running this ridiculous Jekyll and Hyde act, are you?'

'No sir, it's my name. It belongs to me and I can use it if I want to.' I stared back at him, defiantly holding his gaze. His eyes flickered momentarily, betraying some discomfort in that he knew very well that I was aware of his predatory behaviour with Sarah.

'There are regulations against running a business, as you know. That's why you've chosen to put up this stupid double act. It's a pity you didn't have the money to buy yourself out of the service. You've been nothing but trouble since you arrived on this camp. I understand you ran over an airman's bicycle and trashed a fellow officer's car. You seem to leave a trail of carnage and destruction wherever you go. Have you got a driving licence and insurance?'

'Yes, Sir. Only a provisional licence, Sir.'

'Right! Show your particulars at the guardroom. He pointed the pencil towards me. 'You will cease to run this snack bar at the London Inn and you will remove it from the premises. You are not a chameleon. Your name is Aspey, and will remain so till you leave the service. Do I make myself clear?'

'Yes Sir.'

'Now get out of my office and don't ever let me see you in here again.'

The bastard!

Any thoughts of lingering on at the London Inn for another week or two were dashed. Mr Blenham had a real tantrum about his fag money.

'I wants me fag money now!' he demanded. 'You never had permission from the brewers to put your trolley here, as you said. Another thing – you be selling soft drinks and that weren't in the agreement.'

'Well, look,' I said, in the most reasonable voice I could muster, 'I'm not trying to avoid paying you your dues, but the police may still recover the fags, mightn't they?'

'No they bloody won't. As I told you before, and you knows it. I reckon I've been real patient with you, and I ain't standing for any more of this delaying things. I wants me fag money and rent by Friday, or else.'

Friday turned out to be a bad day for paying bills. Mr Blenham would have to wait a little longer.

The Granny said to me on Saturday morning, 'Mr Blenham was real cross, using some awful language. I told him "It's no good you swearing at me Mister, I only work here." I hardly knows how to say what he told to tell you. He said for you to remove your arse and piss-pot trolley off his premises. He said he'd be taking you to court for the fag money.'

'Blimey! What are you going to do?' said Ginger.

'I don't know, Mate. The gods are ganging up on me at the moment. As if I hadn't got enough problems, I've got to produce my driving licence and insurance at the guardroom.'

'That's a problem?'

'Well, yes. I've got two driving licences. One's in my Aspey name and the other's in the name of Uphill. Unfortunately the Aspey one has expired. Oh yeah! And the insurance is in the name of Aspey, which is still current… So I've got… er… a bit of a dilemma.'

'Phew! What a to-do! You don't 'arf get yourself into some scrapes. You can't show them the Uphill licence. That's a real can of worms.'

'Anyway, getting back to the tea trolley. Are you up for a quick getaway job back to the candle factory, late tomorrow night?'

'What about the police? You said they think it's nicked. I don't fancy finishing up in the cells over this, Gordon, and I hate towing that blood trolley; it's dangerous.'

168

'Don't worry, Ginger, the police aren't too bothered. They know the owner is in jail. Leave the talking to me.'

Sarah came up with a good idea. 'Why don't you put the tea trolley in the Bridgwater Fair? It's a massive annual affair, and people come from all over the country. My cousin is a friend of Mr Richards, the market superintendent. I reckon he'll find you a spot all right.'

* * *

Mr Richards removed his grubby trilby hat and scratched his shiny head. He smiled with a glint of mischief in his beady grey eyes.

'So... How long've you knowed Sarah, eh?'

'Hmm... ages,' I lied.

'Well look, young man, there's only one plot left, about a hundred yards down on the left, by the railings. It'll cost you ten pounds for the two weeks. I've marked it out for you and here's the number that'll be on the staked flag. Okay? And good luck.'

The Granny was delighted to be back in employment, but wanted her sister to help as she was worried she might not be able to cope on her own. Her sister was also a granny, with a kind, Florence Nightingale expression. I side-stepped the issue of payment, confirming that it would be linked to the overall contents of the Oxo tin and that I couldn't say any more than that.

Trying to manoeuvre the trolley into the fair proved to be a tricky affair. Ginger became red-faced and unusually bad-tempered.

'I've nearly had enough of this; it's bloody near impossible. You'd think they'd organise things better than this. It's everyman and his dog trying to get in at the same time.'

'Come on, Ginger, don't get your knickers in a twist. Try reversing it in. Look, I'll treat you to a slap-up meal in that new Greek restaurant afterwards.'

'You said that last time, and then you were skint. This time I'm going to hold you to it, you slippery sod... Is this it? Not a good spot for a tea trolley, Gordon.'

'Well, it's the only vacant plot. I'd no choice ... I had to take it, Ginger.'

'Yeah! But you're hidden by that hedge. People won't see you here – and look at all that dog shit. Jesus, I wouldn't buy a cup of tea here.'

'I'm not happy with it, but what can I do? It's this or nothing. I've no choice and they've got my money. Although, wait a minute; did you see that empty barrow at the other end of the site? That's a perfect spot. Why don't we swap places with that?'

'You can't do that, for fuck's sake; the owner'll go crazy.'

'Look at it this way, Ginger. Two feisty old grannies running a tea trolley have big argument with barrow boy. Who's your money on? I reckon we might just get away with it.'

'What do you mean, *we*? You're fast becoming a real criminal. I don't fancy this operation. I think there's a lot of trouble in this move.'

'C'mon, Ginger, where're your balls? Let's do it.'

The barrow had a faded sign fixed to its rear: 'Williams and Sons, established 1732.'

'You might be all right there,' joked Ginger, 'they could be dead by now.'

A few other stallholders were working late and eyed us suspiciously as we wheeled the cart away.

'So what you be doing?' enquired a tall, black-bearded man with a large mallet in his hand.

'Been moved further down,' I said in a voice as calm as I could muster.

'He didn't look too convinced,' whispered Ginger.

'Yeah he looked too curious for comfort. If it's all right with you, Ginger, I'd like to hang around a bit longer before we slot the tea trolley in, and hope he goes home. Are you any good at blowing up balloons?'

'Balloons? What next? And what about that slap-up meal? Yeah, I know; they'll be shut by now, you cunning sod.'

'Well, my idea is to tie a large bunch of balloons to the roof of the trolley. Where there are balloons you find kids; where there are kids you find parents; where there are parents you find the teapot. And that's the most direct path to my Oxo tin.'

Early the next morning I met up with the two grannies on site setting up their display of confectionery, cakes and sandwiches, including sixty chocolate mice. I had some misgivings about the chocolate mice, which were expensive but had a good mark-up. Sarah, however, had insisted, saying, 'You have to cater for children'.

The grannies agreed. 'You have to speculate to accumulate,' they said.

Having finalised the details, I made my hurried excuses to return to camp on the basis that I needed to attend the early-morning roll call. This was genuine, since the Mighty Mouse had issued orders that anyone absent would be put on a charge. Roll calls were not the usual procedure on this camp. It was considered to be a very cushy place until he'd arrived. The other reason for my hurried departure was, of course, to avoid the outcome of my evil overnight deed. I had barely travelled a hundred yards, however, when I heard a commotion from the fairground. There were loud shouts and swearing, and, looking back, my worst fears were confirmed. The bunch of balloons was crazily zigzagging all over the place. Two angry men were rocking the tea trolley back and forth, almost capsizing it. The terrified grannies were screaming and trying to squeeze out of the narrow doorway. I had expected some bother, but not on this scale.

With consideration for my capital investment and the welfare of the two grannies, I returned to the scene.

'Hey! What's going on?' I said, mustering a look of total surprise and innocence.

'That's one of them,' said a tall bearded man.

'So you're the clever bugger that switched our barrow,' said one of the trolley rockers, a man with a large bushy face, as he moved threateningly towards me.

'There seems to be some sort of mistake,' I said in a voice peppered with apology and fear. 'The market superintendent has obviously made a big cock-up.'

'You lying bugger,' shouted the tall man with a beard, 'I saw you last night with a ginger-headed bloke. Going to a new site, you said.'

Realising that matters were about to turn nasty, I tried to reason with the trolley rockers.

'Look! It's obvious there's been some mix-up. I'm sure we can sort things out. But there's no need to take it out on these two elderly ladies. If it's a question of shifting the trolley, that presents no difficulty, surely?'

'That's a load of crap,' shouted the man with the beard, 'you were trying to cheat them out of their rightful plot.'

The bushy-faced man threw a wild swing, catching me on the side of the head. I saw a thousand brightly coloured stars and felt a boot whack me in the groin. I looked around for a means of escape, but a crowd had gathered, denying me any chance of a quick exit. I felt like the proverbial cornered rat. My thought processes were taken over by a confused autopilot that shouted 'run', 'duck', 'scream' and 'attack', all at the same time. I felt another blow on the side of my head and realised I was going to have a really bad day. Fear welled up inside me. Between the gaps of my protecting arms I saw the bushy face moving in with clenched fist ready to strike again. I rammed my elbow into his face and kicked him hard on the shin. He let out an angry yelp and stood hopping on one leg, swearing vehemently. I took a wild swing at his companion and knocked his trilby hat off. I pushed and shoved, trying to get away from the crowd. But a hand grabbed me by my hair and jerked my head backwards.

'Cut it out now or I'll call the police!' shouted a voice right behind me. It was the market superintendent, Mr Richards.

Bushy Face, still swearing profusely, came towards me, dabbing blood from a split lip.

'He moved our fucking barrow,' he snarled.

'I know what he's done, but everyone needs to calm down, be reasonable, and stop this nonsense now or I'll get the police. The Williams barrow must be returned to its proper designated site, and the tea trolley likewise.'

Then, turning to me, Mr Richards said, 'These people have had this pitch for the last two hundred years. Your pitch is down there as you well know, so you move your trolley back there, now.'

Realising that the danger of being impaled on the railings had subsided, I became a bit more bolshie.

'I'm not putting my trolley back there; it's a dog lavatory. I want another site or I want my money back. I've been conned.'

Mr Richards grabbed me roughly by the arm, remonstrating with his forefinger into my face.

'Look!' he cried, his beady grey eyes brimming with anger, 'I tried to help you as a friend of Sarah's. It's people like you that makes an 'ard job impossible. You must've knowed there would be trouble doing what you did.' He lowered his voice. 'You chose the wrong people to tangle with. They have their own way of doing things.'

Then, in more conciliatory mood, he offered what he called an alternative that would resolve the present problem and be a good opportunity for me to make some money. He looked around at the dispersing crowd.

'That was a daft thing to do, young man,' he said. Then, grinning broadly, he continued: 'It was a plucky performance; you've given the big fella a fat lip, but you'd better keep well out of his way. If I hadn't arrived when I did you'd be in hospital right now. I'm not supposed to do this and I'm putting my head on the block in a manner of speaking. I'll get my workers to put your trolley in the sheep fair on that small hillock over there. Vans aren't normally allowed in there, but I am making this one exception. Your ladies will be pretty busy, I can tell you. Now, are we all agreed this be a good solution?' The grannies, still trembling from their ordeal, looked accusingly in my direction.

'I'm really sorry, ladies!' I said. 'How about a chocolate mouse for each of your grandchildren and a little bonus added to the wages? What d'you say?'

They looked at each other, nodding uncertainly, and Mr Richards went round shaking everybody's hand.

I was nearly two hours late getting back to camp, and I was only too aware that missing the early morning roll call would put me back on jankers. I felt sick at the prospect; it would have a devastating effect on my outside interest. Then a thought occurred to me: *if I felt sick, that meant I was unwell. Why not report sick with some sort of complaint?*

The medical officer looked me up and down with suspicion. 'So what's up with you, Aspey?'

'Well, I have a sharp pain in my shoulder, Sir.'

'How long have you had this pain?' he asked with thinly veiled sarcasm.

'Off and on, some time, Sir, though it was really bad this morning.'

'All right, Aspey, take off your shirt ... Hmm, that *is* unusual; you have a perforation in your shoulder. Were you aware of this?'

'No, Sir.'

'This is most interesting. It isn't serious. I can't be absolutely sure, but I think you might have what we call a sinus. I'm going to fill it with some special pellets. They are administered with a gun.'

'Huh! Sir?'

'Don't worry, Aspey, you'll hear a bang and feel some impact, but it isn't painful, you understand. Just lean your left shoulder into the wall and try to relax.'

I felt cold metal on my shoulder and the whole of the medic's weight pressing against me. It was like being in the middle of a corn beef sandwich. There were two sharp bangs and then he was finished.

'All right, Aspey?'

'Er... yes, Sir.'

'Okay, put your shirt on. I'm giving you a light-duties chitty, and you're not to do any physical activity, marching or anything else. You take it easy and report back here in three weeks' time, and we'll see if it's clearing the problem. If it doesn't clear up you may have to go under the knife for a small operation. Nothing to worry about; it's a very simple operation. (The pellets fell out after two days, but the medic was spot on with his diagnosis; I had the operation over thirty years later.)

'What's that large bruise on your face?'

'I walked into a swing door, Sir.'

'Do you wear glasses, Aspey?'

'No Sir.'

'Hmm!'

Flight Sergeant Koch from Admin studied the light-duties chitty from the medical officer with disbelief. 'I would like to look as sick as you, Aspey. I don't believe a bloody word of it, and I'm going to have words with the medical officer. What's all that bruising on your face? Have you been in a fight or something?'

'No Sarge! It was the Mighty Mouse having a tantrum.'

Although I gained much satisfaction from putting one over on Flight Sergeant Koch and the Admin office – we had a well-aired mutual dislike of each other – I also had concerns about the possibility of going 'under the knife', as the medic had put it. I would have been much happier with a fake migraine or slipped disc or something. This was real, for Christ's sake. I really was ill.

The light-duty chitty gave me the perfect opportunity to skive off early to the fair to see how my business venture was working out. My buoyant mood continued on seeing the long queue at the tea trolley. One of the grannies beckoned me over. 'Can you get some more milk? We're nearly out.'

'Okay. How's everything going?'

'Look!' she said, holding up the Oxo tin brimming with cash.

'So how are the chocolate mice doing?'

'Not very well. They started to melt in the sun, so we had to put them away. See – they don't look like mice any more.'

'Christ, they look awful. Can't you just cut them up and sell them as lumps of chocolate? Or sell them as invalid mice or something? I can't afford to scrap them; they're too expensive. Anyway, I'll get the milk and stock up for tomorrow.'

The first week at the fair was a great success ... apart from the chocolate mice. The rain came during the second week and the fair was transformed into a mud bath.

'So how did it go?' said Ginger, grinning with amusement. 'Got a bit damp the second week, didn't it?'

'Well I've got to hand it to you, Ginger, you were absolutely right. You've shown uncanny foresight.'

'So are you taking the mick or what, Gord?'

'No, no. You remember in the cinema car park that you said it was a frigging waste of time? You were right. Do you know how many cups of tea you have to sell to make a fiver? Do you know how many cups of tea you can make with a quarter-pound of tea? The answers are a bit variable. I don't like figures that don't stack up. Sarah was getting nearly two hundred cups of tea to a quarter-pound. The grannies were only averaging seventy cups. There are twenty slices in a loaf of bread, so eight loaves should give you about eighty decent sandwiches.'

'Don't forget the wastage, Gord; there's a crust at each end, and bread goes stale.'

'Not in three hours it doesn't. The Oxo tin is a long way from matching up with consumption. I've been robbed, Ginger. The pair of grannies has stitched me up. I promised them a chocolate mouse for each of their grandchildren, to compensate for that bit of shenanigans. They have managed to sprout twenty-two grandchildren, and they don't want the invalid mice that melted in the sun. You know, Ginger, since I got that tea trolley, I've been robbed, verbally abused, beaten up, sued by a publican, and called a tight-fisted shit by two grumbling grannies. I should have listened to you at the beginning. Tomorrow night we're down to the new Greek restaurant. The tab's on me. By the way, can you give us a hand to get the trolley back to the candle factory? I'm not allowed to do any lifting or anything – I've got a wonky shoulder and according to the medic it's got a hole in it. In fact they may have to operate.'

'Blimey, how long've you had that?'

'Don't know, Mate, but it's a bit of a worry. One minute you're as fit as a fiddle and the next moment someone tells you you're dying. Still, there is one bit of good news.'

'Yeah?'

'I've been promoted. Well, sort of. The engineering officer has put me in charge of the paint store and petrol supplies for the compressors. I'm the man with the keys! He said I was a pain in the arse, but he couldn't find fault with my workmanship. Yeah! And I've got a nice little workshop near that garage in Othery. The garage owner said I could use it if I did his garage facia sign. Could be a bit of scope there, eh Ginger?'

'Jesus! That was an irresponsible decision by the engineering officer. Did you give him a backhander or what?'

'Well I did respray his car on the quiet. Oh, and another bit of good news. You know the licence problem?'

'Yeah?

'I showed them the Uphill licence.'

'Ouch! And?'

'Well, he was a new bloke, and he was so busy telling me to belt up when I was trying to distract him that he forgot to check the name.'

'Bloody hell. Talk about falling in sewers and smelling of violets.'

'Yeah! I never thought I'd get away with it. Mind you, I

nearly wet myself when later on he threw up the window and called out, "Oy, you, airman, just a moment, what's your name?" I pointed to my arm and shouted back, "SAC Aspey." I sure needed that bit of luck.'

A little while later I asked him, 'Something's been bothering me, Ginger. Where did you learn to blow up balloons like that? It took me fifteen minutes to blow one up.'

'I used to play the trumpet. You need a lot of puff for that.'

* * *

One of the less attractive tasks involved on the camp was the certainty of being detailed at some point for fire picket and crash duties. If a jet aircraft crashed on the camp we were somehow supposed to resolve the problem. I can't recall anybody with specialist skills in our group. I hate to think what might have happened if there had been a problem. Five of us sat in a small cluster just staring at the floor waiting for a fire. The idea was that if a fire did break out we would use our initiative and provide a sensible solution. Conversation was sparse, peppered with a lot of disjointed 'ers' and 'ums'. The exception was John, a voluble, burly dark-haired blacksmith, who told us all about the finer points of embroidery. I thought he was joking, considering that his hands were like a pair of extended coal shovels – no way could he possibly do embroidery. But life is full of surprises and he showed us some examples of his work, which left us speechless for most of the day. In true English tradition the weather asserted itself as the main topic of conversation. Rain had been heavy and constant for almost a week, offering some comfort in the certain knowledge that nothing could possibly catch fire in such a damp and miserable environment.

The main gripe was about how we could get to the NAAFI without drowning.

John threw up his expansive hands with a eureka-like yelp. 'I know what!' he said. 'Why don't we drive over there in the water bowser?'

'Yeah! Great idea, John,' chorused the others.

'I can't drive,' said John, looking at each face in turn for a positive reaction.

I happened to be the only one in the group who could drive, but not wishing to increase my jankers record I remained silent.

'You've got a car,' said John, sticking his chunky embroidery finger towards my left nostril.

'Who... me? Yeah, but I don't know anything about water bowsers. I've never driven anything like that. Besides, the guardroom would be on to us in a flash.'

'No, those toads will be muffled up with their Horlicks in this weather. They're not interested in water bowsers.'

'What if we bought you a couple of chocolate Wagon Wheels and a mug of tea?' offered another member of the group with rising interest.

'No thanks. I don't fancy another spell of jankers. I'm fed up with polishing brasswork in the guardroom and washing up in the canteen.'

'C'mon, Mate,' chimed in the others, 'we could be there and back before you know it.'

'I really don't fancy this idea. I'll tell you what, though, make it four Wagon Wheels and I'll give it a go. Any problems and I'm first out of the cab, and I'll deny everything.'

'Done!' they chorused. 'Let's go.'

The water bowser was a cumbersome vehicle with a lot of gears. It needed about four gearshifts just to get it to move at all. Another spell of jankers looked to be in the offing when the rear end became stuck in a freshly created flower border. Wallflowers and sweet williams were being shunted all over the place as I revved up the engine, turning the flowerbed into a quagmire.

'Whoa! Whoa! Steady on!' cried John. 'What'ya doing?'

'Well, for Christ's sake give me some directions; I haven't got eyes in the back of my head,' I yelled. In a wild panic I rammed her into forward gear and drove straight across the freshly laid lawn.

'Jesus!' said John, 'I thought you said you could drive. You've made one God almighty mess of the flower border.' We stood looking at the carnage. 'The shit's going to fly over this,' mumbled John.

'No... no... it looks worse than it really is,' stuttered Tom, the shortest member of the party. 'I used to work for a landscape gardener. With a bit of help from you blokes I reckon I can fix it so no one'll notice.'

The bowser wasn't designed for carrying passengers, but incredibly five bodies squeezed into the cab. Changing gear was a hazardous experience, accompanied by expletives and squeals of discomfort. We trundled along to the NAAFI with the rain hammering down on the metal cab. 'You're nearly over the curb, Gordon – straighten her up,' yelled John.

'For Christ's sake, I can't see a bloody thing. Can somebody switch the windscreen wipers on? Whose leg is this? I can't steer with your boot up my nose.'

'We're nearly there,' whispered Tom. 'Doesn't she make a lot of noise.' I hope we don't wake up the police in the guardhouse.'

Despite Tom's best efforts the following morning, the idea that nobody would notice what we'd done was impossible. I stood munching my last Wagon Wheel.

'Surely I didn't do all that? It looks like a battlefield; it's worse than it was last night.'

We agreed to adopt a mask of head-shaking, horrified innocence if questioned on the matter. We would mumble vaguely about strange noises in the night, hoping to put the blame on badgers, moles or rutting deer. As the day progressed so did the rain, followed by hailstones, and then fog and nightfall. There was much relief that nobody of any importance came near us. The rain continued all night, and by the final morning Westonzoyland was a picture postcard of puddles, cut off from the mainland so as to make lawns and flowerbeds of little consequence.

The law required me to have a qualified driver accompany me in a car until I had passed my test. I had to write to the Foundling School governors to ask them to notify the Motor Tax Department that my name was Edwin Uphill. Techie was well aware of this requirement and exploited the situation shamelessly. 'We can pick up my wife by the cinema. We just need to get a bit of shopping, and I want to go to the post office.'

'Steady on. I'm not your chauffeur.'

'Quick! Turn right here!' yelled Techie. 'There's the post office.'

'Too late,' I muttered.

'You can still do it, if you turn now,' he argued.

A heavy goods lorry close behind sounded his hooter.

'Sod him! Don't take any notice. Take your time, Gordon, you should just make it.' The bumper bar on my Morris Ten saloon was a non-standard unit, a good four inches longer than the original. I had some doubts as to whether it would clear the shop window. 'Keep going,' hustled Techie. Pedestrians scattered in all directions with angry shouts of dismay. 'St... st... steady,' said Techie, his voice tinged with doubt as the car mounted the pavement.

Too late. There was a loud crash as the car entered the Scots Wool and Hosiery Store shop window.

'You daft bugger! What did you do that for?' screamed Techie, his glasses sliding down his reddening face. 'Why didn't you brake?'

'It was your fault,' I argued. 'You told me to keep going!'

A tall lady with gold-rimmed glasses stood with sagging jaw, her hands spread out in a dreamlike trance – like a waxwork in Madame Tussaud's. Panic set in as I tried to reverse the car as quickly as possible. Unfortunately the non-standard bumper bar curled itself round the corner post, bringing down the remaining window with an even louder, nerve-jangling crash.

There were jumpers, socks, and knitted garments dangling over the bonnet, balls of wool rolling along the pavement – and glass everywhere. Twitching with fright, I ran into the shop apologising profusely to the manageress, who was clinging to a display unit as if it were a life raft in a raging sea. She was mumbling incoherently and her glasses were hanging on one ear. I told her not to worry about a thing, I would get it all sorted. The car was now surrounded by crowds of curious people staring at Techie's white face, desperately pleading for me to take over. I waved back to him and ran off at high speed in the opposite direction. Fortunately I was just about in order with my paperwork, having taken and failed the driving test. But I needed to get some L-plates and fix them on before reporting the incident to the police...

After regaining my composure I ambled round to Techie's house and was pleased to see the car parked outside. I fixed the L-plates, and then knocked on his door to apologise for my cowardly behaviour. Techie threw the car keys into the middle of the road and told me to fuck off.

I'd never seen a policewoman before and was startled to have one checking my paperwork in the police station. She had a red nose and was dabbing at it with a handkerchief.

'That's a nasty cold you have,' I said, trying to adopt the most caring and friendly voice I could muster.

'Can't seem to get rid of it,' she said, dabbing more aggressively with her handkerchief. Then she squared her shoulders in an authoritative manner. 'So you're a learner-driver?'

'Yes.'

'So why didn't you have L-plates?'

'I did!'

'No you didn't. I were there. I saw the whole thing – I saw you smash into the window and watched you run off and leave the other person behind. You didn't have L-plates on your car.'

'Yes I did,' I argued, 'but they're not easy to see, because I hadn't put them on very well.'

'Let me tell you,' she said, with her finger dancing around my nose, 'you were seen only half an hour ago by one of my colleagues, tying plates on to the car in Clare Street. So stop telling lies.' Then, rubbing her nose even more aggressively, she added, 'I think you'll have enough problems paying for all the damage. You've made a right mess of that shop. This time, I'm letting you off. Take this as a warning. Next time I won't be so lenient. Now you can go.'

The Scots Wool and Hosiery Store sent me a huge bill, and I quickly engaged the services of a local solicitor. But I heard no more about the matter ... and didn't even receive a bill from the solicitor.

13

I had my fortnightly letter from Renee, telling me she would be spending the Whitsun holiday weekend in Southsea. Could she bring a pal and make up a foursome with Trish, her best friend? There were times when I felt a right rotter. I had promised to marry Renee, and I guessed the long trip from Lancashire was intended to tie up the loose ends. But I was now living with Sarah, and I could see a lot of complications ahead. My excuse for not going to see Renee was that I was always in trouble and on jankers; the real reason was that I didn't want to get married. I liked Renee a lot, but I also liked Sarah and her little boy Michael. The problem seemed insoluble, and I was having sleepless nights worrying about the problem.

Time and time again the same individuals were on jankers. They were those who could not adapt to being pushed around, or who lacked the enthusiasm for shiny shoes or polishing brasswork. Lofty was one such character. A tall, awkward-looking airman with a cooked-lobster complexion and invasive acne, he was the janker king, though I was putting in a serious challenge for the title. Despite his general awkwardness he was an intelligent individual, with a hat-full of higher school certificates. He also had a musical bent, and played saxophone part-time for a local band. He couldn't settle down to the discipline of service life. If he had something to say, he just said it, with little thought for rank or consequence. Like me he had no family ties and had to fend for himself.

I was having unexpected difficulty in finding somebody to make up a foursome. Then it occurred to me that Lofty might be the answer. I was astonished at his lacklustre response.

'Well, what's she look like? Got a picture?'

'Blimey! What do you want? It's a blind date. I've never seen her myself. We're talking girls here, you know, with all the yum-yum and curvy bits. I mean, Lofty, you're hardly a great catch yourself.'

'There's no need to be so bloody personal! Okay, let's give it a try. I could do with some excitement. What's the master plan?'

'Southsea, Saturday night. I've got their address. We'll sort out accommodation for a couple of nights on arrival. There's a problem with my car so we'll have to hitchhike, if that's all right with you.'

'That's a fair old trip. We'll have to go in uniform or it'll be a long walk.' (In those days drivers would stop to give lifts to Her Majesty's uniformed forces, but were much less willing to do so for civilian hikers.) 'I thought your girlfriend lived in Bridgwater – or is this girl somebody different?'

'Lofty, don't you dare mention that; that's a topic to be avoided at all costs.'

We were hardly out of the camp when Lofty started arguing: 'I thought we'd agreed to go in uniform?'

'Sorry. I forgot all about that. Still, as one of us is in uniform we should get a lift okay.'

'You cunning bastard! You had no intention of wearing uniform!'

'Give it a rest, Lofty; no wonder you're always on jankers. D'you argue like this all the time? – Quick! Flag that lorry; he's slowing. Go on, for Christ's sake; you're far too slow.' Tempers became frayed as the sun got more intense and the temperature soared; the cars just flashed by. We stopped at a roadside café for refreshments and I tried to chivvy up his enthusiasm.

'Come on, Lofty. Cheer up, Mate. We're going to meet a couple of birds, remember?'

'Well, if we don't get a lift in the next quarter of an hour, I'm going back to camp – I'm knackered. At the rate we're going, we'll be lucky to get to Southsea by tomorrow. If we were both in uniform we'd be there by now. Drivers are suspicious.'

'Lofty, you're giving me a headache.'

I decided to take more drastic action. I put my feet on the road as if to step into the path of a white van, and then quickly hopped back on to the pavement. The van screeched to a halt.

'That was a stupid thing to do,' snarled the driver. 'Are you fed up with life on this planet, or what? Where're you going?'

'Southsea! Sorry about that, Mate,' I said. 'We're getting a bit desperate; we've walked a long way.'

The driver grinned. 'Yeah I know, I've done it myself many a time; it can be frustrating. Can you squeeze in okay? I'm bound for Chichester, but you'll be pretty near about. So, are you on leave?'

'We're on a blind date – well, Lofty is. He's making up a foursome.'

The driver squinted at Lofty, the perspiration was running down his face and his shirt was sticking to his chest.

'You look a bit hot and bothered, Cock. So you don't even know what she looks like? Hope she comes up to scratch.'

'I don't care if she looks like a fleet of disfigured buses; all I want is to get these bleeding boots off and relax with a pint of beer. I'm totally brassed off.'

'Whoops!' shrugged the driver.

We arrived in Southsea in the early evening. There had been a mix-up with the guesthouse, and the women had been moved to another venue. Directions to the guesthouse were confusing and inaccurate, and I was beginning to have doubts whether we would ever find them. Lofty had completely lost his temper and was on the point of calling it a day and going his own way.

Then there was a shout from the other side of the road and I saw Renee hurrying towards us. Pretty as could be, all pink and stripy like a stick of Blackpool rock.

'There they are.'

Lofty stopped and stared. 'So which one is mine?'

'The one on the left in green.'

'Crikey! The one in green! Is she *really* my date?'

As we came closer, I was taken aback. Renee was an attractive girl with all the attributes any man could wish for, but Trish was in the Miss World category. She was unbelievably beautiful, with the confidence and grace of a mannequin.

Lofty walked towards her in a zombie-like trance, stuttering awkwardly.

'Hello, er... my name is um... Lofty. Pleased to meet you.' He made to shake hands, but she nodded and turned towards Renee.

'Got a headache. See you back at the guesthouse.' Then she half turned towards me with a frosty look of disapproval.

Renee looked shocked and blushed with embarrassment. 'I'm so sorry,' she said, 'that's not like her. I'm sure she'll be all right in the morning.'

'Don't worry,' snapped Lofty. 'I get the picture. You tell your shitty friend to get stuffed. I've seen some really interesting seagulls around here.'

All the guesthouses were full, except for a grotty-looking place with a dank smell and permanent haze of cigarette smoke. Lofty and I tossed a coin to win the only single room. Lofty lost and had to go into a hotel.

Renee, still upset by her friend's rudeness, continued to apologise to Lofty, assuring him it was not like her. 'She's a bit "plum in the mouth" sometimes, but things will be better tomorrow, you'll see. Come and join us for a drink and unwind a bit.'

'No thanks,' said Lofty. 'You look after this awkward bugger. I'm going to find a nice pub and a chip shop.'

As expected, Renee brought up the subject of marriage. Despite my guilt about the promises I had made in the railway hotel about eighteen months previously, I was determined not to be steam-rollered. 'I need to build a solid foundation with some financial security before I can take the final step. I'm sure you understand,' I said.

She clutched my arm affectionately, rubbing her cheek against mine.

'Let's find somewhere quiet.'

We stood huddled in the shadows of her guesthouse, wedged against a drainpipe. The pink, candy-striped frock was held together with four large buttons, cleverly designed to blend in with the frock material, making them scarcely noticeable. The upper two had been conveniently left undone and I felt sure the main gate was now open to me. I didn't need to ring the bell. Her breath became hot and hesitant as I pressed into her. I opened the remaining buttons excitedly, realising she had no bra. With fumbling haste I slipped her panties into my jacket pocket. She let out a long, low sigh as our bodies met and wrapped her arms tightly around my neck, groaning and kissing me. I gripped her thighs and went to make her mine. At long, long last, I thought.

There was an angry shout from behind. 'Oy! What do you think you're doing? This is private property.'

I couldn't speak, or move. I was aware of a light illuminating my backside and a silhouette of my genitals on the brickwork.

Renee, with buttons rapidly secured, said with commendable composure, 'I'm sorry, but we're staying here on holiday. This is my future husband.'

There was a short pause. 'Ah well, that'll be different then,' said the owner's daughter, with torch still lingering on my backside. 'Sorry to have troubled you. Have a nice holiday. Good night.'

All efforts to restore Renee's passion failed. Sex slipped below the horizon with the last dregs of sunset. Yet again I was denied fulfilment with Renee.

'You looked like one of those rude Roman statues. That was so embarrassing,' she said.

'She had a blooming good look too, didn't she, the silly cow.'

'No matter,' she whispered, kissing me on the nose. 'You'll just have to wait a little longer.'

Lofty appeared in the morning with a migraine, wondering what he was doing in a hotel he couldn't afford. As his memory started to recover, he enquired, 'How's the stuck-up bitch this morning?'

Any hopes the foursome would get off to a better start on the Sunday morning were soon dispelled. As we ambled along the seafront, Trish made it clear she had no intention of socialising with Lofty.

Renee became cross. 'For goodness sake stop playing silly hopscotch. You're acting like a five-year-old. I'll walk with Lofty and you walk with Gordon.

Trish grabbed the opportunity to admonish me for my choice of companion, insisting I was responsible for ruining the weekend by expecting her to partner such a pimply-faced gangling gringo. 'He's an insult ... an inconsiderate yob. Fancy coming on a blind date with a face looking like a pus lolly. He's got a problem; he should fix it ... shove his head in a bucket of disinfectant ... see a doctor or something.'

'That's a bit strong. He can't help having a few spots. All young people have them; I had them myself.'

'Not like that they don't. I had them when I was fourteen. My dad said I was to stop moaning and get them fixed. So I did.'

'Well, I think you are being a bit cruel with poor old Lofty. He's a clever bloke. D'you know he's got a load of those those newfangled O levels.

'I'm not interested in his levels, whether spirit, sugar, shit or any other, Gordon. I don't fancy the bloke. I'm not going to waste my time being polite to someone just because it suits convention. The world is full of cruelty and ignorance; I've learnt to accept it and not dwell on it. I've watched my parents being polite and deferential to their so-called betters, and they were totally shat on. Not for me, thank you.'

No question Trish was a one-off. I found myself fascinated with everything about her: her eloquence, her poise, her looks and her bare-boned frankness. I found myself comparing her with Renee and wondered what sex would be like with her. I imagined it would be wild, fast and furious, with teeth marks and socks out the window, and 'Bugger off I've finished' – that sort of thing. Renee was quite different, a compassionate, next-door type. Sex would be nice (whenever), neatly tied up with a ribbon – and maybe a quick whizz round with a dustpan and brush afterwards. I wondered if the opportunity missed the previous evening would ever arise again.

Trish was drawing a lot of attention on the promenade. Her tight-fitting, lime-green two-piece with scarlet high heels gave her extra prominence. Admiring glances followed her, from both sexes. Her darting blue eyes scythed through the sea of faces, with the occasional toss of wavy, jet-black hair contrasting with her full, defiant red lips. She was every man's dream and she knew it.

She clutched my arm and, turning her head, listened intently.

Her face beamed. 'Do you hear that? It's a band; I just love brass bands.'

Members of the band wore smart blue and gold uniforms, and their instruments glistened brightly in the sunshine. Scented flowers mingled with the smell of frying chips in the light onshore wind. We stood with a small crowd listening to the music.

Lofty tut-tutted. 'That trombone ... he's well out of sync.' Trish looked surprised, and nodded approvingly.

'He's not the only one,' she said. 'They've had too much booze with their dinner. My dad's a bandmaster. He'd be whacking them round the head with a cricket bat.'

'Lofty plays the saxophone,' I said. 'Don't you, Mate?'

'The sax?' frowned Trish. 'You actually play the saxophone? You don't look the type.'

'What d'you mean I don't look the type? What's a bloke supposed to look like? I only play part-time at the moment.'

'Only when he's not on jankers,' I laughed.

'Why didn't you tell me this?' said Trish indignantly.

'Tell you what? I thought you were dumb and wouldn't talk to blokes with pimples.'

'Yes, I must try and improve my manners. We northern folk, well, we're a bit direct, like.'

'That's crap! You're an ignorant bitch; I'm from Gateshead.'

'Steady on, said Trish. How long've you been playing the sax, then?'

Lofty paused and scratched his head. 'Since I was about twelve.'

'Hmm...' said Trish approvingly. 'You must be pretty good by now.'

Lofty edged closer to Trish, surprised to find himself in earnest conversation with her. 'I play for a local band at weekends. We have loads of fun. The sax requires a lot of practice to get to a good standard. I like to think I'm pretty good; at least nobody's told me otherwise.'

'I love the sax,' whispered Trish. 'I can listen to Charlie Parker all day. He takes me into another world.'

'Ah, the Bird,' said Lofty his eyes lighting up with excitement. 'He's magic, God's got a bit of catching up to do there. His improvisation! Wow, I buckle at the knees. If I could play a fraction like him I would be the happiest man on earth.'

Trish placed a light hand on Lofty's shoulder. 'I'm really sorry, I've treated you like shit. If you could play one hundredth as good as Charley Parker, well, I'd kiss every one of those horrible damn pimples till they were cured. Gordon says you're a bit of a renegade.'

'He can't talk; he's worse than me.'

'Welcome to the club!' laughed Trish, pecking him on the cheek.

'Can you believe that?' said Renee as we left them in deep discussion on a promenade bench. 'That's a right turn-up. What a transformation!'

'Yeah! You wouldn't think a bucket of pimples and a saxophone could make such an interesting mix.'

* * *

Lofty sat with a dreamy expression on his face as the train gathered pace. We'd decided against hitchhiking back to camp, guessing that if we did so we'd both finish up doing more jankers.

'So what d'you reckon, Lofty? Things didn't turn out too bad for you in the end.'

'I've learnt in life not to expect too much, Gordon. I know I'm not in the Clark Gable category. I hated your guts yesterday and I was really brassed off. But today I'm a new man, completely transformed. I kid you not; this weekend's been an absolute revelation. It's been the best couple of days in my life. Trish is the most beautiful, talented and kindest person on the planet. In my wildest thoughts I never imagined I could latch on to someone like her. You have my eternal thanks.'

'*Kindest*? She's a bitch.'

'No, no, you've got that wrong, Gordon. Look at this: it's her address and phone number. She kissed me full on the lips – a long, lingering smacker. Told me to fix my face, write regular, bring the sax, and visit her soon. She may have a hard shell, Mate, but she's a heart of solid gold.'

'Well, good luck to you, Lofty. Glad to have helped. I would need a sack of Aspirin to keep up with her. I'll grant you she is a real eye-opener, but too overpowering for me. I wouldn't get too carried away with her invitations; she'll have forgotten all about you by Friday. She'll finish up with some fancy millionaire. Birds like that don't belong on our menu, Lofty, so savour the moment, Mate.'

'I see you had a good time with Renee, then?'

'Me? Like hell I did. It was a complete disaster.'

'As bad as that?'

'Worse, much worse. I don't want to talk about it. Your weekend might have been life changing, but mine was accelerating backwards. In fact, mine was zero minus.'

'Come on, Gordon, surely not; it can't have been as bad as that. So what's this frilly thing?' he said, yanking Renee's panties out of my jacket pocket.

'Oh no, hey! Give 'em here. Christ! I forgot to give them back to her.'

'So it wasn't really such a total disaster after all?'

'Look, Lofty, sometimes things aren't always like they seem.'

'So you were just nipping down to the laundrette? Or maybe you're just a trophy hunter. Come on, Gordon, come clean!'

'It doesn't matter what you think, Lofty, but I'll tell you this. If Casanova were aware of my exploits, he'd be wringing his hands with tears of despair.'

14

It was about four o'clock in the morning when I woke up with an arm locked around my throat; a man was trying to drag me out of bed. There was a strong smell of alcohol and stale cigarette smoke, and a hot, rasping breath on my face. In a blind panic I wrenched myself free and lashed out with both fists, trying to fight off my attacker. A hazy beam of light swept through the window from a passing car, and I saw my assailant coming towards me. There was a flash of steel and I felt a thud in my left shoulder. I realised he was trying to kill me and shivered with fear. I needed to get out fast, but the shadowy figure was blocking my exit.

My eyes quickly became accustomed to the light, and I realised the man's movements were slow and cumbersome; he was the worse for drink. I heard Michael crying and Sarah trying to console him in the other room. The figure turned and stumbled towards them. I took my chance and hammered him. I heard him groan as my fist sank into a fleshy part of his anatomy. He fell to the floor with a grunt and I knew I'd hurt him. I gathered my clothes and rushed past into the other room.

'Who the hell is that?' I gasped, hurriedly putting on my trousers.

'I'm her bloody husband,' groaned the angry voice of my assailant. 'You get out of my fucking house now,' he said, as he tried to stagger to his feet, but he fell down again.

'I'm not stopping with him here,' cried Sarah. 'We can drive over to Hazel's place. Come on, Michael luvvy, get your jumper on quickly, and hurry.'

As we got into my car I anxiously felt my shoulder, trying to feel blood or a wound, and was puzzled.

'Did he hurt you?' asked Sarah.

'I thought he stabbed me, but there doesn't seem to be any blood and I can't see any marks of any sort.'

'No, no, he wouldn't use a knife – he's not that stupid.'

'I don't understand. How did he get in? Did you let him in?'

''Course not. He must've forced his way in through the back door or window – I don't know.'

* * *

Hazel called out from her upstairs bedroom. 'What's going on? I'll be down in a second.'

When we got inside, she said, 'Sarah ... you're a fool! That's a silly thing to do. You mustn't let him stay there. The rent book's in your name; you'll lose the house.'

I returned the following morning with Sarah to regain possession of her house and was horrified to see the RAF police outside loading my belongings from the pavement into their jeep. This was because Sarah's husband had called the RAF police when he discovered all the airforce paint. I noticed a stainless-steel watch strap on his wrist glinting in the sunlight, which solved the mystery of the missing knife.

I hurried to the police station round the corner to get help, knowing the military police had limited powers when dealing with civilians and their property. A sergeant accompanied me back to Market Street, assuring me the military police had no right to remove property from civilian premises without proper authority. He explained the legal position to the military police. The corporal shrugged his shoulders.

'This is a military matter involving theft,' he said, pointing to the paint tins covered with arrows, and that takes precedence over civilian matters.'

The sergeant was uncertain of his ground and hesitated. Sarah asked him to remove her husband from the premises as she was the lawful tenant and he'd used violence and broken in. As far as this was concerned he was more certain about what he couldn't do. 'I'm sorry. We can't get involved in domestic problems ... that be a personal matter.

The corporal pointed at me. 'That man is under arrest, Sergeant.'

The sergeant grasped my arm and started to manoeuvre me towards the jeep, assuring me that everything would be fine. 'Now you just climb into the jeep and have a little chat, and everything'll be all right.'

I noticed the tins of War Department paint in the back and realised I was in serious trouble. There was an urgent need for receipts and alibis. I wrenched my arm free and took flight, running towards the timber yard with the sergeant and military police in hot pursuit. I climbed over a six-foot fence and scooted across the railway lines.

'Stop, stop, stop!' shouted the sergeant, pausing at the fence. I rested briefly on the other side to catch my breath. The bulky figure of the sergeant had got stuck on top of the fence and the military police were trying to unhook his trousers. I set off across a field towards a large housing estate and hid amongst a group of dustbins, trying to work out where Hazel lived. 'I saw it all, Gordon,' said Sarah later on laughing, as she'd seen the chase. 'It was like watching a cops and robbers film. To see the sergeant huffing and puffing and trying to get his arse over the fence.' When she'd discovered she couldn't get back into her home, Sarah had made her way over to Hazel's house, which wasn't far away. Later, Sarah regained possession of the house when her husband was at work, with the help of myself, Hazel and a couple of neighbours.

'Sarah, it's not that funny. I'm in real trouble; my freedom's in jeopardy. I might get sent to the military prison.. I've serious problems with the paint. I need receipts and alibis. I've an urgent plan and I need your help.'

'What can I do?'

'The civil police are going to ask you how the paint came to be in your house. You know the alleyway running down the side of your house; the public thoroughfare?'

'Yes.'

'Well. I'd like you to say the paint was in the alleyway ... you thought it was mine and brought it indoors. It's a highly unlikely story, and they won't believe you, but there's nothing much they can do as long as you stick to the story exactly. Will you do that?'

'Okay.'

'I'll be telling them the same story, word for word. They'll try and bamboozle you and trip you up, but just stick with exactly the same line all the time. In the meantime I'll try and get receipts of some sort. I'm going to say I used the empty Air Force tins for mixing purposes. They wont believe that either, but providing we both stick to the same story I should have some chance of a damage limitation exercise.'

We were having a cup of tea when screeching brakes outside heralded the arrival of the military police. Sarah's husband had told the police where to find me. Hazel started to get panicky. 'What if they've got a search warrant?'

'Don't let them in, Hazel,' I urged. 'They haven't had time to sort out a search warrant. They don't have the authority, don't let them in.' I wasn't sure of my facts, but I didn't fancy another cross-country run so soon. I felt knackered. I hid in the lavatory and listened nervously as the police tried to imply that they had every right to search the premises, but Hazel aggressively held her ground.

'I've already told you twice he's not here, and *no*, you can't bloody well come in.'

* * *

When it was dark I drove down to Othery to the garage where I had done a bit of previous business and told the owner of my predicament. He'd little liking for the establishment and furnished me with back-dated receipts, grubbing them with his oily overalls to add more authenticity, and wished me luck.

On Monday morning I walked towards the camp entrance, dressed in civvies as they'd taken my uniform from Sarah's house. From a hundred yards away I could see activity in the guardroom, with heads popping out of the window, and I knew they were

197

waiting for me. I'd gone over the story with Sarah a dozen times to ensure our stories tallied exactly, and with receipts in order I felt I had a reasonable defence.

The way they arrested me with unjustifiable force made me really angry. I was sorely tempted to plant my boot where it might produce the loudest yelp.

The military ritual started to take shape. A long list of charges was read out, plus the one that gets you if all else fails – that is, charged with conduct contrary to the good name of the Air Force, etc. The special investigation unit (SIB) was brought in from Bristol, and they gave me a gruelling time. I had to stand hour after hour with them gulping down numerous mugs of tea while they interrogated me. Their interest centred on several gallons of paint that they insisted was War Department paint stolen from the paint shop. The sergeant said, 'You pinched the paint, Aspey. You're the only one who has keys to the paint shop. We've had it analysed, and it's proved beyond any doubt to be War Department paint.'

Having spent many hours at technical college studying the make-up and constituent parts of paint, I knew this was a lot of bollocks. I argued they were mainly empty tins I used for mixing paint. It was civilian paint, and I had the receipts to prove it.

The interrogating sergeant said he had a good idea, one that would get me off the hook and let him get back home to his family. 'Why don't you admit you only intended to borrow a bit of the paint and that you had every intention of returning the rest of it? At worst you'll probably just get a telling off.'

'I'd like to help you, Sergeant, but surely you don't expect me to tell lies? Although, just a minute,' I said, with a cry of great excitement, 'I vaguely remember Sarah found some paint in the side alley some time ago. She thought it belonged to me.'

The sergeant threw his papers into the air in disgust. 'You cunning little bastard, you're really taking the mick,' he said, and he stormed out of the office, leaving his assistant to pick up the paperwork.

My early optimism that things were going my way was soon dashed. The sergeant returned with a big grin on his face, clutching a spray gun. I realised somebody had shopped me and that they knew about the workshop in Othery. I had borrowed some RAF equipment for some car spraying. The garage had also recommended customers. I remembered a brief association with a warrant officer's daughter in the village that had gone sour. In a fit of temper she had vowed to tell her dad about the workshop.

With no warning or preparation for such a question, my answer fell awkwardly from my lips: 'I bought it from Corporal Trotter.'

I almost bit my tongue off and cursed my stupidity. Snitching on your comrades wasn't acceptable. Corporal Trotter had pinched it from the stores and sold it to me for six pounds.

The SIB people dismissed me from the guardroom, saying their investigations were nearly complete. I was still under arrest and could not leave the camp under any circumstances. I was to remain in the barracks while they gathered further evidence from the witnesses, and I would be dealt with accordingly.

I had to warn Trotter of his unfortunate involvement. As I'd expected, he took it badly and called me all sorts of names.

'Look, Trotter, I'm sorry I got you involved, but we need to get our stories right. I suggest you stick to your story. You say you definitely didn't sell me the gun and you don't know anything about it. Likewise I'll stick to my story and say you did. That way, they can't punish us both for the same offence. I reckon your senior rank will give you the edge and you'll just get a slap on the wrist.'

The camp had a useful grapevine that offered crumbs of comfort. After three courts martial it was usual for the commander to be posted to another station. If I were court martialled it would be number three, and the commander was reportedly worried because it was a cushy camp and he wanted to stay. Trotter also gleaned from colleagues in the admin department that they had spent a fortune on phone calls trying to pin down the paperwork and origins of the spray gun, without success. The general consensus was that the prosecution wasn't as straightforward as had first been thought.

The number of charges was reduced to single figures, and I was marched up to the camp commander's office for suitable punishment. Flanked by two officers, the commander read out the charges to me. When asked, 'Do you plead guilty to the charges or do you elect to be court martialled?' I suddenly became stubborn and elected for a court martial.

The commander's jaw sagged. 'Do you understand what you're saying, Aspey? Do you know what this entails?'

'Yes Sir.'

'Very well, Aspey, you're confined to camp and will remain under arrest. I am convening this hearing to a later date. There'll be a summary of evidence pending the date and time set for your court martial. An officer with some legal experience will be appointed to adjudicate the summary, and you'll be entitled to question prosecution witnesses and produce witnesses for your own defence. Do you understand?'

'Yes Sir.'

From then on things become more complicated, and I began to wonder if I had made a serious error in electing to go for a court martial. I had to supply written statements in answer to specific charges. My mate Techie, with access to admin, kept me informed about the progress and paperwork involved. He gave me one piece of really useful information: they were unable to find any invoices, receipts or gain any further knowledge about the spray gun. It might just as well have fallen off the back of a lorry. There was no evidence of ownership.

* * *

I was marched up to the adjudicating officers' office and told about the procedure.

There were a lot of people coming and going, with all sorts of questions from the officer who was shuffling reams of paperwork. Each time I was asked, 'Have you any questions, Aspey?' I would say no, until it came to the squadron leader in charge of the stores. I was hoping Techie's information was accurate or I'd look a right chump.

The adjudicating officer addressed the squadron leader in charge of the stories: 'You have evidence concerning a spray gun?'

'Yes indeed,' he replied.

'Any questions, Aspey?'

'Er...Yes Sir. I...'

'Go ahead, Aspey.'

'Er... yes Sir. How do you know the spray gun is War Department property? Anyone can stamp a couple of arrows on it, can't they, Sir?'

The squadron leader looked perplexed. 'What do you mean?'

The adjudicating officer intervened. 'I think the defendant is suggesting that the arrows on the gun are not adequate proof of identity.' Then, looking towards me, he said, 'Maybe you are saying there should be more positive proof such as paperwork and receipts, etc. Is that what you are saying, Aspey?'

'Yes Sir.'

The squadron leader butted in testily, 'What sort of idiot would go round stamping arrows on spray guns?'

'Do you have the necessary identifying paperwork in your possession?' enquired the adjudicating officer, scribbling notes in a pad. The squadron leader looked uncomfortable, rustled some papers in his folder, but had to admit that he hadn't anything right then.

The only other witness called was for my defence. He was my star witness who had helped me with my car-spraying activities, and I'd primed him to perfection on what to say and what not to say, but I was horrified by his confused and stumbling performance. On his evidence I could have been sent straight to the glasshouse. He was totally confused and dropped me right in it, introducing all sorts of facts that had not previously been mentioned. He couldn't have done a better job if he was representing the prosecution. I was gutted.

The court martial was abandoned for lack of evidence, but I was charged with the offences described by my star witness that they had previously known nothing about. Accepting the punishment, I lost a week's pay, got demoted, and spent one week in the cells. As I'd predicted, Corporal Trotter received a mild reprimand. The sergeant in the guardroom considered me extremely lucky.

'Just look at it,' he growled at the duty corporal. 'This is WD property and we have to give it back to this thieving little bastard. There are arrows all over it. If it were down to me you'd get six months in the glasshouse and fifty lashes.'

'Yeah! But they couldn't prove it, Sergeant, could they?'

'Who asked for your opinion Aspey? Get back in your cell. And another thing – I want all this paint and crap out of here. It's cluttering up the guardroom.'

My incarceration for seven days in the cells was no hardship. Most of the time I spent playing cards and darts with the guards. It had been a worrying episode and I was relieved it was over. The main sting was the loss of a week's wages and being confined to camp during the enquiries. I hadn't seen Sarah for nearly a month and I was missing the comfort of her bed.

I was lying on my bunk in the cells when I overheard part of a conversation between the guards. There was to be a demob party at the winter gardens at Weston-super-Mare, and a table had been booked to see Ken Mackintosh and his band. They needed a car for six, but despite their urgent efforts to hire a car they had been unsuccessful. I explained to one of the more amenable guards that it was foolish to mention parties, especially demob parties, when talking to the car-hire fraternity. They could be very selective with their clientele. Far better to say in doleful tones that it was for a funeral or a vicar's tea party.

I knew they were getting desperate when the sergeant's distant voice drifted through the bars of my cell. 'That nerd in the cells has got a car, hasn't he? Take that.'

From then on I didn't lose another game of cards or darts, and first names fluttered around like snowflakes. Now and again broad hints were dropped about the need for a car on Saturday night. There were furrowed brows and sighs of despair, and I nodded sympathetically with outstretched arms of helplessness. Then one of the guards who had arrested me, who I'd nearly kicked in the goolies, took a more direct line.

'We want to borrow your car for a couple of hours on Saturday.'

I shook my head. 'No chance.'

'We'll give you two quid.'

'No.'

Actually, a daring plan was forming in my head, one that would enable me to have a bit of free time in Bridgwater and also perhaps some conjugal rights with Sarah. I called the more amenable guard to one side and explained my idea, including the requirement of three pounds ten shillings for the evening. His eyes rolled with disbelief.

'We couldn't possibly do that! The whole guardhouse would finish up in the slammer; the sergeant would crucify us. I'll tell the others, but I know they won't go for it.'

I heard howls of laughter from the main guardroom and guessed my proposition was being discussed. What I wanted was to be let out of the cells on Saturday lunch time when the sergeant went off duty, and to get the car, which I would refuel and return before the orderly officer's inspection at six o'clock.

'That's my one and only final offer.'

In the unlikely event of my not turning up for the six o'clock inspection they could put out an alarm and say I had escaped. At this point I only had a few months left before my demob and would have too much to lose.

Two of the guards came to my cell. They agreed to pay the money after I had collected the car and they would give me two hours absence only. They said they were really putting their necks on the block.

'No.'

The subject was dropped. I started losing at cards again and the air became distinctly hostile. Early on the Saturday morning one of the guards came in with the money, saying, 'Don't you fucking let us down on this or we'll frigging hang you from that fucking flag pole.'

* * *

Sarah wasn't jubilant about my unexpected appearance; she was suffering from an ongoing migraine and her babysitter had failed to turn up. The car was equally reluctant, and showed no enthusiasm for the Ken Mackintosh trip as I pushed it up and down Market Street all afternoon. Totally exhausted, I almost decided to return to camp empty-handed. Then I remembered Techie's remedy of thumping the vacuum fuel pump, and it fired up straight away. I cursed my stupidity in not remembering the sticky diaphragm and returned to the guardhouse with five minutes to spare. The relief on the guards' faces was very apparent as they confessed to passing bricks with worry. They congratulated me on my haggard, exhausted condition.

'You don't half look rough – you must've shagged your socks off,' laughed the amenable guard.

On Sunday morning news began to filter through about the demob party, which had not gone to plan. There was a break in the electrical circuit, with sparks under the floor that kept flattening the battery. The three girls thumbed a lift while their partners pulled up the boards, spoiling their best clothes and becoming quite cross about the whole business. They never managed to see Ken Mackintosh. On their return they congregated in my cell, demanding their money back. I explained it was unreasonable to expect refunds; It was an old car; I'd given no guarantees; it was unfortunate, a bit of bad luck, but I wouldn't refund anything.

One of the more aggressive guards told me the remaining two days in the cells might become extremely unpleasant if I didn't co-operate, but I refused to be intimidated by threats. I wouldn't refund any money as they had abandoned my car.

An urgent phone call was put through to the cookhouse, then, after some discussion I was transported to the kitchen area. The sergeant in the cookhouse seemed pleased to see me. He pointed to a mountain of plates, dishes, pans and cutlery, and gave me instructions about what to do. It looked a huge task for a regiment, never mind a solitary airman. The group then departed with grinning faces.

Two hours passed before the sergeant returned – to see the same pile of washing untouched save for one large saucepan. This saucepan gleamed with a mirror-like finish.

The sergeant lost his temper, accusing me of taking the mick. 'You're on a charge,' he growled.

The police jeep arrived to return me to the cells; the guards wanted to put me on a charge as well after seeing the solitary clean saucepan. The duty officer arrived, and there was a lot of discussion as the gleaming saucepan was passed hither and thither. The sergeant complained he would be up all night sorting out the washing up ready for breakfast in the morning – because he had let his kitchen staff go early. The officer took me on one side and asked me if I thought cleaning one saucepan represented honest toil for two hours' work. I assured him I had scrubbed, rubbed and polished without stopping.

I'd spent a lot of time studying Station Standing Orders, the camp bible. I hadn't broken any military law, and I didn't see why guards should adapt the system in order to administer private grudges. The officer took off his cap and stroked his head in a bid to hide the smile on his face.

'If I were you, Aspey, I would keep your head down. The men in the guardroom are determined to nail you. There are no charges. As you rightly say, no rules have been broken.'

The guards were livid. Their attempts to put me on a charge had backfired. And the cookhouse sergeant indicated he wouldn't be doing the police any favours in the future. I also noticed the spray gun was missing from the items in the guardroom. I put in a request for the return of the spray gun that I had paid for and was therefore my property in the eyes of the law. This entailed filling in a form that required the blessing and signature of the camp commander. The form wasn't well received by the commander, who had me marched up to his office immediately. After much shouting and thumping of his desk and calling me various names, he assured me the spray gun was Air Force property and he didn't give a toss about all the legal nonsense. He had a sworn statement by Corporal Trotter that he'd never sold a spray gun, and there were two arrows stamped on it. The evidence was overwhelming that it was government property. I had caused a lot of trouble and expense since I'd arrived at the camp, and he didn't want to see me again. 'Get out,' he concluded.

Techie recovered the car for me from where it had been abandoned in the middle of a field. He couldn't find anything wrong with it except a sparking wire under the floorboard, and it started without difficulty. 'If I were you I'd get rid of that car, fast,' he said. 'That aircraft octane fuel is not doing it much good.'

One of the trainee pilots showed a keen interest in buying it. He demanded a trial run, and I twitched with disbelief as he grated the gears and shunted my sedate family saloon around the runway like a go-cart racer. My buyer had a terrier-like haggling quality, which involved the clever idea that he would act as both buyer and seller. He set the buying price, which was non-negotiable. My comfort zone was badly affected on realising this crazy madman was entrusted with eight tons of highly combustible material.

Ginger was highly amused at the way I'd been ripped off. 'How could you let him get away with it? I can't believe you've been so naive. You didn't have to accept his cheque.'

'Yeah! I feel a bit of a chump. I was so intrigued with his fancy cheque with a feather on it that I didn't notice the amount. Techie says I should be honoured, because it's the bank used by the Royal Family.'

* * *

Flight Instructor Brill was one of my car respray customers, and was no doubt relieved by the collapse of my court martial. He might well have been dragged into it.

'Aspey,' he said, 'I'd like you to join me on a ventral test tomorrow morning. You'll find it quite exciting.' This was an exercise to see how long the aircraft could remain airborne with extra fuel tanks strapped under the fuselage.

At that time I thought that flying was inextricably linked to dying, an opinion that was well supported by the fatality figures at the camp. According to Techie, who was privy to all the top-secret information, the camp had a 'pilot wastage' (as admin cutely called it) of nearly 30 per cent. Only the previous week an Mk 7, alleged to be the aircraft used by Prince Philip to complete his pilot training, had exploded on the outskirts of the airfield. Rumours were going the rounds that it had been tampered with, but there seemed no evidence to support this. We ground staff had had to gather up the human remains. It had been a gruesome task: there were flying boots with feet still in them and the horrible smell of burnt human flesh hung in the nostrils for days afterwards. It was not a bit like roast chicken. Food consumption in the canteen showed a steep decline as the experience affected appetites for several days afterwards. This was especially so in the case of poor Corporal Knight, who had been ordered to recover a body from the water. He tried to raise the pilot's head, but it came off in his hand.

Another plane had crashed when the dinghy had accidentally inflated and forced the pilot against the console, giving him no chance to haul back the stick. Both the instructor and trainee were killed. Later an instruction was given that every pilot had to carry a knife strapped to his leg.

Against this background I felt reluctant to get involved. I thanked the instructor for the opportunity, but declined on the grounds that it wasn't really my scene. Aeroplanes were not called meat boxes for nothing. The instructor, however, insisted

I should take up the offer – or, to put it more succinctly, that it was an order. His argument was that if the people who work on the aircraft had no confidence in their product, what were the pilots supposed to think? He gave me instructions to report to the crew room at 10.00 hours the following day and collect a parachute and oxygen mask.

I said to Ginger, 'What's so exciting about risking your life to find out how long a plane can fly before it runs out of fuel? And why me? Are they trying to bump me off or something? I'm just a paint dabbler, for Christ's sake, I don't muck about with jet engines and stuff.'

'Yeah!' said Ginger grinning, 'maybe they're going to punish you for all that fuel you nicked out of the bowsers. Actually I'm surprised he can order you to fly. I'd be a bit nervous about those add-on fuel tanks if I were you.'

'Huh? Why's that Ginger? What d'you mean?'

'Well, there've been mutterings by a couple of the fitters that they think they're a bit dodgy. It's like strapping a couple of oversize bombs under your arse.'

'Thanks, Ginger. Now you've really put my mind at rest.'

'D'you know why most planes crash, Gordon? said Techie. They run out of fuel, for God's sake. They don't seem to grasp that the fuel consumption of a Meteor jet bears no resemblance to the piston-engine craft. You take that bloke who bought your car. Several times I've seen him pushing it in the pouring rain. If he lifted the bonnet and tapped the fuel pump, the car would go. He should have learnt by now that a sticking diaphragm cuts off the fuel supply. Cars are like aeroplanes – they don't work without fuel. The RAF has an appalling accident record. Over five hundred crashes in one year, and three hundred fatalities. I think it's bloody scandalous.'

'Yeah, but they didn't all happen here,' argued Ginger.

'You have a look in the scrap yard or, better still, in the graveyard, Ginger. It's full of dead pilots. The vicar has asked that any future pilots who die should be buried in the next

The funeral procession of the RAF pilots

village. Now the Ministry is going to offload the Meteors to South America, and has agreed to train their pilots. With their volatile temperament the figures will get even worse.'

'Well you blokes have been most helpful, and have put my mind at rest. I'm just raring to get up in an aeroplane and kill myself. Incidentally, does either of you know this instructor Brill? Does he have any unusual tendencies?'

'He's okay,' chuckled Techie, 'but you made the mistake of selling your crap car to his best mate. I reckon he's going to punish you for that. He'll probably try and scare the pants off you – it's a grudge thing.'

'Yeah! Or it might be a conspiracy forged with the camp commander and the Mighty Mouse trying to bump you off,' laughed Ginger.

Trying to borrow an oxygen mask in the crew room proved to be difficult. 'You see,' said one pilot, 'it's a very personal bit of gear. If you puke into it – well, it's not nice.'

So I helped myself from one of the private lockers; they weren't locked.

The parachute was less of a problem. The same pilot informed me, 'Your chances of survival with a parachute are minimal, old son. Your prospects would be better jumping off Beachy Head with a bunch of bananas. There are three outcomes when using a parachute: the tail plane chops your head off; the tail plane removes your undercarriage; or – the best option – the chute doesn't open.'

I felt like a condemned man when I made my way to the tarmac. There was something wrong with my parachute and I couldn't stand up straight. The airman refuelling the aeroplane looked me up and down with an amused expression on his face.

'You look like a chimpanzee,' he laughed. 'Your parachute's on wrong.'

'Bollocks,' I said. 'I've just returned from a parachute course.'

'Well I reckon it's upside down and you'll land on your head if you bale out.'

'That might be a preferable option at the moment. Do you know anything about this instructor? Does he do aerobatics and other crazy stuff?'

'He's all right ... he's still flying. Didn't you sell your car to his mate? Hmm... Ah... Here he comes now. Stick your foot in there. I'll give you a shove up. Okay?'

'Thanks, Mate.'

'Right, are you ready, Aspey?' said the instructor.

'Yes Sir.'

'I'll do my checks, then we're away.'

As we sped down the runway, I watched the intermittent stripes fuse into a single white line.

'Now, Aspey, in the unlikely event of something going wrong I'll tell you the escape procedure. When I jettison the canopy you must release your harness and dive out headfirst over the right-hand side. You count to ten and pull the cord on your parachute. Is that understood?'

'Yes Sir.' *Like hell*, I thought.

'Now we're going to be up here for a bit while doing a fuel test and other manoeuvres. You'll get a bit disorientated at times when I bank over, and when we increase height you might get a pain in your ears. You can cure this by holding your nose and blowing hard. If you scream – and I hope you don't – turn the mike off or you will really upset me. Understood?'

'Yes Sir.'

There were other things of more immediate concern to me. There was a gale blasting up my left leg, which showed there was a hole somewhere nearby or that an inspection panel had not been replaced. The instrument panel was shaking itself silly. According to my understanding, there shouldn't have been any vibration in the cockpit area.

The pilot then took to doing some fancy stuff, and the sky was replaced with trees and fields. I felt a searing pain in my ear, and let out a yelp, remembering to switch off the mike as I noticed the pilot's shoulders started to rise upwards.

211

'Are you all right, Aspey? Would you like to have a go at the controls?' He had to be joking. Hadn't they got a bad enough accident record without invitations like that?

I recognised various small notices screwed on to the console displaying my sign writing skills. Momentarily I felt indignant at the way they'd been fixed, without using a spirit level. I'd spent hours painting the tiny lettering and felt annoyed at such slovenly workmanship.

The instructor explained the purpose of various controls, and emphasised the need to be gentle with the joystick, which was very sensitive. I did a bit of twiddling with it – and became aware of the donuts and coffee that I'd previously eaten and drunk gurgling in my stomach. As we reduced speed from 500 knots to our landing speed of approximately 110 knots, my stomach muscles relaxed and I had an overwhelming urge to be sick. I struggled to unclip the oxygen mask and broke the buckle. I was almost puking when the pilot slid back the canopy. The cold blast of air cured the sickness instantly.

One thing was certain: no way would I be doing any more flying on military aircraft, orders or no bloody orders.

15

In 1953 Renee invited me for Christmas, finding me a bed at her Auntie Susan's house. I realised this was the final call for our marriage arrangements. Renee herself lived in a small, two-bedroom terraced house in Blackburn, a grey conglomeration of smoking chimneystacks and steeply inclined cobbled roads.

There was no answer when I rattled the door on Christmas morning, but a jovial voice called out from next door.

'Hello! So you're Gordon, Renee's young man – been expecting you. Heard a lot about you. Renee's still at the mill with her mum. Would you like a brandy?'

'Er… Thanks! She's working on Christmas day?'

'Oh, they won't be doing much work, love. Just tidying up and having a laugh more like.'

No sooner had I finished one brandy than she gave me another – and another. By the time Renee and her mum returned from the mill I was legless. They were not amused, and the good-hearted neighbour got a mild ticking off from Renee's mother.

Renee had changed in her looks. She seemed plumper than I'd remembered. Her hair was shorter and she wore minimal make up. Yet she had a clean, classy look and was most desirable. Her eyes sparkled with excitement and she wafted a delicate perfume around her as she planted a firm kiss on my cheek.

'As you know, we've only got two bedrooms, so we've arranged for you to stay at Auntie Susan's place. I'll take you there later. She'll be cooking you breakfast. Afterwards you catch the number eighteen bus and I'll meet you back here. Susan will show you where to catch the bus; she'll give you all the details.'

Christmas turned out to be a mobile holiday; her aunt's place was at the wrong end of a very long bus journey.

Renee tended to be a bit prim and proper, and had traditional values. All attempts to progress down the avenue of sex had terminated in a cul-de-sac or had been thwarted by circumstances. I'd promised to marry her when I left the Air Force and I was genuinely fond of her. Maybe I loved her, but love wasn't a familiar word in my dictionary. I was also fond of Sarah and young Michael and I enjoyed the homely atmosphere in their house. Now there was something else bothering me. Renee's aunt Susan didn't look how aunts are supposed to look. She was a real eye-opener and so much younger than I'd expected. I was beginning to consider the possibility of something more than breakfast on the table. Her dressing gown had a habit of parting in the middle when she was serving food, revealing a see-through, pale green negligee with hanky-sized panties. I hardly knew where to look when she sat herself opposite with crossed legs, sipping her tea and chatting about nothing in particular. There didn't seem to be a man in the house. I reached for the marmalade as I was considering possibilities, and knocked the Cornflakes packet off the table.

'Sorry, I...'

'Don't worry, Precious. I'll get it.' Leaning forward, her breast burst out of the negligee and bobbled around delightfully.

'Whoops-a-daisy,' she giggled, drawing her dressing gown tightly around her waist. 'I'd better get dressed.'

'Ye... Yes,' I stuttered, almost choking on the cereal, and wishing everything else in her negligee would make a dash for freedom. She'd called me 'Precious'. Could it be that she fancied me?

Renee joined up with a crowd of friends and we went to a football match between Blackburn and Doncaster. There wasn't much to watch, because all the spectators in front of us were tall. All I could see were thousands of heads turning this way and that. I suddenly remembered the lady instructor at the dance academy in Cardiff.

'You have a fine cant of the head,' she'd said. 'It looks most refined, especially from the rear.'

'What d'you think of the back of my head, Renee?' I asked.

214

'Eh! What do you mean? What's the matter with it?'

She had a good look round and asked her friends, 'The back of Gordon's head, it's all right, isn't it?'

'Yeah!' they nodded, 'looks normal'.

Renee had a large circle of friends, but one I was hoping to see didn't appear.

'D'you see much of your friend, Trish? The one you brought with you on the blind date to Southsea?'

'She's engaged to that saxophone bloke, Lofty, the one who came with you.'

'NO! You're kidding; that's amazing.'

'Oh yes. He's got his feet well under the table there. The family have taken to him. They think he's got real talent. They're planning to get married in the spring. It's secret, so don't say anything.'

'Has he still got spots? I haven't seen him since he got demobbed.'

'I don't think so. I don't visit her place much, now. It's like the Albert Hall with all the instruments blaring away.' Then she turned her face towards me. 'Gordon, tell me the truth. What about us?'

'How d'you mean, "us"?'

Her clear grey eyes hardened as she scanned my face intently. 'Do you really want to marry me?'

'Of course, but why do you ask?'

Now her voice developed a hard edge, and her steely eyes bored into me.

'Trish says you are going out with a married woman with a small child. Lofty told her.'

'Well Lofty needs to get his facts right!' I snapped. 'Things aren't always like they seem. I'm really annoyed with him, causing mischief like that. The woman he's talking about used to run a mobile snack bar for me. I had to keep it quiet because we're not allowed to run a business while we're in the service. As I've said before, we'll sort out the marriage when I get demobbed. It won't be long, and there's nobody else. Honest.'

Renee didn't look convinced, however, and I sensed a slight cooling towards me. I was really annoyed with Lofty for stirring things up. I would give him a right earful next time I saw him. Although Renee succumbed to a bit of cuddling and kissing in snatched moments the full passion tap remained out of service. During the long bus ride back to Susan's place, I mulled over my situation at length.

I was becoming more and more confused about women and relationships in general. The thought of marriage was starting to scare me. In only a matter of weeks I would have to make my decision.

On our last night we went to the Tower Ballroom in Blackburn and Renee was disappointed with me. 'I thought you'd learnt to dance last year,' she said. 'You haven't made much progress. Your feet are all over the place. Try and concentrate.'

'I gave it up – I found it too difficult. The woman said I was making good progress and had a good carriage of the head. She said that if I persevered I could go a long way. Mind you, she said the same thing to about ten thousand other airmen.'

'So is that what all that was about at the football match: "What do you think of the back of my head?" Ha! Never mind your head, Gordon, you should've concentrated on your feet. You can't tango on your head.'

I decided to abandon any ideas of making a pass at the voluptuous Susan; if I got it wrong the repercussions didn't bear thinking about. I groaned inwardly at the missed opportunity on the final morning. Her goodbye kiss wasn't a 'Look after yourself' type of kiss, with a Maclean's smile; her whole body had been squeezed into a lingering hug, with her moistened lips planted firmly on my gaping mouth. And she called me 'Precious' yet again.

* * *

216

My brain was in turmoil when I returned to camp after the Christmas holiday. How could I marry Renee when I was lusting after her aunt?! I was dreaming about her every night. She would be at the wedding. Jesus! It wasn't feasible. I was beginning to think I needed medical treatment. I wondered if all blokes had the same problem of a dangling tongue and an uncontrollable, throbbing dick.

During the Christmas holiday I'd missed my new car, a 1936 Triumph Dolomite sports saloon. I loved the smell of the leather, the hum of the engine, and the sheer joy of driving around the countryside. Few airmen could afford a car, which was mainly the preserve of commissioned officers. Unlike most of the recruits, however, I didn't smoke cigarettes or consume gallons of alcohol. This enabled me to put money aside, and this, together with my illicit earnings, enabled me to buy such luxuries. I used to get £15 to £20 for a respray. I had several cars over a ten-month period. I would often respray them and sell them for a profit. The Triumph Dolomite, which needed work, cost me £120 as far as I can remember.

I settled back into my homely routine with Sarah in her small terraced house. Life in the Air Force started to feel relaxed and leisurely, and I started to wonder how I would fare in civvy street. Renee and her auntie Susan temporarily faded into relative obscurity.

But things were about to change for the worse. Sarah told me of her concerns about paying some of the bills since she had put her husband out of the house. My contribution, though generous considering an airman's pay, wasn't enough. The tea trolley robbery had impacted badly on my finances, especially after I'd had to shell out cigarette money to Mr Blenham at the London Inn as well as for other items.

'I've got a part-time job at a country club, as a catering assistant,' she said. 'The pay's not good, but it should help. I have to live in three days a week on alternate weeks.'

'What about Michael?'

'Mum'll look after him.'

One Saturday morning, several weeks later, I was alone in the house preparing a lunchtime snack when there was a knock at the door. A smartly dressed, dark-haired lady stood in the doorway.

'I'm sorry, Sarah's not in. Can I take a message?'

'I know she's not in!' said the woman firmly. 'I've come to see you.'

'Me?' I gulped. 'What d'you want to see me about?' The woman pushed past me, flopping down on the shabby black settee and looking around the room with thinly veiled disdain.

'So this is where the whore lives, is it?' she said, carefully removing her earrings and snapping them into her handbag.

'I beg your pardon! Who the hell are you? I take exception to you talking about Sarah like that. What's this about?'

'Really? Well, I take exception to your Sarah. She's having an affair with my husband; he's her boss.'

I stared at her with mounting disbelief. 'Sarah? That's rubbish!' I shouted. 'You're talking nonsense... Bloody hell. What're you doing?' 'No... no... Stop that now!' Her grey skirt slid to the ground, revealing creamy white thighs with black suspenders and lacy black panties. She unbuttoned her white blouse and was on the point of removing her bra.

Her words darted around my brain like a firecracker. I felt a mixture of rage, jealousy, disbelief ... and now carnal lust started to well up inside me. The woman paused, her dark eyes flashing fire, and she jerked her shiny black hair over her shoulders angrily. 'Rubbish, is it?' she said, removing a photograph from her handbag. 'Well take a look at that; it doesn't need words, does it?'

I looked in horror at the two naked figures in the grainy photograph. There could be no mistaking that the female was Sarah. The look on her face was like a knife in my groin. She was smiling with eyes half-closed.

'Now do you believe me?' hissed the woman, snatching the photograph out of my hand.

'I can't believe it. Why would she want to do that?'

'She's the centre of his world at the moment – till the next tart comes along. She's not the first and she won't be the last. I've had enough of his lies.'

She removed the last remnants of her clothing and lay across the settee.

'Two can play this game,' she said, throwing her panties over her shoulder. 'Now it's your turn!'

I stood gazing at her, unable to move. Slight stretch marks on her inner thighs led to a small tuft of black pubic hair and up to a wineglass waist and perfectly formed breasts. Her blush-pink nipples stood proud like raspberries on a cream cup-tart. Her sparky temper and defiant jaw made her even more sensuous. She was an artist's dream of creamy erotica displayed on a sacrificial plinth of black leather. I hesitated, uncertain about what to do next, and felt awkward about such an incongruous situation.

'Well, are you just going to stand there staring?' she snapped.

I thought of Sarah in the photograph and the smile on her face, and gritted my teeth, thinking, *She wants it, and she can have it. I'll give that husband something to think about.* Unbuckling my belt, I grimly stood over her, slowly undoing my flies, beginning to savour the prospect of such an unusual situation. I roughly pushed the woman's legs apart and started to lower myself on to her. I caught a strong whiff of alcohol as she tilted her face away from me. While she did this I saw that her eyes betrayed a flicker of fear. I looked up and was startled by my reflection in the mirror on the opposite wall. I saw the expression of a lecherous animal; at first not realising that what I saw was myself.

The face immediately morphed into a look of surprise. I could hardly believe I was capable of such an expression. I moved away from the woman and sat on the edge of the settee, unsure about what to do next. I still felt rampant as my gaze swept back and forth over her body, but I couldn't touch her. I noticed that her hands were shaking; she no longer looked defiant and angry but tense and frightened.

'I can't do this,' I whispered. 'Look, I really can't. I'm not Sarah's husb...' But before I could finish what I was saying, she jumped to her feet and pushed me out of the way, clasping her hands to her face. She rushed into the kitchen and violently retched into the sink.

'Are you all right?' I said. I watched her with a mixture of concern and worried fascination. Every time she vomited her body shuddered, making her curves ripple and judder in a titillating way. I turned away as she looked in my direction.

'I'm so...s... sorry,' she spluttered, dabbing her face with a cloth under a running tap. 'You were going to say you're not her husband?'

'No. I'm from the RAF camp, but I'm living here at the moment. She had a problem with her husband and booted him out.'

'That's a surprise!'

'Look,' I said, handing her a bath towel, 'why don't you get yourself sorted, and I'll make a coffee, if you'd like one.'

'I think I could manage that. Thanks.'

'Sugar?'

'Two, please.' The anger and fear had melted from her face, and her eyes had softened with a look of overwhelming relief as she sipped her coffee

'I can't believe what I've just done,' she grimaced. 'I've never done anything like that in my life.' Smoothing her skirt, she said, 'I hardly know what to say. You must think me a right cow. I feel so cheap and humiliated.'

'I can't believe Sarah could do that. How could she do that?'

She lowered her cup on to its saucer. 'You won't like this and I'm sorry, but I wasn't surprised. The way she looked at my husband. I've seen that look before. He had her on the first day.'

'No! That's enough. Don't tell me any more. I'm so... absolutely gutted.'

'It took a lot of courage and half a bottle of gin to get me to do that. I hate the stuff. You strike me as being a half-decent sort of man. You can do much better than her, you know. My hands are tied and I can't leave my children. He keeps promising he won't do it again, but he'll never change.'

'Well, I'm totally baffled with this marriage business,' I said. 'I feel like I should get a book out of the library. It might sound a bit flippant, you know, but his demon lingers in the crutch of his Y-fronts. In the Air Force they stick bromide in our tea – and I can promise you, it works. Maybe if you stick some in his Cornflakes and coffee he might take up train spotting or caving.'

She spilt her coffee and spluttered with laughter. I hadn't really noticed her face before, but she was beautiful. There was elegance in her smile and her face radiated warmth tinged with determination. She didn't look anything like the angry woman who had knocked on the door half an hour before. In fact she looked remarkably composed for someone who had swilled down half a bottle of gin and had completed an erotic striptease only moments ago.

'That's really funny,' she said smiling as she rose from her chair. She straightened her skirt and paused at the door. 'Can I ask you not to tell Sarah what I just did? I feel so... well...'

'Don't worry, I felt more embarrassed than you.'

'And thanks for not ... well, you know what I mean. What was that stuff called again, Bro... what?'

'Bromide.'

* * *

Sarah became flustered when I challenged her about the affair, and her face turned scarlet. 'She's a lying bitch!' she screamed. 'None of the staff like her. I've done nothing!'

'Look Sarah, we're not married. I'm not your husband. You don't need to tell lies.'

'You prefer to believe that lying bitch rather than me. Look, there was a bit of horseplay at a wedding party, that's all. A bit of innocent fun – nothing happened. And that's the gospel truth.'

'Sarah, you're lying. She showed me a photograph of the two of you screwing.'

'A photograph? What do you mean a photograph? – How could she? Who took...?' Her mouth sagged open with amazement. 'Who took a photo?'

'I don't know who took it or where or what, but it's pointless denying it.' She became silent with her head in her hands, staring at the floor. 'So what are we going to do, Sarah? I'm not playing second fiddle to your boss. What about Michael, what sort of a life is he going to have with you screwing around?'

She burst into tears. 'I don't know where I'm going, or what I'm doing; I just want to be able to pay the bills.'

'Your boss is paying the bills?'

'No, no, no,' she said, dabbing her face with a handkerchief. 'It wasn't like that, oh God, I don't know; it just happened. I honestly wish it hadn't, but it did. I feel so rotten and dirty. Are you going to leave us?'

I embraced Sarah, comforted her and stroked her hair, saying, 'Sarah, I've no rights in this, but sharing you with somebody else – I can't do that. If you like, we can try and start afresh tomorrow and we won't mention this again. It's up to you. Let me have the bills and I'll sort them out. We'll manage. You'll see – everything'll be fine.'

I lay in bed unable to sleep. Jealousy and anger roamed around in my thoughts, and I wondered how often she had had sex with her boss. The photograph with her smiling face kept surfacing in my mind like a kick in the teeth. Despite all my assurances that everything would be all right, I knew our relationship would never recover. I thought of Renee, her aunt, and others. How unfair was that? Everything seemed so complicated when it came down to sex. I started to regret not taking up her boss's wife's offer. I'd been on the brink of succumbing to what she'd been offering; she'd looked a real bundle of pleasure ... her creamy, black-stockinged figure reclining on the black settee...

But along with Renee's aunt, and others, she became just another missed opportunity. I seemed to be turning missed opportunities into a marathon.

* * *

I eventually came to my senses when Sarah's husband sued for divorce and cited me as co-respondent. This was one expense I really couldn't afford. The idea of paying her husband damages and all the litigation costs was a real turn-off. I used my dual-name facility to good effect. Sarah simplified matters by becoming pregnant by another man, who acknowledged he was the father.

Any idea of marrying Renee rapidly dissolved after I received a blistering telegram calling me a wicked liar and telling me to stick with Sarah and her little boy. That bastard Lofty.

* * *

After my demob I took up lodgings with Sarah's friend Hazel, who was now an ex-friend because they'd had a big bust up. Hazel was comfortable with the arrangement as she needed the money.

This was not one of my better decisions.

16

After leaving the RAF in February 1955 I decided to stick around the area for the time being, although my options were limited. Bridgwater was a slow-moving town, still steeped in mid-Victorian traditions; anything new was frowned upon. As one old-timer put it, 'They don't like strangers round here. They likes to deal with their own. Many has come here to make a living but they don't last. They soon goes away again.' I would experience this attitude soon enough.

I started my first job at a local motor company. The works manager had a neurotic dislike of inactivity. If you stopped to meditate or scratch your rump, he would ask agitatedly, 'What are you doing?', and then a large broom or a bucket and sponge would be thrust into your hand. A loud siren announced tea and dinner breaks, as well as the beginning and end of work for the day. It was assumed that you had to work to earn your money. There was a massive division and discontent between the white-collar office staff and the manual workers. Even the toilets were of the 'them and us' variety. Everyone seemed to be griping about something. The job lasted for only six months. I got the sack when I was caught drawing some unconventional cartoons of the boss on the reception wall.

Ralph was the hardest-working man I'd ever met. He was the managing director of Westward Ice Cream but had no qualms about doing an early-morning milk delivery to augment his petty cash. I recognised his walrus moustache, and remembered him as the driver who'd sold me the two ice cream cornets when I'd first met Sarah. He jokingly introduced me to his mother as the twin-cornet Romeo. They both knew Sarah and Michael quite well, as they were in close proximity to Starman's yard.

Ralph's mother – generally referred to as Mrs H – had a thing about the law of averages, and whenever there was a problem the solution would include the large brown teapot.

Slightly built like her son, with thick lenses and a permanent cigarette dancing on her lower lip, she would recount her law of averages as she filled the mugs with tea in an attempt to bolster his wavering confidence: 'You can't work as 'ard as you do, Son, without reward. Your turn is a coming ... that's the law of averages.'

They lived in a small house at the end of Starman's yard with an office tacked on to the living accommodation. They were like a pair of sparrows in a privet hedge, darting back and forth trying to boost the ice-cream sales. Mrs H never missed an opportunity for a sale. A rattle on the heavy doorknocker would see her flying down the stairs, belying her advancing years, to dispense lollies to local children. There were three ice-cream vans, though usually only two were serviceable at any given time, and two part-time drivers who claimed to be qualified mechanics, who'd dismantled and reassembled the engines many times during previous seasons.

Ralph was determined to double the turnover and create a dynamic and successful company. 'We've got to put the abysmal summer of last year behind us and make a new start. I've decided on a new strategy,' he said, stroking his walrus moustache. 'Ice cream is seen as a seasonal product; people only eat the damn stuff when the sun is shining. We need to educate the public, get them to understand that ice cream tastes the same in January as it does in August. We need to get people to realise ice cream is food and can be eaten anywhere, any time.' He was certainly a man of ideas. He had me designing ice cream and lolly-wrappers with robins lounging on logs, holly and mistletoe, sleighs and Father Christmases – even skipping lambs. He wanted new livery and signage, together with a whole raft of new ice-cream flavours.

The main snag seemed to be a lack of cash to pay for it all. After several sittings round the teapot he reluctantly decided to get a loan from the bank.

The bank manager wasn't helpful. 'I've never really taken to ice cream,' he said. 'It's one of those things; even as a child I never got to grips with cornets, lollies and that sort of thing.'

'Yes, but a lot of people like ice cream,' argued Ralph. 'Surely you're not letting personal…'

'No, no, I can't let my personal preferences influence my decision, of course not. On the other hand, your sales figures don't suggest a wild clamouring for the stuff. I think it would be better to leave things until next year and re-apply if you're in a more favourable position.'

Ralph was livid, but eventually secured a loan from another bank that accepted his ice-cream factory at Glastonbury as collateral. He kept me busy for several weeks, and with cars and other signwork my future was looking secure. The sun came out, ice-cream sales perked up, and Mrs H was glowing with optimism.

'What did I say, Ralph? Didn't I tell you? Your turn would come soon enough; it be the law of averages.'

But her and my optimism was short-lived. An unscheduled visit from the food inspector shut the ice-cream factory down for two weeks. He ordered the destruction of the entire stock, and refused to let the factory reopen until certain requirements had been fulfilled. The two-week delay and loss of production painfully coincided with a rare and prolonged run of hot sunshine. To add salt to the wound, all three vans were serviceable and roadworthy.

The food inspector had cost Ralph dear, losing production and total loss of stock in the two best weeks of the year. The rains returned with a vengeance. The bank manager at Glastonbury was threatening to auction the factory, and Mr Starman was showing an uncharacteristic tetchiness in the matter of a few weeks' rent.

Mrs H pushed and prodded her son, and kept on repeating her law of averages theory. 'C'mon Son; don't get disheartened; it'll all come right in the end, you'll see.'

Unbeknown to Mrs H, Ralph had a new business project simmering on the back burner.

'You've got a letter,' said Hazel as she served up my evening meal. 'Oh yes, and a friend of yours called. Someone called Joe.'

'Joe? I don't know any Joes,' I said, tearing open the envelope. 'Did he say what he wanted?'

'He just said he'd catch up with you later. He had a posh car. Oh, he's just pulled up outside.'

I was distracted by the letter. 'That bastard!' I yelled. 'You read that. The pig-eyed Mighty Mouse has sent me a reference to give to my employer. Who the hell asked him to send me a reference? You read that, Hazel – they wouldn't let me in Pentonville with a reference like that. I'm going to write and tell him to mind his own business; he can stick his reference up his jacksy.'

'He's here,' said Hazel, hurrying to the front door.

'I don't know him. I've never seen him before. What's his name?'

'Joe, he said.'

'Ah, hello Gordon,' said Joe, scraping his feet on the doormat. 'I've been trying to get hold of you for some time. Can we talk privately?' The last sentence was said in a low voice.

'Yeah, come into the front room.' I was puzzled. Here I was talking to a complete stranger who was acting like a long-lost friend.

He pulled out a note pad and biro. 'I just want to ask you a few questions, Gordon, if you don't mind. Are you insured?' he whispered.

'Well, no. Why?'

'You mean you've no insurance *at all*?' he exclaimed, with a well cultivated 'I can't believe it' look. 'You must be the only man in the world who has no insurance. I think I've arrived in the nick of time.'

I laughed, saying, 'You're a bleeding insurance salesman. What a con. I don't believe in insurance. I admire your technique, but I won't be buying any policies from you, Joe.'

'You need to give this matter serious thought, Gordon. Surely you have aspirations for the future – a nice car, a house, a nest egg?'

'Hmm… Well, yes, that's true. I'd like a nice, big, sea-going motor yacht, a wheelbarrow full of money, and a car like yours. But I don't want any insurance, Joe. No thanks.'

Joe turned up everywhere: in the chemist, in the library, in the café, even at a New Year's ball in 1956, where I was dancing with a dental receptionist I really fancied. He tapped me on the shoulder in the middle of the dance floor.

'I've got a new policy that's just right for you with an escalator facility,' he whispered.

'Joe, I'm dancing for Christ sake. I'm not interested in insurance. I don't believe in insurance. I won't ever be buying insurance. I hate insurance, Joe.'

'Look, Gordon,' he said in his rat-a-tat style, ignoring the gaping face of the receptionist. 'You are my ultimate challenge. I'm determined to sell you a policy before I retire in March.'

'No chance, Joe. It's New Year's Eve! I've got other things on my mind right now.'

'That's just it, Gordon. Now is the perfect time to make that resolution to provide for your future and get that nice boat you dream about. In twenty-five years you will be so grateful to me.'

'Joe! Your partner is yawning,' I laughed. I hadn't known that Joe or his partner would be at the dance. I met them on the dance floor.

'Gordon, I've made my New Year's resolution. You *will* be buying an insurance policy from me. That's a promise.'

The dental receptionist started giggling.

'Joe, I don't want to be rude but NO. NO. NO. I DON'T WANT ANY INSURANCE.'

My evening with the receptionist didn't turn out as I'd hoped. She didn't rate my foxtrot, and she expected me to pay for her friends' drinks. I stood outside the dance hall totally skint and pretty fed up. The rain was hammering down, and I was wondering how I could get back to my digs without a pair of oars.

There was a loud hoot and a shiny Rover pulled up alongside. 'Hello Gordon, d'you want a lift?' I couldn't believe it.

'Joe! I'M NOT BUYING A P...'

'Get in Lad, you're getting soaked.'

In the car Joe asked me about my family. I hated being asked, but it being New Year's Eve, and what with the effects of the alcohol I'd drunk, I spluttered out my life history. I'd done this on only two previous occasions, and both times I'd really regretted it. It was no different this time; I fervently wished I hadn't told Joe.

Jo looked at me sympathetically, saying, 'You really should think about insurance,' and wished me a Happy New Year. He started to accelerate away, but then braked sharply and, leaning out of the window, he cried out, 'You know, Gordon, we have much in common.'

* * *

Hazel's husband, Dennis, was irritated because his garage was being used to store my car spraying equipment. He didn't think it should comprise part of the lodger's facilities. He was a big, lumbering man who worked in the fire service at nights and for a scrap merchant during the day. He wasn't endowed with skill in the small exchanges of everyday life and carried a permanent look of mild disgruntlement. I was keen not to upset him and promised Hazel I would try and get a proper workshop and keep out of his way.

I received a threatening letter from the Mighty Mouse, who took exception to my ideas about what he could do with the reference he'd sent me. His letter said that I was still in the RAF reserves for the next three years. He had certain powers and he would use them if he felt a need to do so. (I'd signed up to do the extra year to get extra money, so altogether served three years in the RAF. I was also in the reserves for three years, but was never called for duty.)

I managed to rent a place from a retired farmer who let out his converted stables to assorted trades people. It wasn't ideal for car spraying, but at least it was a starting point. The retired farmer had been a local squire, with tied cottages and workers to maintain his extensive acreage and tend his varied livestock. But times had changed and all had gone save a pony and trap, his only transport, and an elderly horse nearing the end of its useful life in the end stable. He was a tall man, thin as a pole, with no teeth, sporting the same brown overall-type coat and wellington boots every day. He had a tired, hangdog look, which he used to good effect when he needed assistance with some awkward task. Conversation was best avoided, as it had a tendency to travel long distances over time and impact badly on a working day. Even so, he never tired of saying how much better things used to be; he reminded me of Mr Starman and his candle factory. When in full flow he would get quite excited and orchestrate his thoughts and memories with flashing grey eyes, waving his arms to emphasise a point, and his voice would grow louder and more excited.

His excitement, however, would soon be dampened by a visit from the RSPCA.

* * *

Hazel was having an affair with the tallyman, who called almost every afternoon when Dennis was at work. He was a typical, smooth-talking salesman, and Hazel seemed to be smitten with him. I was shocked when one day she asked me to lend her fifteen pounds for the tallyman because he was in a bit of bother. She assured me the money would be repaid within the month and that he would double it to thirty pounds. He needed the money to repair his car, as he couldn't collect payments that were owing to his company. I knew it was a bad move, but went ahead on the basis that she guaranteed the repayment.

The month came and went without any attempt to repay the money, and when I asked her Hazel flounced off in a huff, saying there was nothing she could do. When I approached the tallyman he shrugged his shoulders and said that things sometimes didn't work out, but that he hoped to straighten things out in due course. I was livid about his laid-back attitude, and realised I would never see my money again.

I decided to approach the tallyman's wife and tell her about the unpaid loan. She was furious, and promised she would repay the money including all the interest. Though I never recovered my money I had the satisfaction of stirring up a right hornet's nest for the pair of them. Hazel, of course, was incandescent with rage and gave me a week's notice to leave.

On the morning of my departure she had the cheek to demand a week's rent. I said I would discuss it when I'd got all my belongings together. The rent man was banging on the door and she became more and more agitated.

'If you don't give me the money now, I'll get Dennis to duff you up.'

I thought he was still at work and didn't fancy tangling with him, so I went to the garage to gather my things together. He suddenly appeared in the garage, and I could see by the look on his face that Hazel had fired him up to knock the stuffing out of me. He leant forward, saying in a menacing voice, 'I'm counting to ten.'

I could see the grim look of satisfaction on Hazel's face and in that instant decided the bitch wouldn't get a penny. Her husband started counting. He got to seven, and broadened his shoulders in an aggressive stance. I ducked as his fist scythed past my head, causing me to trip over a tin of cream paint, spilling it down the sleeve of my nearly new sports jacket. I'd paid a lot of money for the jacket, albeit in a sale. He kicked me in the ribs, shouting abuse and demanding the money. I locked my arm round his knee and reached up and grabbed the collar of his shirt, pulling myself upright. He punched me in the face, but I didn't feel any pain. All I could think off was my ruined sports jacket. I was really mad.

I slammed him against the garage wall and rained punches into his face without stopping. He had no chance to retaliate.

All I could think about was the cost of my sports jacket. The grandmother came out of the kitchen and threw a tin of Ceilingite at me. I read the name on the tin before I had a chance to duck and it slammed into my face. Hazel hit me with a garden spade as her husband tried to hit me again. I turned on Hazel and she dropped the spade and ran into the kitchen with her mother, bolting the door. I could feel blood running down my face and on to my jacket and shirt. One of the neighbours stood staring in horror at something behind me. I turned quickly to see Dennis coming towards me with an axe raised above his head. His face was twisted with rage, a bright red with mottled black and blue bruising and smears of cream paint in his hair. His eyes were almost closed. I felt a shiver of fear and shock at the state of his face; he was hardly recognisable.

With no time to think, I threw my whole weight at him in a desperate rugby tackle, lunging at his axe-carrying arm. He was cursing, pulling my hair, and jerking my head backwards and forwards, but I grimly hung on to his arm. I could hear the two women shouting and the bolt sliding back on the kitchen door. Sensing things were about to get worse, I tightened my grip on his arm and rammed my knee into his groin with all the force I could muster.

'You stupid man!' I said as I panted with relief as he let the axe clatter to the ground. 'That bitch of a wife of yours is screwing the tallyman while you're at work. And she owes me fifteen pounds.'

He paused, and shuffled towards the two women standing by the kitchen door. Ignoring the open-mouthed neighbours I hurried away, leaving my belongings behind. I called in at the hospital. My nose was swollen and painful, and I thought it was broken. They gave me an anti-tetanus jab and applied a few strips of plaster. The nurse tut-tutted: 'Why do you young men always have to finish up fighting? It's so silly. Where's the other one? Is he all right?'

'He's an idiot, and he'll need a lot more plaster. So might his wife.'

Ralph revealed his latest idea to Mrs H. 'Why don't we use two of the ice-cream vans for a mobile fruit and veg shop during the winter? They're standing around in the yard doing nothing and costing money. Those big council estates are an absolute gold mine – we can make a fortune. I'm already doing the milk run, and the housewives are really responding well to my idea. Then we can invest most of the profits we make from the fruit and veg into new ice-cream vans and press ahead with our expansion.'

'What a brilliant idea, Son,' enthused Mrs H. 'I always said you'd do it. It's the law of averages.'

Ralph even managed to gain some respite from the bank manager, who confessed to being amazed at his ongoing optimism.

The fruit and veg idea was a disaster.

'It's my fault!' groaned Ralph. 'It's one thing to be shifting milk bottles on people's doorsteps, there's no interactivity – only a brief moment once a month when they're settling their accounts. Selling fruit and veg is a different matter – you need the customer to be present. Banging on doors is a waste of time … all the women are at work.'

'Stop blaming yourself, Son. It's not your fault; it happens in business.'

'We're not equipped for this market,' sighed Ralph. 'I've had enough. Ice cream is our mainstay. We have the factory – well, I think we do. We also have five thousand bloody wrappers with Father Christmases on them, thanks to that conman of a printer. He tells me it's just as cheap to print five thousand as two thousand, then sends an invoice for nearly double. So all the lollies and ice creams will have Father Christmas wrappers on them for the foreseeable future.'

Even less happy was Mr Starman, who smelt the whiff of failure in his yard from the stink of rotting fruit and vegetables. The showman and his two sisters also complained, saying it was like living in a sewer. Mr Starman's voice had escalated several octaves, and he'd been moved to use one or two unaccustomed expletives. His vilification of Michael Faraday had shifted towards Ralph, now in arrears with his rent. With outstretched arms he proclaimed that the demand for fruit and veg was following the same wretched path as ice cream and wax candles.

* * *

While looking in the newsagent's window at the private ads boards, I felt a tap on the shoulder. I turned to see Joe's grinning face.

'Oh no – not you! For goodness sake,' I said. 'You're the most persis...

'N...no... no! Don't worry, Gordon. I'm finished with the insurance and all the selling. I retire next week. I'm selling up and moving to the Channel Islands. So, are you keeping busy?'

'Not too bad, could be worse.'

'What're you looking for?'

'A decent motor,' I sighed. 'I'm fed up with old bangers that keep breaking down.'

'How about mine?' he said, holding up a photograph of his Rover. 'I was just going to stick it in the window.'

'Wow, that'd be fantastic, but it's way out of my league, Mate.'

'Make me an offer Gordon.'

'No, I couldn't get near it, Joe. I'd spoil your day.'

'I've got to sell it; I can't take it with me. I've got to sell it this week. Look, it's in the cinema car park. Come and have a look – it's absolutely spotless. Make me an offer.'

I stood looking at the immaculate royal blue coachwork and shiny chrome. I opened the door and sank into the luxurious seating, with the smell of leather and polish wafting across my nostrils. I sat back and admired the walnut dashboard with chrome-rimmed instruments.

'You sure do look after it, Joe. Blimey, you've even got a clock! Does it work?'

'Of course, and it keeps good time, though you can't hear it.'

I felt I absolutely had to become the owner of Joe's car.

'What's your rock bottom price, Joe?'

'One hundred and fifty pounds. It's a gift – and you can drive it away.'

I detected a look of worry and desperation about Joe that I'd never seen before. I couldn't imagine him being desperate for money. He'd earlier bragged that he would live the life of old Riley when he retired, and he was going to live in the Channel Islands. I felt that something wasn't right – and that I would take advantage of this if he were desperate.

'I'll give you a hundred pounds, Joe, and that's my top whack. That'll clean me out, I'm afraid.'

'You cheeky blighter, I'm not giving it away. My area manager described you as a typical WOT. Waste of time: young, no money, and doesn't give a toss about anything.'

I shook hands with Joe and wished him well in retirement. 'I'd like to buy your car, Joe, but my wallet is the boss and he says no. A hundred pounds is the maximum.'

Half an hour later I was queuing at a fish and chip shop with mixed feelings about Joe's car. I felt disappointed at not getting it, but at the same time relieved that I hadn't given myself a lot of financial aggravation by running my account down to nothing.

I heard a shout, 'Gordon!' It was Joe again. He looked hot and flustered.

'What's up? Are you all right?

'I've got a proposition to put to you. I'll let you have the car for a hundred pounds if you sign up for a twenty-five-year policy here and now.'

'I don't understand...'

'Just listen a minute. You're getting the car for silly money. I'm virtually giving you your early premiums for nothing. I get to keep my excellent record, giving me the extra bonus and the commission on your policy. But more importantly, I lift my bet from that weasel of an area manager who screwed up my promotion a few years back. I'll still be a bit out of pocket with the car, but I haven't time to be frigging about with it. Is that a fantastic deal or not? You get a lump sum at the end of twenty-five years, and you get your dream boat or whatever. What d'you say?'

'You're on, Joe.'

17

Although I was pleased to be getting plenty of work from Ralph's ice-cream company, I needed to spread my eggs.

There were about twenty workshops in the stable yard that were rented out to a variety of self-employed tradesmen. I had managed to secure the only one vacant. On one side was the old horse, which spent most of the time making strange shuddering noises. On the other there was Fred, an amiable, middle-aged man with two children. He was highly religious and still grieving for his recently buried octogenarian father. Fred came from Birmingham, and told to me in self-mocking tones how he came to be in business in Bridgwater.

'My Dad ran a long-established piano business in Birmingham. The sales figures started to fall once television had been introduced. I suggested we should sell televisions and keep up with the times. "Nonsense, Son!" he said. "D'you seriously think people are going to sit around staring into a little wooden box? They'll go blind and stark staring mad. Forget it; the piano is here to stay." The shop closed down eighteen months later. I decided to start up a completely new type of business somewhere down south where the climate was a few degrees warmer. I settled here and opened a tripe and onion shop. The family loved tripe and onion. Dad argued, "you've got to be joking, Son; they don't eat that type of food down there. They have some of the finest meat in the world – end-to-end juicy steaks on the hoof, as far as the eye can see, just wandering around in acres of green pasture. Not like our fields that are full of blessed cars – that's why we eat offal. It won't work. You won't last twelve months."' Fred laughed. 'Dad was almost right; we lasted only four months. The family was sick of tripe. We couldn't sell it, so we tried to eat it. My children got fed up with it and refused to eat any more. Dad ate much more than was good for him – it probably killed him.'

'So what do you do now?' I asked.

'Well, anything at the moment. We lost a lot of money on pianos and tripe, and now we're trying to consolidate. I sell the odd piano, do tuning, French polishing, sell bicycles, lawn mowers, sewing machines, golf clubs – I've become a general dealer. Anything for a crust. It's not easy making a living down here, you know – you need to be flexible.'

I learnt a few tricks about survival from Fred.

* * *

Ralph had yet another idea. 'I've been thinking, Gordon. You know the real problem with ice cream? It's cold; our climate is cold; the people of Bridgwater are cold; and the whole bloody country is cold. We need another commodity to sell that's warm and cosy. I think I've got the answer.'

'You have? What's that?'

'Logs, Gordon. Logs! That's what people cosy up to on cold winter nights when they refuse to eat ice cream. What we can't sell one year we can sell the following year. We can have these logs for nothing and sell them for whatever price we can get away with.'

'Hmm… sounds interesting… Where're all those logs coming from?'

'Look!' he said with a tinge of smugness, 'I've got a concessionary letter from the Forestry Commission granting me permission to clear a ten-acre woodland site up in the Quantock hills. All we have to do is to cut the trees down, clear the site, and all the thermal units are ours.'

'But Ralph, you don't know sod all about…'

'All sorted, Mate,' he said, tapping his nose with his index finger in a secretive fashion. 'I've bought a load of gear from an old timer who's retiring. It's ancient but serviceable, and I got it on the cheap. The old chap's going to show me the ropes. All we need now are a few willing hands.'

I was anxious to make a contribution, having received a few helpful cheques from Ralph for various signs, artwork, and gallons of Mrs H's tea. 'Is there anything I can do?'

'Well, we're going to need some signage, and we'll have to sort out some advertising, but cost is going to be critical.'

'Tell you what, Ralph. I wouldn't spend any money on signs and fancy advertising. All you need is one line in bold print in the local paper, and only during the winter months. Just LOGS! LOGS! LOGS! and the phone number; there's no need for anything else. Concentrate on what you're flogging. No one gives a toss about fancy names and lettering. Focus on the product. Anyway, it's all going to go up in smoke – and the phone number.'

'That's good thinking, Gordon.' exclaimed Mrs H, starting to say something about averages – till the rattle of the door knocker sent her flying down the stairs.

* * *

My car-spraying activities were developing into a nightmare. The old horse next door turned my workshop into a dust bowl, ruining my work. And he took a dislike to the smell of cellulose. I told the owner, Mr Hancock, about my concerns for his horse and how the smell seemed to upset him.

'Good lord no! He likes the smell; it's like pear drops. D'you know when he were younger and had the teeth he used to eat peppermints by the bucketful. He's got a real sweet tooth and he thinks you're going to give him a handful of peppermints. He's not upset; he's excited.'

I wasn't convinced by his argument, and was relieved when I heard that the horse had been put down by the RSPCA. Mr Hancock was heavily fined for cruelty – something to do with the horse's hocks.

'What a load of nonsense,' he complained. 'The horse was past it and unravelling like me. They ought to come and have a look at my hocks; they're no better.'

Any relief from the old horse's departure was short-lived, however. The new tenant was a panel beater. The incessant hammering on steel, day after day, proved an unbearable torment. I sometimes wondered whether the horse was directing some vengeful punishment from horsey heaven.

Fred was having horse trouble, too, with his Standard 14 horsepower shooting brake. It was a great heavy monster that guzzled vast quantities of petrol and oil. Despite all the expensive pampering and prayers to God on any long journey, it returned little in reliability and service. He was a quiet, even-tempered man, with no hate or hostility in his soul and he showed nothing but compassion for the wretchedness of his fellow man, but there were two things guaranteed to turn him into a frothing-at-the-mouth demon. One of them – the lesser of the two – was the special spanner used for releasing or tightening the terminals on his car batteries when he recharged them. His determination to avoid buying new batteries meant he always needed this. He had a secure place to keep it so that he could always find it. Unfortunately, though, it had an irksome habit of slipping from his grasp and burying itself under all the lawnmowers, bicycles, sewing machines and other paraphernalia. He'd have to unload the contents of the estate car to find it. Then his anger would resonate from one end of the street to the other. He never discovered a satisfactory solution to this problem. But the main thing that made him froth, which was sure set to cause a burst of blood vessels and hat dancing, was a blue rosette and the word 'Conservative'. For him this was like a spear through the heart. His late father and family had always voted Labour, and he couldn't imagine doing anything else. Even the word 'conservatory' would bring him up with a furrowed brow. I had no interest in politics but once casually mentioned something complimentary about the local Conservative candidate, and he went apoplectic. He seemed to be on the point of clasping his hands round my throat.

Fred urgently wanted some help. He had a sudden influx of work, and although I cribbed at the miserly rate I was glad of any opportunity to put money in my pocket and try to balance my failing finances. I'd never shifted a piano before and wondered what on earth they were made of to make them so heavy.

'How come all these pianos?' I asked.

He smiled wickedly, showing me an advertisement in the local paper: 'Wanted urgently, for old people's home! To give them a bit of cheer. Unwanted piano. Can arrange collection.'

'So you're giving these to old people's homes?' I asked naively.

'Of course not!' he laughed. 'If they want one they'll have to buy it.'

'You're a crook, Fred! I can't believe you're doing this. It's downright dishonest. You prattle on about religion and all that stuff, and all the time you're conning people.'

'Steady on, Gordon. There's no need for that sort of talk. The people I've got the pianos from don't want them; it helps them to feel good about themselves – that they've done old people a kindness. They've made me feel good because now I can polish, tune and sell them – and pay my mortgage. They've made my wife and children feel good because the money I earn will help to feed and clothe them.'

'I still say it's dishonest, and I hope you get caught out.'

'Look here, Gordon, the grocer, the cobbler, the candlestick maker will all feel good because I'll be able to buy their goods. You should also feel extra damn good, because the money I'm paying you will help you hang on to that fancy car you can't really afford. It's not dishonest; it's business. I look on it as a scaled-down version of the bread and fishes parable. You've much to learn.'

He was right there.

* * *

Mrs Bridgeway, my new landlady, lived in the road round the corner to Hazel's place. She was an inquisitive character, and really annoyed me with her persistent questions about my parentage and background. She wanted to know all the ins and outs of everything. I told her that my parents worked abroad and that I'd be joining them later on. I knew she didn't believe me when she said, 'They don't seem to be writing, do they?'

She had two grown-up sons in the army and a randy thirty-year-old daughter recently divorced. Mr Bridgeway was a maintenance engineer at British Cellophane, the largest company in the area, which employed most of the local populace. He was a short, shuffling thin-faced man with a permanent puffing cigarette. There was also another lodger, referred to by Mrs Bridgeway as 'Fork Fiddler' because he was a violinist in a BBC orchestra and because of the way he pushed his food around on his plate. He was a quiet, neatly dressed man who seemed to be in a permanent state of deep thought.

My financial situation was getting desperate. Purchasing Joe's car had cleaned me out of funds. I had enough money to pay one week's lodgings, and there was also Christmas. I needed to do something quickly. I went to Middleton's garage, where I'd done the odd spray job, and approached the manager.

'I'm selling my car to a friend and he wants to buy it on HP. Can you arrange it?'

'Sure ... send him along here and he can fill in the forms and sign it in the office. No problem.'

'That's a bit difficult. At the moment he's in hospital, having his appendix out. Can I take the forms and get him to fill them in and sign them in hospital.'

'Hmm... that's a bit tricky. I'm not supposed to do that.'

'What difference does it make where he signs?' I argued. 'I'm interested in that Riley sport you've got on the forecourt, but I'll need to raise the money.'

'Hmm... er... hmm... Okay, I'll make an exception this time.'

I sold my car to Edwin Uphill, and was therefore the buyer and seller of my own car. It was a devious way of raising money, albeit at high interest, but it certainly helped me out of a big hole.

Mrs Bridgeway wanted to know whether I would be joining my parents abroad for Christmas. I told her I wasn't sure. Then a formal-looking letter arrived from the car finance company in the name of Edwin Uphill.

'Who's Edwin Uphill?' she said, scanning the envelope.

'Oh, er... That's me!' All faces turned towards me in amazement.

'You?' she said. 'I thought your name was...'

I went into a fumbling explanation, saying that it was to do with my parents, that it was very complicated, and that I didn't really understand it myself. Mr Bridgeway thought it most unusual and questioned the legality of having two names. He clattered his knife and fork on to the breakfast plate. 'The country would be in a fine old state if everyone went around with two names. You wouldn't know whom you were dealing with.'

Fork Fiddler thought it very funny. 'Just think, Gordon, you could get married and divorced on the same day.'

Christmas with the Bridgeway family was a disaster. Feeling obliged to give Mrs Bridgeway a Christmas present in addition to her lodging money, taking into account the extra food she provided, I gave her a bottle of home-distilled whisky.

I'd done some work – new advertising signs – for an Italian dentist who wanted to get registered with the NHS so he could make some 'real dough', as he put it. He had spent a lot on what he called unbreakable teeth and was short of cash. He showed me an example of his unbreakable dentures, saying, 'They cost me a fortune, so I haven't any money at the moment. See,' he said, chucking the sample across the floor with wild abandon. He stood speechless with disbelief as the teeth scattered in all directions. Even though I was angry about the possibility of not getting paid I couldn't help laughing.

'Oh *no!* My God!' he cried as he gathered up the scattered teeth, 'I've been robbed.'

'I'm sorry,' I said, handing him my bill and trying to keep a straight face. Our voices were soon raised in argument as he shrugged his shoulders, saying he hadn't any money but would give me some of his home-distilled whisky.

'What do I want with bloody whisky? I don't like the stuff. I don't work like that. It's illegal! For Christ's sake I want cash.'

'You Ingleesh... you all the same. Can't do this, can't do that, against the law; you do what you told. What's the matter with you people? You got no balls?'

I eventually agreed to take four bottles of his finest whisky on account, with the promise of full cash settlement after the Christmas.

Mrs Bridgeway enjoyed the odd glass of whisky and thought it would be all right to open her present on Christmas Eve rather than wait till Christmas Day. Mr Bridgeway had a preference for ale and plenty of it, so he joined his two sons down the pub for a lengthy session. I opened a second bottle of the whisky in a gesture of bonhomie and poured out a large tumbler for Fork Fiddler, who said he felt in real festive mood. Mrs Bridgeway was also in festive mood, and her early tune humming between puffs on her fag turned to full vocal expression. As the evening wore on she became ever more inebriated and developed a rowdy duo singsong with Fork Fiddler, who seemed to have abandoned all sense of propriety.

On Christmas Day Mrs Bridgeway didn't get out of bed. She issued groaning instructions to her husband on how to cook the dinner, further relayed to their sons, who also had dreadful hangovers. Fork Fiddler didn't appear till midday. He was unshaven and wearing a Fair Isle jumper back to front. He said something about the hair of the dog and helped himself to another tumbler of whisky. The Christmas dinner was a farce. The chicken was burnt and the vegetables boiled to buggery. There was a lot of arguing and tempers flared. Mr Bridgeway stormed out of the house and once again went down to the pub. The two sons followed soon after, leaving Fork Fiddler and myself to salvage what we could.

On Boxing Day things were no better. Mrs Bridgeway remained in bed, saying she was dying. Her husband wanted to know more about the whisky and took the remains of a bottle to be analysed by a chemist at British Cellophane. Fork Fiddler gave in his notice, announcing that he was going on tour. He whispered that he was interested in the whisky, and how much did I want for the remaining two bottles, so of course I flogged them to him. He thought it was the best drop of Scotch he'd ever had. 'It sort of takes you out of yourself,' he said.

The chemist said it was 90 per cent proof, and that it was illegal, unsuitable and dangerous for human consumption. Mr Bridgeway threatened to sue me for trying to kill his wife and wanted to report the Italian dentist to the police.

18

I missed my mates from the RAF. Both Ginger and Techie had been demobbed and had gone their separate ways. In an effort to kick-start my social scene I had joined a skittle and darts team. The Halfway House, or Disappointed Woman as it was sometimes called, had a magnificent view. In the middle of nowhere, an ancient DC generator supplied its electricity. The hum of happy voices mingling with clinking glasses was always secondary to the noisy diesel. 'Donk-clonk-donk-clonk-donk-clonk.' Often the lights would go out in the middle of a game and the landlady would apply her engineering skills to the problem, which entailed thumping the generator several times with a wooden mallet.

One day Bill Dayfoo, the skittles captain, clutching his obligatory pint of black-and-tan, joined me at the bar, saying, 'Cheer up, Gordon. It's only a game, you know.'

'Yeah, I know Bill, but I really screwed up on the skittles, didn't I?'

'You just need a bit more practice, Mate. We all 'as our off days, you know.' Bill was an easy-going man and well liked by everybody. His nickname was golden bollocks, and he had a knack of winning nearly everything he tried. Even the pub raffles and hamper prizes regularly fell into Bill's lap, which caused a few mutterings and questioning eyebrows.

The football columnist in the local paper described Bill as a terrier in the penalty box, until an opponent breathed on him. Then he would adopt the expression of a tortured spaniel and lie in a groaning heap until the ref gave him a penalty. It was no wonder that he held the highest goal-scoring record for the local football club. This was even though one or two of the more cynical members of the football club had noted that nearly 20 per cent of his goals were accidental, as they were the result of lucky rebounds or unintentional deflections. I liked Bill; he was one of those rare characters that you could never get angry with, even if he crashed you car or accidentally set your house on fire. I was hopeful that some of his popularity and good fortune would rub off on me.

'It's your technique with the darts that worries me,' he was saying. 'No offence, Gordon, but you look like an angry demonstrator throwing bricks. You really scared Ruth; your darts are flying all over the place. You're throwing the darts too hard, Mate. It slows everything down, and people get niggly – that's why you're getting the verbals. All you need is a short, looping throw from the shoulder, like so.'

'Yeah! But it's very off-putting when the lights keep going out. I thought I played really well, all things considered. I mean it's not as if I play darts on a regular basis.'

'Huh?'

'You know, Bill, I sometimes wonder if I've been cursed or something – nothing seems to go right. I seem to have the Midas touch of a bleeding dung beetle. Everything I touch turns to shit. I'm beginning to think I'm just incredibly unlucky.

'Come on, Gordon! I wouldn't call you unlucky. You talk about luck; did you read that article in the local rag about the young couple snogging in their car at Cheddar Gorge? Now *that's* what I call unlucky. Look, here it is.'

'Jesus, Bill, this is unbelievable! That's really bad luck. Absolutely mind-blowing bad luck. It doesn't bear thinking about. Do you think it's true, or d'you reckon someone's having a joke? What sort of a bleeding headline is that? "Unlucky couple", for Christ's sake. It's a life-changing disaster. Can you imagine them, Bill? Poor sods all snuggled up in the back of the car with wafting perfume, soft, sensuous skin, a gentle stirring in the groin – an atmosphere charged with excitement and anticipation. The next minute "wham-splat"! A two-ton boulder and amen.'

'You're not still drinking that crappy orange juice, Gordon, are you? Come on, have a proper drink. I've a proposition to put to you that could really improve your luck.'

'Hmm... Well, okay. I'll join you with that black-and-tan stuff ; I need something stronger after reading that.'

Apart from Bill's fine reputation for scoring goals for the local football team, he had a notorious reputation for being a bit on the sharp side, though he called it good luck, when it came to business. Before I had anything to drink, I had absolutely no intention of getting embroiled in any of his business ideas. Nevertheless I said, 'I'm all ears, Bill. Fire away.'

'Well now, I could've asked one of the local lads, but they ain't particularly far-sighted in such matters, being more inclined towards agriculture, if you get my meaning. An intelligent bloke such as yourself would be quick to recognise a good opportunity and take advantage of it. At the end of this season I'll be thirty-six. I've lost my hair and most of my teeth, and my feet can't catch up with my brain. It's time to hang up my boots and focus more on my finances. My employer is the main sponsor for the local football team, and in recognition of my contribution to the club they've sold me a large plot of land at cost. It's far too big for my requirements, so I'm willing to sell half of it to you for eighty pounds. Then you can build your own house.'

'Sounds great, Bill, but I haven't a clue about building houses. Surely it'll cost a packet to do that?'

'I guessed you might say that, and here's how we get round that little problem. For starters, I and a couple of the lads who're in the darts and skittles team will help you dig the foundations. Then I'll arrange for a useful number of bricks and other materials to tumble gently off the back of a passing lorry, as and when required. This will help you to get the build-up to the first stage. The local council will grant you a mortgage when the house has reached sill level. Thereafter you get three staged payments to complete the project. So all you have to do is get the build up to sill level and you then take as long as you need. In short, we can have a freehold bungalow apiece on the cheap, with the opportunity to make a serious profit. What d'you reckon, Gordon? Is that a good proposition or not? Here, let me top up your glass.'

Three pints of black-and-tan helped cast aside all negative thoughts. With Bill's generous help, I would be propelled up the social ladder into the property-owning middle classes. This could be the beginning of my own modest Fairlawn Estate, like the one in Shipbourne village. The thought of telling Mrs Bridgeway to get knotted and having my own place made me reel with ecstasy. As Bill said, spreading his arms wide as he displayed his big dimpled chin, 'How can you possibly lose, Mate?'

'You're on, Bill. It's a deal. Where do I sign?'

**

After purchasing the land and incurring the costs of legal fees, architect's drawings and so on, I discovered I was insolvent. In the 1950s, tradition demanded smart dress with collar and tie and shiny shoes to approach a bank, especially when borrowing money.

Mr Gilbert was all I imagined a bank manager would be: immaculate in chalk-striped blue suit, gold-rimmed spectacles, greying sideburns, with an occasional flick at imaginary dust on his sleeve. He gestured towards the chair on the opposite side of his desk.

'So, Mr Aspey, I understand you want to build a bungalow? What made you take on this formidable task? You're a bit young at the age of twenty-two, if you don't mind me saying so.'

'Yes, well, I'm fed up with lodgings. I want my own place and hope to make a good profit on what I build, and then perhaps find somewhere else.'

'Good for you! Are those the plans?' he said, pointing to the cardboard sleeve under my arm.

'They've just arrived in the post today. I haven't seen them myself yet.'

Leaning over the desk, he placed a heavy ashtray at each end to hold the drawings in position.

'Is it your intention to employ a bricklayer in the construction, or do you propose...' His voice tailed off as he squinted through his glasses at a blob of something in the middle of the drawing. He drew away from the desk and sat back in his chair. My confidence drained, realising that the blob was a large lump of gooey nasal snot. A look of sheer panic spread over the manager's face as he rose from his chair, eyeing it as though it was a hand grenade. The thought crossed my mind that he wouldn't find a solution to this problem in any bank manager's manual. He edged towards a small iron-barred window and stood looking outside as if something had attracted his attention.

'So how much is this, er… project going to cost altogether?' he enquired.

I couldn't answer immediately as I realised the architect's snot had screwed up my loan application. All I wanted to do was to take the expensive drawings, complete with snot and ashtrays, and spear them up the architect's arse. He'd charged me top wack for the drawings, which were exactly the same as Bill's drawings, because he'd simply stuck them in the photocopier. My thoughts were completely haywire. It hadn't occurred to me that the manager might be staring out of the window to give me the opportunity to remove the problem and avoid any further embarrassment. The carefully prepared costings were no longer in the brown envelope where I felt sure I'd put them. Then I remembered; I'd left them in the glove compartment. Not a single figure surfaced in my memory bank as I sat in goldfish mode. The interview was turning into a nightmare.

'Well, I haven't got much idea, really. I've never built a house before.'

'You don't know,' he said, turning towards me. 'Surely you must have some idea?' Then he made a sudden move towards the desk as though he had received a telepathic memo from Head Office. He planted his left elbow on the drawings with his hand pointing skywards as if challenging me to an arm-wrestle. Then, using his right arm, he deftly scooped up the offending matter with a rubber-topped pencil. With an audible sigh he sank back into his chair, and several times vigorously tapped the snot-laden pencil on the metal wastepaper basket under his desk.

'So how much will the total project cost?' he repeated.

'Well, that depends,' I said.

'On what?' he said, showing signs of irritation, with the tapping on the basket becoming more frequent. 'Mr Aspey, I'm not a mind reader; you don't appear to have answers to my most basic questions. Surely you must know how much it will cost to get to sill level?'

The bank manager's questions posed a problem, since the carefully garnished figures in the glove compartment had failed to surface to my brain. I hoped that most of the materials would cost me nothing, but I didn't think it a good idea to tell him this. The tapping on the wastepaper basket became more frenzied, and it started to sound like an industrious woodpecker.

There was a definite glint of anger in Mr Gilbert's bespectacled face as he said, 'I don't have any clear plan of your proposal, Mr Aspey. I don't know whether you want to borrow one pound or twenty thousand. I think you need to go away and give this matter more serious thought.'

There was a loud snapping noise as he broke off the rubber-topped part of the pencil and threw it into the wastepaper basket.

I tried to flannel my way through the rest of the interview, knowing my application had failed.

'Well, my original idea was to obtain a flexible loan facility to get to sill level, as I don't want to borrow more money than I actually need.'

'Well now, that is very commendable of you, Mr Aspey.' He surveyed the remainder of his rubber-less pencil with annoyance. The lead element had also parted from the main body of the pencil, making it useless. With an irritable sigh he accepted the small dent in his stationery budget and threw the remainder of the pencil into the wastepaper basket. He then closed the meeting with his verdict.

'If you do not know how much money you want to borrow, how can I possibly know how much money to lend?' He went as if to shake hands, but then changed his mind.

* * *

Despite this major setback I was determined to get the bungalow up to sill level somehow. During the weekends I went down to the plot, cutting away the undergrowth and burning all the rubbish. My plot was undulating, muddy and overgrown, with a large puddle in the middle of it. I wasn't overly concerned, as I felt sure I could get it into shape without too much effort. Yet I couldn't help noticing Bill's plot was like a billiard table and looked so much superior on the higher ground. He already had the foundations in place. Even so the view of the River Parrett was a delight, and only five minutes from Bridgwater. I just couldn't wait to get things moving.

The promised help from Bill Dayfoo and his mates to dig the foundations took on a *mañana* quality and I was beginning to lose patience. I leant back on my heels as the bonfire smoke engulfed me. The fluky wind chased the smoke fitfully to all points of the compass, making my eyes water. I loved the smell of dried grass and burning leaves, and the noise of spitting, crackling twigs – and I thought of Mr Tapp, my foster father. I remembered him digging his garden fork into a damp bonfire, trying to get it to burn, and how a rabbit had run between his legs, making him fall over. I could still see him laughing: 'Heh heh! Why didn't you catch 'im, Smiler? Heh heh!'

Through the hazy smoke I saw an old man shuffling towards me. He had a white, bushy beard halfway down his chest. He raised his stick in the air and pointed it towards me. 'What you be doing there, then?'

'I'm building a bungalow,' I said, proudly waving the drawings in the air.

'Thee can't build there. That be a god-awful place to be building anything.'

'What d'you mean? What's up with it?'

'Well it be a burial ground, innit.'

'A burial ground? I'm not having that. The council wouldn't give planning permission if there were bodies buried here.

They've seen the drawings and everything's been passed.'

'Who said anything about bodies, though that wouldn't surprise me neither. Anyways, since when did those daft buggers down the council know something about anything? They only knows what people's prepared to tell 'em. I've lived here all my life, and I knows every clump of grass in these parts. I'm telling you, you'll need a gas mask and oxygen digging them foundations.'

'Gas mask? Oxygen? What are you talking about.'

'Some years back it were an open sewer, running down there towards the River Parrett. Then we had a right bad flood; the whole place was under water. It was terrible. Then some of the locals complained of finding turds in the kitchen. They filled it all in, right to the river bank with lorry loads of rubble and god knows what else, and then stuck a couple of septic tanks down there and they are still there today as far as I know. Afore that it was always a bucket and chuck it site. My family and local folk have been burying here for hundreds of years.'

'So you're telling me this plot is swimming in crap!'

'Well! It sure ain't a place for building houses.'

'What about that plot over there? On the high ground.'

'Oh, that's all right.' He slowly raised his stick and pointed past the puddle at my plot. 'Look at all those mushrooms.'

'What about the mushrooms?'

'Why do you reckon no one picks 'em?'

'What about the other plot over there?'

'There be no mushrooms there, 'cos I picks them regular. I likes my mushrooms with a bit of egg and crackly bacon. Mind you, I'm not a saying there's anything wrong with your mushrooms, but like I says, folk don't pick them. Well you wouldn't want to try, would you?'

I was going off the idea of building a bungalow in Bridgwater.

Bill Dayfoo declined my gift-wrapped carton of mushrooms, insisting his wife preferred the tinned version. When told about the bearded man's story, he vehemently denied any knowledge of the burial ground. 'Honest to God, Gordon, I dunno nothing about any septic tanks and other stuff. I'll give you your money back as soon as I can. You might have to wait a bit, because I'm totally cash-strapped at the moment. I'm really sorry, Gordon – although, Jesus! It could have been a lot worse.'

'For Christ's sake Bill, what do you mean it could be worse? How can you say that? I've thrown away a small fortune on snotty-nosed architects, legal fees and other nonsensical bills; I'm unable to pay my landlady; I'm about to be chucked out in the street. For fuck's sake, Bill, I'm penniless and destitute. I'm saddled with a giant crater of Jurassic shit and you're skint! For Christ's sake, Bill, how can it get fucking worse?'

'Well, I was looking at it from my point of view. I could have easily sold you my plot. The truth is, Gordon, I'm honest to God sorry. I hardly knows what to say. You have been so incredibly unlucky.'

* * *

I was getting fed up with the car spraying, which was really hard work and a messy business. Also I found the continuous banging from the panel beater next door very depressing. Even worse were the continuous interruptions from Mr Hancock, who had time on his hands and wanted to regurgitate the past and tell me how wonderful everything used to be. He seemed to think he was still the village squire, not realising that time was money and that people needed paying for their services. He asked the plumber to do some work down at his house and gave him ten shillings and a box of apples. When the plumber sent him a bill Mr Hancock went berserk and gave him notice to quit the workshop.

I was on the lookout for a small business with minimal hassle – a business where somebody else did the work and I collected the money. I investigated several small projects, and a business making leather studs for football boots looked quite promising.

The owner produced a client list, sales figures and profit margins; it seemed a genuine opportunity. The main advantage was that the leather came in the form of off-cuts from a local shoe factory, therefore costing nothing. The only other materials were small packets of nails. The owner had six housewives working from home, each equipped with a one-armed punch. You would place a nail in a slot, then lay a piece of leather over the top and bring the arm down with a thud. After four thuds you had a complete football stud ready for action.

'I don't pay 'em much,' chuckled the owner, 'but it keeps 'em out of mischief, don't it?'

I decided to buy the business when I got my money back from Bill and collected a decent cheque for some lucrative exhibition display work. I met Bill in the Halfway House.

'I'll have yer money next week, Gordon,' he said, thumping a pint of black an' tan on the counter. 'So, how'yer doing, Mate? What's new?'

'Ah, cheers, Bill! That'll be real handy. By the way, how often did you change your studs when you were playing football?' I enquired casually. I was nervous about getting involved with him again after the building-plot saga.

'Well, I started using them new plastic studs. They don't seem to wear out so easy. Why d'you ask?' he said, looking increasingly curious.

I muttered, 'No reason. I Just wondered, that's all.'

I bought a small mail-order business called Flockspray Ltd from an accountant based in Weston-super-Mare. He produced an impressive list of clients, including schools and councils from all over the country. What was interesting was that they were regular repeat customers. The sums of money were hardly impressive, but he described the potential as 'mind-boggling'. Flock spray was a product recycled from old clothes. The material was shredded down to tiny, almost dust-like, particles. It was then dyed to the required colour, with a range of about twenty-five colours, some of them quite intense. There was a small stock of flock fibres in various colours, together with literature, flock guns, plus all the regulatory bits and pieces for running a limited company. There was even a large lump of red wax, company seal and articles of memorandum.

A company in the north of England supplied the flock in large, five-pound bags, which I used to fill the small, specially customised and printed cardboard boxes. The standard kit also included a tin of white, rubbery glue, together with a 'flock gun', which was like a bicycle pump with a cocoa tin welded in at one end. You had to apply the liquid rubber to the surface and then fill the cocoa tin with the desired colour and apply the flock with a pumping action, as if you were pumping up a bicycle tyre.

'As the sole shareholder, you would be the managing director,' said the accountant.

'I would actually be managing director?'

'Sure, It's a limited company, and you would be in total control.'

Crikey! I'd suddenly become an important person. I only knew one managing director, and although Ralph didn't exactly sparkle with importance he had an aura of status about him.

My only concern was why the accountant was selling.

'So why are you selling this "mind-boggling potential"?'

'Well,' he said dolefully, 'I've spent most of my working life clocking up profits for my clientele. I haven't paid sufficient attention to my own finances. I need every penny I can lay my hands on just to survive.'

We sat in a café drinking tea. He pointed his sugar spoon at a small hotel opposite, with men in white overalls assembling scaffolding.

'That's my final throw of the dice. Last year was the pits. The weather was appalling, bookings were low, and the staff were lousy. This year I have higher rates, health and safety, higher wages, redecoration – and the same lousy staff. I've had diabolical luck. You wouldn't believe the terrible luck I've had these last few years. If things don't improve this year I might swallow dive out of the attic window and bring everything to a peaceful conclusion.'

I resisted unzipping my own portfolio on bad luck, but reiterated the story of the young couple crushed in their car while necking at Cheddar Gorge. 'That's what I call bad luck,' I said emphatically.

'I'm not so sure,' he sighed. 'I wouldn't mind going like that. Eldorado to oblivion in one fell swoop.' He continued with his tale of woes all afternoon. I didn't have the heart to turn down his business and bought it without a quibble.

I also paid for the tea and biscuits.

I told Ralph about my new flock spray business and, puffing out my chest, I informed him that I was now a managing director just like him. At first he seemed mildly impressed, then, looking thoughtful, he said, 'Y'know, Gordon, I wouldn't get too excited. The difference between a dustman and a managing director is barely perceptible, but the dustman gets regular wages. Tell you what, though, it might be worthwhile to get a sales rep with that product. Get someone calling on the schools and handicraft shops on commission and expenses only.'

'I reckon you could do well with that,' said Mrs H, filling the teapot.

There were many problems with the flock spray. The adhesive liquid didn't do what it said on the tin and was absolutely useless. The flock sprayer was an insecticide gun with a transfer stuck on it and was almost useless. Even worse were the difficulties of parcelling and postage. The gun had the shape of an over-inflated crucifix, causing the postmistress to mutter with irritation when trying to wriggle it into the postman's sack.

'Surely you can wrap this up better? What on earth have you got in here, for goodness sake?'

'It's a gun.'

'A what?' she yelped.

'It's actually a flock gun.'

'Well, whatever it is, it needs to go into a box and be properly wrapped. You'll get a lot of complaints from your customers.'

She was right there.

When I realised the product had too many glitches I produced an instruction manual offering an alternative method of application.I had found out that a white japlac enamel with a little linseed oil was a much better fixative. Also that a tea chest or any old box with the use of a vacuum cleaner could replace the pump. By placing the object in the box with a given amount of flock, the vacuum cleaner could be reversed to blow, with the hose fed through a reasonably well fitting hole in the box. Once the vacuum cleaner was switched on the flock would be efficiently circulated around the object. When this process was finished the vacuum cleaner would be returned to suck and you would then recoup all of the unused flock. The product was used in handicrafts for making pictures, firescreens, coasters, cutlery drawers and all sorts of gifts.

19

After selling his tripe and onion shop, Fred had bought the old customs and excise premises overlooking the River Parrett in the heart of Bridgwater. I'd made an arrangement with Fred that he would let me use his address and phone number on my business cards and letterheads. In return, I would help him when he was busy with his French polishing, and help shift pianos for nominal wages.

Things started to go wrong when the French girl I was going out with at the time started telephoning at all hours. Fred grumbled.

'I don't want you running a dating agency from my home, Gordon. You tell your French lady this must stop. My wife is nervous answering the phone after that awful message last night. She's very religious and isn't used to that sort of thing.'

'She left a message for me, Fred?'

'Yes! It was in broken English and greatly embarrassed my wife. As far as I could make out, she was saying, "Please to tell Gordon I go back home on Friday. I want to spend last night in hotel and he make beeg fuss of me. I want nice bed and him to be hungry for me. I want him make beeg, beeg fuss of me." What sort of a message is that to leave with a straight, God-fearing woman?'

'Sorry about that, Fred. She does have a picturesque way of putting things. If she's going home you won't have to worry any more. So she's going back on Friday?'

'So it seems. And another thing, Gordon, we're getting a lot of calls from people complaining about your flock spray business ... some of them are very rude. My wife is threatening not to answer the phone at all, and that would cripple my business.'

His wife's indignation would soon be elevated to a much higher level.

Mrs Bridgeway, still grumbling about the dodgy whisky, was also highly indignant about my late nights. 'I ain't having it,' she said, 'being out half the night like that … the neighbours'll think I'm running a brothel. I knows what you're up to. I found half a haystack in your bed this morning. Eleven o'clock is plenty late enough, and then I'm bolting the door.'

The French girl was adamant her last night would be in the hotel. 'Gor-don, you think more of your landlady than me. You can easy get new landlady. Please, we go to the hotel.'

I spent an arduous night in the Railway Hotel, and Mrs Bridgeway gave me notice to find somewhere else to pursue my nocturnal activities.

* * *

I had one reply answering my advertisement for a representative for Flockspray Ltd: a semi-retired teacher with a posh voice and an elderly BSA saloon car.

Ralph was impressed with the woman. 'You've hit the jackpot first time, Gordon. Absolutely perfect! She'll be able to winkle her way into all the educational establishments. I reckon you'll do really well with that flock spray stuff.'

Jennifer didn't seem too excited about the commission only element and tried to push for a basic salary plus motoring costs. I wouldn't agree to a salary, but did agree to modest motoring expenses and an extra 5 per cent commission.

I requested she make a list of all the schools she visited, including the names of the principals. We shook hands and she left, clutching her notebook liberally filled with notes about the product and prices. I watched her drive away in a cloud of thick, black smoke. I felt an inner glow of satisfaction, convinced my future was at last truly on the up. The orders and profits would soon be flowing into my account like the bore up the River Parrett.

* * *

Ralph was having mixed fortunes with the log business. Mr Starman insisted he would have to pay extra to store all the logs in his yard since it deprived him of the opportunity to improve his income. Ralph responded by storing the logs in a field in the Quantocks, which cost him nothing. He also filled one of the three ice cream vans with logs to keep dry. But an unexpected spell of warm winter sunshine generated a demand for lollies and ice cream. The ice-cream vans were alive with woodlice, so they had to be hosed down inside and out, and then disinfected. Ralph confessed to being totally bewildered by the way things were going. But he did say he thought his winter ice-cream strategy was paying off.

Soon afterwards a sharp drop in temperature witnessed a big demand for logs, with the telephone ringing incessantly. Conditions were so bad it was impossible to get to the log store in the Quantock Hills. Mrs H couldn't hide her frustration. Her teapot went into overtime, and the law of averages was put on the back burner.

'I can't believe it,' she wailed. 'We've got all those orders and logs coming out of our ears, and we can't get near them because of the weather. You're so unlucky, Son.'

Ralph decided to drive as far as he could to the log site and then walk the remaining half-mile or so. Mrs H joined him. He had left one of the ice-cream vans on site loaded with logs to keep them dry for their next visit. The steady hum and whine of the circular saw broke the still air of the Quantocks as the logs began to pile up. Then Mrs H had an awful accident. Ralph plucked at his moustache as he related the nightmare story to me.

'It was cold but the sun started to shine through, and I was rubbing my hands together with satisfaction. "This is the life," I said. "We've got a whole stack of orders. This little lot are all spoken for once we get them back to the yard."

'She looked up at me with a smile. "Its like I've always said, Son, you can't work hard like you does without..." and then she let out a horrible scream. She had been feeding the logs through the saw without a proper guard. When she looked up, having briefly lost her concentration, she'd cut off half her middle and index fingers on her right hand. At first I wasn't sure what had happened. Then she held up her hand, streaming with blood. I didn't know what to do; I completely panicked. "Oh God! G... g... get into the van," I said.

'She squeezed into the ice-cream van with blood dripping all over the place. I wrapped my jumper round her hand and draped my overcoat around her shoulders. How I got that log-laden van down to the hospital I'll never know. It was the most terrifying experience of my life. I felt certain we would both finish up in the mortuary. Mrs H fainted and lost her spectacles, which we never found. She had to stay overnight in the hospital as the doctor said she was suffering from shock. The doctor also said she would suffer from what he called "dead finger syndrome", a condition where the patient doesn't realise her fingers are missing.' He paused and with a weak smile added, 'She's broken every cup, saucer and plate in the house. This morning she even dropped the blasted teapot.'

* * *

My visit to the sales rep's home address was a most depressing experience. Any thoughts of a big improvement in my finances were soon quashed. Our meeting developed into an ill-tempered shouting match. She gave me a bill for three new tyres and fuel receipts that could have taken her twice around the world in a double-decker bus.

'The average mileage for a tyre is fifty thousand miles – and how come you've only been driving on three wheels?' I said sarcastically. 'These petrol receipts ... some of them have the same date. You couldn't possibly have used all this fuel; you've been picking receipts up off the petrol-station floor. You're taking me for an idiot.'

'Don't you talk to me like that,' she said loftily. 'The agreement was that you pay me expenses and commission.'

'This list of schools you've visited. You couldn't have covered more than one hundred and fifty miles, and that's being generous. What orders have you managed?'

'Orders? Surely you don't imagine orders materialise just like that! It takes time and patience, with follow-up visits to get things moving. You've got a lot to learn.'

'You're telling me you haven't got one single order? I can't believe it! I can't afford to pay you on the basis that something might develop in the long term. I need orders now, for Christ's sake. I'm not paying this fancy bill; it's ridiculous. I'll pay you for half of the petrol, which I reckon is generosity to the point of stupidity, and we'll call it a day.'

'That's what you think!' snapped the sales rep, her face contorted with rage. 'You haven't seen the last of me. I'll take you to court. You'll be hearing from my solicitor.'

'That's fine by me. Goodbye.'

* * *

I was stopped when I was driving my car – a regular occurrence for me – and the police sergeant studied my driving licence. He looked me up and down with suspicion. 'This ain't your name. I knows you – your name is Arspee. You're from the air force camp. You're the smart arse that dreamt up that cock-and-bull story with the woman from Market Street when you were court-martialled.'

I recognised the sergeant who had tried to arrest me and hand me over to the military police just before I was demobbed. It was he who had chased me across the railway and become stuck on top of a six-foot wire fence.

'Yeah, that's my name, but I've two names – and I'm perfectly entitled to use them.'

His bushy eyebrows twitched with disbelief. 'Two names? I'm not having that. Only important people have two names ... like film stars and such-like. It ain't for the likes of you. Anyways,' he said with an air of triumph, 'you only 'as one birth certificate.'

'No, I've got two birth certificates.'

'Two certificates! – Two certificates!' he repeated. 'That can't be right. Anyways, the inspector wants to see you about some other matters. You better take your licence and them certificates with you and report down the station.'

I was sent to an upstairs office where the inspector was engaged in conversation with a plain-clothes detective. The two men stopped talking as I entered. 'Well, well, if it isn't Mr Uphill ... or is it Mr Arspee?' said the inspector with thinly veiled sarcasm. 'We've been getting a lot of bad reports about you. So you've still decided to settle down in these parts despite our earlier request for you to move on. Is that right?'

'I might; it depends how things go.'

'Oh no. You're not settling down here. As far as I'm concerned you're nothing but a petty criminal. We don't want you on our patch, so you'd better be moving on.'

The detective pressed his pockmarked face close to mine. 'What the inspector is saying is that you've got one last chance to get out of town.'

'I'm not going anywhere. You can't treat me like a criminal; I've no convictions.'

'Not yet,' said the inspector. 'But we're looking into a number of things. There's the question of a stolen tea trolley, stolen paint and grievous bodily harm.'

'"Grievous bodily harm"? I don't know what you're talking about.'

'You attacked your landlord and didn't pay your rent.'

'That's a load of rubbish! His wife owed me fifteen pounds. It was self-defence. The man was going to knock the shit out of me. His wife was whacking me on the back of the head with a garden spade and his granny was throwing missiles at me. What was I supposed to do, Kneel and pray to God? He started it and got what he deserved.'

'What about the paint you stole from Cecil Oliver's, the builder's merchants?'

'I was fed up with their lousy service, keeping me hanging around hour after hour. I told them I was trying to earn a living. I told them to send me the bill.'

'So what about all the trouble in the air force camp and all the lies you hatched with that woman from Market Street?' said the inspector. 'And demolishing the Scots Wool and Hosiery Store? You seem to have an answer for everything, Arspee, or whatever your name is. Everybody else is in the wrong except you.'

'The wool shop was an accident. That could happen to anyone. I was a learner driver.'

'Well, according to my sergeant who was on traffic duty yesterday, you nearly collided with a bus because you were so busy ogling two girls outside the butcher's shop. No doubt you've a good excuse for that as well. Let me tell you that if you decide to stay in town we'll give you a very uncomfortable time indeed.'

Soon afterwards a policeman called at my lodgings accusing me of stealing an RAF compressor from the camp. 'According to my information you were seen loading the compressor on to a van near the runway last week,' he said.

I was getting increasingly angry at the ongoing harassment, while Mrs Bridgeway was getting very fired up and counting the days to my departure.

'So how come these RAF policemen just stood and watched me load this compressor into a van? Why didn't they arrest me? I haven't been anywhere near the camp since being demobbed. What's more, you might just tell the inventor of this cock-and-bull story that an air compressor weighs over half a ton; it wouldn't be possible to get it into an ex-post office van. I'm keeping a record of all this harassment and I'll make sure it finds the right department if it continues.'

'Don't you start getting cocky with me. As I told you before, I'm just doing my job.'

* * *

I had an enquiry from the owner of the Greek restaurant who recognised me from earlier visits with Ginger before we got demobbed.

'Ah, Mr Gordon,' he said, shaking my hand. 'How are you? And your friend with der ginger hair.'

'He's married and now lives in Scotland.'

'Ah! I see.' The Greek was a large, jolly man with a permanent smile on his lips. He told me I'd been highly recommended by Jock the car salesman who'd done a deal with me on the tea trolley and ex-post office van.

'Mr Jock say you vera good artist and only charge peanuts.'

'He said that? The bastard!'

'I think he mean you not charge me so much. What I want, my friend, is how you say ... a romantic setting to attract the younger people for my restaurant. What you think?'

Later that day I had a good look around his restaurant and realised it might be a good opportunity to push the flock spray technology. I pencilled in a few sketches and ideas in my notepad. I described my idea of painting the ceiling a midnight blue and sticking cut-outs of half-moons, stars and silhouettes of dancing couples sprayed with a bright yellow flock.

'You think that look good, Mr Gordon, eh? It would make the place look very romantic, huh? Yeah! I like. You please go ahead and do quickly, yes?'

The overall effect was most pleasing, and the Greek restaurant owner was overjoyed. He paid me in cash with the promise of a free meal any evening.

Meanwhile, I was getting a lot of complaints in the post about the inefficacy of the adhesive. There were also complaints about the telephone response from Fred's house. He had been telling customers I'd gone abroad; I'd moved premises; ceased trading; I was in hospital. One customer even sent his condolences and asked if he could speak with someone else about his flocking problem. I was really annoyed with Fred as he was crippling my business before I'd hardly started. I went down to his house to complain that it wasn't a very Christian way of carrying on.

Fred answered the door foaming at the mouth. He shouted at me as though I was selling blue rosettes and had pinched his battery spanner. 'You're finished here. Don't ever show your face again. Hoppit.'

'Steady on, Fred. What's happened? What've I done?

'What have you done? My wife took a phone call from a madman. His language was unrepeatable. He called her a lying bitch and said we'd ruined his restaurant. He called round here an hour ago. He's a raging monster. He said he's going to kill you. My wife's had enough. I've had the telephone disconnected and we're selling up.'

The job I did for the Greek had looked very impressive when first completed and I couldn't imagine what had made him so angry. I was later told that young people had come to the restaurant in droves, but had later left with bright fluorescent yellow hair.

20

It was 1957, and I was beginning to realise there was no easy road to success in business. Ralph appeared to be doing all the right things and working his guts out, but was going nowhere. Jock, the freelance car salesman, puffing nonchalantly on his ever-present cigar, was really living from hand to mouth. Fred worked all hours and appeared to be going backwards. All the entrepreneurs I knew were having an uphill struggle to survive. I, on the other hand, wasn't interested in survival; I wanted success.

It was at this point that I saw what the real problem was – Bridgwater was twinned with the Bermuda triangle. I needed to get out quick, and my exit would have nothing to do with the police, angry Greeks, Italian dentists or fuming flock spray complainants – or even Jurassic shit. The problem was the headline in the local paper when the falling boulder at Cheddar Gorge had crunched the courting couple. 'Bad Luck' they called it – strewth! The geography was all wrong. Bridgwater was simply too far from the flight path of Lady Luck. Contrary to Mrs H's unswerving belief in the law of averages, I was convinced the town's inhabitants were banging their collective heads against an impervious red brick wall.

In confirmation of my pessimistic outlook, Mrs Bridgeway, who was eagerly looking forward to my weekend departure, told me that two visitors urgently wanted to see me.

The first was a man with one arm and a bundle of papers who muttered something about a stolen tea trolley. 'I think he was the bailiff,' she said, crossing her arms disapprovingly. 'God knows who the other man was. Some sort of foreigner effing and blinding. He says everybody's got yellow hair and he's going to kill you.'

I was beginning to think the police inspector who had given me a week to get out of town had been trying to do me a favour. There seemed to be only one sensible solution: to scarper.

I decided to make a dash for London, so after a few carefully selected goodbyes I loaded all my worldly possessions into the Rover, including Flockspray Products Ltd and all Cecil Oliver's unpaid-for paint. It was the August bank holiday when I crept out of the house in the early hours of the morning and headed for Bristol. One of the things I enjoyed about the Rover was the tendency for fuel-pump attendants to call me 'Sir' and their offers to wash the windscreen, on occasion even offering to check the tyre pressures – in sharp contrast to the surly treatment I'd received as the driver of old bangers. I patted the highly chromed radiator of the Rover with satisfaction. Joe the insurance salesman had done me a big favour, and although I'd no idea at the time I was destined to get a lot more than mileage out of his car. The holiday traffic was building up, so I decided to stop at Weston-super-Mare and have a stroll along the promenade. I bought some corned beef sandwiches and sat on a bench to enjoy the sunshine. There were children playing football on the beach with their parents. I watched them for a while. They seemed so happy and contented; I'd missed out on all that.

The musical chimes of an ice-cream van stopped the football as the kids ran to buy a cornet. I watched a father playing cricket with his young son; he was about Michael's age. The father looked with mock astonishment as the boy hit the ball with a delighted yelp over his head. The mother sat close by with her giggling young daughter sharing an ice cream.

I wondered how Sarah was getting on. I'd enjoyed the homely atmosphere with her and Michael, and realised that that's what I really wanted from life: a proper home with a wife and kids. It dawned on me that I didn't belong to anybody or anywhere. I was nothing. If I disappeared overnight no one would miss me, or even be aware I'd gone.

The memory of Mr Drawl, the upholsterer in Sheerness, surfaced angrily: 'Stop whining! Stop feeling sorry for yourself, nobody's interested in your problems. Show a bit of backbone!' His words still made me wince, but they never failed to chivvy me on. I squared my shoulders and muttered in angry tones that

I would have my own business, my own house, a nice boat, and that my family would want for nothing. It was a promise I was determined to keep.

*** *** ***

I stopped overnight in Bristol and checked out an advertisement in the local paper: 'Commercial van driver wanted urgently'. It seemed sensible to try and boost my savings before tackling London.

'Can you start now?' asked the boss.

'I can work for you on a temporary basis, if that's any good.'

'That'll be fine,' he said. Initially I was paid cash and wasn't on the books, but the company secretary told the boss that that was illegal, so I then became an employee.

My accommodation was in a posher guesthouse than I was used to, but I felt I could afford something better. The other guests were six students studying for entrance to Bristol University and a commercial traveller with red hair from Yorkshire. Yorkie had a very loud voice, more suited to addressing large crowds or selling newspapers than ordinary, everyday conversation.

The guesthouse was a family set-up, with landlady, daughter, and sombre son-in-law attending our table. The students came second in the pecking order and ate on a separate table. They would scrutinise every morsel of food put before us and would watch us munching till their own food arrived, which they would then gobble down as if they were starving.

In the local pub I said to Yorkie, 'I'm a bit concerned about the food in this place; the portions are more like emergency rations. Is it like this all the time or have I just struck a bad patch?'

'Funny you should mention that. I was talking to my wife on the phone this morning about the same thing. I told her I've had to take a food hamper to the office to sustain body and soul. She thinks I'm joking.'

'Christ! Is it as bad as that? Why don't we tackle the landlady?'

'We could bring the students into it as well; they looked ready to eat the tablecloth last night.'

'Yeah, she's a miserly old bat; perhaps we could get them to join us tonight at the snooker hall.'

I'd already experienced a taste of the landlady's temper when she discovered I'd stored a lot of my stuff in her garage.

'I didn't give you no permission to store your flock spray and all that paint and rubbish in my garage. We couldn't even get to the lawnmower. You'd better move it quick, or I'll be adding storage charges to your account.'

In the 1950s, verbal combat with landladies required steely courage, so we decided to let the students do most of the complaining. They agreed that something had to be done. Robert, a six-foot bespectacled scruff with a couldn't-care-less attitude, spearheaded their argument.

'We're being ripped off. She must be making a packet. The trouble is she won't take any notice of us. I think Yorkie should handle things.'

'Who, me?' said Yorkie with a start. 'Why me?'

'You have the voice for such a situation,' said Robert.

'You really think so?' said Yorkie, pleased at the unexpected flattery.

'Yeah! Gordon's in the doghouse with his stuff bunging up the garage; I reckon he's anyway going to get chucked out. We'll all back you up, Yorkie. Isn't that right?' he said, turning to the students.

'That's right!' they chorused.

Back at the guesthouse, several pints of bitter hadn't improved the way Yorkie spoke. He stuttered through his Oliver Twist impersonation of 'Can we have some more?'

The landlady stood wide-eyed and motionless as she listened to his oratory. She seemed to bear some resemblance to my landlady in Duxhurst who used to dish up marmalade sandwiches, and I wondered whether the two of them might be related.

'I can hear you; I'm not bloody deaf!' she yelled. Then she turned towards the head-nodding students with some ferocity. 'What do you think I am? Some sort of bloody charity? Food is expensive. You won't find anywhere within a thousand miles giving better value. I don't make no money out of you lot. As far as I'm concerned, if you're not satisfied you can bugger off – the lot of you.'

After Yorkie gave in his notice, there was an immediate improvement in the food at breakfast time. Not only were the portions noticeably larger but the smiling son-in-law did two circuits with the Cornflakes and doubled the toast on the table.

The students were winking and giving the thumbs up to Yorkie for his brave display.

* * *

One of the traditions of the period was the annual works outing. The boss would hire a coach and the entire workforce would go to the seaside, each bobbing in and out of as many pubs as he or she could manage within the time available. This was usually followed by a rowdy sing-song on the coach returning home.

Though usually curmudgeonly, my boss was very generous with this annual outing. Paper money would flutter across the seaside bars with total abandon. Supported by unsteady legs and muddled brain, he had a high regard for this occasion, and it was considered unwise for any staff to abscond or engage in some other activity. According to one of the old-timers, anyone who didn't turn up for the annual outing could expect a few difficulties when work resumed. Already forewarned, I nevertheless decided to be sick for the day. My interest was focused on Irene, an attractive secretary in a nearby office. I had arranged my first date with her, which conveniently coincided with the works outing. We decided to visit Burnham-on-Sea and have a picnic. Irene loved my Rover and luxuriated in the deep leather upholstery, gliding her elegant manicured fingers across the highly polished walnut dashboard.

'It's a beautiful car,' she murmured. 'It looks almost new; it's the poshest I've ever been in.'

'Me too!' I laughed. Then I told her the story of Joe and the insurance policy.

'You've kept the insurance running?' she laughed,

'You bet! I'm determined to keep that going to the bitter end.'

We were sitting on bar stools enjoying the warm summer evening, when we heard a commotion and shouting. Glancing over my shoulder I was horrified to witness the unsteady progress of my boss and the entire works entourage heading towards us.

'Oh, no!' groaned Irene, crumpling her empty crisp packet into the ashtray, 'this is going to be awkward.'

'You're not kidding,' I gulped.

'I thought you were supposed to be ill,' said the boss's son accusingly, pointing a wavering finger in my direction. His father looked as though a Kalashnikov would be more useful than the glass of beer he clutched in his hand.

'What's going on, Irene?' he demanded.

'I'm just having a drink with a friend,' she snapped.

The boss tugged at his heavy-buckled belt, trying to cover his distended beer belly, and turned towards me, saying, 'So how long has this been going on?'

'Well we only...'

'Look! I can go out with anyone I like,' argued Irene, 'I'm not married to your son yet. It's not definite, you know.'

The remainder of the party had dispersed to all parts of the pub, laughing in their beer. I hadn't realised I'd been with the son's bit of fluff. The boss, half turning, fixed his withering gaze upon me.

'I can't stand bloody liars.'

'Blimey!' I said after they'd gone. 'What a turn-up! Why didn't you tell me he was your boyfriend?'

'Well, everybody takes it for granted we'll marry, but I'm having second thoughts. He's so boring. I didn't know you worked at his place, or that his army were coming here, did I? Anyway,' she giggled, 'he hasn't got such a nice car as you have.'

On our return to Bristol, Irene sighed aloud, saying, 'I enjoyed today, but you know he's going to give you the sack.'

'That's crazy! He wouldn't do that, would he?'

'That's for certain. He doesn't mess about; he's absolutely ruthless.'

'Ah well; it doesn't matter that much. I was going to London anyway.'

'That's a shame. We were getting on so well. I think I could get to like you. Do you have to go to London?'

'I could hang around a bit longer if you like. Would you really like me to?'

'Only if you want to.'

Before I could tell Yorkie what had happened, he delivered a bombshell of his own.

'Guess what!' he said, chalking his snooker cue, 'you're not going to believe this! I had a heart-to-heart with Moira, the landlady's daughter. She thinks I'm a real hero. "You put my Mum's nose right out of joint," she said. "It's about time somebody told her how mean she is." And do you know what she said to me?' He lined up his cue with the black. 'She said she herself was much, much more generous. At first I wasn't too sure what she meant, and then she said, "I don't sleep with my husband any more – we have separate rooms."'

'Shhh! Christ! Keep your voice down, Yorkie; everyone's looking at us. She told you that?'

'She did! And, wait for it,' he was whispering now, 'she said, if either of us fancied... you know what... she'd be happy to oblige!'

'I don't believe you. You're telling porkies!'

'No, honestly, Gordon – those were her actual words.'

'Are you telling me she said "either of us"? Maybe she wants paying.'

'No, It's not like that; I think she's brassed off, and wants a bit of fun. She feels a bit of a prisoner and has nowhere to go. It can't be much fun working in that place seven days a week. I think she just wants a bit of old-fashioned dick.'

'So, if I said to her, "Excuse me, Moira, I have a large bone in my trouser pocket and I would like to share it with you. Can you pop upstairs for a minute?" she would be in my bed in a flash, huh?'

'Look, Gordon, I'm only telling you what she told me; I'm not kidding, okay? She's not the bee's knees in the beauty stakes, but all the bits and pieces seem to be in the right place. My wife would put a meat cleaver to me if I got involved. You're fancy-free, Gordon; you can do the lady a favour – bring a bit of sunshine into her world.'

I lay in bed that night thinking about sunshine and Moira. I reckoned she was in her early thirties, with a kind, plumpish, hospital-nurse quality about her, and the thought of a pleasurable interlude with her left me twitching with excitement. I thought about a casual swashbuckling approach:

''Scuse me. I've just nipped in for a bit of nooky, if that's all right with you,' and then I'd scramble into her bed. After all, she really must be gasping for it, to tell Yorkie and be willing to share it out like that. Then I winced at the possible outcome if Yorkie had got his wires crossed or was playing games. I considered a better alternative was a polite invitation to join me in my room.

'I don't suppose you'd fancy joining me, if you're not doing anything special?' That would give scope for flannelling my way out of an awkward scene. Then I heard a guttural throat-clearing from Yorkie's room, followed by grunting and slapping noises. I couldn't believe it. I'd half a mind to knock on his door and ask him to keep the animal noises down. He was married, for Christ's sake. There was a strange hissing noise like cold water being poured on to hot coals. *What on earth was he doing to the*

poor woman? I thought. *He's so coarse. He's got no manners at all.* Then there was a loud gargling noise, and I buried my head under the pillow almost choking with laughter when I realised Yorkie was only washing and cleaning his teeth.

The students had finished their exams, and the landlady told Robert, 'There's no way you'll pass. Serves you right, you lazy devil; spending all your time in the pub.'

Only two students passed – and one of them was Robert, who showed more surprise than either the landlady or his parents.

* * *

The boss called me into his office. 'I've no further use for you,' he said, throwing my wage packet on the table.

'No notice?' I said.

'I told you; I don't like liars.'

I gave a week's notice to the landlady. She showed an almost indecent pleasure at my decision to leave.

'Now we might be able to mow the lawn,' she muttered. 'By the way, a man came looking for you yesterday; something about some paint. It looked like a summons to me.'

This brought about a rapid change of plan, and I had to abandon the idea of giving Moira a bit of sunshine. I left a note in the garage for the landlady, saying she could have the paint, and left early the following morning for London.

21

I left Bristol to go to London in Ocotber 1957. I needed to get a job quickly to protect my slender savings, but this proved more difficult than I'd imagined. The jobs available were poorly paid and would hardly cover the cost of my accommodation in a seedy hotel near Earls Court.

At that time brewers were spending large sums of money refurbishing public houses. Eventually I managed to get a job with an expanding company who were starting a new branch in London. They had a large contract to renew all the signage for one of the major breweries.

I had to go to Brighton and do a trade test and meet the owner, who told me that this was a marvellous opportunity and that I was getting in on the ground floor. Unfortunately he failed to warn me that a lot of the work would be above the top floor. The use of triple-extension ladders would be a regular feature, challenging my still largely untested fear of heights.

The workshops were near the Kennington Oval cricket ground at the back of a builder's yard. I needed to get more reasonably priced accommodation, and somewhere within shouting distance of the works to save on fuel costs. I stood outside the workshop and looked across the road. There was a large Victorian house with a blue plaque on the wall, saying that a famous artist had lived there. It amused me to think that were he still alive he might approve of my cheek of enquiring whether there were lodgings available in his nice house. A petite lady in her late twenties answered the door. Her grey eyes flashed with indignation.

'Who told you to come here? We don't have lodgers and don't intend to do so in the future.'

'I'm sorry to have troubled you, but I'm in a bit of a rush and thought I'd take a chance. Well, you never know your luck,' I laughed. 'You see I start work across the road tomorrow morning.'

'I see.' Her face softened. 'Can you come back later this evening when my husband's home? I can't make any promises, but we do have the middle rooms empty; we won't do meals or anything.'

'That would be great. Thanks very much.'

John and Jenny became my landlords. John worked at the War Department most of the week away from home. He was a tall man with a striking appearance and a sharp sense of humour. 'These are the rooms,' said John. 'They're a bit basic and need tarting up, but you can have them at a reduced rent if you like. I can't afford to spend any money at the moment.'

'They're just the ticket for me,' I said.

The bedroom was enormous, with large sash windows that rattled angrily with every passing lorry. I was able to store everything I had with ease in the bedroom: all the flock spray equipment, tools, books and everything else. There was another huge room, a kitchen-diner, in which I cooked and ate that emphasised my solitary situation when I sat at its long table. I had to share the toilet facilities with the rest of the household. There was an old-fashioned bath and sink and marble sanitary ware. On the inside of the heavy brass-handled door hung a familiar coloured print, 'When did you last see your father?'

The following evening John introduced me to the other tenants, who lived in the top flat. Sylvia hadn't been married long, and her husband, Tom, was on leave from the merchant navy. He spent long periods at sea, but was on the point of giving it up. Like me they were in their early twenties.

* * *

There were only three of us at the workplace. A teenage apprentice who implied he wouldn't be staying long and my boss, who was only twelve months older than me.

The work turned out to be extremely hazardous. The equipment was often in a poor state of repair, but the worst thing of all was my fear of heights. I started smoking in an attempt to disguise my fear, getting up to forty a day on Capstan double strength. There were times when I felt physically sick, worrying that I might fall and get injured or even be killed. But I needed the money and I tried to convince myself it wouldn't be for long. Most frightening of all was a contraption consisting of two triple-extension ladders linked by a scaffold board and length of rope, with the board resting on the appropriately named cripples, metal brackets clipped on to the ladder rungs that have long been illegal. Working on this set-up and painting intricate lettering at first seemed impossible; it was like trying to thread a needle on a rocking boat.

Many of the signs were on solid mahogany, large, heavy and high up. The usual practice was to repaint them in situ, but if necessary they were removed and repainted in the workshop.

One day I was sent to a pub in Battersea with the young apprentice. We had to remove a large, heavy sign that was fixed to the brickwork four storeys high. We were on the flat roof immediately above the sign we had to remove. I had loosened the securing steel pegs so that I could get two rope slings around the back of the sign at both ends. The two ropes were then pulled around the chimneystack on our right to prevent the sign from falling to the ground too fast. The idea was that I would knock out the two remaining pegs so that only the ropes supported the sign. The apprentice would hold the ropes tight when the pegs were gone and I would then take his place, so that he could rush down the internal stairs and keep the public clear of the pavement. I would then gradually release the ropes around the chimney so that the sign would be gently lowered to the pavement.

'Hang on tight!' I warned the apprentice. 'I'm going to knock out the last peg. You might feel a tug, but then I'll take over the rope and you rush downstairs and keep the pavement clear while I lower the sign.'

'Okay.' He nodded hesitantly and I could see the fear on his face.

279

'I'll change places with you if you like. You can knock out the last pin if you prefer. I'm shitting bricks too, but we've got to get the job done.'

'I'll manage,' he muttered. The last peg stubbornly defied my attempts to knock it out. I was beginning to feel dizzy, what with my exertions and with looking at the ground below. I gave the crowbar one almighty whack with the mallet and quickly stepped out of the way as the rope whistled past my ankles.

I heard a yell and turned to see the apprentice about to disappear around the chimney. His eyes were bulging, there was blood on his shirt, and his arm was red and raw.

'Bloody hell! Hang on, hang on!'

I grabbed the ropes and wedged my full weight against the chimney. 'It's okay, I've got it! I've got it!' I gasped.

The apprentice stood studying his arm and dabbing it with his handkerchief.

'For Christ's sake!' I yelled, 'go down and keep the pavement clear of pedestrians. We don't want this falling on someone's head. Hurry! This is bloody heavy.' I gradually lowered the sign in short, jerky movements, which became easier as I got used to the weight.

'Don't let it swing into the pub window,' I shouted, suddenly aware that the movement was becoming more erratic and difficult to control. I strained my ears trying to hear his reply. Then I heard a loud thud, followed by a clattering noise. The rope went slack and everything went strangely quiet – even the traffic seemed to have stopped. I felt beads of sweat running down my forehead and my shirt was wringing wet. My mind was struggling with a horrible scenario as I nervously edged towards the parapet, still clutching the slack rope in my hands. I peered over the edge and sighed with relief on seeing the apprentice at the back of the van attending to his bloodstained arm. The sign had slipped out of the rope noose and had fallen just two metres from a railway track, buckling the iron railings.

'I'm sorry, Mate! I made a right pig's ear of that. I'll run you down to casualty. That looks nasty. Does it hurt?'

'Don't bother,' said the apprentice in a quivering voice. 'I've fucking had enough. I'm jacking it in and going home.'

'Yeah! But you ought to get a tetanus jab and get it looked at.'

'I'll manage.'

I gradually adjusted to the risk and fear levels, learning to occupy my mind with other thoughts. But one day while working off a ladder that was too short I overstretched – and the ladder lurched sideways. I dropped my palette and brushes and slid down the ladder, collecting splinters by the handful. I just managed to prevent the ladder from falling into the road.

My boss wasn't impressed when I told him the ladders were dangerous. 'You need proper scaffolding for those jobs. The work's bloody dangerous,' I said.

'Look, Gordon, you're the same as me in this. We've got two options – take it or leave it! Ladders are part of the job – you must have known that right at the start.'

I decided I'd leave when I'd found another job, but the man gave me a week's notice – with the promise of glowing testimonials if I needed them. The sense of elation and relief on realising I had no ladders to climb left me on cloud nine. Being unemployed seemed a minuscule worry in comparison.

* * *

My first six months in London had been disappointing. I found the place grey, cold and clammy, with thick, choking smog that often lingered all day. I was used to the pubs in Somerset where even as a total stranger you'd be greeted in a friendly way, but here it was very different. I was thankful for the company in my flat. Tom and Sylvia upstairs were very friendly, often inviting me to dinner. We would sit and watch the Flintstones on their television, which made me roar with laughter. John and Jenny were also friendly, inviting me downstairs for tea and biscuits and a good laugh. They enjoyed my stories about the ice-cream factory, flock spray and the Italian dentist who distilled his own whisky.

Even so I felt lonely. I needed to perk up my social life. With tongue in cheek I decided to advertise in a dating paper. At the time this was considered very infra dig, but to me it made sense. My advertisement brought a good response, ranging from fluffy teenagers to thirty-something divorcees. On reflection I realised my choice of words was misleading. 'A twenty-four year-old highly successful managing director wishes to meet,' etc. For the most part the applicants melted away very quickly when they realised that the reality didn't quite live up to the advertisement.

As one high-flyer put it, 'I had no idea what to expect; I've never done this sort of thing before. But if you're supposed to be a highly successful businessman, I'd hate to meet one on his uppers. A bag of chips and a trek round the park is not my idea of a night out. Goodbye.'

My next job was with Macleans Toothpaste as a stock checker and general dogsbody. The wages in London were much lower than I'd expected, and living costs very much higher, My stock checking wasn't very good either, according to the works manager. 'How on earth did you arrive at this figure, Gordon?' he demanded. 'According to your figures we have enough toothpaste to last half a century. We might as well shut the factory down and all go home.' I conceded my maths was a bit rusty and that I must have overdone the zeros. He demoted me, and thenceforward I was given the task of unloading sacks of chalk and other commodities. After one month I had muscles in places I never knew were there. I could feel my short-sleeved shirts cutting into my biceps.

Although my landlord John had a great sense of humour, there was one thing he took very seriously: the subject of money. Like everyone else I knew he seemed to be very short of the stuff. I told him it was cheaper to go to the cinema every night rather than feed silver into his finely adjusted electricity meter to keep warm. At that he straightened up his six-foot-something frame and said with an unsympathetic grin, 'Make the most of it, Mate, because I'm putting the rent up soon and you won't have any money for feeding meters.' On the plus side he said he was going to decorate my rooms in nice warm-looking colours to compensate for the odd bout of shivering.

'Anyway,' he said, 'what's the idea of using my address as your head office for Flockspray Products? I should be charging you a commercial rent for that.' My idea had been to generate a bit of interest, get some sales going, then try and sell it.

'Well, I'll tell you what, John, when I sell Flockspray I'll stick another one of those blue plaques on your wall saying the managing director of Flockspray stayed here at colossal cost and died of pneumonia.'

Jenny was more sympathetic, and suggested I might like to get someone to share the flat with me. 'After all', she said, 'it's a big flat to be rattling around in on your own, and we won't mind.'

Jenny's parents lived across the road; they were very kind and often invited me over for coffee. Her younger sister Chris also lived with them. She was an attractive girl and I really fancied her, but she had a boyfriend who used to call for her regularly on his motorbike. She asked me to teach her to drive, as she'd noticed I was teaching Tom upstairs.

John and Jenny started to decorate my rooms, and it became apparent that neither had much idea about DIY. The constant dust irritated me, with putty and wallpaper all over the place, and it looked as though it was going to be a long operation. Jenny cunningly tried to get me to help, and asked what colour I would like the kitchen and breakfast room to be painted.

'I'm not bothered; whatever you're comfortable with,' I said.

I considered offering to help, but I knew that immediately the decorating was finished my rent would increase.

Tracey was my last remaining date from my dating advertisement. She was a buxom, peroxide Diana Dors blonde in her late teens, with pouty lips and a determination to enjoy herself. She was becoming impatient. I couldn't invite her back to my place as it was covered in dust, putty and paint everywhere.

'Why don't you come over to my house?' she whispered, nibbling my ear. 'Dad is working nights this month and you could stay till five o'clock in the morning.'

'What, you mean a pyjama job?'

'Yes! But you'll have to take them off,' she giggled.

I hadn't had any fun for quite a while and her invitation was just what I needed to pep up my life a bit.

She lived well out in the countryside, with no street lighting. The whole area was completely black. My car headlights were the only source of light, which gave a ghostly eeriness to the place. 'Park further down under those trees, and don't slam the door,' she whispered.

'Are you sure this is all right? What about your mother?'

'Stop worrying,' she teased, pinching my bum, 'nothing will wake her up. She's worse than me. I'm starving. What about you?' she asked, pulling out the frying pan once we were in the house.

'Well, if you're sure...'

'Egg and sausage?' she said, coyly undoing the buttons on her blouse.

'Yum, yum,' I stuttered, scarcely able to contain myself as her bra fell to the ground.

I sat drooling over the prospect of bedding her as she slowly undid her skirt, gyrating her thighs and juggling her ample breasts. I reached forward to grab her panties.

'Now, now, be patient, Sweetie! Let me finish the frying.'

'Bugger the frying, I want...'

There was a deep guttural harrumphing and throat clearing from upstairs.

'Jesus! Who the hell is that?' I gulped. 'That can't be your mother.'

'Hell! It's my Dad. We better get out,' Tracey said, rapidly donning her clothes. 'Quick! Shove the egg and sausages in some bread; we'll take it with us.'

We dashed back to the car and sat panting in the back seat. 'Phew! That was close. My Mum definitely said he was on nights this week.'

'Ouch! Ooh… Oh sod it.'

'What's up?'

'Bloody hot fat… Oh no! My new shirt is ruined. Grab these sausages; they're burning my nuts. God! It's all over my trousers as well.'

'They'll clean up. I'll rinse them through if you like. I can borrow a pair of Dad's trousers; it won't take long.'

'It's okay; I'll sort it when I get back.'

There was something else bothering me. 'Tracey, was that a helmet I saw in the hall?'

'Yes.'

'Your father, he isn't a policeman, is he?

'Well, yes he is.'

'That's nice. That's bloody great! Why didn't you tell me?'

'Well having a policeman for a dad is a bit of a turn-off for most of you blokes. But my Dad's all right. He's not like some of them, you know.'

'Tracey you're so naive! Can you imagine how he'd react if he caught us humping on the kitchen table? "D'you take sugar, Lad? Want another sarnie?" Like hell. "Want to borrow my trousers, Lad?" He'd grill me with these pork sausages; I can't bear to think of it.'

* * *

The toothpaste job came to an end and my finances became so stretched that I had to go to the pawnshop in order to pay my rent. It was a humiliating experience standing in a wire-caged cubicle grovelling to get the maximum return for my limited assets.

I did a deal with a bombsite car dealer in Ealing. His site was conveniently situated and I passed it each day on my way to work. I knew it was a risky thing to do and I could almost hear Joe's voice screaming in my head, 'Gordon you fool – don't do it.' I handed over my car and signed the hire purchase forms. I drove away in my new acquisition, a horribly cramped Morris eight. About half a mile later I made the worrying discovery that my new car couldn't do a left turn. The leaf suspension was badly damaged and it turned about six degrees but no further. If I therefore wanted to make a left turn, I had to drive past, turn around, and take it as a right turning.

The proprietor of the bombsite garage was a chunky, fast-talking man with a Burberry coat who stood with a cigar welded to his lower lip. He sighed with disinterest at my ranting and raving, puffing a cloud of smoke into my face, and signalled to one of his cauliflower-eared henchman to relieve him of the aggravation.

'Look Matey! The Boss don't like people shouting at him; he gets upset. And when he gets upset, so do we, so piss off while you can still walk.'

'Don't you threaten me. I'll call the police. It's illegal to sell a car in an unroadworthy condition like that. I want my Rover back.'

'The boss has sold it!'

I was seething with rage and almost on the point of smacking him in the mouth. I'd bought the small car on HP and paid part of the cash for the Rover as the deposit.

'I won't be paying the hire purchase for that heap of junk, and you can whistle for your money.'

His two henchmen squeezed up against me, making a human sandwich. The more aggressive one pushed his face into mine.

'We have a solution for that little problem; we come and take the car away. Now get your arse out of here.'

'Not another penny and you won't get the car either – that's a promise,' I shouted.

The Morris eight continued to give me a lot of aggravation and I was getting fed up with London. It was too expensive; it was impossible to park anywhere; and I was finding it a thoroughly depressing place to live in. I persevered with the steering problem, preferring the inconvenience of not being able to turn left rather than cough up for the eye-watering cost of repairing the problem that I had been quoted.

Tracey was appalled by my new car, and thought it was a right comedown from the Rover.

'It's like sitting in a shoebox,' she complained. 'So where we going?'

'I thought we'd go down to the river and have a picnic. There's a dance at the YMCA in Putney in the evening. Maybe we'll have a couple of drinks and relax in my place. How does that sound? By the way, what happened the other night with the hasty fry up? My shirt was a write-off.'

'Look where you're going... Gordon! That bus driver is signalling you.'

'It's all right. I've seen him. So... you were saying?'

'Oh yeah! Well, nothing really. I went back and it was all dark. I cleaned up and put everything away, then went to bed. No problem. Then I heard them arguing at breakfast. Mum swore she had bought some sausages for dinner and thought Dad must have eaten them. Dad started swearing at her: "No I didn't! You silly daft moo, you probably left them in the bloody butcher's. You're always losing things." I felt a bit guilty over that,' she giggled.

'Can you wind your window down, Tracey? It's getting hot in here. It looks as though there's another traffic jam brewing. It gets worse week after week. Hang on a minute, I'll have a look and see what the hold-up is. Oh no! We've got a real problem; I've got to try and turn the car round somehow.'

'Hey! What're you doing?'

'There's a policeman up front who's making all the traffic turn left at the river. This car doesn't turn left.'

'Doesn't turn left? What d'you mean? Why not?'

'The leaf suspension is busted; it's going to the garage on Tuesday. If I can get right over the other side of the road, I might just manage a diagonal left.'

The driver in the car behind started to hoot its horn, then closed the gap so I couldn't reverse. Then a car came flying at me from the other direction sounding its horn. In no time at all we had mayhem. The policeman's eyes grew larger by the second and his arm paused in mid-air as my car gently edged towards his kneecaps.

Tracey pushed her head out of the window and yelled at the constable, "Scuse me! This car doesn't turn left!'

The constable removed his helmet and pushed his head inside the window. His eyes still flickered with the fear that he was going to be run over. 'What do you mean, this car doesn't turn left?'

'Well I turned the wheel and it wouldn't go left,' I said.

'Hmm... Can you turn right?'

'Oh yeah! No problem.'

'Okay. Park over there on the grass verge. I'll have a word with you later.'

We waited and waited. The temperature soared. The policeman kept waving all the traffic to the left with no further problems. Tracey fidgeted, perspired, and got angry, threatening to have words with the policeman. 'He's taking the piss,' she said.

'No, don't do that; you'll only annoy him, and he'll take it out on me.'

'Well I'm not spending the bank holiday in this piddling little bathtub. I can hardly move, and it's like an oven in here. Fancy having a car that doesn't turn left! It's ridiculous; I've never heard anything like it. Sod it! I've had enough and I'm going home. Don't bother ringing me – we're finished.'

'Hey, steady on Trace...' But she got out of the car and slammed the door. I watched her striding away with a defiant sideways glance at the traffic constable, who paused to ogle her shapely retreating figure with a smile.

Soon afterwards the policeman came over grinning. 'Can't turn left, is that right?'

'That's right, I can't turn left.'

'So why not?'

I realised I had to be careful with my answer as any suggestion of it being a long-standing problem wouldn't be helpful. I needed to be apologetic and totally ignorant about anything to do with cars. I gave the constable a look of total surprise.

'I just don't know what happened. I turned the wheel to the left but it just kept going straight. It was really terrifying.'

'Hmm... You've got a serious problem there. You'd better get it to a garage and get it sorted. You can't drive around like that. So you haven't had a very good bank holiday?' he said, grinning like a Cheshire cat.

'Bloody awful!' I groaned.

'What happened to your blonde lady friend?'

'She got fed up and went home.'

'Oh dear! So we've really messed up your bank holiday,' he chuckled.

'Yep! Still, we weren't serious. I didn't fancy her much anyway – she's the daughter of a policeman.'

The policeman's grin vanished and his eyes hardened. 'Get this heap into the garage, clever dick. I'll be keeping a lookout for you.'

* * *

'Cheer up Gordon! Where's that big beamy smile of yours?' said Jenny. 'We'll be painting your rooms over the weekend. John has bought a job lot of emulsion. We've got enough to do our place as well. It's a lovely blush cream.'

'It's a *what*?'

'Blush cream. It looks really nice; you'll like it.'

'Jenny, I hate blush cream ... I hate it.'

'What do you mean? What's the matter with you?'

'It's unlucky!'

'That's ridiculous! John has bought it. How can paint be unlucky? By the way, we had a chap came round about your advert to share the flat. He's going to call this evening.'

Ron described himself as a sales team leader.

'So what d'you actually sell?' I asked.

'Anything – absolutely anything. At the moment we're doing a big push on vacuum cleaners.'

I showed him around and pointed to the large sideboard in the breakfast room. 'There's no fridge so I use that as a pantry. I'll put my food in the left compartment and you put yours in the right, if that's okay with you.'

'I won't be around a lot; I do a lot of travelling. So what do you do?' he enquired with interest.

'I'm between jobs at the moment. I've a couple of interviews next week.'

Tom in the upstairs flat had only been in his packaging job for six weeks when he gave Sylvia the bad news that he had been made redundant. He wanted to go straight to the labour exchange in Brixton and sign on to get the dole money.

'Why don't you come, Gordon?' he said. 'It beats going to the pawnbrokers. You're entitled to it. Come with me and sign on.'

I'd never been on the dole and I wasn't very keen, remembering my only other attempt to sign on five years earlier. There was a long queue at Brixton labour exchange, mainly West Indians who'd been encouraged by Colonel Lipton, the local MP, to come to England to fill job vacancies on the buses and railways. We queued for hours, and when I finally arrived at a cubicle a woman told me that I wasn't eligible for unemployment benefit as I'd previously been self-employed and would have to reapply in six months. Tom couldn't believe it and neither could I.

Just when things were looking really bad and I thought I would have to cash in Joe's insurance policy, give up the flat and move into lodgings, I had a stroke of luck. My advertisement to sell the flock spray business came up trumps. An accountant in Fulham was interested but wouldn't be hurried into making a quick decision.

'I'm an extremely careful sort of person, and I want to make a thorough inspection of the books, stock and client base. I'll let you know in one month if I'm still interested,' he said.

I feigned a casual, not-too-bothered attitude, and suggested I'd leave the whole business with him, stock, books, client base and everything else, on the basis he paid me a twenty-five-pound refundable security deposit. He hummed and hawed, but finally agreed. Several weeks later he telephoned to say he might be interested and was prepared to pay cash if I would accept six bubblegum machines and some stock as part payment.

He told me the bubble-gum machines had a massive potential, were the up and coming thing, and that I could make a lot of money. The deal was done after the guy did some furtive gymnastics in his front room to disguise the secret safe set into the wall.

'I'd like to give you a bit of advice, Mr Aspey,' he said with a lofty smile. 'When selling a business, never leave your books and client base with a prospective purchaser. You leave yourself wide open to getting fleeced.'

'Blimey! I'll have to remember that,' I said. 'Still, I'm only a learner you know.'

I thanked him for the advice, counted the money and made a hasty exit, knowing he'd made a mistake.

I was scrambling to get into my car when he yelled out of the window, 'Just a minute!' and came rushing down the stairs. 'I've overpaid you,' he said. I forgot to deduct the twenty-five pounds deposit.'

'Yeah! You made a mistake there. So what d'you reckon I should do?'

He paused, gaping with disbelief. 'Well, give it back to me, of course. You should have told me. You were obviously aware of my mistake; that's why you were in such a hurry to get away.'

'We all make mistakes. I made one earlier, as you told me. I think it's accepted practice in business that we have to pay for our mistakes. I've got an idea – why don't I pay you half the money back and you put the other half down to experience?'

'Sod that!' he snapped. 'That's stealing. That's my money and I want it back.'

I didn't feel comfortable driving off. I gave him half the money back, and reckoned he had good cause to feel disgruntled, but his inflexible stuck up attitude got up my nose. He confirmed what I'd felt for some time, that accountants are the worst people in the world when it comes to money.

22

Tom told me that he was a bit suspicious of Ron, my new flatmate. 'There's something not quite right about that bloke, Gordon. I was in the flat reading a book when I saw a shadow pass the door. There was no sound ... it was uncanny. I rushed out and couldn't see anything. I looked over the banister and saw his head passing underneath. Although I can't be absolutely certain it was Ron because it happened so quickly, I'm almost positive it was. The thing that amazed me was the speed he went down those stairs – like a greyhound – and not a sound.'

There were other things about Ron that were beginning to annoy me. There was never any food on his side of the cupboard, and he was helping himself to my rations. Several times I'd come back late to an empty cupboard – with not even a slice of bread. I was determined to have it out with him. The trouble was he was never in the flat long enough. Luckily there was a small grocer's store in Brixton that unofficially used to stay open day and night where you could always get something to eat.

One of the treats I used to enjoy at my foster mother's was her treacle puddings. I just loved them. Late one night while buying groceries from a West Indian shop in Brixton, I spotted a tinned treacle pudding and decided I deserved a treat. I had it heating up on the gas stove when Jenny called up the stairs, 'Phone! Gordon!'

The phone call lasted longer than expected – a mild argument with a prospective partner in a new business venture. I was still on the phone when there was an almighty bang.

'What the hell was that?' said John, racing up the stairs. He paused at my kitchen door. 'Good grief! Come and look at this, Jenny.'

The saucepan, now a grotesque mangled shape, lay in the middle of the floor, and treacle pudding had been scattered to every corner of the extensive kitchen.

'What a dreadful mess!' screamed Jenny. 'Look at all our work; it's absolutely ruined. I'm really cross with you, Gordon. You'll have to pay for it.'

'I'll redo it,' I said without much conviction. 'I'm really sorry; I forgot to punch a hole in the tin. Mind you, I told you blush cream was unlucky.'

* * *

One of my prize possessions was a second-hand voice recorder, one of the early ones made by Sound. I had used it twice to raise money at the pawnshop. The instructions were complicated and difficult to follow, but I'd had a bit of fun with it. I secretly recorded the antics of a house party game with John, Jenny, Tom, Sylvia and myself. We each had to give an authoritative talk on a subject for four minutes. I remember that I was a founder member of the Flat Earth Society, John a veterinary surgeon with a mock-Chinese accent, Tom a bus inspector, and Sylvia a dental receptionist. The recording was a hoot, far funnier than the real thing, and I intended to surprise them with it.

While playing it through I discovered sections of it were missing and there was a lot of gobbledygook, scratching noises and different voices. I realised somebody had been tampering with it.

Then I heard Ron's voice, 'Yeah, it belongs to the jerk I share the flat with.'

'What's it worth, d'you reckon?' said the other voice.

'Dunno, maybe twenty quid top wack,' said Ron. The voices started to fade and I turned the volume to maximum. I picked up Ron's voice again, 'Well, her old man's over six foot tall. He's away a lot, but she's a good shag. I've got a date with her sister across the road. She's quite tasty.' Then the voices faded out altogether. I stood in a daze, hardly able to believe what I'd heard. There couldn't be any doubt he was talking about John and Jenny and her sister Chris.

How could they fancy such an ugly weasel like Ron, let alone have sex with him? I thought of Chris, such an attractive girl with a lovely personality – surely not! It must be hot air or wishful thinking. Her parents would be apoplectic, and so would her boy friend.

I spoke to Tom upstairs, who confirmed that he already knew Ron and Jenny were having sex. Then I told him about the tape recording and how Ron was supposed to be having a date with Chris. 'He's such an ugly bleeder; what can she possibly see in him?'

'Beats me,' said Tom, 'but I'm not too surprised. I think they're both a bit on the flighty side. I don't understand women; they're so complicated and unpredictable. I've given up trying.' He squinted towards Sylvia in the kitchen. 'You had two visitors last night, Gordon. A right pair of dodgy characters, bent noses, cauliflower ears, the lot. They wanted your car.'

'Oh blimey. There could be a bit of trouble brewing there. It's in the garage at the moment having its springs done. The bastards. They should have done that themselves.'

'I spun them a yarn, I told them you'd gone on a ten-pound ticket to Australia.'

'They'd never believe that, Tom, but I like the idea.'

'Gordon, you forget that I was in the merchant navy for eight years. I gave them a lot of information about sailing times, your cabin number, and I showed them some of my paperwork. They asked if I knew anything about your car. I said it had been taken to the police compound pending an enquiry. I said it was involved in a serious accident, something to do with the steering, and that that was why you'd scarpered. That seemed to unsettle them a bit and they left in a hurry. I think you might just get away with it. They weren't O level material; in fact they looked a bit gaga.'

'I'm very impressed, Tom; you're a born storyteller. I don't fancy a rough and tumble with those two. They wouldn't stick to the Queensberry rules. Thanks, Mate, I owe you.'

* * *

It was the Whitsun bank holiday in 1959 when I first met Babs. On the day when Tracey dumped me, I tried to get into the YMCA dance during the evening. The bolshie attendant refused me entry, saying that the dance was only for couples and that it was anyway too crowded. I went to a pub a short distance up the road with the intention of trying to sneak in later. Then I heard music on the other side of the road and noticed a large banner stretched across the church wall: The Ewell and Cheam Scooter Club dance.

Babs was taller than average with shoulder-length fair hair. She wore an emerald-green dress with a bright yellow cardigan. She reminded me of a daffodil stretching towards the sun. Her manner seemed relaxed and natural, and she appealed to me immediately. Not a beauty queen but a striking freshness unsullied by lipstick or mascara. We shuffled around the crowded dance floor to the music of Mantovani, with the obligatory question-and-answer charade that two people play when they first meet.

I established that she was an ophthalmic optician, and that she worked in her dad's practice in Peckham Rye, south London.

'So what do you do?' she enquired with a shy smile and honest grey eyes that demanded the truth.

'I'm unemployed.'

'Oh,' she said.

'But I've a couple of interviews next week.'

'Good luck with them,' she said, and smiled. 'What sort of scooter do you have?'

'Scooter ... me? No, no, I don't reckon scooters; I think they're dangerous. I've got a car.'

A look of mild irritation came over her face as she retorted, 'So what are you doing here if you don't like scooters? I think they're marvellous. You have fresh air, they're economical, and you don't have parking problems.'

As I was leaving I saw her get into a newish Standard Pennant saloon. I suddenly decided I wanted to try and date her. I tapped on the window. 'So what sort of a scooter is this, then?'

'It's my Dad's car,' she laughed. 'I've got a Lambretta.'

'How about a date next week?'

'You don't believe in hanging about, do you.'

'Is that a yes or no?'

'Okay, why not? Wait a minute and I'll give you my phone number.'

* * *

Ron apologised for messing about with my recording machine. This was very unlike him, but he was really piling on the smarm so that he could borrow my car. He also apologised for scoffing my rations. 'I'll tell you what, Gordon, I've been well out of order. I'd like to make amends. Why don't I get a bottle of Scotch, some best rump steak and chips, and we'll make right pigs of ourselves?'

'I think that's the least you can do after calling me a jerk.'

After the third glass of whisky he confessed to having it off with Jenny, going into lurid details that, had she heard what he was saying, would have left her munching her handbag with embarrassment. He followed this up with more rapturous details of another gorgeous blonde girl not a million miles away who had fallen for his charms – whom he was bedding across the road. The whisky lubricant reached a climax when he slapped me on the back in a 'you're my Mate' fashion, and asked, 'Is there any chance I could borrow your car over the weekend? I promised this bird I'd give her some driving lessons.'

I gave him a polite refusal. 'Not a chance, Ron. The insurance people won't allow it.'

'Oh, come on, Mate. I'll pay extra for the insurance.'

'Sorry Ron, no can do.'

John also wanted to borrow my car. 'It's such a business,' he complained, 'me and Jenny staggering around with the shopping on a Saturday, waiting for a bus.'

'Sorry John, it's the insurance; it's a real problem.'

'No, you're all right there, Gordon. My insurance covers it.'

'Well, I don't know, John. I tell you what, though, why don't I pick you up when you've done your shopping? Just phone and I'll come straight over.'

'I'd rather borrow the car, Gordon. It's not much to ask, is it? How're you getting on with redecorating my kitchen?'

I was sick of blush cream and bloody treacle pudding. Everything I touched seemed to have a sticky film of treacle on it. 'Oh, all right then.'

Late in the afternoon John came into the breakfast room with a downcast look on his face.

'What's up, John? Had a row with Jenny?'

'No, it's your car, Mate,'

'Oh no! What's up with it?'

'It's only a small dent, and it's okay because it was his fault. It was an ice-cream van, and he was coming the wrong way down a one-way street.'

'Have you got the company name and details? Your insurance company will want that,' I said, hurrying down the stairs.

'Oh yeah! No problem there. There's only one snag, though...'

'What's that?'

'Well, I've only got a motorbike licence, so I might have a problem claiming off my insurance. But if you say you were driving at the time, you could claim off your insurance, and then there'd be no problem.'

'For fuck's sake, John, I can't do that. The driver will know it wasn't me.' I could see a lot of grief over this.

When we got to my car I exploded. 'Jesus! Is that what you call a small dent, John? The front's mangled. It's nearly a write-off.'

'Don't exaggerate, Gordon. Let's get down to the ice-cream company's offices and sort things out.'

The management denied all responsibility. 'We ain't got no vans in the area,' said the manager, 'and we don't know nothing about any accidents. You must be mistaken.'

I couldn't help feeling that Ralph at the Westward Ice Cream Company in Bridgwater would benefit from a manager like him. He was totally dismissive of any suggestion that his company was responsible for the write-off of my car. He hitched up his trousers over his beer belly, watching John's dance of wrath with mild interest as though he was watching advertisements in the local cinema.

'No you've got it wrong, me old Mate,' he said, dragging hard on his cigarette, 'it weren't my van.'

'What a toad,' fumed John. 'He knows it was his van.'

'So what we going to do about the damage, John? I don't mind doing the paintwork, if you pay for the panel repairs.'

'I can't agree to that, Gordon. I reckon it's even stevens: you messed my kitchen and I bounced your car.'

'Jesus, John, there's a hell of a lot of difference in the sums. All that damage compared to your bit of crappy blush bleeding cream.'

The end result was a stalemate.

* * *

After the Whitsun dance I had my first date with Babs, and we seemed to get on well enough. I wasn't interested in the glamorous type that plays havoc on building sites; previous experience had cured me of that. Neither did I believe in the misty-eyed 'love at first sight'. Though not ready for marriage, my thoughts for the future were directed towards a more practical relationship. My experience of life, and the misery and deprivation experienced by my young mother, had taught me the need for a solid base to build upon. I would only get married to a woman who had the ability to support herself and not be dependent on me. Babs was an only child living with her parents in the stockbroker belt in Ewell. Her father was a bully who dominated mother and daughter, and it was clear they were afraid of him.

My appearance was greeted with unfettered disdain. 'Who are you?' Babs's father at once made it clear he didn't like me. He had suffered with gas poisoning during the First World War and took an assortment of pills for chronic arthritis. His main interest was playing cards with a couple of his regular cronies, and he had a surprising talent for conjuring tricks despite his arthritic hands. My acceptance in the household was measured in percentages, which tended to go down most of the time, although I had the odd blip in my favour. One of the positives was a clever joke about a Rolls Royce, which he utilised to good effect at a Rotary Club dinner.

* * *

There was huge excitement when Ron was discovered in Chris's bed by Jenny and their parents. Their mother screamed at John and Jenny, demanding to know how long the sordid business had been going on. Jenny had a few problems of her own with her liaison with Ron and didn't like being dumped for her sister. She knew she was on perilous ground. The mother stormed into my flat demanding a few facts from me. She prodded her finger angrily into my chest.

'Are you trying to tell me you know nothing about all this, Gordon? Do you really walk around this place with your eyes closed? I'm disgusted with you, after inviting you over last Christmas and you accepting our hospitality. So this is how you treat me.'

'You're being very unreasonable,' I argued. 'Ron is rarely here, and I genuinely didn't know he was sleeping with Chris. Anyway, it's none of my business.'

'You're all liars, all of you,' she yelled, slamming the front door with an almighty crash.

Ron took Chris away to Ireland for a holiday and gave her a huge emerald engagement ring. On their return they moved into a commune. According to later conversations with Tom and Sylvia he was arrested for burglary and got three years. The engagement ring was part of his last haul before going to

Ireland. It turned out he was a professional burglar with previous convictions and a lengthy record.

I moved out of the flat and rented rooms at Dulwich so that I could be nearer my work at an exhibition firm at Crystal Place, where I was now working on point of sale signs that later went bust.

23

I landed a job with Rootes Commercial Vehicles at Ladbroke Hall in London in October 1959. The job was a real joy. There were no ladders to climb, nothing to fear, and I had my own workshop with all the facilities I could possibly need. I just sat on my backside all day, with palette, sables and mahl stick, signwriting vans and lorries. It was a really cushy job.

The only worry was the emphasis on punctuality. Any individual late for work on two consecutive mornings would be instantly dismissed. Babs's enthusiasm for a scooter rubbed off on me and I decided to give it a try, so I bought one to try and maintain better punctuality, and weave in and out of the burgeoning traffic jams. But fear returned with a vengeance. Whizzing back and forth across London in the rush hour was a nightmare. Sometimes I even went up on the pavement to avoid an impatient and angry motorist who seemed to regard anything on two wheels as a menace and appeared to be trying to introduce a culling operation. I soon reverted to the car.

A colleague and I set up a small part-time business selling old bangers. The idea was that we would jointly purchase the cars, and he would use his expertise to sort out the mechanics while I would do the paintwork and cosmetics.

We came to grief on the first purchase. He had trouble finding his half of the purchase price, and reckoned it would be best to deduct his half from the profit.

'No way!' I argued. 'That means I take a hundred per cent of the risk. It's fifty-fifty profit and loss, or nothing.'

My colleague promised he'd give me a bad time if I tried to cut him out of the operation – and he did. I bought a Standard Drophead Coupé that couldn't be relied on to get from one end of the street to the other. It kept cutting out every ten minutes or so. I eventually discovered he had been putting little tufts of cotton wool in the tank that got sucked up into the fuel supply. Sometimes the cotton wool would drop back when the engine stopped, making it difficult to diagnose the problem. I managed to stop these antics by fitting a locking fuel cap. Shortly afterwards the fuel consumption soared alarmingly. I discovered this was due to a small hole made in the fuel tank, which had the effect of leaving a neat trail of combustible fuel following me around – just waiting for someone to chuck a fag end out of the window and blow me and the Standard sky high. My stock of bubble gum, which, in spite of what I'd been told by the disgruntled accountant, didn't seem to be all the rage, came to the rescue. It required some heavy-duty chewing before becoming sufficiently pliable to effect a temporary repair. A more satisfactory and permanent repair was achieved with a couple of kettle washers and Bostik filler, which worked a treat.

* * *

Babs's parents were going abroad on holiday, and I thought it would be a good time to extend the kiss-and-cuddle routine. Babs had displayed the same elusive characteristics as Renee.

'D'you fancy a name change?' I asked.

'What's this? Is it your idea of a romantic proposal of marriage?'

'Well I'm not much of a romantic, but I can promise you an action-packed future, and a choice of names. How d'you fancy Mrs Barbara Aspey, or Barbara Uphill, or maybe a nice double-barrelled moniker like Barbara Aspidistra-Aspey-Gordononi-Uphill?'

'I like things nice and simple. Let's drop the Uphill – it sounds too much like hard work. I'll settle for plain old Aspey; that'll be fine. So, do I get a nice, chunky engagement ring?'

'Huh? Of course. I'll make an appointment with Aspreys.'

'There's no need to be sarcastic. What sort of a proposal is that? With not even an engagement ring.'

'All in good time, Babs.'

'Dad's going to go mad when he returns from holiday; he really doesn't like you.'

'There are times when I don't like me! But I've learnt to lump it, and so can he.'

I thought my proposal of marriage, coupled with her parent's absence, might open the gates for a rehearsal. My previous attempts had been tactfully sidestepped and this time, too, her Victorian upbringing prevailed – she locked me in the kitchen all night.

Her parents' holiday abroad did nothing to endear me to them when they were told of their daughter's impending marriage.

Her father asked me how much money I had in the bank. I was so gobsmacked by his audacity that I could only manage the much-delayed answer of, 'Would you like to see a bank statement?'

He insisted I should have asked his permission, and said he would cut her out of his will if she went ahead with the marriage – and did so. Her mother also expressed disappointment, by saying, 'Babs, you could have done so much better, dear.' Unlike her husband she'd always been polite to me without displaying any real enthusiasm – 'It's lovely to see you Gordon' – but I was shocked and angry at such a withering statement. As I had no relatives and being very short of friends, I asked Tom and Sylvia to be my representative duo at the registry office, and to try and balance things up at the reception.

There were some concerns as to whether I would turn up for the wedding. We had arranged to get married on 16 November 1959. Babs's father had told everybody it was a waste of time and wouldn't last six months, Tom confessed he had some doubts about me being the marrying sort of bloke, while Babs was getting concerned, despite my assurances. The latter devised a plan to ensure I turned up at Epsom registry office.

'Auntie Freda needs a lift to the wedding, as Uncle is unwell. Can you give her a lift? You can stay at her house overnight.'

The journey to the registry office did not go smoothly. Auntie Freda was accustomed to a better class of transport. Her observation that the tax disc was out of date was rapidly superseded by the more pointed remark of, 'You're going the wrong way!'

Things got worse. During a three-point turn the exhaust pipe embedded itself into a muddy bank, causing the engine to stop. All efforts to restart it failed, and Auntie Freda's voice went up several octaves as she cried out, 'Gordon! We're going to be awfully late!'

After scooping handfuls of mud out of the exhaust pipe I finally persuaded the engine to stutter into life. Meanwhile, Auntie Freda had signalled to a heavy goods lorry with a give-us-a-lift sign. The lorry driver reversed his vehicle to give us assistance but, realising I had managed to start the car, gave us a friendly thumbs-up and accelerated away, enveloping us in an enormous black cloud of choking diesel fumes. Auntie Freda coughed her lungs up.

'You're a bad lad, Gordon. I feel like a criminal, driving around like this. I hope the police don't stop us.'

'Sorry about that, but it was a toss-up as whether to buy a suit, or tax and insure the car. I couldn't afford to do both.'

'Oh no,' she groaned, gazing at my smart new suit, and then spent the rest of the journey looking nervously over her shoulder fearing the police.

Our honeymoon was short. Babs's father thought one day off work was quite enough time for us to sign a document and for me to shove a ring on his daughter's finger. My manager at work had not been very generous either. Instead of congratulating me and wishing me well for the future, he had said, 'Oh no! Do you have to get married *now*? We're very busy. Can't you leave it for a couple of weeks? We've got to get this Joe Lyons contract sorted.'

After we'd got married we went to the pictures to see Alistair Sim and Ian Carmichael in *School for Scoundrels*, which had us busting our sides with laughter.

The following day the police were called to my workshop. A lorry that I'd been signwriting at my workplace in Rootes, which was bound for the Earls Court commercial vehicle show, had a serious problem. The driver thought the battery was flat when the engine wouldn't start, but further investigation that revealed that somebody had stolen the batteries. There was worse to follow: a gaping great hole where the engine used to be. The driver was apoplectic.

'That's impossible,' he exclaimed. 'How can anyone pinch an eight-cylinder Dodge engine, for fuck's sake?'

There was, however, a light-fingered contingent, which I knew about – although I was never involved with it – that was blessed with the power of such magic. They could supply anything from a pair of Hush Puppies to a lawnmower at unbeatable prices, although the mystery of the Dodge engine and batteries was never resolved.

Babs's father had an accident with his Standard Pennant car. He knocked over and killed a twelve-year-old boy on his bicycle. The parents were distraught with grief and came to his house to complain about the verdict of accidental death, but all he did was shrug his shoulders and say, 'The verdict is confirmed – it was accidental death.' Having a police inspector for a neighbour and being a Grand Master Freemason were thought to have been helpful in his defence. I was appalled at his apparent lack of remorse and his inability to show compassion to the grieving parents.

They might have gained some small consolation from knowing that he had contracted lung cancer and that he died soon afterwards. Just before his death in late December 1962, he confessed that expressing emotion wasn't easy for him. He also apologised to me, admitting that his behaviour had been deplorable.

* * *

It was during the late 1950s when house buying started to take off. At that time there were few properties for sale. Those that were on the market were often owned by the large insurance companies as leaseholds, and they tended to get snapped up quickly. I had been against buying a house, on the basis that everything was being made in plastic, from football studs to motorcars. I thought the price of houses was set to tumble and reckoned it was initially better to rent a place and see how the market went.

Our first experience of a really greedy landlord soon changed our plans, however. Babs rang the owner of a terraced house in Balham that was selling for £2,500 with a thirty-five year lease. He told her there were forty people interested and that he would make a decision at seven o'clock that evening about who he thought the most deserving.

We devised a plan to milk the human kindness thing.

Babs, heavily pregnant, would concentrate on being the wife, sticking out her belly a bit further than she really needed to and acting a bit weepy, saying we were being evicted by a greedy landlord. I would concentrate on acting the husband – I would give him a cheque for fifty pounds and tell him we didn't need to look over the property, we just loved the place and wanted to buy it. This wasn't the usual way of doing things, and there was some risk attached. But I thought that the offer of cash in hand might be a big enough temptation to swing things our way.

My confidence evaporated somewhat when we witnessed the continuous stream of people going back and forth. I decided to act fast and sidelined the husband in the kitchen. 'I know it's not the normal procedure,' I said, pulling out my cheque book, 'but we don't need to view the property. We just love the place.'

He looked over my shoulder as I wrote out a cheque for fifty pounds.

'Hmm… I'll have a word with my wife,' he said, practically snatching the cheque out of my hand. 'I can't promise, but I think it'll be all right.'

Shortly afterwards Babs came into the front room beaming all over her face.

'It's ours,' she whispered. We couldn't believe our luck. We celebrated with a slap-up Indian supper on the way home.

'There you are!' I boasted. 'Sometimes the unconventional approach can be a winner.'

With only two weeks to go before exchanging contracts I nearly had to eat my words. The local council rejected our mortgage application, leaving us in a very precarious position. I was livid. I'd spent hours on the phone trying to find out why we'd been rejected, all to no avail, and I was about to lose my deposit. At the last possible moment I managed to get a mortgage with a small building society at a higher rate of interest. Babs was nervous about some of my answers on the building society's application form.

'You can't say that! Or that. And we certainly don't earn as much as that.'

'They're forms, for God's sake,' I argued. 'These people lend money and charge immoral interest. Most of these questions are none of their business. If we jumped through all the hoops like they want us to, we'd never get a mortgage.'

We finally bought the house and moved in on 12 November 1960. We had a bad scare when Babs had a haemorrhage and was told she would have to go into hospital to have a scrape. The nursing sister, however, advised against the procedure, saying the baby was okay. Victor was born a month later on 13 December 1960, nearly two weeks premature. He was a fine, healthy lad with a great thumping heartbeat, which was why we called him Victor.

24

One of the first things we discovered with our very own terraced house was that you get neighbours, usually one on either side. The retired schoolteacher on our left gave us her version of the rules of the road: 'You mustn't park your car outside our house as my son often comes to see me.' She also said, ' Don't light bonfires in the garden. I find the smoke most offensive.'

Our neighbour on the right was a retired major with lingering memories of the Battle of the Somme, and he had an equally strict rulebook. He had a penchant for painting rockery stones white, and flowers had to be of uniform height. Weeds were subjected to verbal abuse and violent dismemberment. He wanted me to remove all the dandelions from my garden as the seeds blew into his plot, thus creating needless labour for him. And he also asked me not to park outside his house.

Although Babs and I were both working – we employed a babysitter to look after Victor –and we let out the upstairs rooms, money was still tight. At that time mortgage interest rates were 15 per cent, and our repayments on the loan of fifteen hundred pounds were sixteen pounds a month. Hire purchase was frowned upon; cash was the only acceptable currency of the period. All the furniture, including our bed, was second-hand. Even so, I was determined we'd have a holiday. We hired a thirty-five-foot cruiser on the River Thames, and took Victor with us. I took it for granted that Sam, a South African ex-navy friend, was an expert in boating matters and that we could depend on his expertise. He later explained at length, after a few prangs, that he didn't know anything about boats. 'I was a stoker in the navy. I only saw the sea twice on each trip, getting on and off the boat. Give me a shovel and a coal bunker, Mate, and I'll do a real good job, but I don't know anything about boats.'

We had plenty of problems, including the threat of legal

Hire boat 'Corinthian' with baby Victor on my lap

action from someone in a dinghy we capsized. We weren't able to establish whether it was a man or woman. Mavis, our other crew member, a lady unsullied by the pressures of trying to make a crust with an ongoing devotion to many charities, expressed her sympathy. 'Of course it's a woman,' she said, as we voiced our doubts. 'I didn't understand what she was saying, but there were plenty of biological clues.'

'I'm not convinced,' muttered Sam. 'I spent twenty-five years in the South African navy. I'm used to the odd colourful outburst, but I've never heard anything as tongue-blistering as that.'

Despite the problems it was a fantastic holiday, and it was to be the forerunner of a lifelong fascination with boats. Victor immediately adapted to boating and hardly cried at all. Both Mavis and Sam took their turn in bottle-feeding him and bringing up his wind.

In the early 1960s central heating was a luxury, and there was no need for a temperature gauge. Telltale signs of the cold in winter were the vaporous cloud on breathing out in bed, icicles on the inside of the windows, and the heart-stopping shock of bare feet on lino. One of my earliest experiences as a landlord came in the small hours of a freezing morning when a loud knock on the front door brought me sharply out of bed. Clutching my vest around my privates, I 'Oohed' and 'Ahhed' my way along the lino-laid hall to the front door. A full-blown policeman, helmet and all, said, 'Have you got a Mr O'Malley living here?'

'Er... I think so.'

'You don't seem too sure, Sir. Can I come in? I'd like to see his room.'

'What's he done?'

'He's in police custody for attacking an officer. I can't be certain when he'll return.'

When I opened Mr O'Malley's door I was shocked to find three men sleeping in the room and the room a complete tip.

'Who the hell are you?' I demanded. They were rubbing their eyes sheepishly and pulling on their trousers.

The policeman took out his notebook and said, 'This may take a little while, Sir. Perhaps you'd like to put some pants on.'

Trying to get rid of non-paying tenants was a hazardous business as it ran the risk of intimidation and threats of physical violence. O'Malley had been using the room as a resting-place for all his mates. I had to change the front-door lock and stick some hefty bolts in place.

There were other hazards to negotiate as a novice property owner. A man who lived opposite introduced himself to us on his return from the pub one Sunday morning.

'I'm a bricklayer,' he said. 'Your garden wall's in poor condition. It wants knocking down and rebuilding. I can do it for you cheap.' We agreed on the price and he set to knocking it down. The work continued at a leisurely pace between numerous visits to the pub.

'Well, I'm celebrating,' he would say. One day, concerned about how long the job was taking, I asked whether I might be able to celebrate the completion of my wall some time soon. In a few hours he had demolished the remaining wall and dug a two foot six trench for the foundations. A long delay followed. Notes were pushed through our front door warning us that this was a serious hazard. The coalman was more forceful.

'I ain't delivering no more coal here until you sorts out this wall. It's bad enough trying to get coal down your cellar; it ain't easy, but I ain't going to bust my leg doing it.'

The major from next door came knocking on bonfire night. 'I nearly fell in your blasted trench with my bike,' he fumed. 'With your trench and those God-awful fireworks, it's like being back at the Somme. There are people who would gladly hurl themselves into your trench in order to improve their finances. You'd better fix the problem now.'

After an acrimonious discussion with the bricklayer, who could scarcely stand after yet another 'extended celebration', as he put it, I delivered my ultimatum: 'You finish the job by next weekend or I get somebody else.'

His raised voice and language opened all the front doors in the street.

There was a master builder who bewailed the downturn of standards and spiralling ethics in his industry. 'I'll start nine-o'clock sharp on Monday morning,' he said. Then, in more apologetic tone, 'Afraid I'll have to ask for 50 per cent advance payment – cost of materials, you understand?'

'No problem,' I said, filling his outstretched hand with cash.

I never saw him again. There were times when I felt I must have a sticker on my forehead. 'I'm an idiot and I want to be robbed of my hard-earned cash and insulted by cowboy builders.'

Another builder quoted to finish rebuilding the wall. I asked him if we were on the same planet and whether he was getting confused with Hadrian's Wall. Rather desperately, as we needed coal to keep us warm, I agreed to an inflated price, but refused to pay in advance. Soon afterwards he knocked on the front door, with a sweaty bill in one hand and a sweeping arm indicating the finished wall. I looked in disbelief at the gently curving wall.

'Don't take no notice of that bow in the middle, Mate. Once the sun gets on it, them bricks'll all straighten out, you'll see.'

'We don't get a lot of sun in January,' I said, and even before I'd finished speaking the whole lot collapsed on to the pavement. The bricklayer who lived opposite was convulsed with laughter and nearly fell out of his bedroom window. The red-faced bricklayer who'd created the bow wall had another go, to loud shouts of encouragement from the bricklayer opposite.

Sam, the ex-navy man who knew nothing about boats, used to do the football syndicate for Rootes Motors. The other workers were sceptical about his knowledge on picking draws. 'We haven't had a sniff of a win for months,' was the outcry. Several members withdrew and the syndicate was on the point of closing down.

'Look Sam,' I said, 'I think I'll bow out as well. We don't seem to have had any luck.'

'Gordon, we are going to win, I promise you. Hang in a bit longer and you'll see.'

The week after I withdrew he won seven thousand pounds, followed by a further four hundred pounds two weeks later.

'We never have any luck,' I groaned to Babs. 'Look at us, coming up to our second Christmas, working our nuts off and we can't even afford a chicken.'

But the week before Christmas we took in a new tenant and our luck changed dramatically. She worked for Fortnum & Mason.

'Would these be any good to you?' she said, opening two large carrier bags full of exotic goodies. Inside were dented tins of salmon, fruit, chocolates, fancy biscuits, crackers and cakes. I also won twenty-five pounds on the premium bonds, so we did manage a modest turkey. The only slight disappointment was the 'fill your own sherry bottles' facility at the local off licence. The sherry was so sharp, even Auntie Clare – who could quaff anything – complained. Nevertheless we had a wonderful Christmas.

* * *

With the coming and going of tenants there was always the danger of vacant rooms leaving a dent in the finances. We were into such a three-week dent when we had a journalist from the local paper apply for a room. He was a short, quietly spoken, unassuming character.

In my eagerness to please, I said to him, 'Just ask if you have any problems; I'm here to help.' Then to Babs, 'That's more like it; he's a better class of tenant. Well spoken, respectable, reliable; he won't be threatening us and duffing up policeman.'

He had an enormous Austin Princess saloon that took up three car spaces. The car suffered from one of the regular features of cars at that time: you would turn the ignition key; there would be a faint, flickering red light; and then and a noise like a magistrate clearing his throat. The tenant would sit his diminutive figure in the comfy driving seat tickling the throttle pedal, while I applied my energies to a metal handle inserted into the front of the car. When he said 'Go', I'd turn the handle hard until the engine fired. When it fired, the engine would kick the handle backwards with enough force to throw me over several rooftops, if I didn't disengage the handle fast enough.

It turned out that the new tenant took the term 'liberty taking' to its highest level.

'He's a real scrounger!' fumed Babs, studying my bruised wrist. 'He's always on the cadge. He borrows things but never returns them.'

'Well he's helping to pay our mortgage. We need him more than he needs us.'

Then I overheard him dismissing the headmistress next door.

'No, Madam! I can't move my car. I pay my road tax and this is a public highway.' Then, in more tetchy voice, 'You don't even have a blasted car.'

A more serious problem developed later, when I had to park my car two streets away. After a rotten day at work and a

314

shouting match with a belligerent driver near Vauxhall Bridge, I was in a bad mood.

'Any chance of borrowing a fiver till Friday?' asked the journalist. 'I'm a bit short at the moment.'

'No!' I growled. 'And I can't park my car outside my own bloody house, either. Another thing while we're at it: why don't you buy a battery, or get a car to match your shoe measurement? I've had enough of your starting handle.'

'Dear oh dear! We *are* upset!' I could have killed him but I was worried he might give notice after my angry outburst. I needn't have worried, however, as he was too thick-skinned to let a minor altercation like that upset him.

The garden meant something special for me. I had always had a keen interest in gardening ever since I'd had my own plot at school. I aimed to supply all the fresh vegetables we needed, as well as a sweet-smelling galaxy of colour to have the neighbours grinding their teeth with jealousy. One day, on returning from work I discovered a carpet of half-opened flower buds in the breakfast room. Victor, who was then nearly three years old, had successfully cleared the lot.

Our journalist tenant continued to aggravate the neighbours with his big car, and threatened the retired schoolteacher saying, 'I'll park it in your bloody living room, if you don't stop twittering on about it.' I was beginning to realise that being a landlord had many disadvantages. I received an invitation from her. 'Take a seat,' she said, once I was inside her house. I looked around for the sherry glasses, but the frosty tone of voice confirmed there would be no drinks. 'I've kept a diary since you moved in,' she said, reading out excerpts: '22 February 1961 at 4.30 p.m., lit bonfire, mainly wood cuttings, newspapers and a piece of old lino measuring 4 feet by 3 feet approx. March 4 Friday1961 at 10.30 a.m., two large cars parked outside my house all night, one blue, without tax disk, the other black with dirty windscreen and a broken number plate. These are just two examples of your inconsiderate behaviour, stretching back over nearly three years. In 1962 I recorded thirty-three incidents. Only yesterday, on December 22 at 9.30 in the morning, I was subject to verbal abuse from your pygmy tenant, who threw his empty cigarette packets into my garden. He told me to eff off.'

'So what's the purpose of this meeting?' I asked.

She straightened her bowed shoulders and snapped the diary shut. 'This is a warning. I will take proceedings in court against you and the pygmy, if you persist with your bad behaviour. The major is also willing to testify against you. Do you understand?' I glared at her defiantly.

'It's my birthday, for Christ's sake. Goodbye.'

The coalman had been grateful when the trench was filled in, and he'd even commented favourably on the quality of the workmanship of the wall. But he still had trouble getting to the cellar, and asked me to get the owner of the black funeral wagon to shift.

Our journalist tenant seemed to have a regular army of beautiful women calling on him, which was not a problem for me. Remembering my own experiences with landladies in the past, I thought *good luck to him, as long as it doesn't adversely affect us.*

'I don't understand what those girls see in him,' said Babs. 'He reminds me of that burglar you shared your flat with in Brixton.'

'Hmm... It's funny how some women like those short-arsed men. I reckon it's their inbuilt maternal instincts. P'raps he's wearing one of those fancy after-shave lotions.'

Another possibility surfaced when we witnessed an elegant brunette swinging the starting handle on his Austin Princess.

'I reckon he's running some sort of fitness and body management course. Can you believe the man's cheek? I bet the diary next door is getting quite interesting.'

Unbeknown to our tenants and the neighbours, we were soon to be on the move. The daily grind of working the other side of London was starting to wear me down. I needed a change; I wanted to be my own boss again.

Babs asked awkward questions about my past, and I finally agreed to show her my old school on top of Chesham Hill in Berkhamsted, now called Ashlyns School. The then headmaster was most obliging and let us wander around the two-hundred-acre site at will. There were no foundlings as Berkhamsted council had taken over the premises and had now been turned into a modern secondary school. We entered the chapel and memories came flooding back of being caned for playing hide-and-seek within its walls. The sun was shining through one of the stained glass windows, splashing multicoloured patterns on to the oak pews below. The church felt awesome in its silence.

One of the maintenance staff recognised me and invited us to have tea with him at his house, which was just outside the school grounds. 'Things have changed a lot since you were here; the place used to be spotless.'

'You're right there,' I laughed, and then said, 'I remember spending hours on my knees polishing the corridors and dormitories.'

We spent a good hour reminiscing about old times, while Victor got a lot of pleasure from rolling down the deeply sloping lawn.

Mrs Tapp would often drift into my thoughts. I still couldn't forget the last words she'd said to me, 'You mustn't come here any more'. I promised Babs I'd take her to see my foster mother. It was in April 1964, nearly fifteen years after I'd last seen Mrs Tapp, that I decided to go and see her. I felt sure she would welcome me with Babs and Victor.

* * *

We turned off the Tonbridge Road into Back Lane, past the old village school, past Jim Jenner's meadow and on to The Brookers. The cottage hadn't changed at all. It was exactly as I remembered it, with whitewashed walls, grey slate roof and a cobblestone path with arched trellis canopy. A short bowed figure with silver-bunned hair stood leaning against the gate. Mrs Tapp straightened her back as I drove on to the verge. There was a smell of freshly cut grass mingled with the fragrance of scented wallflowers. Dotted around the pond, which had nearly dried up, were daffodils looking well past their best.

Her twinkling cornflower-blue eyes closed to narrow slits as she cupped her hand to her face and looked up at me, saying, 'Bless my soul! What a nice surprise. Smiler! How are you, Son?' Then she raised her arms towards me.

'I'm okay. This is my wife Babs. I hope you don't mind us calling on you like this.'

'Not at all, my dear. I'm delighted to see you. So this is your little boy, eh? Well isn't he a bonny young man? He's got that same wavy hair you had when you were little. What's your name, Sonny? Victor? Now that's a nice name. Well, Victor, we'll have a nice cup of tea and then you and I will feed the pony, if your Mummy doesn't mind. How about that?'

Victor smiled at her with wonderment, as her lilting voice weaved its magic, capturing his complete attention. The past came flooding back as I walked along the cobbled path and under the rose trellis arch. I looked up at the window from where I had fallen as an infant. The protective steel bars that were put in place after I fell out of the window some time during 1937–8 were still in place. The wireless aerial I had tried to grab to stop my fall stretched across the garden to the now disused privy, covered in a rambling rose bush.

'Ouch!' I grunted with pain as I banged my head on the doorframe entering the porch.

'You boys do that every time. You forget you're all growed up and left school now.'

'Well I'll be blowed! It's Smiler,' said Uncle Dave, stroking a brown and white spaniel that wagged its tail with excitement.

His sallow face broke into a wide smile stretching almost from ear to ear, displaying the jagged remnants of teeth.

'You're looking well.' He shook my hand limply.

Uncle Dave had never liked kids and had usually made no secret of his feelings. Yet he'd a wonderful sense of humour and would often make my ribs ache with laughter. He accepted he was ugly and unattractive to women, and didn't seem to mind one jot.

Mr Tapp had died from a heart attack and had fallen headfirst into the coalhole. Uncle Dave had taken over the running of the house. He now tended the garden, did all the shopping, and generally looked after Mrs Tapp, who must now have been in her early eighties. The local squire had told her she could remain at The Brookers for the rest of her life for a nominal rent of half-a-crown a week. The Cazalets were very generous to all the tenants in their tied cottages. After selling Fairlawn they only charged them pepper corn rents until they passed on. I glanced around the main living room and noticed that the antlers had been removed from above the door, as had the large gun that had been suspended above the mahogany table. Some concessions to the modern world were an electric toaster, a yellow plastic radio and a large table lamp.

'I'm not the hard-nosed beggar I used to be, Smiler,' said Uncle Dave. I can't skin a rabbit or even swat a fly now. Yeah, I'm a right soft in the head daft sod now. Ever since coming out of hospital; they took all my guts out y'know. God knows what they did with them – probably finished up in the kitchen. My insides have never felt right since.'

'We've got mains water now. We've had a lot of changes since you were here last,' said Mrs Tapp. 'We've done away with the old iron pump; we're all electric; and we don't use candles now.'

'Yeah, and the Cazalet's aren't here any more,' interrupted Uncle Dave. 'He sold the Fairlawn Estate to some Arab sheikh who was fed up with desert sand and oil and came here to enjoy a bit of old England.'

'Guess what,' chuckled Mrs Tapp there's rumours going around that 'They've discovered oil on the estate. Tell them about your guide job at the castle, Dave.'

Uncle Dave propelled his hand-rolled cigarette from one side of his mouth to the other. 'I used to show tourists around and give a running commentary. It was a right boring job. I had to repeat the same old thing over and over, so I introduced a bit of variation, just to make it more interesting. Then some American came with one group and gave me a right roasting. He was a well known historian and he got me the sack.'

I knew it would be the last time I would see my foster mother. I felt this last visit was somehow the end of a long chapter of my life. Mrs Tapp had become an idyllic memory that would stay with me for the rest of my life, but I somehow had to get the hard words she'd said to me as a child out of my head. I didn't ask her why she had told me never to visit her again, because this now no longer seemed important, and I felt I could totally concentrate on the most important things in my life, which were my family and my work.

As we turned off Back Lane I recognised a man standing on the other side of the road. He called out and hurried across the road towards me. Sam Mould was also a foundling. His foster mother was Mrs Tapp's sister, who looked after several foundling boys.

'Sam! How are you?' I said, shaking his hand. 'D'you still live in the village?'

'I'm in the airforce, but right now I'm home on leave.' It turned out that Sam had travelled the world, but he admitted that he liked nothing better than Shipbourne, the place he regarded as home. He knew all the goings on in this little village and rattled off the names of many famous people who'd enjoyed the hospitality of the Fairlawn Estate. Gregory Peck used to fly from America to open the local summer fair. Richard Burton, Elizabeth Taylor, Noël Coward and many others had been regular visitors. Going back in time there had been Emily Pankhurst, Rudyard Kipling and even Queen Victoria who had spent many winters there. Sam reckoned that sometimes there were more Rolls Royces in the village than villagers. He was the self-appointed village historian, and later attended Mrs Tapps' funeral when she died aged ninety-six on the 12th of December aged 96. She was interred at Tonbridge Wells Crematorium. Her funeral was very well attended with the whole village turning out to pay their last respects.

*　*　*

Just before we visited Mrs Tapp we moved to Whitehorse Road in Thornton Heath in Surrey. It was a three-bedroomed chalet bungalow, with large cellar workshops and a double garage. Doubling the mortgage was a huge gamble for us, and our second child was on the way. Caroline was born in February 1965, with a dusting of snow on the ground. Our expenses spiralled ever upwards, what with private school fees, rates, and regular increases in utility bills. I was working seven days a week, which I did for many years, while Babs was working part-time, and we had a regular babysitter who looked after the children. I let part of my workshops to a local carpenter, thinking that I might gain his services at favourable rates. In addition to sign work I had become involved in small shop-fitting contracts.

When Babs's father had died in December 1962, his assets turned out to be far less than expected. His wife, Babs's mother, had no income and had to get a job to pay the service charges on the recently purchased leasehold flat in Sutton. She couldn't babysit for us so we decided to get an au pair. Mauricette was the first of several, a shy seventeen-year-old who couldn't speak any English. We soon learnt that good communication was vital when dealing with a child minder who couldn't speak our language.

Babs gave Mauricette five shillings to take Victor to the Crystal Palace zoo, which was only a short bus ride away. Late in the afternoon we received a phone call from the police station near Regent's Park zoo on the other side of London. The sergeant gave me a right roasting.

'I have here a young lady with a small boy,' he said. 'You are totally irresponsible sending a young foreign girl with an infant to London with no money. Both are in a very distressed state.'

I tried to explain that the au pair had misunderstood the instructions she'd been given, but he yelled down the phone, 'You come and collect them immediately!'

London isn't a good place in the rush hour. My nerves were in shreds when I arrived at the police station. I received an even bigger rollicking from a finger-wagging desk sergeant and, to complete a truly miserable day, I had an ill-tempered exchange with a foul-mouthed lorry driver.

Another au pair was Rosetta, who arrived just after Caroline was born. She set the carpet alight in the front room after using the vacuum cleaner to Hoover the fireplace. She rushed into the garden hugging the Hoover while Caroline was coughing up her lungs in the front room. We soon got rid of her.

Despite my determination to distance myself from my past, sometimes I couldn't avoid it. There was one day when we were enjoying a sunny afternoon in Dulwich Park when a voice called out, 'Fancy seeing you here!' I turned to see Chatterton, a lanky character dressed in the brown uniform of a park attendant. I remembered his foster mother also lived in Shipbourne near the village green.

'Blimey! It's a small world,' I said, and laughed.

We invited Chatterton over to Sunday lunch and he was able to tell me what was going on at Shipbourne. He also told me about many of the other foundlings from the village such as Loveridge, Redmayne, Endsleigh and Grinley. Fortunately he didn't know about the more murky details of my birth mother and family. All that was a completely closed book to everybody as far as I was concerned.

We had a visit from Katie, Babs's granny, who was looking for somewhere more permanent to live. Her children took it in turns to accommodate her for three months of every year. Her eyes lit up when I pointed to the lush green local park and jokingly complained about how long it took me to mow the front lawn. I then had to quickly confirm that we only had three bedrooms and had no room to put her up.

Our next au pair, a vivacious, dark-haired nineteen-year-old, was called Pom. She was extremely efficient and loved the children, especially Caroline. She had a good grasp of English and displayed an instinctive understanding of the requirements for running a home with young children. She was a wonderful cook and treated us to French cuisine. Then however, she blotted her copybook when she announced to me in a husky voice full of promise, in earshot of Babs, 'Mr Gordon, I 'ave made love to a German, a Spaniard, a Frenchman and a Greek, but I have never 'ad an Englishman.'

After a very awkward silence I mumbled something about how Englishmen are more reserved, and I would like to confirm that I wasn't able to help her regarding her problem but that an American put a ring on her finger three months later.

I had another surprise when Cleaver, one of my younger foster brothers, knocked on our front door. He'd found my name in the phone book. 'There aren't many Aspey's in there,' he said. He'd brought his girl friend with him – a bright-eyed, bubbly woman with a good sense of humour. Her dad owned a granite business making tombstones and suchlike. Cleaver was a strapping big bloke and did a lot of heavy work.

I never saw them again.

Babs told me some surprising news. Although we'd both agreed that Babs would not take the Pill – I remembered my teacher Mr Bavister's advice about pills – we had nevertheless been very careful. Even so she was pregnant again, and Robin was born in September 1967.

* * *

My business continued to grow steadily, and I expanded into silk screen printing, exhibition work, shopfitting and machine engraving. I used one or two tricks I'd learnt from Fred in Bridgwater: always be flexible and ready for change. I had a growing band of self-employed tradesmen working for me. I didn't want the hassle of employing people direct, paying for their holidays and stamping their National Insurance cards; I'd been lax enough stamping my own cards. The Inland Revenue, however, was not happy with this arrangement, insisting that I should either forward all names and addresses of my self-employed employees to the tax office or make them full-time employees of my own. This suggestion didn't go down well at all, and half the workers quit. My accountant was concerned at my reluctance to fulfil the Inland Revenue's requirement. He warned me that I would become liable for the self-employees' tax bills and that the revenue people could make life very uncomfortable indeed. They certainly did so.

I was in the workshop one morning when I heard a voice calling, 'Anybody in?' Before I could deliver a warning, 'Mind the steel girder,' there was a thud and anguished cries of pain. I recognised the bald-headed dancing figure as Jack, an estate agent I had met earlier in Tooting. He was expanding his business, and I'd done much of his shopfitting work. He had the reputation of being a bit of a rogue. He was a likeable man, with what I thought at the time was a preference for making a bent half-crown rather than an honest pound, but later I discovered that this description was well wide of the truth. He was a professional crook, and he was going to give me one very big headache.

One of my business ventures involved electric advertising panels for vans. They worked off small DC inverters powered by the vehicle's batteries. A key element in the design was the use of tiny transistors, an innovation at the time, imported from Hong Kong. I tried to get the product patented but was unsuccessful. Jack, the estate agent, was highly impressed by it.

'Tell you what, Gordon. I'm franchising my estate agents' offices. I can also franchise this product for you; you'll make a packet. Just leave it with me.'

In a short time I had twenty eager agents scattered around the country clutching contracts that promised the earth. The difficulty was that Jack hadn't consulted me; I knew nothing about them. He had creamed off one-third of the franchise fee as commission. Not content with that, he and his dodgy cohorts had run up hotel and bar bills all over the place and had charged them to my company account. Any hope of resolving these issues with Jack was quashed when I saw his picture in the *News of the World* above a report of his three-year jail sentence for fraud. He'd had some scam going with Spanish property. Soon afterwards he died in prison from a heart attack.

The police authorities were not happy with the idea of Vanlites zooming up and down the motorways but had to agree there weren't any laws banning them. (I ran a company called Vanlite Limited that was separate from my main business.) I had enquiries from some of the country's leading companies and the future was looking good. My first big order came about the time Murdoch purchased the *Sun* newspaper, previously the *Daily Herald*. Vanlites were stuck on their delivery vans all over London. Despite the dodgy contracts with the franchisees and other problems, I was convinced I was on to a good thing and heading for early retirement, but Prime Minister Harold Wilson had other ideas. The devaluation of the pound, coupled with restrictive fiscal issues such as freezing bank lending, calling in bank overdrafts, and imposing import restrictions on foreign goods, proved to be a disaster. Businesses were going bust all over the place, orders were cancelled and, worst of all, the transistors required for the inverters were not going to be available until the following year because of import restrictions.

I had a five-year period with many challenges. I had a stack of orders I couldn't complete, an army of angry agents, hefty bills for advertising, and materials I'd purchased that were worthless without the transistors. Then I received a copy of the contract sent by one of the agents contemplating legal action against me. Jesus! If all the agents got together I would be trussed up like the proverbial turkey. Jack had really stitched me up. I was sitting in Pandora's Box cuddling a hand grenade. I needed legal advice fast.

My solicitor took me to see a barrister in Temple Chambers, London.

'The barrister is a rally driver enthusiast,' said my solicitor. 'He might prattle on a bit about cars, but he's got a reputation for winning. If anyone can sort this out, he can.'

'Ah yes, Mr Aspey, we do have a problem,' said the spindly-looking barrister, scrubbing his nose with a handkerchief. 'I've had a close look at your paperwork. It doesn't look good, does it? The contract is a cannibalisation of two or three existing contracts made to form one. It's been put together to make the most attractive package for a would-be franchisee. People would pay good money for a contract like this, in fact I wouldn't mind a contract like this myself. The main content is heart-stopping stuff, with obligatory national advertising and very generous commissions.'

'Yeah, but I didn't know he...'

'Yes, yes. I know you didn't know anything about it, but the law will see things differently. Presumably you banked the franchise fees?'

'Yes. But I've spent most of it on promoting.'

'That's not the point. You are culpable, recklessly so, in law. I'm afraid you have displayed astonishing naivety in the matter.'

'Well how was I to know he...? I had other things on my plate.'

'This man, Jack what's-his-name, has signed the contracts on your behalf, as a representative of your company, and that is binding. He hasn't done you any favours. You see, Mr Aspey, I know you feel you are an injured party in this matter – and indeed you are – but the judge's sympathies will lie with the agents, who are also injured parties ... and there are twenty of them.'

The barrister did a lot of scribbling and tapping with his pen on a writing pad. Then he offered an amazing variety of solutions in quick succession. He set out what he thought would be the best defence.

'Jesus Christ, I can't say that! It's just not true. Nobody would believe me.'

The barrister looked perplexed, his face brimming with concern. 'Mr Aspey! You can't afford to tell truth – it'll ruin you. You'll need an honest-to-goodness alternative.'

My solicitor nodded fervent agreement, 'Yes, yes; you'd be unwise to get bogged down in that area.'

After a two-hour session the barrister settled on a solution he thought best suited to my moral predicament.

'We'll call it my Rally module.' His voice quickened with excitement. 'Lots of Scandinavian flicks, handbrake turns, hill jumping, left-foot braking, slamming doors, looking and sounding really ferocious. Of course, we *are* talking metaphorically.'

'This rally thing – will it get me off the hook?'

'Nothing is certain, Mr Aspey. But I do think we must try and avoid a tight court circuit at this stage. We would crash on the first bend with that contract. We need to attack and wear the plaintiff down. The first thing is to introduce a genuine contract. Then perhaps intimate that the agent has had something to do with falsifying this contract, even colluding with Mr what's-his-name to defraud the company. Dead men don't lie. Make him so fed up and fearful of his own costs he withdraws his claim. If he persists, we can fall back on the Time module.'

'So how does that work?' I asked.

'Well, documents get lost, there are postal strikes, people go sick, bank holidays intervene, memories fade, people die like your what's-his-name, which can be quite handy, and so on. Time can be a wonderful asset.'

'Another possibility is to create a barrow-load of unpaid invoices payable to you as the main creditor, and bankrupt the company, before the agents get started.'

'So what's all this going to cost?' I asked nervously.

'That's tricky. It will take two, maybe three, years to get sorted. You said twenty agents, didn't you?

'That's right.'

'Well, there's only one of me. The reality is, Mr Aspey, you will be paying somebody to get you out of this mess – either them or me.'

My visit had been an education. I now had a much better understanding of the legal establishment and how it worked. I was most impressed with the barrister and his tactics, but not with his closing statement: 'You will be paying somebody.'

Like hell I would! I developed my own module and called it 'Return to sender'. I returned all the business letters, changed my telephone number, dumped all the stationery and erased anything to do with Vanlite from the company work premises. I went to Malta to try out a bit of boat charter work. This, however, never really got off the ground: the boat wasn't suitable; the red tape considerable; and the rewards unreliable. The agent dropped his action against me, I think because it became too expensive for him to continue. Another agent took action against me that was undefended, and he won his case. He put in the bailiffs, but they were unable to claim any assets and the case just fizzled out. I had paid my solicitor £50 up front, but I never heard another word from either him or the barrister again about additional fees.

* * *

I was back in Thornton Heath after a few weeks, and this seemed to be a good time to move house. We sold the Thornton Heath bungalow privately at a good price and moved to Birdhurst Gardens, south Croydon, in January 1968. Our new house had five bedrooms and was a detached property with a huge garden. Even so, it only cost us £2,500 more than the Thornton Heath bungalow. There was a large garage that to begin with I used as a workshop, but somebody in the road complained and a surveyor informed me that there was a codicil in the property deeds that expressly forbade any commercial activity on the premises.

It was about 1969 when I rented a three-storey shop with a showroom from the local council. The garage was in any event too small for the type of work I was doing. The business started to expand quite rapidly at this point, and I was earning good money. Litigation was a regular feature of my business, but I usually defended the actions against me myself, with modest success and minimal cost.

I felt a little self-conscious when first moving into our posh new neighbourhood, with my rusting Hillman Minx reclining in the drive. Our neighbours were from the higher echelons of the commercial world. The houses were of sturdy Edwardian design, built within the fruit orchards of the former Horniman Tea Estate. Malcolm Muggeridge had spent his youth in the house next door. The neighbours occasionally gave wine and cheese parties, and I knew we'd arrived when the first invitation flipped through out letterbox. Any ideas of a flower and vegetable garden with a sweeping manicured lawn were soon abandoned, however. Our back garden became a recreation ground for all the local kids.

Babs delivered a bombshell when she said in hushed tones that her mum was wondering if she could come and live with us in our new house. The service charges on her Sutton flat were becoming unmanageable. She would pay one third of the total cost and babysit for us. What did I think?

I did a bit of wondering myself. I'd previously never hit it off with Babs's mother, and felt we needed a serious chat to make sure that such an arrangement would work. The two of us sat down and agreed to try and get on. I had the house adapted to give her maximum independence, with her own kitchen and living area. Katie arrived on the scene soon afterwards with two suitcases and a Parker Knoll green velvet armchair, announcing that this would be her final move. She stayed with us for nearly two years, but then had a stroke and had to go into a home. The arrangement with Babs's mother worked very well, and before her death in 1980 she confessed that the time she'd spent with us had been some of her happiest years.

We had a letter from Auntie Olive and Uncle Jerry, who were on Babs's side of the family. They wanted to come and visit us. Jerry was the manager of a gold mine in Yellowknife, Canada. He gave us an egg-sized rock with seams of gold glinting on its surface. He was now retired and wanted to learn more about his own family, the Claytons. We drove to various places in the south, looking in churches and studying gravestones. Jerry was delighted when he discovered his family had been prominent in the Westerham area in Kent. A member of his family had been the mayor on Tenterton, and there was a commemorative stained glass window in the local church. The vicar opened the church out of normal hours to show him. After that Auntie Olive and Jerry came to see us every year.

We kept Jerry's rock on the mantelpiece where it glimmered handsomely when the sun flooded through the large window. I regarded it as a good luck talisman, and on the whole our luck was rather good. I enjoyed the rock's cool feel in the palm of my hand, and imagined the clang of machinery, the rattle of heavy wagons with their cargo and the toil and sweat of the men underground as they clawed the valuable metal out of the earth.

An awkward question often cropped up at the wine and cheese do's: 'So what do your folks do, Gordon?' The problem was that I had to remain consistent with my answer, which had often varied over the years. I'd then make a dive for Jerry's rock.

'You see that?' I would say, holding it up to the light. 'That's real gold! Babs's uncle manages a gold mine in Yellowknife, Canada.'

'Really?' would be the wide-eyed reply.

I would then regale the people we met at length with the stories Jerry had told me about how the mineworkers had tried to smuggle the gold out of the mine and past security. By the time I had finished they would have forgotten their original question about my folks. Our social standing went up in leaps and bounds. I became the leading authority on gold mines in the Yellowknife area, and pretty soon we were handing out invitations for our own wine and cheese do's.

When the children were young we spent most of the summer holidays on the southeast coast in cheap and cheerful caravans in Ramsgate and Margate. In those days the motorcar was the new status symbol that represented real freedom ... this being reflected in the traffic jams on the way to the seaside. They were happy times, but the urge to do something more adventurous kept surfacing.

My hankering for a boat was always with me. I bought the *Exchange and Mart* every week and got to know about all the boats in the market place. I also read many books about boat handling and maintenance, and did a six-month course at a technical college near London about diesel engines. I'd been procrastinating about buying one for a long time. Victor was now in his early teens and had the confidence to air his own view on matters. 'Dad,' he said, 'you've been going on about buying a boat for as long as I can remember.' Then somewhat grumpily he added, 'I don't think you will ever, ever buy one.' On the first of January 1976, however, the year of the unbelievably hot English summer, I bought my first boat, a seventeen-foot cabin cruiser. I told the bank manager that I was expanding my business and that I needed to buy a new engraving machine. I actually bought both a boat and an engraving machine, but inflated the cost of the second-hand engraving machine, which was only a fraction of the cost of buying a new one, so there really was more than a grain of truth in what I said to the bank manager. We were so excited. I had the boat parked alongside the house on its trailer. We photographed it from every angle and discussed at length all the fabulous holidays we would have with it in the future. We soon discovered, however, that there was a steep learning curve in the matter of boats and their watery environment.

Auntie Olive and Uncle Jerry invited us to visit them on Vancouver Island in Canada. The cost was too prohibitive for the whole family, but we agreed to let Victor, aged sixteen, and Caroline, aged eleven, go on their own. Robin, who was aged eight, stayed with us and we enjoyed a memorable summer holiday cruising the River Thames – without a winter woolly in sight.

Babs continued to work as a locum for various opticians, working many extra hours to help send our children to private schools. We were determined to avoid the nearby state school that had a deplorable record. We followed the well-worn trail of parenthood, struggling to pay the ever-increasing utility bills and to meet the cost of school uniforms, holidays, school trips and birthday parties. We did our share of trying to keep up with the Joneses. Christmas time, though, was much more awkward for us than for most other families we knew. Our children's friends would come round, excitedly showing off armfuls of presents. But we were a small family, without the usual entourage of aunts and uncles to share the load. We nevertheless decided that they wouldn't miss out and so every Christmas we would buy one expensive present in addition to each child's smaller presents. The children would take it in turn to receive the expensive present. This arrangement worked very well and I cannot recall any arguments.

* * *

It was time for some serious study. Initially our little boat never went past Teddington Lock on the River Thames, but I started navigation lessons at night school. I wanted to go to sea to try out my new-found skills. By now the boating bug had really taken a hold. I enjoyed nothing better than the smell of ozone and the slap of water against the boat's hull.

Three years later I told the bank manager I was expanding again and bought a thirty-foot, twin-diesel, sea-going motor cruiser. The boat cost double what we had paid for our house, and this was even though property prices were now going crazy. (Our Birdhouse Gardens house was now worth £130,000, which was a huge increase on what we had paid for it.)

Malacca opened up a new world for us. I liked the boat's name and Babs agreed that it had a wonderfully mysterious edge to it. As a family we crossed the Channel many times and explored the canals of France, Belgium and Holland. We also used the boat to help Victor with his dissertation, which was based on the true cost of pleasure boating on inland waterways and offshore cruising. In 1981 he obtained his degree in maritime studies in Cardiff, which was presented by Prince Charles, and it was a proud moment for us parents.

Victor started work with Lloyds shipping register after he finished university. He also started up his first part-time business venture with a work colleague, teaching navigation and sailing, and using his late Granny's quarters in the house. Sometimes I

Malacca, my twin diesel boat

would help with the practical classes that he ran throughout the winter and summer. Often thick fog would blanket the Thames Estuary. We had no radar or automatic pilot, just the steering compass.

It was while we were returning from one of our holiday trips across the channel that we were told by the Harbour Master about the name of our boat. 'When I was in Greece it was a commonly used expletive,' he said with a smile. 'It meant effing wanker.'

'Oh no! You must be kidding. Are you telling me that every time I use that VHF I'm telling the world that I'm an effing wanker?' I groaned.

I moored the boat in Brighton for a while, soon after the marina was built, and were surprised to see Arthur Lowe's boat, *The Amazon*, moored alongside. It was a delightful, copper-bottomed wooden boat from an earlier period, with coal-burning stove – a true gentleman's yacht. There were often celebrities around the marina, but I felt obliged to respect their privacy and pretended not to notice them. In any event I've never been a celebrity-worshiper, apart from briefly swooning over Veronica Lake in my teens. But Arthur Lowe was different. *Dad's Army* was my favourite comedy, and I was tempted to try and engage in some small talk with the famously funny man. He often nodded at me on the pontoon, but the expression on his face seemed to say, 'What are you staring at, you stupid boy!'

Late one summer's evening I was hurrying towards the toilet block. Arthur Lowe stood on the end pontoon with gin and something in his hand. He grinned and pointed his glass towards the name on my boat. I often wondered whether he'd cottoned on to what the word signified.

'Good evening! Are you on holiday?' he said, and then jerked his chin to one side in that characteristically funny way of his. Jesus! He wanted to talk to *me*!

'Yes,' I puffed, crossing my legs. 'Ooh! I must dash. Good evening.'

It was then that I decided to sell Malacca.

* * *

Victor collected several useful commissions while teaching navigation, and then decided to give up his Lloyd's job and strike out on his own. This included overseeing a catamaran being built in Southampton and delivering it to Florida. There was also a new build in Rio de Janeiro and full-time skippering on a large yacht in the Greek islands. These contracts came a little later. Our first delivery together was for one of my customers. We did several deliveries together, but went out own way. For me it was more a question of fun, but for Victor it was serious business and the way he earned his living.

'How much would you charge to get my boat from Shoeburyness to Ramsgate?' asked the owner. 'I've been quoted one hundred pounds.'

In best Tesco tradition, I volunteered to do it for twenty-five quid. It was not a journey of any great magnitude, but there was some urgency.

'Could you do it tomorrow?'

'No problem.'

Apparently, near-mutiny had broken out on the original voyage from Teddington. Surrounded by the bright lights of Clacton, with big ships en route to Tilbury Docks and tugs whizzing all over the place, a 'Where are we?' problem had developed. The owner wanted to turn left, where he could see land, whereas the navigator was adamant they should continue heading east. The owner grabbed the helm and aimed the bow at top speed towards the nearest light bulb. This happened to be the groyne of Her Majesty's Gunnery Station, used for target practice. It was a mystery to the locals how he'd steered his boat through the middle of the groyne unscathed and buried his anchor on the other side.

With high water at 2300 hours being the only window of opportunity, we had to scurry back and forth with heavy jerry cans to refill the near-empty fuel tank.

'I'm starving,' complained Victor.

'Me too,' I said. 'Let's find an eatery.'

Shoeburyness wasn't a good place for hungry mariners on a late Wednesday night. Even the British Legion club found it impossible to muster up a couple of sandwiches. The railway station didn't provide calories either. But there was an advertisement for a taxi.

'Where to?'

'Well, we're at the railway station. Is it possible for you to get a takeaway for two, bring it to the station, and then take us to our boat? We have to catch the midnight tide.'

'What sort of takeaway? Indian, Chinese?'

I decided to short-circuit the salt-sprinkling, ketchup and other time-consuming issues. 'Look, Mate, we haven't got much time, anything as long as it's hot and edible.'

'Be right over!'

As I replaced the phone I realised I'd left my wallet on the boat when I'd got changed. 'Have you got any money on you, Vic?' I shouldn't have asked; he never had any money on him. 'Can you dash back to the boat and get my wallet in my other trousers?'

'We haven't got time, Dad; the tide's already well in.'

'If you're really quick, we can just about make it.' I nervously waited for the taxi driver and his reaction to the 'My wallet's on its way' story. A train pulled into the station and a small queue formed behind me. There was a screeching of brakes and a large black saloon pulled up with a wild-eyed driver shouting, 'Chinese! Chinese!' (I had forgotten to give him my name.)

'Over here!' I cried, 'over here!'

A row of heads turned towards me and I became aware of my face coming under close scrutiny. The driver puffed angrily on his cigarette when told my wallet was in transit and would be arriving soon.

'Look, I've got a living to make. I can't hang around waiting for your bleeding wallet; you'll have to pay. It's a good job I didn't buy the Chinese.'

'What? You mean you haven't got any food, for Christ's sake?

'I ain't using my money to feed you! I'm running a taxi service, not a bloody take away!'

'Ah! Here he is,' I said, as Victor staggered into view, breathing heavily.

'Here's the wallet, Dad!' he panted. 'The tide's on the turn.'

'Jump in Vic. We can still make it, can't we?' I asked, looking at the driver.

'I'll do my best,' he said, chucking his cigarette out of the window. 'You'd better hang on.'

At the Chinese restaurant the cook started a lengthy discussion about the menu.

'Anything that's cooked will do,' I pleaded. 'But not too many bean shoots. I always feel a bit cheated with those tangly things.'

'Maybe soon?' she smiled, and disappeared into the kitchen.

Although gratitude should have been on my lips for the driver's efforts in getting us back to the boat in time, I assured him I would rather face hurricanes and hell than endure such a terrifying and irresponsible bout of driving again.

In the shadowy darkness I could make out several youngsters who appeared to be throwing stones at a lager can on the beach.

'I hope they're not going to be a problem,' muttered Victor. We removed our shoes and socks and rolled up our trousers, and warily waded towards the boat, which was now well afloat. We could hear the youths laughing as the water came up to our chests and we had to hold the precious food cartons above our heads.

'I think we're about to be stoned, Vic, but don't drop the grub for Christ's sake.'

Then one of the kids shouted, 'Ooh jer fink you are? King Bloody Canute?' We nearly dropped the cartons for laughing. We clambered aboard with some difficulty, and after a rapid change of clothes scoffed the Chinese food and prepared to scarper.

'C'mon, hurry up Vic, or we'll lose the tide.'

'The anchor won't budge, Dad. You'll have to give me a hand; it's well and truly buried.'

I was anxious about leaving the controls for fear the tide would sweep us on to the moored boats, or on to local fishermen in their dinghies close by.

'For Christ's sake. Tell you what, Vic – I'll drive over the anchor and release it that way. You keep an eye on the outdrives and give us a shout if the chain starts to foul up the props.'

I gently eased the throttles forward, squinting into the darkness and trying to fathom where the fishermen were.

'She's clear, Dad. Go steady till I get the anchor on board. Blimey, look at all that gunge; she was well and truly buried.'

The rest of the journey went smoothly and it was the forerunner of many over the coming years. The only harrowing part was the vertical twenty-foot steel ladder in Ramsgate outer harbour. I was unfortunately destined to use this facility on many occasions. At low water it exposed treacherous slimy rungs covered in seaweed.

Predictably, someone had to die before the harbour authorities installed a proper gangway.

25

It was during the early 1980s that we started to take in students from the nearby Cambridge Tutors College to help prop up our finances. We had Egyptians, Saudis, Turks, Japanese and even English. My interest in boating was increasing at the same rate as my interest in business was diminishing. I read an article in the paper where a businessman insisted he would be financially much better off if he invested his money in a bank deposit account and got rid of his business and all the hassle. This struck a chord with me. The banks were paying 10 per cent interest on deposit accounts at the time. After a couple of days studying my accounts, the idea made a lot of sense. I decided to sell my main business and work from home. I had always done some work at home, but my main workshop was at the premises that I rented from the local council. At this time the council was trying to build up a case against me to ensure I paid for renovations to the property, but never completed the action.

* * *

Our forays around the English coast in the family boat were beginning to look less attractive. We had spent too much time holed up in expensive marinas dressed like Eskimos trying to avoid the bad weather, but I still wanted to get into the boating business and seek out the sun. I had experience of chartering and a bit of boat delivery work and had read all the books I could find, so I volunteered for boat deliveries and crewing jobs on both power and sail.

* * *

There was a small band of watersports enthusiasts in South London who treated their leisure activities with great solemnity. If the tide was good and the wind was favourable, telephone lines became busy. There would be a procession of vehicles towing jet bikes, sailing dinghies, colourful surfboards and such like. Funerals, weddings, elections, matters of state became secondary to the business of a bit of fun on the water. I had been accepted into this group, and life started to get more adventurous. Babs, however, didn't have the same enthusiasm for boating after a lumpy sail in the English Channel. She had a preference for large luxury liners such as the QE2 with her long time friend Lisa.

'If I'm going to have a fright in a boat,' she said, 'I want it to be in the biggest boat around. I want to be comfortably seated in the lounge bar with a suitable drink and be able to snap my fingers and call for help in a dignified manner.'

My first experience of real sunshine boating came in December 1986. I had a call from Boris who ran his own roofing business and had often sailed with me.

'Hello, Gordon. How d'you fancy a bit of sailing in the Med? A bloke I know has been left a load of money by his granny and he's bought this fancy yacht. He wants a bit of help in a shake-down sail, if you're interested.'

'Count me in, Boris. Who else is coming?'

'Jasper – you've met him; he's the ginger-haired bloke who dabbles in drains. The owner is Charlie. He's been driving buses for the last twenty years. I don't know much about him except the secretary says he's a manic depressive and he's got the distinction of being the only man in the yacht club that's been kicked out and told never to return.'

'That's charming. Are you sure about this, Boris?'

'Don't worry. Everything'll be fine.'

The thirty-eight foot yacht wasn't the most luxurious boat on the block, with paraffin cooker, no shower, and cramped accommodation. As Charlie explained, 'This craft is designed to sail round the world, Gordon. You've got to keep everything simple.'

We weren't that ambitious. We happily sailed out of Benalmadena harbour and headed towards Gibraltar. The conditions were perfect and there was nothing about Charlie's behaviour to suggest we might have a problem. We rafted up against an expensive-looking yacht on the visitors' pontoon in Gibraltar. The owner, Jimmy, was a solicitor, and he invited Boris and me to join him and his wife Wendy for 'drinkies', as he called it. We then discovered that Jimmy was a member of the same yacht club as Boris and Jasper and he was amazed that they hadn't met in the club house. Charlie and Jasper had wandered off to investigate the town. Jimmy was feeling sore at the theft of his brand new dinghy, which hadn't been insured.

We left Gibraltar on 16 December bound for Estepona. This would be our last port before returning to Benalmadena and flying home. As we waved goodbye to Jimmy and Wendy, a speedboat crept alongside our starboard side in the early morning mist. The sole occupant touched the peak of his cap, which covered most of his face, and nodded a sort of acknowledgement. He remained close to our starboard side.

'So what's his game?' whispered Jasper, eyeing the row of six engines clamped on the back with disbelief.

'Drugs,' said Boris. 'He's hoping our mainsail will hide him from the customs people. Fibreglass doesn't show up well on radar, and customs will probably think we are towing a dinghy abreast. When we get to Europa Point he'll open the throttles and be gone.' Soon afterwards the motorboat roared off as Boris predicted.

We were making good progress with the mainsail and engine, which was giving us a steady six knots, when we heard the drone of a plane coming towards us. It swooped down to tree-height level then with a roar banked sharply to port and disappeared over the horizon.

'What the hell was all that about?' asked Charlie.

Boris looked thoughtful. 'Hmm… I reckon we've had our photos taken.'

'Photos taken?' said Charlie. 'Who'd want our mug shots?'

'Could be customs,' said Jasper, with a look of mock consternation. 'I reckon they picked up on that speedboat and think we're connected to a drug-smuggling gang.'

'Cobblers!' growled Charlie.

'I dunno, Charlie. There could be some truth in that. Look at it this way,' said Boris, 'you've graduated from being a skint bus driver to a yacht-owning yuppie. I can't see them believing your story: "I got the money from my Granny". They'd think she'd been bumped off by a rival gang.'

'Well I would make sure you three buggers went down with me.'

The temperature started to rise as the sun burnt through the early-morning mist. The sea and sky became a perfect duo-blue. The slight breeze gradually dropped away and the mainsail hung limp and lifeless.

'Might as well drop the main, Charlie. We're going nowhere,' said Boris.

'I'll leave it to you blokes,' he yawned, stepping down the hatch.

I was sitting on the foredeck chatting with Jasper when I became aware of some activity in the cockpit. Boris, noting that the breeze had returned, decided to leave the main hoisted and let out the genoa. Apart from blocking out our share of the sun, there wouldn't have been a problem. But in a moment of absent-mindedness he'd failed to warn Charlie of his intended course change. This decision coincided with the wash of a passing speedboat that created a problem with an otherwise uneventful manoeuvre.

Charlie burst into the cockpit with hot coffee dripping off his chin. 'Look what at you've done, you idiot!' he said, pointing to his shirt.

'It wasn't my fault,' argued Boris.

His apologies were to no avail, however, and we witnessed Charlie in his first angry fit of malevolent abuse that continued as we tied up in Estepona.

I liked Estepona. It seemed strange but wonderful to be walking down a shopping centre with orange trees either side, full of fruit for the taking. The main street had a large crater extending to about a hundred feet. We were told a bad storm had created havoc and had swept much of it into the sea. The number of red, black and gold flags fluttering in the marina was testimony to a large German contingent.

We stayed out of Charlie's way for the rest of the day and sneaked off for a meal in town. Boris had been practising a few Spanish words plucked out of a phrase book, and we reckoned we could rely on him to resolve our language problem.

A tall, dark lady with a beaming face swept down on us. Before Boris could utter one syllable she asked, 'How're yer doing love? O'right?' They were a friendly family from Rochdale in Lancashire looking for a better life, but were finding it quite difficult in their new restaurant venture.

'We need all the business we can get,' sighed the woman. 'it's been really hard this last year.' They were concerned about Spain joining the European Union and how the tax increases would affect them in the future. Many of their regular expat customers were heading for the Eastern Mediterranean where the cost of living remained relatively cheap.

As we motored out of Estepona harbour, the white-capped waves and freshening wind promised a lively sail back to Benaldamena and the lack of a spray hood ensured an uncomfortable wet ride. The ill-conceived sheet blocks sent gallons of water into the cockpit to dampen our spirits. I tried to catch Boris's eye, and indicated with a spinning of my forefinger that we ought to reduce sail. I wanted to avoid any confrontation with Charlie on our last day. Boris nodded and I could see that he, too, was getting worried.

Jasper stood clinging to the shrouds and called out to Charlie, 'Are you going to furl the genoa?'

Charlie shook his head. 'We'll leave it a bit longer.'

Boris snapped at him angrily, 'You're crazy. For God's sake get this canvas down now.'

Charlie had no time to reply, as a haymaker of a wave lifted our stern into the air and laid the boat on its side. There was a loud clattering noise of shifting objects and water everywhere. I was under water without time to take a breath. I groped around, gasping for breath, and grabbed a stanchion rail as the boat righted herself. Charlie was furiously winching in the genoa. Jasper had managed to cling on to the shrouds, wild-eyed and wringing wet as he had been completely dunked. Boris was clinging to the mast, trying to reef the main, but was having a struggle. Charlie screamed at him, 'Get the cringle over the rams-horn!'

Boris had never been one for sailing terminology, and with a deeply furrowed brow asked 'Put the what over where?'

Jasper crawled forward to help him and yelled back at Charlie, 'Turn her into the wind, you idiot!'

Once all the sail was down, I ventured into the cabin to assess the damage. My belongings were stored on the starboard side, and had sustained no damage apart from a slightly soggy sleeping bag. Boris and Jasper, however, were less fortunate. Charlie came off worst. He groaned with disbelief as he discovered the mayhem in the navigation area – almanacs and expensive pilot books ruined, and instruments broken.

Jasper remonstrated with Charlie, wagging his finger angrily in his face. 'You put our necks in jeopardy there.'

'Okay,' sighed Charlie. 'Maybe I should have reefed earlier, but everyone makes mistakes sometimes.'

'Not like that they don't,' snapped Boris, trying to contain his anger.

On the way to the airport, Boris announced, 'I never ever want to see that miserable sod again.'

'Me too,' growled Jasper. 'He ruined what should've been a nice holiday.'

I met Charlie again the following year – when we weathered the English Hurricane in Gibraltar.

26

Round about March 1987 we sold the Birdhurst Gardens property and my business and moved to Kingsdown in south Croydon. We bought a three-bedroomed chalet bungalow with an added self-contained flat. This enabled us to let the flat and have extra financial security. Jasper offered to help with the move, using his large Black Maria-type van. Boris came along for the ride. On the day of the move the rain descended in earnest. We trundled along to our new house, which we had bought without the help of estate agents and solicitors, only to discover that the previous owners were still living there. Two removal vans were parked outside, and nobody was going anywhere. We occupied the house at about 3 o'clock the following morning. Boris and Jasper accepted the horrendous inconvenience with their usual good humour. 'Don't worry, Gordon,' laughed Jasper, 'We always get up early.'

'I tell you what, Gordon,' said Boris. 'Join us for a sail at Brighton on Sunday. The forecast is good, a nice 3 to 4 southwest variable.'

Sunday was even better than the weather forecast.

'Come on, Boris! Give her a bit of welly, for God's sake! We'll be here all day.'

Boris looked puzzled. 'I dunno what's wrong with it. I'll try and take her in backwards. She seems to have more power in reverse.'

The lock keeper at the new lock built in Brighton Marina yelled 'Oy! You can't come in like that. Turn her round.'

'Take no notice,' said Jasper. 'She'll spin on a sixpence.'

We bumped into every boat in the lock. The air turned blue with the language used and the lock keeper continued to boom out his disapproval. Once outside the harbour we nearly wet ourselves with laughing.

'So what speed are we doing, Gordon?' asked Boris, still wiping away tears of laughter.

'Five knots,' I said.

'Blimey! She should do better than that?'

'Well, look at all this gear you've got, Boris. This antique direction finder is a waste of space.

'He won't get rid of that,' said Jasper. 'It's too pretty.'

'If you cleared out some of this old-fashioned crap you'd get another three knots,' I said.

'By the way, there's something I meant to tell you, Gordon. Remember that couple who had their dinghy stolen ... we went for drinks on their boat in Gibraltar – Jimmy and Wendy, the solicitor bloke, remember?

'Yeah?'

'Well, we bumped into them in the yacht club. They're talking of emigrating. He's fed up with his job, complaining he's never got any money. Then Jasper pipes up and tells him we're going to take three months off cruising around the Balearics. That really upset him. Then he had a good moan. "I don't know how you chaps do it. I worked jolly hard for my degree, and I've made huge sacrifices. Look at me now. Poor as a church mouse! In heaven's name, what am I doing wrong?"'

'Then Jasper puts on his philosopher's hat,' said Boris, laughing. "Look here, Jimmy," he says, "this is an old argument. I've heard it all before. We're all working in the same field, in a manner of speaking, you know. Our creator has seen fit to give you a degree, which is like a shiny red tractor in agricultural terms. If you sod off for a couple of months – well, all the work grinds to a halt, doesn't it? Everybody's asking, 'Where's he gone? Where's that nice tractor man?' But with the likes of us, well, we've a minor part to play. If we go, nobody notices. So there you are, Jimmy. That's your dilemma. Your degree equals responsibility and hard cheese." "That's rubbish!" argued Jimmy. "After all, Leonardo didn't have a degree. Whoever built Stonehenge, the pyramids, Brunel – those chaps didn't have degrees, did they?" "Yes, but Honey," piped up Wendy, "they didn't have a £60,000 loan on a boat either!"'

'How's your mother Flossy getting on; is she out of hospital yet?' asked Boris, changing the subject.

'Yes, I've promised to drop in and see her next week. She's moved to a nice flat in Weston-super-Mare. I don't like that car journey, and it's expensive staying in hotels during the holiday season, but Babs likes a break.

'She's a spunky old girl!' laughed Jasper. 'She gave me a right telling off when we were decorating your dining room. "Look what you're doing, you daft bugger," she yelled when I nudged her walking stick with the steps.'

'Yes, she's been giving me a whole lot of grief about some writing I'm doing for her. These old people are all the same; they think you've got all the time in the world. They forget that we have to make a crust sometimes. Still, I expect we'll be just the same.'

* * *

Later that evening I met up with a builder who wanted his boat delivered to the Greek Islands. It was being built in Norwich and I was told it would be ready in May 1988. Dick confessed to not knowing anything about boats. His idea was to make the delivery trip a holiday for him and his two workers. We agreed to meet a few times in the interim period so that they could learn a few of the basics of navigation, rope work and general handling. This idea, however, foundered in the Blue Anchor over numerous gallons of lager. They weren't remotely interested in my adventure of the previous year. Just talking about the 'English hurricane' seemed to unsettle them.

After fixing a few electrical problems, we left Poole in early August 1988 on a flat sea. The electronics failed in mid-Channel and we diverted to Cherbourg. Dick, the owner of the boat, suffered from seasickness and reckoned a little ripple on the water with a bit of wind over tide was a hurricane. The boat was up for sale before we reached the entrance to the River Seine, and we were now destined for Malta. The crew, whose names escape me, emphasised that they were 'on holiday', and the running of the boat was secondary to the main requirements of a plentiful supply of lager, sun lotion and a place to lounge. Dick spent much of his time on the telephone. Each phone call was more worrying than the last. He announced that the Inland Revenue was taking an unreasonable interest in his accounts and that the accountant had told him the they were going to shut him down if he didn't return immediately to answer some questions.

We were in the old port of Marseille, waiting for a break in the weather. The harbour master told us the wind worked in cycles of three. He suspected this was a nine-day version, so we might as well relax and enjoy ourselves. This seemed to be a good idea. Then out of the blue Boris and Jasper appeared. The temperature was in the middle seventies and they were dressed in motorcycling gear and sweating like pigs. They had parked their huge black motorbikes next to the harbour master's office. He wasn't very keen, but the linguistic problems of dealing with two aggressive-looking Englishmen in leathers left him shrugging his shoulders in despair. They made good use of the shower and other facilities and came aboard for drinks and a chat.

'We've bought a motor-sailer from a bloke at the yacht club and sailed it down to Mallorca,' said Boris. 'Yeah! We've had a great time. Now we're biking round the Med for a bit, then we've got some mates coming over early September to do a bit of serious sailing, and then my nephew and his mate are coming over for a week.'

'Blimey! Don't you blokes ever do any work? No wonder the country is in such a state!' I said, laughing.

Jasper placed his helmet on the cockpit floor and scratched his gingery thatch of hair. 'You only live once, Gord.'

'That's right,' agreed Boris. 'We're a long time not here. Why don't you and Babs come and join us for a week? You'd love it. It's a lot different from that Charlie trip. It isn't the most luxurious boat, but everything's there. What we do is use the hotel facilities, including the swimming pool across the road. They don't seem to mind.'

'I'll have a chat with Babs, but you can put my name down for certain. I'll give you a call when I get back.'

The delivery became a real worry. My crew, permanently under the influence, seemed unaware of the potential hazards involved. My wish to get the trip over and done with led me to take risks I wouldn't have normally considered. These included anchoring overnight in open water, because I was too exhausted to continue. Their wide-eyed discomfort during the early hours when the wind piped up finally sharpened their interest in what I was doing. They insisted that if I ever intended to drop anchor again in open water I should drop them off on the beach first.

I felt a great sense of relief on returning home. The trip had been far more hazardous than I'd expected. I told Babs to expect a call from Boris or Jasper, who'd invited us for a week's sailing around the Balearics and asked her to check available flights and times.

We were enjoying a glass of wine after a late dinner, with the ten o'clock news droning on in the background. Then Babs gasped, saying, 'What did he say?'

The newsreader mentioned the *Edith Carol* and two lost at sea, presumed drowned – and he gave out the names of Boris and Jasper. We sat staring at each with disbelief. The report on the television gave no details of the loss apart from the fact that they were caught in a storm returning from Ibiza to Mallorca.

The British consulate reported that *Edith Carol* had been sunk in collision with *Sirius* that belonged to the Greenpeace organisation. *Sirius* had come to their rescue when *Edith Carol* fired her flares. Boris had been at the helm when a wave swept him overboard. Jasper went forward and clipped himself on to the mast, while the vessel circled in the darkness to locate him. Jasper's nephew was at the wheel and his friend was in the cabin; both were complete novices. The nephew was still at the wheel when *Sirius* came alongside. There was a collision, and *Edith*

Carol sank almost immediately with Jasper still clipped to the mast. The nephew and his friend jumped into the water and were saved by Greenpeace. It was thought Jasper was killed instantly when he was hit by *Sirius*'s bow. Boris was never found. The rescue operation took over four hours, and included the rescue of the Greenpeace wireless operator who'd taken a whack from *Edith Carol*'s mast.

The full details were never reported.

D E C L A R A T I O N

Merchant Shipping Act, 1970 (Section 61)
and
Merchant Shipping Act, 1979 (Sections 28 and 29)

PRESUMED

Relating to the death of .....1).. DAWSON, John Mr................................ 2) DAVIES, Ronald Mr ....
(Surname first, in block letters)

Rank or Rating   ) 1) Part Owner and skipper of MY EDITH CAROL
Profession or   ) 2) Friend of above and navigator of MY EDITH CAROL
Occupation   )

On Board the vessel ...Missing at sea.. Official No. of vessel ....

I, ...Anthony BRAND .... Age 18

Home Address ...12 Genoa Road, Anerley, London SE20 ....

Rank or Rating   )
Profession or   ) ...apprentice engineer ....
Occupation   )

Vessel (if not the same)... Official No. ....

whose probable future movements are: ....

....

do declare that:- The report I jointly made with Simon Marshall for the enquiry being
conducted by the Spanish Naval Authorities and of which a copy is appended hereto (and
initaled by me) is a true statement of the circumstances surrounding the loss at sea
of Mr Ronald Davies and Mr John Dawson. I am not an experienced yachtsman. When we
sailed from Ibiza sea and weather conditions were suitable. At that ime I was aware
that the radio was not working to full capacity, but I believed that the skipper and
navigator thought it was adequate for the journey. Mr Ron Davies was not using a
safety line or buoyancy aid other than his wet suit top at the time he was washed
overboard. The Edith Carol was under engine power when struck by Sirius. John Dawson
was wearing a safety belt and line but I cannot be sure the line was attached to the
Edith Carol when she came into collision with Sirius. I would have expected him to
have been using the line. I do not know for how long Sirius continued the search: I
was below decks and without a watch. I was at the wheel at the time of the collision.
I believe the Edith Carol sank almost immediately after we abandoned her.

P.T.O.

NOTE: This form is to be attached to Form Inq. 15/72 and should be signed and dated by the Superintendent or Proper Officer. In cases where the
Superintendent or Proper Officer experiences any doubts or difficulty in getting the witness to write the statement himself, the Proper Officer
Superintendent should take the statement down in full and in the words used by the witness so far as possible. Any space for the Declaration
either side of this form which is not used should be deleted by two lines.

351

27

It was 1993 and I was approaching my sixtieth birthday. Our intention was to downsize and cash in on the property values that had taken a knock with the housing crash. Our Kingsdown property had been devalued by £80,000. Even so, we were ready to lick our wounds and fulfil a long-held ambition: to spend twelve months on a pre-retirement sabbatical cruise, meandering through the French canals, and then winter in southern Spain. This would be topped with a family Christmas aboard our new thirty-three-foot cabin cruiser *Kingsdown*, named after the street we lived in, with all the trimmings of the season. I promised Flossy that I would phone her regularly and try to finish the remaining chapters of her book.

As a change from the regular noisy parties of our offspring, we had our own special party, with corks popping all night as we celebrated our final mortgage payment. We were now free of all encumbrances. Our children had got their degrees; Babs had given notice to her long-time employer; while I was hovering on the 'shall I retire, or not?' escalator. The good life could begin. There was just one thing worrying me. After our move to Kingsdown I couldn't find Jerry's rock. It had completely vanished. I've never really been superstitious, but I couldn't help noticing that a lot of things were going wrong. My bad luck seemed to have returned.

The stockmarket crash of the previous year – 'Black Wednesday' in September 1992 – had messed up our original plans. I began to wonder whether the devil had put his mark on me. My only insurance policy had matured shortly afterwards and had been devalued by £5,000. I cursed Joe and his policy. Even worse, the Inland Revenue deducted tax on the reduced profit. At least the money, along with our rental income, would give us a reasonably comfortable living for the next twelve months. We wouldn't be scrimping and scraping our way through life.

Or so we thought.

We met Peter and Molly in Brighton Marina, where they treated us to a grand farewell lunch in a posh restaurant. We had sailed with Peter many times in his fifty-one foot C *Kip*, a hefty trawler-type yacht, but now he had decided to give up boating after Molly broke her leg getting off the boat. Peter was a crusty but knowledgeable old sailor, with a short fuse. He liked everything to be shipshape. His crew turnover was legendary, but we got on with him rather well.

'Trouble is, Babs, you can't get decent crew these days – they're so bolshie, they just won't do as they're told. I even had one bloke smash my boat up. Would you believe it?' He glanced towards me with a broad grin – he was referring to an incident in Brighton Marina, when I'd left one of the flying bridge controls slightly in reverse gear. They worked independently from the console in the main cabin, which I'd always thought was a dangerous set-up. He started the engines in the main cabin, opened the throttle, and we careered backwards at a rate of knots, demolishing the waiting pontoon and causing over twenty thousand pounds of damage. (The insurance company paid for this; Peter had more faith in insurance that I did.)

* * *

We left Brighton for Calais on 5 June 1993. The Channel crossing was a real joy: a millpond sea, in warm sunshine. My previous visits to French canals had always been gloriously free of licences and mooring charges, but now things had changed. There was a complicated form to acquire, and the tariff depended on how long you spent in the canal system. Trudging around trying to find out where to buy the thing was a trial in itself. Anyone contemplating the trip we made would be well advised to spend plenty of time sorting out the necessary paperwork before departure.

Working our way through the lock system was spoilt by continuous heavy rain. I realised it was a lot to expect of Babs, working the ropes on her own. We really could have done with another crew member.

Fortunately the weather changed for the better and we had a magnificent trip through the heart of Paris. Hundreds of students crowded along the embankment enjoying the sun. Several waved to us, and I took up a pope-like stance with bowed head and raised arm in acknowledgement. Then the whole crowd latched on to my papal pretence and reacted with a popified Mexican wave. There was much laughter and humorous banter.

After leaving Paris we entered the canal system that passes through endless French countryside. I remembered a lot from earlier trips, but was still fascinated by the size and wildness of the surroundings. Each day offered a change of scenery, with different people, allied to a variety of problems. I was reminded of the need always to stop to fill up with water, diesel and food supplies – just in case. Holiday closures, sickness and breakdown can play havoc with essential services. Then there were the daily queries and intelligence tests:

How do you flush the loo? Is it push, pull, remote control, work in progress, or what?

What's this bit of string dangling in front of the lock for? Where's the lock keeper?

Why are the ladders on one side of the lock and the bollards on the other?

How come the water hose is always one inch too short to reach my tank?

Why is the supermarket always on the other side of a railway, entailing an eight-mile walk?

Why is the water-ski run next to the marina moorings? What were they thinking of?

Why is the lock keeper ignoring me while he's eating his lunch?

Why don't the gas bottles fit my connections?

Most of these things I knew about, but that still didn't make them easy to deal with.

We met people of every nationality roaming around the French canals. In many cases their boat was their home, and despite the oft-repeated need for more money, they seemed to be happy. It was often the culmination of a long-held dream. They had finally made the escape. The dreaming and talking was over, and they were now doing it. In fact almost everybody we met on boats seemed serenely happy. It was as though just being on a boat calmed people down. I had made this observation several years previously, when sailing with Boris and Jasper.

'Well, you know why it is,' said Jasper. He was a bit of a philosopher.

'Okay, tell me.'

'Well,' he said, 'behind those happy, smiling faces in the boating world lurk monsters. In their work and offices they aren't be so popular. Their guts are a topic of violent discussion from Monday to Friday. Getting away on a boat for a few days, mixing with people who smile and even appear to like them – well, it's like an opium overdose.'

When I asked some of the boaters how things were in their respective countries, the reaction was always the same: spread-eagled arms, rolling eyes and groans of despair. It was the same with the French.

We'd settled down to a lazy, lolling routine, mingling with hire boats, enjoying the food, the wine and the general ambience. We often tagged along behind a large passenger boat for a while to save fuel. Its powerful thrust would pull us along, enabling us to leave our engines just ticking over. Babs was enjoying the regular trips for provisions, fresh croissants, coffee and socialising with other boaters. Then disaster struck.

There was a horrible rending of metal, followed by a crunching, clanging, knocking noise. The bow rose into the air, then dropped back again with a splash. I became totally confused. I couldn't think or imagine what had happened, although I immediately managed to switch the engines off. Babs and I stood looking at one another in total shock.

'What's happened?' she cried.

'We've hit something pretty big!' I looked over the taffrail and saw a trail of plastic material hanging from the stern. I walked down the deck towards the bow sections and could see some twisted metal. I felt numb and confused and wondered what on earth we'd hit. I managed to ease the boat away with the boat hook and clear the plastic material. I nervously tried to re-start the engines. The port engine sounded dreadful – the prop shaft had buckled and the propeller was mangled. The starboard engine seemed undamaged.

Later we discovered that we'd collided with a submerged car. My discussion with the insurance man involved a long phone call.

'Sorry, Sir, we don't insure cars. You have the wrong phone number. We deal with marine insurance.'

'I'm not claiming for the car; I don't care about the car. I'm claiming for my boat and I'm insured with your company.'

'But you said you crashed into a car.'

'Yes. It was in the canal.'

'In the canal? What was it doing in the canal?'

'Well I don't know, do I. I presume it had been abandoned.'

'Oh I see! You mean it was submerged and you couldn't see it.'

'That's right.'

We continued along the Canal du Loing on one engine, with me exercising my helmsman's skills to the limit. On the positive side, there was some advantage in using one engine. Trying to maintain the low speed limits along the canals causes the pistons to glaze up, reducing the engines' efficiency and storing up problems for later. A diesel engine needs to be worked hard to arrive at working temperature quickly to achieve maximum efficiency. In our case the one engine was doing the work of two, thereby achieving the desired result and avoiding glazed pistons.

We were told of a good barge mechanic at St Jean de Losne, turning upstream from Chalon-sur-Saône. This would take us eighty kilometres out of our way, but we'd no choice. Soon afterwards *Kingsdown* was lifted by a crane and lowered on to six steel drums. The mechanic hurried round making notes, with the occasional loud hissing noise and clucking of the tongue.

'Sounds as though it's going to be expensive,' sighed Babs.

'Yeah, it's all an act. Every time he hisses like that it's another five hundred francs. Still, he's got us by the goolies – and he knows it. We are perched up here and going nowhere.'

The next day the shaft and propeller were removed.

'Monsieur? Le papier before you start?'

The mechanic shrugged his shoulders, saying, 'No understand,' and disappeared. There was a time when we were altogether ignored, despite my angry shouts from my elevated position, 'Hey! I say!'

This was all to no avail. I was contemplating putting on Babs's bra and knickers and dancing on the foredeck to attract attention. Fortunately at the last moment such action was not needed.

'Bonjour,' grinned the mechanic, handing over the estimate. It was in English and put great emphasis on the word *approximate*. Worse followed. The next day he gave a cheery wave to us on our steel-drummed perch and announced he was off on his summer holidays. The whole firm shut down. We were six weeks on our perch before the work was completed.

Determined to enjoy ourselves regardless, we became immersed in the local boating scene and had a great social life with barbecues on the banks of the Canal de Bourgogne. There were a number of expats who used a bartering system in preference to money, exchanging skills for services and provisions. I had a haircut for a bottle of wine and some home-made scones.

We spent many a happy hour sipping wine and howling with laughter, all witnessed by a herd of white cows that regularly came in close to study us. The locals had organised holiday amusements, including a race between a dozen steel canoes with two men in each canoe, one carrying a paddle and the other a parasol and a pole with a padded glove on the end. We were honoured with a grandstand view of this event, since it started immediately below our boat.

There seemed to be some uncertainty as to what the contestants were supposed to do. I was much more certain and assertive as to what they could not do, after discovering that all the boats were tied to the steel drums supporting our boat.

'Not a good idea, Monsieur.'

'Not a problem,' he said through his megaphone.

'No way!' I said, determined to spoil the fun.

There was further uncertainty concerning a huge firework show further downstream commemorating Bastille Day. According to all the posters it was on the Saturday. But some eager administrator fired them all up on the Friday instead. The French contingent was not amused.

The final bill for the repairs took a huge bite out of our finances, as the insurance company would only pay on the receipted bill. But at last we were on our way again.

'We don't want anything else going wrong or we'll never get to Spain,' said Babs.

I then remembered we hadn't bothered with medical insurance and hoped to God we didn't get ill.

The previous year on a boat delivery, I had a crew member who'd suffered a stroke in the lock at Decize. He lost all power of speech and movement. A local doctor came and wanted immediate payment. He ordered an ambulance, and the ambulance crew also wanted their money straight away. The lock keeper had to refill the lock to enable us to lift the patient out of the boat and into the ambulance. The hospital was anxious to know that he had funds or was insured before giving treatment. Fortunately the man received excellent treatment in a spotlessly clean hospital. The doctor spoke English and the nurses were efficient and pretty. Then they spoilt things by dropping him on the tarmac at the airport when loading him into the aeroplane. He recovered his speech quickly. Movement was slower, but eventually he made a full recovery. We didn't want to go down that road.

We continued on our journey, with a stop in Lyon. The moorings were crowded, but we managed to squeeze into a tight berth that guaranteed a worrying exit. I was shocked at the change from the previous year. I recalled a busy, bustling place, shops and cafés bulging with people. Now it was almost empty and had the appearance of a deep depression in progress. The heavy rain didn't help, and this followed us to Vienne.

'There's a lot of history round these parts,' said Babs. 'Do you know that Pontius Pilate was the governor of this place?'

'Who?'

'The one in the Bible who washed his hands and had Christ crucified.'

'Oh him! Well, he wouldn't have had any problem washing his hands here. He could have had a power shower.'

We moved on to Avignon marina, but didn't stay. Floods had created extensive damage the year before and it still looked dodgy. The locks are massive in the Rhône but easier to negotiate than the smaller, hand-operated ones. They have traffic lights for entry and departure. The bollards move up and down with the water levels, making a strange groaning noise. The crew stay on board without the need for climbing ladders or leaping around on the deck. There's usually very disturbed water just outside the exit where the sluices empty. It's prudent to give it a few moments to settle before leaving, even if the lights are green. Barges and large pleasure boats have priority with entry. Generally it's better for smaller craft to tie up towards the rear of the lock, if possible.

The Bollène Lock is twenty-three metres deep, a most impressive piece of engineering. That's an awful lot of water to shift. Arles, another historic venue, came into view as we contemplated where we would enter the sea. Port St Louis would be the quickest exit, but I had recollections of the bridge becoming stuck and of long delays. The walled city of Aigues-Mortes sounded much more interesting, but I was uncertain of the depth of water and didn't want any more mangled props.

We branched off down the Petit Rhône through the Camargue, admiring the pink flamingos and wild white horses. We saw beautifully coloured bee-eaters, kingfishers, herons, lizards and buzzards. There were grasshoppers large enough to pull a rickshaw, dragonflies like Tiger Moths, horseflies of Olympian stature, and the ubiquitous mosquito with the buzz of a chain saw. Unlike the French labour force, mosquitoes had a 24/7 work schedule and they got stuck into us before breakfast each day. We bought special candles, reckoned to be the answer to the problem. We were nearly asphyxiated, but even so the mosquitoes had a banquet.

I knew it was illegal to use the cheap red diesel for pleasure boats in France, but decided to take a risk when I spotted a refuelling barge. The fuelling attendant waggled his finger and made a few clucking noises. Looking around to make sure we were unobserved, he filled the tank and grinning all over his face stuffed the cash into his pocket. Soon afterwards, however, we were told by a friendly Norwegian that police were dipping the tanks of pleasure boats for red diesel, and one offender had had his boat impounded.

This really put the frighteners on to me, and I decided we had to get out of the canal system and into the open sea as quickly as possible. We finally settled on Sète, with its awkward three bridges, where you cannot be certain of their opening times. When we arrived it soon became clear that not much had changed since my last visit to the place.

As we were leaving the first lock in the Petit Rhône, the steering failed. I turned the wheel to left and right but there was no response. The boat was out of control, drifting all over the place. The lock keeper started shouting instructions and pointed to the rocks on our port hand side, warning us of the danger. I in turn pointed to my steering wheel and spread my arms in despair. What the hell could we do? But the thought of a further six weeks sitting on steel drums brought about a sudden burst of energy. With my tool box I squeezed into the lazarette, where I could get to the steering. One of the large nuts holding the pantograph-type assembly had dropped off – probably removed by the barge mechanic to refit the shaft and prop and not tightened properly. Of course it had to be out of my reach by some six inches, but with many expletives and one wire coat hanger, which turned out to be the most useful item on the boat, I managed to sort things out before we were dumped on to the rocks.

A waiting mariner assured me the first bridge would open the following morning. We moored up on Mistral Quay, which displayed a large yellow sign: '*Mouillage interdit*'. Earlier experiences had told me that all the best moorings in French waterways had this most offensive sign on display. I had the impression that there was a small gang of men with a job lot of yellow paint whose sole purpose in life was to annoy the pleasure-boating fraternity and me. This particular mooring would be the beginning of a small nightmare. We could only utilise one of the bollards to attach our mooring line, because they were spaced too far apart. It seemed this mooring was reserved for much larger vessels, though they were not showing much interest while we were there. I decided to attach my bowline to a sturdy-looking vertical steel pole nearby. I hopped off the stern, unravelling my neatly coiled line and humming a tune as I contemplated whether to use a clove hitch or a bowline. A door slammed in the small cottage opposite, and a frail old woman with her mouth full of clothes pegs looking like crocodile teeth came hurrying towards me. She had a heaped basket of washing and her expression needed no translation. I would not be tying my boat to the sturdy steel post of her washing line.

Instead I settled for a two-metre concrete flowerpot, sporting half a dozen tired-looking geraniums. The old lady watched me indignantly out of the corner of her eye as she pegged out her clothes. Then, for no apparent reason, she swung her foot angrily at a clump of dog's pooh. She shook her spindly leg back and forth in a poor rendering of the Hokey Cokey to no avail, then hobbled over to the only clump of grass on Mistral Quay, which was struggling to survive in a patch of crumbling concrete. All attempts to clean her shoe were frustrated by the existence of numerous earlier deposits. Like me, she was probably beginning to think dog pooh was the only growth industry in the whole of France. She hobbled back to her cottage red-faced and angry. There was a clattering of pegs hitting a hard place, then a loud yell, followed by a whimpering dog that flew out of the front door.

We were studying a chart on the saloon table when there was a loud, screaming rattle of a high-speed train. We stood looking at each other with disbelief.

'Well, we're not going to get much sleep tonight, that's for sure,' groaned Babs. 'That frightened the living daylights out of me.'

We sat in the aft cockpit sipping a glass of wine, watching the *moule* gatherers in their narrow craft whizzing back and forth. Their faces seemed to be a slightly seaweedy green, perhaps from spending long periods of time under water gathering the mussels. We had come across one in the salt flats walking on the canal bed with a line attached to a rather nice floating fender. Fenders are expensive and come under the 'finders keepers' category. I prodded it with the boat hook to haul it aboard, only to discover an angry *moule* man on the other end.

'Isn't it peaceful?' said Babs. 'D'you think they're all having an early night?'

'Hmm... maybe they know something we don't. I reckon it's got something to do with that big cigar-shaped cloud up there. That gives warning of the Mistral winds.'

There was a loud howl and a whoosh.

'What the hell was that? said Babs. Then there was another such sound, even louder. It wasn't a train but the Mistral wind. Out of the corner of my eye I saw the concrete flowerpot leap off the quay and into the water. The boat swung around one hundred and eighty degrees and smashed into the yacht in front of us with a horrible thud. I danced around the deck with spare fenders and extra mooring lines in a state of pure panic.

'Throw me your line,' shouted a voice in broken English. I started the engines and used full power to turn the boat against the wind, then another man arrived, and we heaved and pulled on the lines until we had hauled her back into position. Within ten minutes the wind disappeared – and so did the helpers before I had time to thank them. I felt sick as I nervously scanned the yacht and was convinced it was sinking. For the next hour I kept looking to see if it was any lower in the water.

'It's a good job the owner wasn't on board,' said Babs.

'That was a hell of a bang. It must have done some damage,' I said.

I started to wonder about French prisons and what sort of sentence I might expect for using red diesel, sinking a yacht and vandalising a geranium display. I wondered if they played billiards and had all the extras, as in English prisons. I trained my binoculars on the cottage opposite. They hadn't pulled the blinds, and the old lady was sitting in an armchair watching television. Cigarette smoke drifted across from another chair, where the occupant's feet were just visible.

It was a good size television, and I was able to establish that a murder mystery was in progress. I've never been a great fan of murder mysteries, but based on my limited knowledge I felt sure it was the man in the wheelchair with a yellow neckerchief who'd done it. I was assembling my facts to prove my case when the adverts came on. The first one was a beautiful young girl holding up a tin of dog food and patting an excited-looking poodle on the head. There followed a loud yelp, and the dog of the house flew out of the front door with his tail between his legs. Much to my annoyance the old man came to the window and drew the curtains across shortly after the mystery had restarted. I took one last long look at the yacht, which still hadn't sunk, and went to bed.

A train awakened me at some unearthly hour and, unable to get back to sleep, I sat in the cockpit peering in the half-light at the yacht. I was relieved to see it was still afloat. Sleepy-eyed, I watched the sun come over the horizon and endured the racket of another train. I made a mug of tea and climbed into the helm seat to survey the activity of road sweepers and early-bird workers. I became aware of the terrier dog from the house opposite standing on the quay staring at me. He had a querulous look on his face as if he had an insurmountable problem.

'What's up with him?' enquired Babs, stretching her arms with a long yawn.

'I'm not sure. He keeps running back and forth then stops and growls at me. I can't think of anything I've done to upset him.'

'C'mon boy, what's the matter?' coaxed Babs with outstretched hand.

'Hey! Don't encourage him, Babs; we don't want the mangy thing ... Oh no! The dirty bugger, he's going to crap on our mooring line. Shoo! Get off, you dirty mongrel.'

'Well, now you know what his problem was,' chuckled Babs.

'Yeah! The geranium pot. Can you imagine how you'd feel, getting up in the morning to discover your lavatory had vanished overnight?'

'Or discovering some idiot has sunk your yacht,' said Babs.

'I think I'll take a crafty look to see if there is any damage to the boat.'

I gingerly climbed aboard and made a quick survey. 'Thank goodness for that! There's not a scratch on her. It's a really solid boat made of steel. The worst the bump could have done was upset the sugar bowl. All that tossing and turning and worry for nothing.'

'Not quite,' groaned Babs. 'Take a look at the damage on our boat.'

'Where? Oh no! It's ripped out the rubbing strake and buckled the stanchions. That's going to cost us a few quid.'

'Don't look,' whispered Babs, 'There's a police boat stopping just behind us.'

'Get down in the cabin quick. We'll pretend there's nobody on board.'

'Bonjour!' There was a thud as somebody jumped into the aft cockpit and rapped on the cabin door.

'Oh... er... b... b... bonjour,' I said, with a vision of handcuffs being applied and being hustled off to jail.

'Vous êtes capitaine, Monsieur?'

'Oui... but I don't speak French.'

'Huh,' said the policeman arching his finger at the first bridge, 'you go... yes?'

'Yes... yes, yes,' I said, furiously nodding my head.

Babs stepped in and assured him in her dubious French, 'We'll be leaving on the first bridge-opening, weather permitting.'

He touched his cap, 'Merci Madame,' and climbed back on to his boat.

'Phew! Well done, Babs. I'm going below to change my underpants.'

After much delay we finally got through the three bridges at Sète. I felt ten years older after the Mistral Quay experience. Now at last we were on the open sea. I opened the throttles wide and pushed my head out of the glass side-screen to feel the delight of stinging spray on my face, breathing in the salt and ozone. We were free!

'This is the life,' I crowed. Then we smacked into the back of a wave with a bone-crunching shudder.

'Slow down!' yelled Babs, 'you're going much too fast.'

'Whoops!' The sea gradually flattened and conditions became ideal. We tucked into fresh cheese and ham baguettes with queen olives and a bottle of chilled white wine. The sun, the sea, and a bit of classical music on a cassette smoothed the edges of our frayed nerves.

For eighty miles we enjoyed Utopia, but then there was a dramatic change. We were about five miles off the Spanish coast when a wind came up from nowhere. It wasn't the Mistral from the north but the Sirocco from the Sahara. The seas became short and steep and very uncomfortable. I headed in towards the coast, trying to identify the nearest harbour. Foolishly I'd thought I could manage with the smaller-scale voyage chart. A larger-scale chart with all the extra detail would have saved me a lot of hassle. Eventually we made a hair-raising entry into a posh marina and on to the fuel pontoon. I discovered we still had a steering problem with one of the rudders. This created a lot of nervous interest for some of the owners sipping their G & Ts on their hugely expensive crafts.

The marina had been built thirty-five years previously on a swamp surrounded by farmland, without planning permission, or so we were told. But money has a way of getting round such obstacles; the investors filled in forms and carried on building anyway. The idea was to create a number of canals so that each house had its own mooring at the bottom of the garden. According to the hype it was supposed to be the largest marina in the world with more waterways than Venice. We had hoped to get further west, past Barcelona and on to Alicante, to benefit from the better climate, but the steering problem convinced me we should stay. We managed to secure six months' mooring with a jolly boat manager at a bargain rate.

'For you, Mr Gordon,' he said, 'I give you the best mooring in the marina.' (He did as well.) Even though we were now close to the snow-capped Pyrenees we were able to spend most days lazing in the sun. For our daily exercise we would walk for miles along the beach and into the countryside. There was an airfield close by, and we spent many happy hours watching the skydivers at play with their rainbow-coloured parachutes.

Nearly all the inhabitants of Empuriabrava were German. At that time Germany was in deep recession, which was reflected in the large number of boats and villas for sale. There was one other English couple with their sailboat in the marina who were trying to drum up some interest in a sailing school. They lived in a small villa in the next bay and invited us back for Sunday lunch, filling us in with all the local information. They showed us an empty villa close by, in a poor state with overgrown shrubs. We were told that an English family who had perished in the

Herald of Free Enterprise ferry disaster had bought it. They were on their way to take possession of the property, but sadly never arrived. Nobody had been near it since.

As Christmas approached we were surprised by the lack of festivity, and the idea of a Christmas tree, crackers and a turkey on the boat started to fade.

Caroline and her boyfriend came to visit us, and treated us to a weekend in a four-star hotel. They pampered us something rotten.

'Well, Mum,' said Caroline, 'I don't like to think of you and Dad roughing it on a boat all this time. Not at your age.'

We visited Salvador Dali's museum in Figueres, forty minutes away from the marina. I found it amazing and well worth all the parking problems. There were also other historical attractions in the mountains. Occasionally we had lunch in a well-attended small café run by a family from Yorkshire. They cooked roast beef and Yorkshire pudding every Sunday, but the idea of a Christmas tree and decorations in the boat cockpit was abandoned, and the nearest thing we could find to a turkey were some enormous purple-looking drumsticks.

We became acquainted with an English couple in a small café on the marina. They invited us back to their luxury villa for coffee. On discovering it was going to be my birthday on 23 December and that I would be sixty years old, the husband treated us to a celebratory dinner at his favourite restaurant. Victor flew in with his girlfriend in the evening, and we had the best food and wine the restaurant could offer. Later in the evening we went back to their place and related humorous anecdotes about times gone by. Somehow I got on to the subject of funfairs. I was describing my favourite ride at the Kursaal, a huge funfair in Essex. My family had taken me on a paddle steamer from Sheerness. I was sixteen at the time and found the water-chute very exciting. I was sitting right in the front and I remember whizzing down an almost vertical slope and then wham! When we hit the water at the bottom it was like hitting concrete, and I got absolutely soaked.

'Ah yes,' said C J, the husband. 'Yes, I remember buying that. We had to make some modifications on it for health and safety reasons. Yes, we did quite well with that.'

I just laughed, thinking he was joking and that the wine had gone to his head. They invited us to join them on Christmas Eve and Christmas morning, but I told them I would be cooking Christmas dinner on our boat. Victor stayed in bed on Christmas Day with an immense hangover. The turkey drumsticks took forever to cook, but eventually got burnt. Although the dinner turned out to be a disaster, nobody was hungry or bothered, and the day became a foggy memory of slurred voices and laughter. On Boxing Day C J invited us for a sail on his yacht that was moored at the end of his garden, and lunch at the nearby yacht club. We awoke the following morning with a rat-a-tat on the coachroof of our boat.

'Oh, hello. You're up early!' It was C J's driver.

'C J wondered if you and Babs might like these leftovers. We're going home later today; it would be a pity to waste the food.'

'Blimey, are you sure?'

'Don't worry, Gordon,' he whispered, with a finger raised to his lips, 'he's a millionaire.'

It was a large but satisfying step from Christmas in the workhouse to Christmas in the Med with a millionaire. It might have taken sixty years, but I was on the right track.

I set about preparing *Kingsdown* for the return journey to the UK. I managed to fix the rudder problem, bleed the fuel system and change the filters. Against all good advice, I was contemplating a return before April, because the marina had increased the mooring fees to £200 a week. No way was I prepared to accept such extortion. Then Babs received distressing news. Her best friend Sylvia had died unexpectedly of a brain tumour and Babs had to return immediately for the funeral.

The Mistral flag warning of dangerous winds had been flying for nearly three weeks in perfectly calm conditions. I was determined to get out, so I took a chance. I set forth with a man and wife volunteer team looking for experience. They certainly got that! They hardly spoke for a week.

The melting snows from the Pyrenees filled the canals and rivers. The rush of water carried with it trees, shopping trolleys, old prams, furniture and anything else not nailed down. Also carried were the 'always with you' problem of plastic bags that cut off the cooling system and disabled your propellers. On seeing the volume of water climbing the buttresses of the bridge at Arles I nearly wet myself. I needed full power to get past Chalon-sur-Saône. Thereafter everything went smoothly until Le Havre, where one engine overheated. We crossed the Channel with just one engine operational, which had the volunteers and me biting our nails for a while.

Our sabbatical had been a wonderful adventure, and at times the adrenaline had flowed faster than the Rhône. We met and made many friends; we had the time of our lives; and we were so pleased we'd done it.

28

After our return to the UK we decided to downsize. In March 1997 we bought a three-bed semi in Hampshire near the sea. Our finances had taken a bit of a hammering: I had become involved with Victor's house that he was working on in Rio; the exchange rate had gone mad and he was having difficulty getting his wages. I bought out his interest in the house and let the property. I also had a difficult tenant who caused all the other tenants to leave. She didn't pay the rent and went on social security. Even so we were reasonably sound.

Then Flossy's problems came to the fore. She had moved to Weston-super-Mare, a council exchange from her Sheerness flat. At first she had a very nice two-bedroomed flat with warden control and a communal area to encourage her to make friends. At first she seemed happy, but after she broke her wrist, followed by two bad falls, the authorities decided she could no longer stay in the flat and look after herself. My half-brother Bernard made a very rare visit to see her and organised her move into a nursing home, and then I took over.

Babs looked astonished.

'Put Flossy in a nursing home? You can't do that; it's ridiculous. You can't afford it!'

'Well, what am I supposed to do? She's my mother.'

'I feel sorry for your mother, but you don't owe her anything. She abandoned you at birth, remember. You can't be expected to support her in her old age. It isn't right. You're nearly a pensioner yourself.'

'You can't blame the old girl. She was just a kid; she had no choice.'

'I think she could have done much more to help herself. She never tried to exert herself or improve her lot. She could have learnt to drive or take up a hobby or something. She just sat around like Queen Victoria waiting for the world to come knocking on her door. She wouldn't even get on a bus, for heaven's sake. She worried the bus would go past her stop. She preferred taxis.'

'Supposing I'd adopted your attitude with your granny and mother when they used to live with us? You didn't seem to have a problem then.'

'That's different.'

'I don't see why. Your mother didn't think I was good enough for you.'

'Maybe she was right! But no way am I going to spend my retirement looking after your mother.'

'Look, Babs; I agree with everything you say. You're right. Flossy is a stubborn, incorrigible pain in the butt. She's been driving me nuts over this history book thing, but I will finish it as I promised her I would. And I think you should know something else. When I was in that Atlantic storm nine years ago, I thought about her a lot. As you rightly say, I hardly knew her, yet it's funny, I had a clear picture of her face. I could see her blue eyes and every line, freckle and feature. I could see the tears rolling down her cheeks. I felt as if I could almost reach out and touch her. You might think it's a lot of bloody nonsense, but I could actually feel her breath on my face. I wanted to hold her, and say sorry for leaving her like I did. Now Flossy is experiencing her own Atlantic storm. She's been forced to give up her flat and her independence, and she feels abandoned. There isn't anybody she can turn to or talk to; all her friends are dead. She has nobody, and she is very alone and very afraid. There's not much I can do for her, but I'll do what I can. You don't have to be involved. I'll contribute a small percentage of what I have for her care; I'll manage that.'

'Wow, Gordon! You've missed your vocation; you should have been a preacher! That was so touching... I thought Flossy had brown eyes.'

'Eh? Er... no. She had blue eyes; she was my mother; I should know.'

'Well I'm not going to get into an argument, but I think you're getting confused with Mrs Tapp. She really did have blue eyes.

* * *

My high-minded thinking started to wear thin, however, as Flossy became more and more difficult. For several years we travelled down to Weston-Super-Mare with grapes and other goodies and tried to cheer her up. Despite all attempts by the nursing staff and benefits people, she refused to sign any documents or pay any bills. My patience was sorely tried with all the coming and goings to the nursing home, to her bank (not overly helpful) and to the benefits people, who were a real pain. Then there were all the travelling and hotel costs. Worst of all, Flossy was more miserable than I had ever seen her. Funnily enough, though, the nurses didn't seem to think she was miserable at all.

'She's a real feisty old girl,' laughed one of the nurses. 'She tried to beat up the nursing sister with her walking stick, and she refuses to be pushed around. She spends most of the day in the lounge or her bedroom reading some documents. Sometimes she's giggling like a schoolgirl and the next minute she's crying her eyes out. I asked her "What's that you're reading Floss?" but she gave me pretty short shrift. "Bugger off and mind your own business," she said. I was dying to find out what she was reading, but she kept it locked up in her suitcase, and kept the key on a chain round her neck. The sister had a peep while she was having her bath. "It's some sort of life story," she said. Flossy had a phone call from somebody in Sheerness yesterday who told her her uncle Bob had died. He was over ninety-nine years old. She was a bit upset about that because apparently he was determined to get a telegram from the Queen.'

I told the nurse that it was my story and that I had the last two chapters in the car. I was pleased Flossy was reading it and, I hoped, enjoying it.

I decided to build an extension on to our new house, to do away with the prohibitive travelling and nursing home costs.

On the plus side it would put extra value on the property. On the downside I knew Babs would be angry.

'We moved here and downsized, and now you want to go back to a four-bedroomed place. It's ridiculous. It'll cost thirty thousand pounds or more. Where's the money coming from?'

'I've sold the boat!'

'You've *what*? I don't believe it. That's really stupid! I'm not spending my retirement looking after your mother. She's a nightmare and your responsibility. Leave me out of it!'

It cost over £1,000 for the surveyor's drawings and council permissions, all of which took forever, but after all that the extension was never built.

During the summer of June 2003 Flossy had an accident and broke her hip. She went into hospital but never really recovered. She lingered on through the winter and died in July.

Later, talking to one of the voluntary workers at the hospital, I asked whether she had suffered. She told me that Flossy did have some discomfort with her leg, but that she was a remarkably positive lady. The voluntary worker said that she kept on saying that she'd had a very full life and a wonderful family. 'I held her hand to the end,' she said, 'and she died quite peacefully.'

The saddest thing for me was Flossy's funeral. Only three people were present: the nursing sister, Babs and myself.

* * *

There were two things I couldn't put into Flossy's book because I felt it would be cruel. The first was that my children did not regard Flossy as a member of the family. They were polite and respectful to her because she was an old lady who had some connection with their dad, but nothing more. Even worse was the fact that my own feelings towards her were not that much different. The gap in time during the early years had been too great, and the feelings I should have had for her had been given to Mrs Tapp.

The second thing I couldn't tell Flossy about was Caroline's wedding. We had a call from Caroline in January 1995, telling us she was getting married. At that time Flossy was unwell and the problems of getting her to London and back to Weston-Super-Mare seemed to be insurmountable. She didn't like trains or buses and was a poor car passenger, and I felt the venue for the reception would have been too upsetting for her.

Caroline insisted the wedding had to be white and Anglican. The groom was equally adamant it had to be Catholic. I thought that it was a good omen for the longevity of their proposed marriage when they agreed to compromise and get married in a hot air balloon in Africa. Babs wasn't keen on this idea, while I was totally against it. I had to take into consideration my long-established fear of heights, as well as my dentures and spectacles. These expensive items would be vulnerable in a hot air balloon. Besides, I didn't consider it to be a fitting environment for a true English rose, exposed as she would be to copulating elephants, creepy insects and noisy wild animals.

I decided that if our daughter wanted a white Anglican wedding then she should have it, and to hell with the cost. She would have a London wedding. There were many obstacles to be overcome, not least an Anglican padre willing to marry an agnostic girl to a young Catholic with a difficult Dublin accent, and all this was not helped by an unbeliever for a father.

Eventually, I persuaded a priest to give his blessing to the couple. The groom was encouraged to speak in murmurs, and to smile liberally with a nodding head. The venue for the reception proved more difficult, with everywhere seemingly booked up for months ahead. There was one very grand hotel near the church that said it might be able to help, but after seeing the estimate I hastily backed off.

Looking up with despair I saw the street name 'Brunswick Square', and realised with a start that I was standing less than a hundred and fifty yards from the offices of the Foundling Hospital. It was the place where I had been baptised and given a new name at the age of three months, and the place that had held the documents of my secret past that I had hidden from my family for all these years. A wild idea started to sprout in my head. Maybe I could hire the courtroom and picture gallery. That would be a wonderful and unusual venue for a wedding reception. It was only a short walk from the church, and it would give me an opportunity to shake off the stigma associated with my past. I could even tell my daughter the origins of her Christian name: a portable clothes line for caravans. It was a magnetic contraption I'd invented but not perfected.

Babs had said to me in an off-hand manner shortly before she was born, 'So what are we going to call her if it's a girl?'

I was thinking of clothes lines at the time, and mumbled, 'Caroline'.

'That's a nice name,' said Babs, 'I like that.'

Caroline had no idea of my background, and pertinent questions had always been evaded. I have often been asked why I had found it necessary to hide my past for such a long time. Surely it doesn't matter these days? Protesting voices air their modernistic views with sunny-faced assurance. Nobody blames you for the failings of your parents; it really doesn't matter. But oh yes it does. From a personal standpoint I no longer give a toss about what people think of my past. That's unimportant. But I remember very vividly the shock, anger and shame I felt when Mrs Lowe told me about my father. I didn't want my children to know about this. I had agreed with Babs soon after we were married that our children should not be told about my past, and there were still many things that Babs herself didn't know. But now the children were grown up they could manage the details of my life in their own way. They would be able to tour the premises of the Foundling Hospital and discover all about foundlings and their upbringing.

I think that when you are young, bad beginnings are best buried. Sympathy is often a burden. But after reaching a certain age you can savour the delights of that golden enclosure where people don't care any more; where you can speak out of turn and make faux pas daily, and nobody is going to tell you not to do this. This is now my pleasure; I can scramble eggs instead of foxtrotting on shells.

Caroline's reception was to be held in the plush Georgian baroque setting of the courtroom, the precursor of the National Gallery, displaying its fine collection of famous paintings and a wealth of history about Captain Coram, Handel, Hogarth and the Foundling Hospital. I could open my Pandora's Box in style, perhaps even embrace the past with pride.

We were blessed with unbelievably hot sunshine in the middle of February. The church service, reception, catering, speeches, and the whole ambience were delightful. Caroline's beautiful wedding dress and her school friends as bridesmaids dressed in emerald satin looked a treat.

As we climbed the stairs towards the courtroom, Babs pointed to the trailing ivy daintily wrapped around the balustrade.

'That looks familiar,' she said, pausing with a furrowed brow.

I stared at the ivy with disbelief. 'The cheeky beggars,' I whispered. 'That's the trellis from our front garden.' We later discovered that the best man had pinched it in a frenzied last-ditch attempt to decorate the approaches to the picture gallery.

The huge courtroom table, the centrepiece of many historical sagas, was now heavily laden with poached salmon, canapés, champagne, wedding cake and other delicacies. The air was filled with the scent of flowers mingling with excited voices and laughter. A golden-haired harpist sat in a corner plucking her strings. I couldn't hear the music because of the background noise, but she looked absolutely right for the occasion. The portrait of Captain Coram clutching the royal charter painted by William Hogarth hung on the wall behind me as I delivered my speech to a receptive audience. If Hogarth had had the power to add speech to his painting, Captain Coram would surely have given us his blessing. He might perhaps have had a quiet word with the photographer, who looked far too cheery for such an important assignment. He was a touch unsteady on his feet as well, and this was reflected in the number of photographs with missing heads and nasal close-ups. Worst of all was the picture of the bride and groom cutting the three-tiered cake, which looked more like the leaning Tower of Pisa.

A local pub was commandeered in the evening, and someone had hired a band at short notice. The dancing continued all night. The happy couple then flew to Africa to spend their honeymoon in a hot air balloon. Fifteen years later they remain happily married, living in the south of France with their four beautiful children.

They decided not to sue the photographer.

The Courtroom at the Foundling Hospital

29

The telephone rang.

'Does Gordon Aspey live here?'

'That's me. Who wants to know?'

'Is that you, Gordon?'

The voice sounded tired, wheezy, and faintly familiar.

'You won't remember me. My name's Joe. I sold you a car many years ago.'

'Blimey, Joe! How could I forget? The insurance... Crikey, I thought you'd be dead.'

'Heh, heh. Well, according to the doctor I should be, so you'd better not interrupt and let me finish what I need to tell you. I did something wicked many years ago. I befriended an old man who was terminally ill. I sorted out his utility bills and did a bit of shopping for him; he was a real loner. I discovered an insurance policy amongst his papers. The temptation was too much; I won't go into detail.'

'That's terrible, Joe. I'm not sure I want to hear any more.'

'Just listen, Gordon, because it concerns you. It wasn't a vast sum.'

There was a noise like air being let out of a tyre: 'cough... cough... ssh... ssssh.'

'Are you all right, Joe?'

'Yes, yes. I need a few squirts of this stuff now and again. Let me finish. Shortly before I saw you at the newsagents all those years ago, looking at the car advertisements, I had two visitors call at my flat. I thought *Oh my God, I'm going to prison*, but they turned out to be officials from a finance house. The car I sold you was still on HP from the previous owner, and they'd come to repossess it. I told them I'd sold the car to you.'

'So you sold me a car that was still on HP? That's charming, Joe.'

'Did they take it back Gordon?'

'No. I really liked that car. It was the best car I ever had.'

'You were very lucky, Gordon; I'm surprised. Still, I guess the paperwork wasn't so organised in those days. I remember you telling me about your early life as a kid. The night I gave you a lift from the New Year's Eve dance. D'you remember?

'Well, vaguely. It was raining, wasn't it?'

'Yeah! Chucking it down. I had a few sleepless nights over that. No, really I did. Just a minute, (ssh… ssssh…) Anyway, I put your car money with the old chap's insurance money into some mining shares. I read somewhere that the price of nickel was on the up, so I unloaded the lot into Poseidon, a small mining company. I felt nervous about the whole business and quite expected it to unravel. My broker thought I was crazy. He kept advising me to spread the risk – heh, heh, if only he'd known. Well, I almost forgot about the shares, because I wasn't short of a shilling. I suppose I was what you might call bread-and-butter comfortable. But a few years later, right out of the blue, I get a phone call from my broker. He says, "Joe, you've hit the jackpot." I didn't know what he was going on about. Talk about the devil looking after his own! My ill-gotten gains had mushroomed. I only paid twenty cents a share in Poseidon and I sold them for three hundred dollars. Can you believe it? By the way, I'm not holding you up, am I Gordon?'

'No, I'm all ears, Joe. I'm just puzzled about where I come in to all this.'

'I'm coming to that. Well, I started doing the stocks and shares with my windfall, and everything I invested increased in value. I became seriously rich. But I had a conscience about the money and wanted to return it to the old geezer somehow, although I guessed he would have passed on by then. I found out that he died intestate shortly after the policy matured, so I didn't feel so bad about things then, but I had a niggling worry about you and that car. You might not think so, but I'm basically an honest bloke – and I knew you were scratching around for a living. I sent you an apology and a cheque for five thousand pounds to buy a new car.'

'H... h... hang on... hang on a minute. You sent me a cheque for five grand?! I can't believe that, Joe. When was that?

'It was chicken feed to me, Gordon, but I wanted to clear my conscience. My memory isn't so good these days, but I guess it must have been round about the early 1970s.'

'It's unbelievable, Joe.'

'(cough, cough.) The cheque was returned in the unopened envelope, with your fancy writing on the back, "return to sender".'

'I sent it *back*?!' Then I realised it must have been at the time when I saw the barrister, the bailiffs were banging on my door, and I was in my 'return to sender' mode.

'I recognised your writing immediately. You're such a slippery bloke; you seemed to have vanished. I was totally mystified. Soon afterwards I went to live in the States and had a fantastic time. But time catches you, and we all finish up at the same bus stop. I'm unravelling fast (pssssssssh).'

'Have you got any family, Joe?'

'It's my biggest regret, Gordon. Now, that's something I really would have cherished, but things didn't turn out that way. To be honest, I was probably too selfish. Mind you, I'd never experienced family life. I was brought up in an orphanage, and what a miserable existence that was. My father went bankrupt and blew his brains out. I don't know what happened to my mother; she just disappeared. I can still see him now, his twisted body on the lounge floor, his eyes like giant marbles staring up at me. There was blood, hair and bits of flesh everywhere; I'll never forget it. You can't imagine what it's like, Gordon. One moment you live in a house with a mum and dad like any other normal family, and then suddenly you're bundled into a huge building full of strange kids. I was about seven years old. That took some getting used to.' He paused momentarily. 'I've never told anyone that before. Well, you don't tell people that sort of thing, do you. You have to keep it to yourself. It's like a shadow, a bloodstain on your passport that stays with you forever. It's an awful legacy for any parent to leave a kid. But of course I forget; you're a foundling. You're sure I'm not stopping you from doing anything, Gordon?'

'No, no, time's not a problem for me any more. I'm really very interested in what you're saying.'

'I see you renewed that insurance policy after you defaulted on the premiums.' I then remembered that Joe used to retain an interest in all the policies he sold and how they performed. He stayed in touch with the area manager who gave him the information.

'That got a bit complicated, Joe. They credited me with all the premiums I'd made, but insisted on issuing a new policy and sticking another ten years on the maturity date. Okay I did get a bit behind with things, but I was bloody furious, and it wasn't my fault that they didn't have an agent in my area.'

'That was crafty, Gordon. It's all about commission. I see that when it matured it was a bit awkward for you. A couple of days after "Black Wednesday".'

'I won't deny I was gutted, Joe. I lost quite a bit. Still, that's life.'

'Gordon, why did you send the cheque back without opening the envelope?'

'I have one or two skeletons of my own, Joe, and at that time I had a situation where I had to return all my business mail. It's a long story, and I'm not proud of everything I've done in my life … Especially sending you that bloody cheque back!'

'Don't worry, I'm going to sort that. Did you get your boat?'

'I did, a thirty-three-foot twin-diesel motor cruiser.'

'Oh, nice. Married? Kids?'

'Yep, two boys and a girl. They're grown up now. They've been great. Never on the dole and never been in trouble. All three with university degrees; we're very proud of them.'

'Y'know, Gordon, dying is a miserable business. I'm eighty-seven years old and falling apart. It's all injections, pills and bloody pain. I hardly know you, Gordon, but selling insurance – and that's all I ever did – you learn a lot about people. There's a lot of psychology involved. You always had a grin on your face, but I knew it hid a few scars. It's a hard slog trying to stand on your own feet, making your own way in life.'

'You're right there, Joe; it's tough.'

'You get used to the whining and people feeling sorry for themselves, but you never did – and I liked you for that. You were a stubborn, impossible devil to sell insurance to, but you were never offensive and always had a ready smile.'

'You've got that wrong, Joe. I fell out of a bedroom window as a kid. I look just the same when I'm furious.'

'Ha, ha (cough... cough...). Right, now let's get down to serious business before I fall off my perch. You need luck in life – never mind all that stuff about hard work and other nonsense. Luck is the big thing, and sometimes you have to bend the rules. I made my luck, Gordon, and my circumstances gave me the tools. I've had a helluva good time, a real roller-coaster, and I don't regret anything.'

'Blimey, Joe. I don't remember you being philosophical like this.'

'We've a lot in common, Gordon. We've both had to claw our way out of the gutter, and we've had to learn how to survive the best we could. There's no charity for people like us; we've had to stand on our own two feet and grab at any good luck that comes our way. I'd like to send you a banker's draft, but promise me you won't send it back.

'I'll eat my Cornflakes in the letterbox, Joe!'

'One more thing. If I kick the bucket before you've cashed it, matters will get horribly complicated. So cash it quick. You shouldn't have anything to worry about, because the money's... er... relatively clean. Though I'd strongly recommend you keep your head down and don't tell *anyone* how you came by it. We are the only two people on this planet that know about this money and it is imperative for you that it stays that way. So keep it to yourself Gordon.

'I promise, Joe.'

'You'll need to be bit creative. I won't be around, if you get my meaning. This'll be the last time we'll speak (cough... cough...), Gordon. I'll get it sorted right away.'

'I hardly know what to say, Joe... Keep your spirits up.'

'You stay happy, Gordon. Keep smiling.'

37

When Joe's money came through, I couldn't believe it. I dared to hope there might be enough for a new car, but in fact there was enough to buy a fleet of new cars – with cash to spare. I started to worry he might have made a mistake or gone slightly loopy, yet on the telephone he'd sounded self-assured and coherent. He'd said I should pay it in quickly, and that's exactly what I did. The cashier in the bank looked askance at me when I presented her with the banker's draft. She knew me well, and cocked her head on one side as if to demand an explanation. I smiled back at her as casually as I could.

'We've flogged everything; we're emigrating,' I said.

'Wow! Somewhere nice?'

Then one of the other cashiers intervened with a query and saved me the need to elaborate.

I telephoned the bank a week later, asking for a statement. My bank statement confirmed that the money had been credited to my account. I checked the balance several times, hardly able to contain my excitement. I sat on the bottom of the stairs and counted the six-figure digits over and over, just to be absolutely sure. I very nearly showed the banker's draft to Babs, but realised that if it hadn't gone through the disappointment would have been unbearable. And Joe had insisted that I shouldn't tell *anybody*.

I decided to take a gamble and buy a present that I'd promised Babs four decades ago. I hoped it would make up for some of the rows we'd had over Flossy.

'Cup of tea?'

'What's come over you?'

'A little present. Better late than never, eh?'

'I don't believe it! … Is it a real diamond?'

'Of course!'

'Oh... Gordon... I don't know what to say! It's fantastic! It must have cost the earth.'

'It's only money, Babs. Look after it. One day we might need to visit the pawnbrokers; you never know. After breakfast we'll do some proper shopping. Then we'll sort out some winter sun.'

As I unloaded the shopping from the car, Babs went quiet. Worry was etched all over her face.

'Have you done something dodgy? Where's all this money come from?'

I grinned, saying, 'Don't worry; it's bona fide. All in good time,' and then handed over the shopping bags. I needed to think up a convincing story.

'There's a bottle of fizz in the fridge,' I said later. 'We have something to celebrate. This might come as a bit of a shock.'

'POP ... fizzzz.'

'This is a special toast to Flossy, my dear departed mother, who has devoted her life to make up for the deprivations of my youth by leaving me a golden egg to enjoy in the future. I'm glad I finished her history book. That was becoming quite a trial. Apparently she was a bit of a wizard with stocks and shares.'

'Flossy?' spluttered Babs. 'I thought she was skint.'

'So did I. But...'

'You've got to be kidding!' interrupted Babs, spilling the champagne down her blouse. 'Your mother wouldn't know stocks and shares from a shovel of sh-sugar. She was eighty-seven-years old.'

'There's no need to denigrate her. We both underrated her. She kept her portfolio secret all these years.'

'Her port-what? I can't believe I'm hearing this!'

'Yes. That's why she wouldn't hand over her pension book or sign anything. She was busy investing all her money. That's why she rarely paid bills or went anywhere. You remember all those newspapers we cleared out of her flat? They were nearly stacked up to the ceiling. All those *Evening Standards*. I reckon she was studying the City news and the footsie index.'

'Gordon! Your mother had the brains of a pregnant lemming. Okay, if she was so smart, how come she was living in a council house?'

'Can you think of a better head office to milk the system and live on the cheap? Come on, Babs; you can't argue with the money. Look at the rock on your finger. It's not a mirage.'

'Gordon! How long have we been married?'

Her face was creased with angry indignation. The words were stamped in capitals on her forehead and didn't need translating. My creative thinking wasn't working.

'Do you really expect me to swallow that load of old Garbage?'

I then realized I had two choices; breaking my commitment to Joe, who was probably dead and would never know anyway, or upsetting Babs.

'Okay! Babs. An insurance salesman left me the money and insisted that I shouldn't tell anybody and Oh! Here's my bank statement. Now you know why I can't tell anyone.'

'Good God! All that money! Where on earth did it come from? Look Gordon, I don't want to spend my retirement going back and forth to Parkhurst Prison.'

'I've done nothing wrong honestly. I've merely helped a petty criminal ease his conscience before he finally meets his maker. That's the least I can do.'

'Hmm! So, we can afford to pay these bills and replace that old boiler.'

'Babs!!! Bugger the bills and the boiler; we've got a plane to catch ...'